MEMOIR

OF

GEORGE EDWARD LYNCH COTTON

BISHOP OF CALCUTTA, AND METROPOLITAN

MEMOIR

OF

GEORGE EDWARD LYNCH COTTON

BISHOP OF CALCUTTA, AND METROPOLITAN

WITH SELECTIONS FROM HIS JOURNALS AND CORRESPONDENCE

EDITOR-MRS. COTTON

GYAN

Published by

Gyan Publishing House
5, Ansari Road
Daryaganj, New Delhi-110002
Phone: 011-47034999, 9811692060
E-mail: books@gyanbooks.com

Distribution Network
gyanbooks.com
India, USA, Canada, UK, Australia

ISBN: 978-93-7097-291-9 (PB)
First Published, 1872

2nd Impression 2025

Printed at: Gyan Press, Delhi.

MEMOIR OF GEORGE EDWARD LYNCH COTTON-BISHOP OF CALCUTTA, AND METROPOLITAN
Editor-MRS. COTTON

BISHOP COTTON.

E. U. Eddis. pinx^t

H. Adlard Sc.

London: Longmans & Co.

MEMOIR

OF

GEORGE EDWARD LYNCH COTTON, D.D.

BISHOP OF CALCUTTA, AND METROPOLITAN

WITH

SELECTIONS from his JOURNALS and CORRESPONDENCE.

EDITED BY MRS. COTTON.

NEW EDITION.

LONDON:
LONGMANS, GREEN, AND CO.
1872.

PREFACE

TO

THE FIRST EDITION.

A FEW words are necessary to explain the change of editorship which will be apparent in this volume. When in 1866, the sincere regard or warm friendship entertained towards the late Bishop of Calcutta passed into mournful and affectionate reverence for his memory, a desire was expressed within the circle of his intimate friends that a published Memoir should make the story of his life more widely known. In behalf of the Indian Church this desire was echoed in India. Through the kindness of the present Dean of Westminster it was partially met; and to him are due the first three chapters, which contain a sketch of the Bishop's early years and English career, with reminiscences of him gathered from various sources. It was a work of greater difficulty to provide for the editing of the second and more important section of the biography, that, namely, which was to give an account of the episcopate. There were very few persons in England sufficiently acquainted with Indian ecclesiastical matters to undertake the task, and of these few none could command the necessary leisure. When at length, after long delay, all hope of securing a more able editor faded away, the question of the Memoir became a personal one for myself. The moment arrived when, had I stood aloof, the project must have fallen to the ground. Under these circumstances it appeared to be my duty to face the responsibility of carrying it out, rather than to yield wholly to self-distrust. It seemed right to make an effort that might in some measure express my sense of that loyalty towards the Bishop which, unchilled by years of separation, seemed to acquire a yet brighter glow when no renewal of earthly intercourse could be looked for. Thus the work of compiling the greater part of the following pages passed unavoidably and almost insensibly into my hands. In discharging this trust, my aim has been to make the Bishop's words the record, as far as possible, of his mind and work, and to introduce supplementary matter only as the framework of his journals and letters, or as links of connection or explanation. Some subjects and incidents seemed to demand a closer and more concentrated treatment than isolated letters could supply. In all such cases I have desired faithfully to exhibit, in a more expanded narrative, my husband's sentiments and motives of action, so far as these could be drawn from a large amount of public and private correspondence and from my own knowledge of his character.

I have to acknowledge obligations to various sources whence materials have been derived. I am much indebted to Lord Lawrence, who, as Viceroy, permitted me to have the use of the ecclesiastical correspondence with the Government of India; to private friends in Calcutta, who undertook to superintend the tedious labour of copying the large official correspondence left in Bishop's Palace; and to many others, both in India and England, who have contributed a large collection of the Bishop's more private letters. I lie under an obligation of a different kind to Professor Cowell and the Rev. J. N. Simpkinson, who furnished respectively a brief sketch of the Calcutta University, and a review of the Bishop's second charge. Except for aid in these two instances, most kindly rendered, and by myself gratefully appreciated, the work has derived scarcely any advantage from the direct assistance of others. If I abstain from a more specific acknowledgment of some valued criticism on one or more isolated sections, it is because I desire to bear the undivided responsibility of blemishes and deficiencies of which I am fully conscious.

S. A. C.

1870.

PREFACE

TO

THE SECOND EDITION.

ON the first appearance of this Memoir, an opinion was expressed by many readers that such portion of it as related to the Bishop's connexion with Marlborough College had been inadequately treated. There were grounds for this opinion, inasmuch as this special section, in common with the whole account of his life in England, had been sketched, advisedly, in a brief and general manner. Such a criticism, however, coming from several quarters, and having reference to a marked period in the Bishop's English career, called for attentive consideration: it is in deference to the wishes of those who initiated this criticism, or concurred in it, that a republication of the book has been decided upon. The direct purpose, therefore, of a new edition is to bring into greater prominence, and to describe with more detail the work carried on during the tenure of the Mastership of Marlborough College. The new matter contributed for this purpose, and now introduced as supplemental to that put together in the first instance by the Dean of Westminster, has its place between pp. 15–30. The compiling of these pages has been a joint work, kindly undertaken by some who were closely connected with the school and were familiar with its history during the years 1852–1858.

A fresh issue of the book likewise furnishes a means of correcting an error in the Appendix to which the late Archdeacon Pratt called attention, so soon as it came under his notice in India. The error related to figures only, and arose out of a misapprehension of his financial statement of the Hills Schools Fund. It was, however, of importance, as involving the question of the principle which regulated the administration of that Fund. The first part of the Appendix has now been altered in accordance with the Archdeacon's corrections as set forth in his letter in the *Indian Church Gazette* of March 18, 1871.

Lastly, the early exhaustion of the first edition opens the way for a second edition at a reduction of price, which may be favourable to a more extended circulation. A republication of this Memoir will not be lost work, if, in days when men pass rapidly out of sight, it serves to preserve yet awhile the record of an earnest and guileless life. It will not be unfruitful if, in an age of haste and unrest, it wins any reader to gather some lessons for daily life from a study of that tranquillity, steadfastness, and truth which so essentially characterised the public and private life of the late Bishop of Calcutta.

S. A. C.

1872.

CONTENTS.

CHAPTER VI.

CHAPTER VII.

CHAPTER VIII.

CHAPTER IX.

CHAPTER X.

CHAPTER XI.

CHAPTER XII.

CHAPTER XIII.

CHAPTER XIV.

CHAPTER XV.

LIFE

OF

BISHOP COTTON.

CHAPTER I.

BIRTH — DEATH OF HIS FATHER — EDUCATION AT WESTMINSTER SCHOOL — UNDERGRADUATE LIFE AT TRINITY COLLEGE, CAMBRIDGE — HABITS AND PRINCIPLES — EARLY FRIENDS — VAUGHAN — CONYBEARE — LETTER FROM MISS MITFORD.

George Edward Lynch Cotton was born October 29, 1813, at Chester, at the house of his grandmother, the widow of Dr. Cotton, Dean of Chester. On November 13, a fortnight after the child's birth, his father, Captain Cotton of the 7th Fusileers, and major of brigade to Major-General Byng, serving in the second division of the British army, was killed at the head of his brigade, while in the act of storming a redoubt on the left of the enemy's intrenchments, before the village of Ainhoué, in the battle of the Nivelle. His son was baptized in the cathedral, and spent his childhood in the town of Chester.

To his mother, in the belief of those who knew him best, he owed his chief early stimulus to those literary and intellectual tastes which he never lost. His marked capacity for humour, on the other hand, though doubtless fostered by her acuteness and vivacity, was rather an inheritance from his father's family. But thrown as he necessarily was from the peculiarities of his early childhood most upon himself, the sweetness of temper and even balance of mind, which distinguished him through life, and the power of absorbing the good and eschewing the evil of surrounding circumstances, were gifts peculiarly his own. He had a keen interest in his father's family. He much enjoyed the only visit he ever paid at Combermere while the veteran head of his house, the first Viscount Combermere, was still alive; and it was with the truest pleasure that he revived in India a long dormant claim of cousinship with Sir Arthur and Sir Sidney Cotton. But it was with his father's brothers and sisters that he was chiefly thrown, for they were fondly attached to him from his earliest infancy, and regarded him as a child of much promise. He was full of delight in family recollections. 'Certainly,' he says in a letter to a much-loved pupil, 'the friendships which we form for ourselves are great sources of happiness, yet there is a charm about relationship which other intimacies rarely have. It is so extremely delightful to call people by their Christian names, and talk over all the old stories of one's childhood, and do exactly what one likes.' In 1845, he married his cousin Sophia Anne, eldest daughter of the late Rev. Henry Tomkinson, of Reaseheath in Cheshire, and family ties were thus in after days strengthened by a yet deeper bond, which can only be appreciated by those who knew the blessedness of that undivided union of twenty-one years.

When he was between eleven and twelve years old, that is to say in January 1825, he entered Westminster, in the Lower School, and was admitted upon the Foundation at Whitsuntide 1828. Some of his Westminster contemporaries, one of whom was amongst his earliest and most intimate friends, have thus described their recollections:—

'College was at this time an abominable place in point of the hardships and tyranny to be endured, and on the score of morality also very bad indeed. The fags, fewer in number than their masters, were simply menial servants wholly in the power of the seniors, and partially of the "third election," which rank Cotton had attained when I entered college. Cotton himself had suffered much under this system in the earlier stages of his course, and had contracted a retiring and guarded manner. Being of a weakly constitution and unadventurous spirit, he had never thrown himself with zest into the games of the school; and the college rules, which forced the juniors to take their part in cricket, football, hockey, and boating, with plentiful application of punishment to bunglers, had unfortunately created a distaste for these exercises, fostered further by his own studious and somewhat diffident disposition, and by his repugnance to all that was brutal and degrading which was perceptible even then. And the dry quaint humour of his peculiar genius was used to soften the harsh and repulsive character of the life that was so distasteful to him, to soften it for others as well as for himself. Surrounded as he was by associates with whom he had little sympathy, he fell spontaneously into a method resembling the "Socratic irony." Talking with those who were too strong for him to check, when bent on some cruel or discreditable act, he would lead them unawares into some admission which showed their conduct in its true colours, and he would drive home this conclusion by some remark which I hesitate to call sarcastic, because it was never unkind. And he would talk to the juniors in a tone of pleasant banter which cheered them under their task-work, and which but expressed that considerate sympathy which the atmosphere of the place forbade to be shown more openly. It was always a relief to me when my turn came round to be assigned to the service of the "third election," chiefly, though not wholly, because of the pleasure of being thus brought into contact with Cotton.'

A similar account is given by another friend who was a contemporary of Cotton's at school, and was also at Cambridge with him: 'He was not considered a boy of first-rate abilities, though standing well and studious and persevering. He was an insatiable reader, not only, as generally is the case with boys, of works of imagination, but he had read far more widely than most of his age the best histories and standard works. He was very fond of theatrical amusements, and he and I generally used to contrive a visit to any celebrated performance, and especially to any good opera. Cotton's discursive reading and vivid imagination made him in great demand as a teller of stories; he would go on for hours, either from recollection or inventing as he proceeded. Even when a senior he never bullied the younger boys, but if his fags offended him he used to invent odd, harmless punishments. He acted in the Westminster plays, I think twice. I remember him particularly as an old nurse in the "Eunuchus," and he acted capitally. He was full of odd fun. I remember once, when he was out of school in the boarding-house (i.e. either really or fancifully unwell), our concocting at his suggestion a supposed translation from the Danish, and sending it to the "Gentleman's Magazine." When it appeared in the venerable publication his glee was extreme, and especially when, a few weeks after, there was an editorial note wishing to hear from the translator again.' After some remarks about the 'very low ebb as to religious tone' at which the school was, he continues: 'But according to the standard of the day, Cotton always stood high. I remember he always said his prayers at night.'

Another friend writes: 'My recollections of Cotton at Westminster, scanty as they are, are still very definite, though I was but twelve to fourteen at the time. When-

I got into college myself in 1830 he was "third election."

'He was certainly a very odd boy at that time, as peculiar in character as in manner and appearance.

'He had very little sympathy with the ways of boys in general, did not care for games, and had been knocked about a good deal, I fancy, in his earlier college days. His quaint and grotesque humour was more demonstrative at that time than in after years; and it was formed on him, I think, as a sort of shell, by which he protected himself from intrusion, and vindicated some independence for himself, amongst companions who were stronger and more resolute than himself, but whom he did not care to follow, and wished to keep at a certain distance. There was no privacy procurable at that time in college, even the seniors and third election having no better approach to studies than the "houses," i.e. the great green baize enclosures round the three fires in the dormitory, in each of which they formed a kind of common room.

'Cotton was most kind to us wretched juniors. Beside him I only remember two or three who took any pains to be so, especially ——, blessings on his head! I wonder where he is now, and ——, a loose and disreputable fellow, but a thoroughly warm-hearted one. It was a great alleviation to the miseries of our Helot condition to have Cotton's kindly humour playing continually about us. He was our good angel in the "middle house." And while his way of treating us showed a sympathy at all times with our outcast state, it had also a softening effect upon the other potentates of the pale. I remember, too, how he would get some tyrant of ours into conversation about his threats or his summary proceedings, and by a Socratic process draw from him some very damaging admissions against himself; breaking, when he had achieved this triumph, into that half-suppressed chuckle which was so characteristic of him at all times.'

His name still remains carved in large letters on the stonework of the school doorway. He never lost his interest in Westminster. At one time it cost him many a pang to surrender the thought of being the head master of the school; and even in India it was curious to trace the traditions of Westminster permeating the ecclesiastical intelligence, which under his supervision appeared in Indian periodicals. Thus, when Archbishop Longley was raised to the See of Canterbury, it was told there probably alone, amongst all the numerous announcements of that appointment, how Longley, the only popular monitor in the midst of an unpopular generation, had fifty years before been greeted in Westminster school with the cry of 'Rose amongst Thorns;' 'Rose amongst Thorns;' and when he wrote from the same distant shores to the dear friend who had become Dean of Westminster, it was with the fervour inspired by his own early recollections: 'I think of you as ruling the noblest and grandest of English churches, the one to which in historical and religious interests even Canterbury must yield; the one in which I worshipped as a boy, in which I was confirmed, and in which I was consecrated to the great work of my life.'

He went up to Trinity College, Cambridge, as a Westminster scholar, in 1832, taking with him, if his own account of himself is to be trusted, no great attainments in scholarship, no eager thirst after knowledge for its own sake, rather narrow views of work, but a well-defined resolve to get a good place in the classical tripos if it could be got by steady diligence. He used to laugh at himself for the scorn with which he and others had treated the suggestions of the tutor that they should of course read the history of a particular period in Niebuhr—'as if Niebuhr had anything to do with the tripos.' As an example of his steady adherence to rules once laid down for his work, he said, 'When 12 o'clock struck, I used to shut up my books, though I was in the middle of a Greek play.' This regularity, however, could not always be maintained by a man who had so large a number of acquaintances and of such various kinds. He has sometimes described in his own humorous way a breakfast, 'which I gave to a party of my rowing friends. Hoping to get rid of them in tolerable time in the morning, and yet wishing to be hospitable, I bought a box of cigars for the occasion, though I never smoke myself. Unfortunately they liked my cigars so much that they stayed smoking in my room from breakfast till hall, utterly discomfiting my plans for reading.' The records of his college life, in his journals, were most enlivening. In later years he sometimes read passages from them to his younger relations, and the reading never failed to excite shouts of laughter. He was always in the first class in his college examinations, and he also got the prize for reading in chapel, and a declamation prize.

By that time his character, such as we all think of it now, had received its final bent, and was already formed in its main outlines. Principles and aspirations distinctively Christian were manifest and prominent in all his words and ways. He was a teacher in the 'Jesus Lane Sunday school,' a member of various religious associations among the undergraduates, and an adherent avowedly of the Evangelical school, which indeed was the only one at that time recognised at Cambridge as inculcating devoutness and devotedness of life. But there was much in the Evangelical system which he distrusted and objected to, and the teaching which had already won his full sympathy and adherence was that of Arnold. It was a delightful and a surprising thing to Arnold's pupils to find one who was as enthusiastic an admirer as themselves of their great master, and this common feeling became of course a special bond of union. Cotton got to know several of the Rugby men well; Charles Vaughan above all, who soon became well-nigh his chief friend. But no one was ever allowed to supersede or even rival the most cherished of all, W. J. Conybeare. His conversation on all serious questions was always thoroughly reverent—its fault being, perhaps, that he exacted rather more confidence than he gave. On personal and other secular matters it was tinged with that indescribable sort of humour, which was all his own, delighting in quaint analogies, in bluntness purposely carried a little too far, yet always stopping short of rudeness, and in rather incongruous fancies constantly mixed up with the realities of the moment, yet withdrawn at once whenever any moral consideration made them out of place. One of his strange fancies was to make out every term a 'Tripos' of his friends and acquaintances, the three classes being carefully arranged in the exact order of his *liking* during that particular period. The Tripos was decorated with (A) (B), (1) (2), &c., as in the Cambridge Calendar, to represent Chancellor's medals and Smith's Prizes. The Medals were for *agreeableness*; the Smith's Prizes for *goodness.* Apparently this was done purely for his own satisfaction, and for the pleasure of alluding to it, as he was careful to conceal the list from everybody, though fond of telling them that he had been 'setting a paper' for it, during a walk with some unsuspecting friend, or that his Tripos was 'coming out the next day.'

The present Master of the Temple had a share in a ludicrous episode that grew out of this whim, and thus records a story still fresh in his mind:—'One day when Cotton was in my room he let out that his last new Tripos was lying on his writing-table. I made some excuse for leaving him, went to his room, seized the paper, and with a fork from his gyp-room stuck it into the plaster of the wall at the foot of his staircase. I returned to Cotton, and presently told him what I had done. He, not knowing what eye might read the fatal paper, was aghast, flew to the spot with stifled shrieks of laughter, and tore it down. He was too late, however, to anticipate the gaze of another friend who, happening to pass by, had of course studied a document thus conspicuously displayed, and, uninitiated in its mysteries, had been already lost in conjecture as to the meaning of a Tripos in which he saw his own name in an unexplained place.

Another of his favourite amusements was to challenge those who, like Vaughan, prided themselves, as he too did, on their knowledge of the Cambridge Calendar, to a contest of mutual examinations, 'more *Westmonasteriensi*.' 'Who was tenth wrangler in 1829?' 'Who was the first Browne's medallist?' or, passing from 'book-work' to 'problems,' to propound with high glee such knotty questions as, 'When would it next be Sidney's turn in the "cycle of proctors"?' 'When would "second tripos day" fall in leap year, if Easter Day were on March 21?' After taking his B.A. degree he continued to reside in college, reading for his fellowship and taking pupils. 'Among these,' says the same friend who has furnished recollections of his school life at Westminster, 'I remember especially Lord Edward Howard, in whom he was very much interested, and who, I think, was in turn much attached to him. He had a great power of influencing younger men, less by force of character, or attractiveness of manner, or genial sympathy, than by the interest he showed in them, accompanied, I may add, by a *curiosity* which did not offend them, being evidently so innocent and so unassuming. This often drew them out, and gave him an opportunity, which he used with great kindness and faithfulness, of remarking on what he observed, and giving them useful counsel. Vaughan was the first to divine what special capabilities were in him for the work of a schoolmaster which I should hardly have thought, and was the cause of his going to Rugby.'

This brief notice of George Cotton in his school and

college days will close with the following singular incident, which has come to light through the letters of Mary Russell Mitford.*

Miss Mitford to the Rev. W. Harness.

September 1829.

I have got the 'Bann of the Empire,' the real words in German and English; and after the great chain of literary connexion which has been set in motion on this question, the libraries that have been ransacked, the German historians and law professors that have been written to, the document has been discovered and sent to me by a Westminster school-boy! Perhaps you know his mother, a Mrs. Hutchinson Simpson, living at Frognal, Hampstead, and the youth, my friend, is her only child by a former marriage, a boy of the name of Cotton.

The letters both of mother and son are very interesting; hers especially remind me much of Mrs. Hemans. The lad heard that I wanted the document from a friend, and sent me first the 'Ecclesiastical Bann,' which he found in a French book. When I told him with many thanks that it was not the thing wanted, he set about learning German, and by the help of a Saxon friend has actually sent me the undiscoverable prize, as I have told you. We shall hear of that youth himself in literature some day or other. In the meantime, I am more touched and pleased by the interest which he has evinced in the matter than I have ever been by any compliment in my life.

* 'Letters of Mary Russell Mitford,' edited by the Rev. A. G. K. L'Estrange.

CHAPTER II.

DEGREE AT CAMBRIDGE—MASTERSHIP AT RUGBY—DR. ARNOLD—COURSE OF LIFE AT RUGBY—INFLUENCE ON BOYS IN HIS OWN HOUSE—SELECT PREACHER AT CAMBRIDGE—ELECTION TO THE MASTERSHIP OF MARLBOROUGH COLLEGE—HIS WORK AT MARLBOROUGH—REMINISCENCES BY JOHN CAMPBELL SHAIRP—CORRESPONDENCE.

In 1836 he took his degree, and was a senior optime and eighth in the first class of the classical tripos. In the same year he was appointed by Dr. Arnold to an assistant mastership at Rugby.

The influences of this appointment on his after life were incalculable. First amongst these must be counted the impression produced upon him by the character and teaching of his great chief. It is not too much to say that there was none of all the direct pupils of Dr. Arnold on whom so exclusive a mark of their master's mind was produced as on Cotton. They received this mark on minds more or less incapable of fully appreciating the force of his character; and in later years, in many instances, its particular effects were more or less rudely effaced, either by the impulses of their own growing thoughts, or by the disturbing attractions of other men and other schools of thought. But Cotton came into contact with him after his mind had been already formed, and yet before he had been swayed by any other commanding influence.

He had received from his intercourse with his Rugby friends at Cambridge a strong predisposition to admire and to love the man whose fame they were proud to spread amongst their new acquaintances. Indeed there grew up at Cambridge a circle of disciples, to which no exact parallel could be found at Oxford—not that the Oxford Rugbeians were themselves less enthusiastic than those on the banks of the Cam—but that the receptive elements which they found at Oxford were fewer or less responsive. All who remember those days will recall the delight with which they found in such men as Conybeare, Howson, Freeman, and others, willing listeners to all they could pour forth of their beloved master, friends who seemed to gather like a new undergrowth beneath the parent tree which had sheltered them. But amongst all those Cotton was chief. From the moment that he first made Arnold's acquaintance, he never wavered in his loyalty. He may, after his manner, have criticised and deprecated parts of his character or career. But no other hero ever took the place of the image which had thus been enshrined in his heart; there was never either in his own mind, or in the circle of his later acquaintances, any force sufficiently powerful to disturb its pre-eminence. His long continuance within the direct sphere of its influence, first at Rugby, then at Marlborough, tended to keep it intact; and when he entered on the wider field of India, the inspiring force of Arnold's genius and goodness only found a new channel in which to work, and all that was most elevating and peculiar in those bright recollections of his early youth stamped itself on every part of the task which he there undertook. There is no proof of Arnold's practical influence so undivided, so unquestionable, so little alloyed with any baser matter, as the blameless and fruitful career which will be described in the following pages. In the book* which beyond any other will keep fresh in the minds of future generations the picture of school-life at Rugby, it will be remembered that the crisis of the story is brought about by

* 'Tom Brown's School Days,' part i. chap. ix.

the wise suggestion of a young master, 'the model young master,' lately come. That 'young master' was Cotton.

'There are those,' so writes a younger friend, 'who can 'still recall the picture of the two men, as they have 'seen them side by side in the school-close, or met them 'in the hedge-grown lanes of Warwickshire, the one 'in the very prime of vigorous middle age, tall, stal-'wart, dark-visaged, with keen eye that flashes still through 'the mist of years, and swinging stride and prompt 'utterance, and under lip and lower jaw that spoke of 'suppressed energy and will, the king of men as he seemed 'to his loving or trembling pupils; the other tall also, 'and younger, and with a face interesting even to boys, 'but of hesitating and awkward gait, slow in speech, dry 'in manner, somewhat slouching in figure, short-sighted, 'and playing perpetually with an eyeglass, as unlike his 'companion in physical gifts as in force of character and 'fire of genius.

'Cotton's success as a schoolmaster was by no means 'rapid or unchequered.

'His Rugby life extended over fifteen years: a time of 'slow and gradual growth, in which the foundations for 'some present and much future success were laid with 'daily toil and patience. His keen and boyish sense of 'life's mirthful side never left him. He was often the 'most amusing and laughter-moving of companions. There 'was a natural and quiet flow of genial humour that over-'ran and freshened, like a mountain spring, the dry places 'and arid relations, the numbing cares and anxieties, of 'scholastic life. The visitors at that hospitable house 'will remember the quaint reminiscences of books and 'travel that reproduced Vitellius in the denizen of his 'pigsty, the Semiramis of Prague in the Libussa who drew 'his carriage, the Norman invaders' dog in the whelp 'Hardigras, and which transformed two faithful household 'servants from a Ramsay and a Packwood to a Criologus 'and Xylosagus. But with all this he was never frivolous 'or self-indulgent: the vein of ceaseless humour which 'played beneath an exterior somewhat grim and saturnine 'was combined with an intensity and earnestness of reli-'gious life which formed the chief feature in his character. 'The pastoral relation in which a clergyman should stand 'to his pupils was never out of his sight. To deepen and 'quicken the Christian side of public school life was the 'deliberate purpose of his life. It was now that he drew 'up and published manuals of devotion for school-boys, 'which have stood the tests of many schools and many 'generations of boys. It was now that he laid the founda-'tion for his future excellence as a preacher by his carefully 'prepared addresses to his house on Sunday evenings. 'It was now that, in occasional sermons at Rugby and 'elsewhere, and as a select preacher before the University 'of Cambridge in the year 1843, he gave evidence alike of 'his powers, and of his promise as a preacher. It was 'now that, in his preparation of his pupils for Confirmation, 'he learnt to find his way to the often closed casket of an 'English boy's thoughts and feelings. It was now that by 'his minute and careful study of all the details of education, 'he laid the foundation of the powers of organisation which 'afterwards developed themselves elsewhere. It was now, 'finally, that by systematic reading and laborious self-'cultivation, he trained himself to become what he was in 'India, the teacher not of boys, but of men.

'Yet he had many difficulties to contend with, and his 'self-development was slow and lingering. It was not at 'once that he acquired the art of enforcing discipline, or 'controlling unruly and turbulent boyhood. He was in 'some respects before his age, and his very efforts to 'become acquainted with his juniors were for a time re-'sented by the stolid conservatism of boys, if not of men, 'as a revolutionary encroachment. His dry humour was 'branded as sarcasm: his interest in his pupils was de-

'nounced as favouritism. He had little of the charm of 'manner which in some men is itself a passport to the 'hearts of others, none of the ready address and super'ficial tact which come unsought to less earnest spirits. 'But he won his way, and the circle of his friends widened 'yearly, and the devotion of his pupils yearly gathered 'strength. There was about the man a simplicity and 'earnestness which went straight to the hearts of those who 'had once come under his spell. After the death of 'Arnold he became the attached friend and trusted coun'sellor of his successor. His pupils, among whom might 'be mentioned the late Professor Conington at the one 'university, the present Lord Derby at the other, carried 'with them to other scenes their warm and affectionate 'homage. And the man himself was growing, not merely 'his reputation and influence. "He seemed," it has been 'said of him often, both before and since his death—"he 'seemed, as time went on, to develop new faculties, to 'become master of fresh gifts: decision, promptness, know'ledge of mankind, came to him as gold comes to the 'patient miner;" and when twelve years had passed, and he 'had vainly offered himself as the successor of Dr. Tait 'to the chair of Arnold, it was felt that he had accumulated 'powers and gifts which might well be exerted in a larger 'sphere. That sphere was found at last, and his Rugby 'life ended in 1852 with his election to the mastership 'of the large school at Marlborough, known as Marl'borough College. It was a post at that time of anxiety 'and difficulty, and a man of less quiet confidence and courage might have shrunk from it.' *

The system of the English public school is so well known that there can be but few who do not understand how much the working of that system in any case,

* Article in 'Macmillan's Magazine' for December, 1866, 'The late Bishop of Calcutta,' by the Rev. G. Granville Bradley, Master of Marlborough College.

however thoroughly it be apprehended and applied, depends on accumulated experience and tradition; how the spirit and tone of such a school must grow, rather than be created by any sudden effort; how sensitive these are and liable to deterioration if sound influences be not unceasingly at work to maintain them. If even long-established schools have had their periods of difficulty and decadence, it must be apparent that to build up a new public school from the very foundation is no easy task even under the most favourable circumstances. The experiment which was practically first made, in its complete form, at Marlborough, was undertaken under some peculiarly unfavourable conditions. To bring the terms within the reach of persons who could not afford to avail themselves of the older institutions, it was necessary to reduce expenses by massing boys together to an extent unknown at any institution of the modern public school type. The old schools were aggregates of small manageable communities; Marlborough proposed to house, feed, discipline, educate, a whole school as one body; and the very success which it met with in its first years in attracting from time to time as many boys as it could accommodate aggravated its difficulties. How these necessarily arose at its very commencement cannot be expressed more forcibly than in the words of Mr. Cotton himself, who, in speaking in his own day of the past history of the school, observed that 'the difficulties of Marlborough commenced when on the first morning of its existence 400 shoes vainly endeavoured to find their owners.'

To organise the domestic economy, discipline, studies, the very games, of 200 boys, all strange to each other and to their masters, could not but be a task of no ordinary difficulty, requiring time for its completion. From the original 200 the numbers increased with the additional accommodation provided, and the problem of fashioning a public school with the tone, opinion, tradition essential to its success, was complicated rather than simplified by the apparent prosperity. When it is added that, in the absence of all experience of the economy of such an institution, the terms were found to have been fixed at too low a point to admit of the school assuming the true character designed for it, and that, in the effort to carry it on upon the original basis, a heavy debt was incurred which still further crippled its insufficient resources, it may be understood that after nine years of existence the task of placing Marlborough in the ranks of the public schools of the country still remained to be performed. It was Mr. Cotton's mission to lay the solid foundation on which an able and brilliant successor reared the superstructure of a flourishing public school. To use his own words, he entered on this mission 'with trepidation and misgiving,' and a success that all acknowledged was neither rapid nor easy. The new head master was not distinguished by the physical qualities or the genius by which the admiration of the young is won, nor had he that force of will which subjugates other wills to its own views and purposes. On the other hand, his own peculiar gifts displayed themselves early and conspicuously amidst the perplexities of a trying position. A calm patience in accepting difficulties; powers of conciliation which went far to disarm opposition; the blending of humility with self-reliance, always leading him to seek counsel on every side, but never to abdicate responsibility; firmness in vindicating law and order, tempered by unbounded sympathy with the young; an intuitive comprehension of a boy's nature;—all these qualities, the task which he had undertaken brought out into high relief. From the highest point of view, the principle on which Mr. Cotton carried out his six years' work is best expressed by the text of his first sermon in the school chapel: *Wist ye not that I must be about my*

Father's business? The certainty that his own daily work was his Father's business had become so completely a part of his moral being, that it would have been unnatural to him not to try always to act upon it. Those who saw him with unprejudiced eyes, saw no theory of religion or morality, but a living proof of the truth of one. Those who saw, may be allowed to speak for once of the strength, the vital force which it gave him.

It was now, too, in a new and arduous field of work that his powers for administration and organisation came into full play. Their action may be illustrated by a few details of the measures which he adopted for remedying some of the disadvantages under which Marlborough, with its new and peculiar features, laboured. Of these a prominent one has been already noticed, the massing together of the whole school in one body. School life became under such circumstances necessarily subject to somewhat stern and hard conditions. Quiet, retirement, opportunities for private intercourse between friends, all the various conditions of life which different dispositions would require for their best development, were unattainable where only one common public life was known. Arrangements were therefore made for extending the subdivision which had been already begun so far as to give a few of the oldest boys studies. The number of studies was increased, and gradually rooms were provided for small groups of boys, to whom such a scene would be more congenial than the larger common life of the great schoolrooms. The youngest and lowest boys were congregated apart in one of the three large blocks of buildings; a measure especially necessary at Marlborough, owing to the fact of boys entering at an earlier age than at other public schools. Work, discipline, comfort, and closer supervision of the younger boys were thus promoted.

In a somewhat similar direction, modifications in the form of government were introduced. The same theory of administering the whole school as one body had caused the management of everything except what came under the head of finance to be concentrated in the hands of the head master. A mass of business connected with details of discipline and oversight monopolised valuable time, and burdened him with a maximum of responsibility while it left his subordinates with a minimum of independence. To remedy this defect, the buildings other than that assigned to the younger boys were divided into six sections, called 'houses,' though one roof covered three of them. Each 'house' had its own class-room and its own house-master, who was specially responsible for its discipline, and communicated regularly with the parents of the boys. By these changes, society was broken up into manageable portions; wholesome rivalries and attachments grew up, and the assistant-masters obtained each his independent sphere of work.

It is worth noticing, as illustrating a breadth of view, wisdom of mind, and freedom from prejudice which would endeavour to find and readily recognise any good feature even in what seemed to require reform, that Mr. Cotton always acknowledged a good side in the large public life of Marlborough so unlike what he had been accustomed to at Rugby. Its power of creating and maintaining a strong public opinion, bearing on the whole community, of excluding some bad tendencies of school life in the forms with which he was familiar, were often discussed and dwelt upon. Feeling keenly how the power of influence for good or for evil was intensified by this feature in the school, he never wished to abolish it as a source of evil only, but rather to make it operate, subject to such modifications as have been indicated, for the general good. For the government of the school, there was another principle to which one, thoroughly imbued with the associations and traditions of the Rugby of Dr. Arnold, could not fail to look as the fundamental support of a sound system; viz. the governing the school in a great measure through its own members. In the head boys—prefects as they were called—Mr. Cotton at once sought, and in many instances found, successors in his confidence and affections to the præpostors who had so largely shared in the rule of his house at Rugby. That the authority thus delegated should have been, at first, not always discreetly exercised or fully acquiesced in by the mass of the school, can be no matter for surprise. An incident that occurred during his first year illustrates alike the difficulties attending the assertion of the principle, and his mode of dealing with them. Some boys indulging, in rather a lawless form, the love of field sports to which boy nature is prone, and for the gratification of which the surrounding country offered great opportunities, had taken to poaching as a diversion, and kept a dog to aid the sport. The prefects were directed to stop this practice. In a short time three of them came upon the boys with the dog, in or near a preserve. The prefects seized the dog, and being perplexed to know what to do with it, they killed it. Of course the outcry on the part of the school was loud against the new authorities, and in favour of the injured poachers. An outbreak seemed imminent. Mr. Cotton at once took a step which will seem hazardous to those who know English boys: he summoned the whole society into the Upper School and made a short speech, which is said by those who were present as boys, and clearly remember the occasion, to have answered its purpose completely. 'The dog is dead, and I am inclined to think that its death is due to excess of zeal'—a grotesque sentence which occurred in the speech—had the sort of magical effect which is attributed to dust thrown upon a swarm of angry bees; the ferment subsided, or was turned into amusement; 'The dawg is dead' and 'Excess of zeal' were chalked up all over the school walls, and became familiar expressions when an 'accomplished fact had to be accepted, or a ludicrous excuse made. This incident is related at length here, partly because it was at the time an important step towards establishing the authority of the prefects and securing order in the school, partly because the mixture of gravity and grotesqueness was particularly characteristic of the man.

Besides thus seeking to associate the elder boys with himself in the discipline of the rest, he lost no opportunity of establishing more intimate converse with those who came to be intimately known. One pupil or another constantly shared the long walks which were his chief recreation. Much of the pleasure of these walks was derived from his keen enjoyment of a fine and varied country. In this respect Marlborough could claim undisputed superiority over Rugby. One there was who, in a moment of mental rebellion against the monotony of the midland counties, had once compared a certain Warwickshire road to 'the driest form of rationalistic Pro testantism.' A criticism which so entirely met Mr. Cotton's innate and peculiar sense of humour was never forgotten To the latest days of his life it used ever and anon to come back upon his mind, fresh and pungent as in the hour of its first utterance, awakening for the moment vivid memories of days that had been. Cheering and invigorating, from the contrast with sameness and dulness thus denounced, were the outward features of the new Wiltshire home. With a zest and enjoyment which increased as years rolled by, he used to drink in the fresh breezes of the open downs on one side, or luxuriate in the exquisite glades of Savernake Forest on the other. Sometimes on a long half-holiday he would wend his way to a distant, but choice and favourite spot, the Roman Camp at Martinshill, a fine commanding point in the range of chalk hills, and overlooking as fair a reach of true English scenery as the eye would wish to rest upon.

It was in these opportunities for familiar converse that the master reached many a secret spring in a young mind; that the boy found the treasure of a friendship which he knew to be invigorating and elevating; which he felt would remain most faithful and satisfying. Many other times for private or social intercourse were turned to account. He used to look over the composition papers in his own study with each separately. Some of his old pupils as they remember those half-hours say that 'they trace back to them the first germs of real intellectual life.' Some of the Sixth Form usually met at his house on Saturday evenings to dine and read Shakespeare. After the lapse of years they still speak of his amusing renderings of many comic characters. He attended the meetings of the Debating Society when invited, and sometimes spoke himself as a visitor, after the boys had made their speeches. In school he was a careful and painstaking teacher: here as elsewhere it is worth observing how his characteristic union of graver and lighter qualities was exhibited. His lessons in divinity and history made a lasting impression: his genuinely Christian spirit, clearness of statement, sound sense and thoroughness, had full scope in this part of the work; in construing Tacitus and Aristophanes, his satirical tendencies, his fondness for epigram, and his humour were brought out; the memory of these lessons too is still fresh in the minds of those who heard them. During the half-year the number of the more serious blunders made by each boy in his composition was entered against his name in a note-book. At the end of the half-year the head master used to give an address to his form about the performance of their duties during the past weeks, and besides reading out their order according to the half-year's marks, he also produced a tripos, arranged in order of demerit, on the principle of a donkey race, in which the greatest number of bad mistakes secured a first class, which it was a great disgrace to obtain, and the least number a third class, which was a coveted distinction, while to be plucked was to ascend a pinnacle of glory aspired to only by the most soaring spirits.

We may here insert from the pen of one of his most attached Sixth Form pupils a testimony to the force and reality of the influence that was diffused by his daily life among them.

'. . . . It is no figure of speech, but the sober truth, to say that among us, to know him at all, was to venerate him; to know him well, was to love as well as to venerate him with an ardour and depth of devotion to which I have known no parallel. He was a man of few words, except when among his intimate friends, but truly his silence was more eloquent than other men's speech. We knew that underneath a calm exterior there was a heart overflowing with genuine kindness; there was a rare humour, the outcome of a mind that could regard every aspect of life and character with sympathy; it was no succession of flashes, rejoicing in their own brilliancy; it was a genuine under-current of the soul, a subdued mirthfulness of disposition, a something into which his whole nature dissolved itself, till he could say "*Homo sum, nihil humani a me alienum puto.*" . . . .

'A sympathy such as this, evidenced not only by his manner, but by his whole life among us, was, I think, one great secret of his success. We felt that when he condemned, it was not the condemnation of one who had never failed himself, or who could look down from a lofty eminence on all that fell short of the right, the beautiful, and the true. It was a condemnation tempered by love, and by a close and sympathetic appreciation of all the difficulties and temptations of school life. So too, when he approved, we knew that his approval was no cold encouragement to those from whom he was himself far removed; it was genuine sympathy, bestowed by one who worked *with* us as well as for us; one who was ever ready to see good intentions where good intentions failed of success; to gauge the act by the motive rather than by the result.

'His self-command, combined as it was with an almost uniform gravity of presence and of countenance, was appreciated most by those of us whose duty it was to assist him in governing the school. And under the most trying circumstances, when the gravest errors of judgment had been committed, when those upon whom he depended most, appeared for the time to fail him, not even calumny itself could say that he acted with anything but his unvarying calmness and allowance for extenuating circumstances. When everyone else was hurried away by excitement, one felt sure that discriminating and impartial justice would be met with at his hands. Not that he was ever what friend or foe would describe as a man of tact; he was far too great for that: indifferent alike to popular applause and censure, he saw the thing that was right and did it. His skill in governing was not that of a man who can thread his tortuous way between dangers upon this side and that, by taking now a longer, now a shorter step; now coaxing this opponent, now that, till both thought they had him on their side and both alike went with a good grace where he would have them. He never wantonly offended prejudices, but neither did he tamper with them or with his own sincerity. He went straight to his mark, regardless of what others might say or think. His was pre-eminently a candid and judicial mind: he was never hurried away by a cry, never joined an unreasoning clamour; he loved the truth, and the truth made him free, and made him also love freedom. A sweeping assertion made in his presence by one of his pupils, he would not contradict at the moment; he would even regard it with sympathy, as an evidence of intellectual energy; but that same sympathy, under the guise of humour, would enable him at some future time to suggest the modifying circumstances which vitiated the theory. . . . But in truth the greatest lesson we learnt from him—what we have treasured in his absence, and treasure now more than ever, when we can see his face no more—was the lesson of his life. With him we always felt that morality and religion went hand in hand; his religion was not a cut and dried system; it was not a theological dogma; it was the life of Christ that he set forth to us in his sermons, and that he evidenced in his own life. His sermons, his Confirmation classes, his solemn addresses to the Sixth Form at the close of each half-year—all were laden with the same burden, the task of working our religion into every action, however small; and blending duty with religion till the two were inseparable, alike in fact and in thought. This, if anything, he taught us then; and this, if anything, will be the moral of his untimely death.'*

The head master's intercourse with individual boys below the Sixth could of course be only slight and occasional. He came chiefly into contact with them through 'Reviews' or *viva voce* examinations, for at least an hour, of every form every five weeks. Besides this, he examined every form *viva voce* at the end of the half year in Divinity and History, and on each occasion he wrote a short comment on the performance of every boy. A half-holiday depended on the monthly 'Reviews' being satisfactory, and thus a considerable stimulant to industry was provided. They made the head master fairly acquainted with the general state of work throughout the school. A full report of them was always written for the benefit of the form masters: those who valued the test, and wished to enlarge their experience, could attend the review, and hear the form taught or examined by an older and more practised teacher. By this means something was done to improve the school work; a good deal

* *Marlburian*, Oct. 1866.

too was gained by making examinations more frequent and more thorough, by providing increased facilities for reading and inducements to take advantage of them; and by instituting a 'modern School' for those boys whose interests or tastes led them to other than classical studies. Another link with the general mass of the school was formed by his sermons. These were not eloquent or striking from a literary point of view, but they did their work, and to some of his hearers were always impressive, from their earnest piety and forcible application of the truths of the New Testament to the facts of school-life. As in dealing with any marked topic furnished by public events, so in a school crisis, his preaching at once rose in vigour and impressiveness. Far more potent than general denunciation, or mere exercise of discipline, for stopping some new bad practice, or turning into a channel some sudden current of excited school feeling, were the plain-spoken but temperate and wise words of the Sunday sermon. Well remembered, too, are the special short addresses delivered only to the annual candidates for Confirmation, in addition to the class and individual preparation always so carefully, so earnestly carried on by himself and the house-masters.

Relations with those under-masters who are in memory chiefly identified with Mr. Cotton's Marlborough life rested on the sure foundation of mutual trust and friendship. The repute of the school was not sufficiently established, nor were the salaries sufficient, to attract older men, or indeed any except those who felt real attachment to the place and work. As vacancies occurred, appointments were made mainly of young men whose college career was just closed. It was precisely what the school at that period needed. Young men with no family cares to share their attention threw themselves into the life they had accepted. They mingled freely with the boys, and shared the foot-ball, cricket, racquets, paper-chases of the school. 'No doubt,' it was said, 'this contact with youth and prolongation of our own youth was a real inducement to some of us to stick to our work at Marlborough.' A curious form of school life was developed which need not be described here, but it often surprised the masters themselves. The general result, however, was most salutary: manly games flourished far more than they had before, taking the place with many of the boys of desultory or even lawless pursuits; the 'natural enemy' idea of a master was greatly weakened. These fellow-helpers, fellow-workers with the head master in reforms which, without their aid and sympathy, must have been very imperfect, were drawn from various sources. Some of the new-comers were old Marlburians, resolute to secure, if possible, the prosperity of the school; others were old Rugby pupils, who felt, some of them at least, that the labour of their whole life could not do more than repay what they owed him; some were college friends of his own pupils, and knew him indirectly through them. 'Our reward was great,' says one of those who accepted a mastership when the prospects of the school were uncertain; 'we helped in a work that was worth doing—this in itself was no small compensation for drudgery, anxiety, and disappointment; those of us who wished to know him, found in him such a friend as we have never had before, and are not likely ever to have again: on the subjects in which we were most deeply and sometimes most painfully interested we could talk freely with him, and were sure of sympathy always, very often of help. Others must speak for themselves: I only know for myself that often as I join in the Prayer for the Church Militant, it hardly ever happens that he is not in my thoughts as I repeat its final thanksgiving and supplication.'

Among the adversities with which the young and novel institution had to contend in its early years have been mentioned the financial difficulties which arose before the necessary experience of its economical working could be obtained. Few would have thought Mr. Cotton qualified to cope with a position of grave financial embarrassment. The success of the measures which he advocated may be no inappropriate illustration of his work at Marlborough. Among plans for reducing expenditure so as at all events to keep it within the income and not increase the debt before referred to, which had reached the large sum of 40,000*l.*, for which liabilities had been incurred under bonds to various persons, a reduction of the assistant-masters' salaries was proposed. This was a step strongly deprecated by Mr. Cotton. He felt instinctively that anything tending to impair the staff and the quality of the education given would be fatal to the prosperity of the school. He had neither the nature nor the training of a man of business, but he was by no means devoid of a power of mind and of imagination to discern a crisis and to grapple with it. In this fresh branch of heavy responsibility, he turned to the masters as the real allies by whose co-operation, financial as well as other, remedial measures could be effectively carried out. One of these consented to act as general treasurer or bursar, his school work being somewhat relaxed, to enable him to discharge the two-fold office, and thus the separate office of treasurer was dispensed with. With the whole staff of masters, including the head master, an arrangement was made which, in lieu of any direct reduction of their stipends, gave each a distinct interest in rebuilding the fortunes of the place. They were asked to become partners as it were in a co-operative society, and to accept not so many pounds sterling, but so many shares in whatever surplus might at the end of each year be found available for the purpose. If the profits of the year should prove such as to enable the shares to be paid at par, well and good; if not, salaries would be diminished accordingly.

This plan was accepted by the whole staff without exception. The result of the measures taken to reduce expenditure and increase income without detriment to the efficiency of the school was that in no single year did the value of a share fall below the point necessary to assign to each master the amount of his nominal salary. As a further evidence of the spirit of co-operation generally diffused, and the strength of the influence at work on the whole body, it may be mentioned that as the financial condition improved, and the available surplus proved more than sufficient to pay salaries in full, the claimants on the fund readily agreed to surrender the excess, receiving in lieu thereof rights of nomination; and funds thus obtained were rigidly applied to the reduction of debt, although money was greatly needed for erecting studies, and effecting improvements in the buildings. The school had other friends in its times of peril besides those who worked within its walls. One generous and wealthy man connected with the school as a member of the council, pledged his credit for the floating debt. A financial statement was drawn up and forwarded to bondholders, with an earnest appeal to their forbearance to accept temporarily a reduced rate of interest. The charge for education was raised for all new boys; the parents of pupils on the old terms were asked to accept the new charge if they could afford it. More than four-fifths of the bondholders and a large proportion of the parents acceded to these requests; and to all these is due the hearty gratitude of all who, at that time or since, have derived benefit from Marlborough College. Through this liberal and generous acceptance of a position of affairs full of difficulty and uncertainty, and through the unsparing economy that was practised, the accounts showed in June 1855 a credit balance sufficient to pay off one bond. Since that day, in matters of finance, as in many others, the College has never looked back.

Thus, from a somewhat detailed narrative, it will be gathered how slowly but surely Mr. Cotton battled with adverse circumstances. The intellectual life of the place remained, it is true, for long feeble and inert. It was left for the finished and stimulating teaching of later years to win a harvest of University honours, and to kindle something of a genuine literary ardour. But Mr. Cotton's six years' work was no less necessary, no less real. He accomplished the task of transplanting the best elements of school-boy life from an old institution to a new one; he invoked a general sense of moral responsibility; he awakened new modes of thought and action; he made the boys respect their school and respect themselves. His ever-increasing influence rebounded on himself in the personal devotion which was his great success, his great reward. Such devotion was no fitful enthusiasm, now rising, now falling; it was the steady, consistent homage of many to a nature essentially true—the natural expression of reverence towards one who drew them insensibly to himself, by his just but gentle rule, by his odd mirthful humour, by his unfailing sympathy, by his hearty appreciation of excellence in characters most opposite to his own and to one another.

This section of the life now under review may be fitly closed by reminiscences from the pen of an intimate friend.

Reminiscences of the Rev. G. E. L. Cotton at Rugby, from 1847 *till* 1852. *By* JOHN CAMPBELL SHAIRP, *Principal of St. Andrews.*

'There are few things that I look back to with such pure satisfaction as the privilege of having known intimately the late G. E. L. Cotton. In trying, however, to recall those years of familiar intercourse with him I find it hard to do so. The throng and pressure of that busy time have so jostled the incidents and blurred their outlines. It is only the total impression, for the most part, that remains.

'Towards the close of 1846, by the kindness of the present Archbishop of Canterbury I went after leaving Oxford to Rugby, to undertake one of the masterships there. During the first few days, while I stayed as guest at the school-house, Dr. Tait told me a good deal of the new life and work that lay before me, and spoke of the colleagues I should meet with. I can still distinctly recall the way in which he spoke of Cotton, as one whom it might do anyone good to know, whose whole life and work were a great example. Dr. Tait had at that time been a little more than four years head master, and I could see that he had formed for Cotton a peculiar admiration and affection.

'I cannot quite recall the first impression Cotton made on me. Only I think it was of one who stood calm and self-possessed in the midst of a great whirl of work and many more excitable persons. In general he received strangers quietly, and it was not at first sight they were most taken by him. In due time, by our mutual friend Bradley, we drew to each other, and began to have walks together on half-holidays and Saturdays. Having lately left Oxford, I was full of views and thoughts which were then seething there below the surface. In these Cotton was much interested, partly from intelligent desire to know what way the currents were setting in the University, partly from kindly sympathy with young men, and whatever engaged their thoughts. In these conversations, two things in him soon struck me: first, the large tolerance and perfect fair-mindedness with which he tried to understand and judge ways of thinking that were different from his own; and, secondly, his stability—while opening his mind to new views he was not carried away by them. He held fast without effort by his old fixed moorings—those truths, few and simple, which were the roots of his being.

'During those early years of our intercourse I remember a characteristic trait of his mingled humour and practical downrightness. Mr. Mill's "Political Economy" had just been published, and several of the masters agreed to read it, and discuss it together afterwards chapter by chapter. Cotton was one of these. In one walk, the early chapters on Productive and Unproductive Consumption formed topics for discussion. The truth was brought out very clearly, that all that was spent in recreation, banquets, &c., beyond what goes to invigorate body and mind for fresh productive labour, is so far wasted and a loss to the community. With most persons it would have stopped there. Cotton, partly from love of a joke, partly from his earnest practical turn, began to press this truth home. Banquets among the masters had at that time in some quarters grown to rather large dimensions; he urged that all banquets should straightway be curtailed within the limits prescribed by political economy. This proposal to square practice by speculation caused much discussion and amusement, and gave rise to one humorous incident. The present Oxford Professor of Political Economy may perhaps remember these things.

'Our intimacy once begun was ripened into friendship by some time spent together abroad, in the summer of 1849. We met at Dresden, where Cotton and Mrs. Cotton were staying, two of his sixth form pupils accompanying them. Together we all travelled to Prague, spent some days there, and returned to Dresden. 'It would be impossible to find a more delightful travelling companion than Cotton was. His entire unselfishness, his perfect temper, placid and even, always interested, the continued play of his quiet peculiar humour on all the little incidents and traits of character we met with, his unwearied love of things and places historic, the thoroughness, the kindliness that prevaded all he said and did, made his society at once calming, strengthening, and exhilarating.

'Prague, I remember, greatly charmed him. He was struck by the Eastern look it had, which was something new to all of us. There was the palace and church of the Hradschin, with its tombs of the Bohemian kings nine centuries old; the bridge with its crucifix and ever-burning lamps supported by a fine laid on the Jews; the mouldy synagogue, one of the earliest in Europe; while in the shattered windows and battered walls of the houses were freshly seen the marks which Winditzgratz and his Austrians had left on the town when quelling last year's revolution. It was the enlargement it gave to his historic sympathies that formed to him the greatest charm of travel. One occurrence at Prague greatly amused Cotton. On the first evening after our arrival we were invited to a party which turned out to be made up of German-hating Czechs, the name of the Sclavonic inhabitants of Bohemia. We had never till that day exactly known of the existence of this small race of Sclaves. But that evening we found ourselves sitting with a number of fierce patriotic Czechs, toasting in German wine "Auf die Bruderschaft der Czech und der Engländer." When Cotton was at Rugby, his summer vacations, often his Christmas ones too, were laid out methodically, not merely for ease and pleasure, but to combine needed relaxation with some increased enlargement of his knowledge of men and of places famed in history.

'In the summer of 1850, while Cotton and Mrs. Cotton were in Germany, he had a severe attack of rheumatic fever, which prevented him from returning at the usual time to his school duties. As I had then no boarding-house of my own, Cotton wrote asking me to undertake the charge of his for a time. After some weeks he was so far recovered as to return to Rugby, still quite unfit for work. He and Mrs. Cotton came for a week or two, and lived in their own home as guests, the name and character he insisted on assuming. After a short stay he left again for the rest of the half-year; but I still vividly remember with what playfulness and good feeling he maintained his position as guest, converting what might have been an embarrassing situation into a most pleasant and friendly visit. During the weeks I took this charge I had an opportunity of seeing what I had always heard, the excellence of Cotton's work as head of a boarding-house. It was a house in all things well ordered, filled with a prevailing spirit of quiet industry and cheerful duty-doing.

'Good as was Cotton's work in his form, it was only in his own house that his full influence was manifest. What Arnold had been to the whole school, that Cotton was to his own house, the boarders in it, and his private pupils out of it. No two men perhaps were ever more different in temperament than the calm, unimpassioned Cotton, and the resolute and vehement Dr. Arnold; yet notwithstanding this, of all Dr. Arnold's pupils or followers none imbibed more largely his spirit and acted out his system more entirely than Cotton did. The præpostor system, as Arnold conceived and re-created it, he thoroughly adopted and carried out. To get hold of his sixth form pupils, win their confidence, mould their views of life and conduct, and through them to reach and influence the younger boys—on this idea, by which Arnold governed Rugby, Cotton threw himself with his whole heart, and by it made his house what it was, one of the best, not only in Rugby, but in any public school. It was his habit to live in great confidence and intimacy with the præpostors in his house, and they with few exceptions returned his confidence and, as far as boys could, entered into his views. And so they became the channels by which his mind and character reached, more or less, every boy under his roof.

'In the routine of his daily work there was "unresting, unhasting industry." Method, orderly but not pedantic' each duty done punctually and faithfully. Yet he never seemed to be in a hurry, almost always to have leisure. If a boy's prose or verse copy was looked over in his study, this was done as carefully as a sermon to be preached in the chapel. Some parts of a master's duty—for instance the scratching of innumerable copies daily—I knew to be painfully irksome to him. Yet I often wondered with what cheerfulness he did these things; the pupil never knew how irksome he felt it. For when the work was done he would take the opportunity of speaking a few friendly words to the boy, and so getting to know him better. Many men who may try to go through these details with something like the same exactness, find themselves, when the long routine is over, so wearied out that they have no heart for further intercourse with boys, but must seek leisure or silence. It was not so with Cotton. Whether in his study correcting exercises, or afterwards in his drawing-room, he sought every opportunity of conversing with his pupils, and showing them that he took interest in them. A laborious life of this kind leaves most men no leisure for reading. But Cotton, even in the busiest times, had generally, besides lighter reading, some solid book on hand. And from his vacations he generally came back having along with his relaxation mastered one or more important works with which he had enlarged his knowledge.

'The custom of reading or speaking some practical words to the boys assembled for Sunday evening prayers was in most boarding-houses occasional. With Cotton the "sermonette," as he used to call it, was an almost invariable institution every Sunday night. This way of teaching suited his turn, and he was a great master of it. These were not formal like church sermons, but brief, plain, home-going words. Some part of school life and daily duty was reviewed before the boys in the light of Christian principle, and that with such plain directness that there was no getting past it. These I believe had much effect on his pupils—partly from the plainness with which they were put—still more because the boys felt that they were entirely in keeping with his own life, and truly represented the spirit in which he himself lived and worked, and which he wished them to share with him. He used to say jokingly himself, "I think that I am a shepherd, not a goatherd." By this he meant to say that it was not by throwing himself into their games, playing cricket and football with them, as some masters do, that he could influence boys. Unless there was something else in a boy than animal spirits and love of games he felt that he could not reach him. He required some degree of thoughtfulness or some sense of duty—at least some common sense—to be stirring in a boy before he could find a point of contact with him. If he could only be got at by his animal sympathies Cotton felt that he was not the man for him. And so it was to their higher nature—mainly their conscience, or intelligence, or affection—that his character commended itself. When, however, any of these had once been touched, then they found other things in him which they had not expected. His humorous sayings, quaint remarks, and jokes, were to those who knew him well, colleagues and pupils, a never-failing fund of amusement, which became the common property of the whole school.

'To his house there came many pupils from the most serious homes in England. He used to say that he thought it was his calling to take boys who had been brought up in the strictest Evangelical system and fit them for contact with the world. He endeavoured to expand their minds and remove their prejudices, while he tried to confirm and deepen whatever good religious principles they had brought from home. If in some cases he did not succeed, if there are instances in which pupils of his have since wandered wide of their first faith, the fault was not in him or his teaching. It is but one result of that spiritual tempest which of late years has so cruelly strained young minds in the English universities, and stranded, as has been truly said, many of the finest spirits on every shore of thought. Of one thing I am sure, that those who have since been led to differ from him most widely still look back on Cotton, as they remember him at Rugby, with unaltered respect and affection.

'His house work, and the impressions he made on his own pupils, formed the centre of Cotton's influence in Rugby. But it did not end there: elder boys in other houses, seeing the effect he had on his own pupils and their attachment to him, were drawn towards him and welcomed any opportunity of knowing him. He thus became a rallying-point for whatever was best in the school, and also in a great measure the upholder of the Arnoldian spirit in it. If in some things, as in the stress of responsibility which it threw on the præpostors, this spirit was overstrained, if it pressed too strongly the spring of "moral thoughtfulness" (the peculiarly Rugbeian virtue, or vice, as some would call it), so as in some cases to provoke an after rebound, Cotton, though not unaware of this possible result, would, I think, have said that he notwithstanding accepted the system, and threw himself into it as the best that had yet been discovered for working public schools.

'I have noticed the methodic way in which he went through each day's routine of work. Neither rapid at it, nor slow, he always seemed to have each thing done at the proper time, and most days to have some leisure over, and this leisure he employed, partly in social duties, partly in reading. He always had on hand, as I have already said, some solid work—historical, theological, or other. This he read in the most systematic, exhaustive way, so that when he was done he could reproduce all that was most valuable in it for the information of others. I never knew anyone who could give a clearer, more well-ordered digest of anything he had read, heard, or seen; hence his knowledge, even in that busy life, every year made a steady increase.

'His imagination too, not originally I should think one of his strongest faculties, grew richer every year he lived. This is one of the mental gains that seemed to grow out of a moral nature true to itself. You see many a time a naturally fervid imagination divorced from moral purpose burn brightly in early youth, but grow fainter as time goes on; while the imagination in other men, originally stiff and bald, as the meaning of life deepens to them, expands and deepens with their years. This growth of imaginative power is observable in Arnold's later, as compared with his earlier, writings. And I think the same was the case with Cotton, and the cause was the same in both. But in most other respects no two men holding the same views, and governed by the same aims, could be more unlike each other.

'If Cotton lacked much which Arnold had, one thing he possessed which Arnold wanted—the humour that oozed from him and gave unfailing zest to all he said. This was closely connected with his temper, which was the most placid you would meet with in a lifetime. I do not suppose anyone ever saw Cotton in a rage. I never saw him even approach to being angry, though I have seen him deeply pained on hearing of some baseness of action or falseness of word. His perfect temper arose in a large measure from his great unselfishness. The "heart at leisure from itself" was in him untroubled by those feelings which spring out of self-regard and make up most men's annoyances.

'The attachment of his elder pupils, especially the

sixth form boys, to him was wonderful; not less deep were his feelings towards them. The earnest side of his character drew out their reverence, the humorous and jocular side interested and amused them. His jokes and quaint sayings were a kind of possession of all his house, and through them of the whole school.

'During his vacations he visited at the homes of his elder pupils or took them with him on his foreign travels. I well remember his return from seeing off in the train a favourite pupil, leaving school for the university, in whose future he felt a special interest. Cotton had seen much of him during his later schooldays, and now on the last had gone with him to the train. When Cotton returned he told me a good deal of what they had spoken about, their last words, the parting, and then he added, with a wave of his arm and the tears in his eyes (strange to see in one usually so calm), "And so passed the greatest interest I ever had in Rugby."

'To this power of attaching his pupils, and through them winning the regards of others like-minded, it was that he owed his greatest success at Marlborough. It enabled him to draw round him a band of young masters fresh from the universities, who went to Marlborough not for salaries, for these then were insignificant, not for the attractions of the place, for hard work was its main characteristic, but drawn solely by love to Cotton himself, and through him to the work he had taken in hand. That work was to re-organise Marlborough, according to the ideal he had learnt from Arnold's work at Rugby. Single-handed, with merely average masters going through a routine duty, he could have done little. But he was enabled to regenerate the school mainly by the personal magnetism which attracted, and the devotion with which he inspired his following of young masters, men of as good ability and as high character as the large-salaried masters of Harrow or Rugby, and with the first ardour of youth on their side.

'It was early in 1852 that he accepted the headship of Marlborough. His going from Rugby was the greatest loss it could sustain. But he felt that his work there was done, and that he could put forth fresh energy in a place which he could mould to his own mind. That summer, just before he went to Marlborough, he came down to Scotland and visited at my father's home. All there, though most of them did not know him till then, greatly relished his society, his naturalness, his quiet drollery, his unpretendingness. On Sunday, I remember, he accompanied us to the small Presbyterian parish church. He felt much interest in being present at this form of worship, which was new to him, but he joined in it as naturally, and with as little constraint, as the humblest peasant there. English clergymen when in Scotland, if they go to the Presbyterian church at all, are apt to do so as if they were condescending. No doubt they are not aware of it themselves, but the natives are, and feel it offensive. Cotton had nothing of this about him; indeed, nothing was more remarkable in him than his entire freedom from the common clerical weaknesses. About many of the most excellent clergymen there is a sort of professional enamel which they cannot get rid of. Those of the broad school, seeing this, sometimes fly to the other extreme and play the layman. They are continually, as it were, taking off their white tie and flinging it in your face. From both of these extremes Cotton was equally removed. You could speak to him about anything, express difference or doubt, just as if he were a layman; indeed, with far less hesitation than you have with most laymen. And the consequence was that with all laymen his influence was much stronger than that of most clergymen, because they felt, in what he said, that there was nothing professional, but that it simply was the honest conviction of a single-hearted, truth-loving man.

'When we left my father's house, he made me lead him

through the vales of Tweed and Yarrow. Dryburgh Abbey we visited in the beauty of a summer morning, then Melrose and Abbotsford. In the afternoon I took him up Tweed through the beautiful woods of Yare to the ridge of the hill behind it. There pausing, and looking westward, we saw beneath us the whole course of the Yarrow, as it winds from the lochs down through the green interlapping hills. The westering sun was streaming down the "bonny braes." Two nights we stayed by still St. Mary's lake, and all day we wandered among the hopes and side-glens that come into Yarrow, the Douglas and Kirkstead Burns, by Blackhouse and Dryhope Tower and other mouldering Peels, while I told him the traditions and ballads that still haunt these places, and make more than half their charm. We then walked down Moffat Dale, and parted at Moffat. Sometimes during this short tour, as we wandered among the green hills, Cotton would begin to discuss some difficult question of education or scholastic management. The enterprise of remodelling Marlborough, now close before him, was evidently much on his mind. After one or two conversations, I bargained that these topics should be left till we had reached our inn at night. Savouring as they did of the work-day world, they seemed alien to the dreamy stillness of those green pastoral uplands. To this, in his good-natured way, he readily submitted. In a letter which I received from him soon after we parted, he told me that his enjoyment in this short tour had been only second to that he had felt in seeing the two or three great world-sights of his life.

'Somehow I regret to say I never made out a visit to him at Marlborough, though often invited. But I saw him from time to time at Rugby, when, during the holidays, he came to visit others and myself there.

'After his consecration as a bishop, while he was on his last visit to Rugby, just before sailing for India, a quite unexpected occurrence brought me from Scotland to Rugby, and there we met. It was on a Sunday we were there, and I remember the impression it made on me when, at the close of the evening service, Cotton rose, and as bishop pronounced the benediction in that chapel where for years his voice had been so familiar. On the Sunday we saw as much of each other as we could, but of course he had many friends to see. We agreed to meet early on Monday morning, as I had to leave at 8 o'clock A.M.; we met at 7 o'clock in the close, walked several times up and down there—walks we had so often paced together in former years—then at half-past seven said farewell. As we parted he gave me a copy of his Marlborough Sermons, just then published, and below my name and his own wrote, "Rugby, Sept. 6, 1858. School close, 7.30 A.M."

'After he went to India, I had a letter from him every now and then, one every six months or so, till the last year or two of his life, when they intermitted. How this arose I cannot now remember, whether from irregularity of writing on my part, or from some other reason. Only I know that very pleasant, friendly, and instructive his letters were, full of the facts and thoughts you wished to know, told in the clearest, most orderly, and often quaint way. He had more the gift of the real old letter-writer than anyone else one knows now-a-days. In his letters he expressed himself almost as fully as one can conceive it done, his life, the things he was doing, the books he was reading, the thoughts which most engaged him at the time he wrote.

'In thinking of Cotton as he was, the thing that most comes back on me is his entire truthfulness and uprightness. The love of all that was good, the open conscience toward all that was right, amounted in him to the very genius of goodness. Whatever other talents and faculties he possessed, this, the central moral power in him, at least doubled his other powers. He was, I think, the most candid man I ever knew; he was almost the only man I have met who, if anything he said or did was objected to, would not try in the least to defend himself, but would hold up himself and his action in the light of unbiassed reason, and judge it with strict impartiality, as if it were the case of a third person. If, after consideration, he was convinced that the objection was true, he would at once get himself to correct his view, and conform his thought and word and deed to his new conviction.

'Another side of the same quality was his love of truth in all its aspects, his desire to know the best attained truth in all matters, and ever to be increasing his knowledge of it. Whether the matter were fact of history, or political opinion, or interpretation of Scripture, or philosophical question, or truth of theology, in all alike he used conscientiously the best helps within his reach, strove to attain the best light extant, and then to turn it to practical account. But the first thing he sought was to know what was true. With him, however, the end of this search was not speculative knowledge. He desired to know, that he might be and do. The open eye for truth and knowledge ministered to the love of goodness—Christian goodness—and all the truth he saw he used in the service of the goodness he loved.

'He had no fear lest truth and goodness should conflict, convinced that at the bottom they were in perfect harmony. So well balanced were these two habits in him that no access of fresh critical knowledge ever weakened his heart's hold on its fundamental moorings, nor did his firm hold of these narrow his mind against perceiving any new truth that might be presented to him. Indeed, while he continued to the last to be interested in all the critical and theological questions of the time, his faith in those great evangelic truths with which he began life was growing every year till its close. For speculation as an end in itself he had no caring. His strong love of practical goodness kept his thoughts solid and healthful.

'He was eminently a friendly man, and one whom friends only could know. Mere acquaintances were very likely not to know or to misunderstand him. His plain, undemonstrative manner often disappointed persons on first seeing him, when they had heard much of him beforehand. You required to get beyond mere acquaintance and within the range of intimacy, before you got a glimpse of the real man; but then every step you took within that range revealed his true worth more fully. Under that calm (what strangers sometimes thought cold) exterior you found one of the truest, most devoted hearts that ever beat. Steadfast and devoted he was to his friends, whether those of his own or of a younger generation, and of such friends no one had more; devoted to his duty, whatever it was, and to the good of the place, wherever it might be, in which his work lay, yet without the narrowness or unsociableness that often accompanies strict duty-doing; devoted not to the romantically, but to the morally heroic, in whatever form he perceived it; devoted to the memory of Dr. Arnold as the best embodiment of this which he had known on earth. But all these forms of human affection were deepened and hallowed by a more central all-pervading devotion still—devotion to that Divine Master whom with his whole heart he loved.

'Of this central affection he seldom spoke—it expressed itself in his life far better than in his words. But no one could know him without knowing that this was the strongest power within him, that which moved his whole being. What made it more remarkable was that it existed in a nature which was so entirely unexcitable, in a heart which had fervour to give not to small or transient things, but only to the most important. All the more concentrated was the devotion it gave to these. Those who knew what Cotton was at Rugby were quite prepared to see the good and arduous work he achieved at Marlborough. They had seen in him a singleness of eye and a concentration of aim which doubled all his natural powers, and drew forth ever new reserves of power to meet each new emergency as it arose.

'Therefore they were not surprised when they heard how steadily and surely his influence in India grew, and how by sheer dint of Christian character he had come to be the acknowledged head, not of the Anglican Church only, but of all the Christian Churches in that empire.

'They were prepared to hear that all laymen as well as all ministers of every communion looked up to him as one of the best of bishops, because they had known him long since to be one of the best of men.'

LETTERS.

To a former Pupil.

Rugby, October 31, 1842.

I was very glad to receive your letter, and to gather from it that you are comfortable in your new home. I hope that I shall hear from you with tolerable frequency, for I can assure you that I regard intercourse with my old pupils as one of the freshest springs of my life.

For myself, I derived such great benefits from Trinity College, and feel to it so devoted an attachment, that I am most sanguine as to your also being in all ways the better for your residence there, particularly if you bear steadily in mind the truth that college life (at least to an undergraduate) is only a part of education, and therefore concerned with the future, rather than the present.

The practical view of which is what I told you before you left Rugby—that you must not allow yourself to be carried away by the desire of present usefulness—the amount of which can be but small—to the neglect of the preparation for that future in which you must fight against evil, not only in your own heart, but in that of many others also. And as certainly there never was a time when the Church of Christ stood more deeply in need of the spirit of wisdom, as well as of the spirit of zeal—with so many foes attacking her without, and strange opinions disturbing her quiet within—so is it the time when the accurate and vigorous cultivation of the mind can least be dispensed with by any of us.

But when I say this, of course I am far from meaning to advise you not to adopt all means which you find necessary to keep alive religious feelings in yourself. In a place so much devoted as Cambridge is to the idolatry of intellectual power, you will surely find it most useful to live always as in God's presence, and to humble yourself before Him, by whatever means are most likely to remind you of your weakness and sinfulness, and of your duty to your Christian brethren. So I think that visiting the poor, and Sunday-school teaching, in moderation, may be very profitable to you; and I also hope that you will steadily keep up the Rugby habit of making the study of the *Greek* Testament an important object; and above all things beware of the great sin of Cambridge—I mean of the more outwardly respectable part of it—that abominable pride of the understanding which leads men who are fond of literary society to ridicule and despise those whom God has not made capable of shining in it.

You will not be angry at my still speaking to you *a loco superiori*, after all my right to do so has been resigned. But I do not think that you are so anxious to get rid of the Rugby connection as to be offended at being still considered as one of our own body.

What happiness your stay at Rugby, as my pupil, caused me, I need not say, nor express to you my earnest hope that it has been the foundation of an enduring intimacy between us, which will have the only sure pledge of permanence in being consecrated to the glory of God. I shall long to see you again, and in the meantime to hear from you whenever you can spare time. I quite approve of your reading arrangements.

We are all going on very quietly and happily here, and Norris, I think, is gaining ground with the house. Your brother is well and prosperous.

To the Same.

Liverpool, February 6.

I was very much interested by your letter, and delighted to receive it, as I always am to hear from you; this one, however, I think gave me greater pleasure than usual. Only, is it too great a favour to ask you to put in your corrections in ink, to write on larger pieces of paper, and more legibly? One or two sentences, I grieve to say, I have not even yet deciphered.

As to Ireland, it seems a *locus desperatus.* Shiel's speech did not please me so much as it did you, and I cannot at all agree with you about O'Connell's goodness and patriotism. His agitation is preventing altogether the investment of English capital in Ireland, which would, I suppose, diminish the misery of his unhappy country. He surely does not always speak the truth, constantly panders to the passions of the mob, and derives so comfortable an income from his patriotism that we cannot believe him disinterested.

I think it would be well if the Queen spent about six weeks there every year; and if the Lord-Lieutenant's office was either abolished or placed on a different footing. But we ought to grant (1) the exclusion of Irish prelates from the House of Lords, and the institution of four new English bishops, who are much wanted. (2) The suspension of all appointments to livings in Ireland, where the number of Protestants is not some fraction of the population, to be fixed by Parliament. (3) The devotion of these funds to general education. (4) I think, but am not quite sure, the endowment of the Popish priesthood. (5) A revision of the Landlord and Tenant law. But the error of establishing the Protestant Church in Ireland was so fatal that it is hard to say what can now be done about it.

But though Ireland is, England is not yet, thank Heaven, a *locus desperatus.* There I believe that the Church system, properly carried out, would relieve us from almost all our evils; and therefore I never cease to regret the abandonment of the Education Bill of last session, as an immense step towards doing so. Another great step in the right direction is the raising of a fund in London for district visiting, under the control of the clergy, but extending help and relief to persons of all religious persuasions, which exactly fulfils my notions of the meaning of an established Church as distinguished from a sect.

To the Rev. A. P. Stanley.

Rugby, September 14, 1846.

I should not have been satisfied to attend the service yesterday anywhere except in the place which is so associated with ——. I do not think that till this week I have half felt or appreciated his excellence, and how unworthy I was to be his teacher. At the same time, I never lost a friend in whose death I more entirely and thankfully acquiesce. I candidly agree with what you say about the happiness of thinking that he is now safe from any evil influence at Oxford or elsewhere; and, as far as I am concerned, the picture and the lesson is now quite perfect. Had he lived, I do not doubt that there would have been little to distinguish him from other good and holy men. Probably many now at Rugby would have been as active and useful clergymen as I had hoped to see him.

But I certainly never knew a boy like him, and so for this reason also I could not wish him back again. This example teaches boys how to live, and also how to die; and having from his childhood loved God, and worked for Him so heartily as he began to grow older, there seems a fitness in the circumstance that he has been called to his eternal portion at the very time of his removal from the school where he exercised so extreme and blessed an influence. So again I delight in thinking of him as having been strictly a Rugby boy. For his religious opinions were greatly influenced and modified by what he heard here, and he was fast losing the peculiarities of Evangelicalism, and learning to think for himself.

The following letter to a former pupil was written in the last year of his life at Rugby:—

Rugby, October 19.

On this Sunday, the first of your Oxford life, I feel more vividly than I did when we parted in June, that you have really left Rugby, that you have fairly ceased to be my pupil, and that the responsibility of these years is, for better, for worse, actually over. So it seems the right day, even though I saw you so lately, to send you the assurance that, though the responsibility is over, my interest in all that concerns you is not over, but greater than ever; that you have been much in my thoughts to-day, and, let me add, in my prayers also. Most earnestly do I hope that Oxford may complete any good which Rugby has begun, and supply any which it has left undone; that you may grow in all goodness, and in all knowledge; that Christ's kingdom may be set up in your own heart, that thus you may be fitted to extend it among others.

You have sometimes, long ago now, but I distinctly remember it, during an autumnal walk on the Dunchurch Road, talked to me about wishing to be a clergyman, and even a missionary. Latterly you have not spoken much upon such subjects; but I do not know that this makes much difference, for every Christian is in fact called to be a missionary. Wherever he is there are people for him to benefit; not only, as Arnold says in his sermons, in Africa or India, but close around you, are there souls to be saved, which are in infinite danger. And so, whether it please God to call you to the actual work of a clergyman or missionary, or not, you can never escape the responsibility which lies on you already by the fact that you have been called to the knowledge, and therefore to the duty of spreading the knowledge, of His Son. And a new period in the preparation for this work is now begun; so let us join in the hope and prayer that God may bless this coming period, and make it really one of preparation, in the truest sense. For, that you may be ever of any use to others, it is necessary first that good should be done to yourself; that your mind should be strengthened as well as your heart fitted for the work. And in this time in which we live, above all others, is an intellectual as well as a moral preparation necessary; the wants of our age can only be met by the spirit of wisdom, added to the spirit of zeal. I entreat you therefore to make a thoroughly good use of these three years at Oxford, and to remember that they furnish, probably, the last opportunity which you will ever have of carrying on systematically your general education.

A laborious profession is probably before you; if you take to the Bar or any (so to speak) secular calling, you will be prevented by necessity—if the clerical or educational profession, by your own sense of duty—from giving up very much time to study. So that really these three years should not be frittered away. Believe me, it is no mere question of emulation and competition and first classes, but a plain and simple case of duty, that you should now store your mind with knowledge and thought, extracted from the great works of great men.

The large extension lately given to the Oxford course gives you ample room for choice as to your line or lines of reading: only determine them soon, and stick to them. I always fear in you a little too much tendency to pick up knowledge as easily as possible; such knowledge is rather superficial than systematic, and a mere knowledge of facts, though indispensable, is not of much use if it remains unproductive. What you should steadily carry out is the thorough, accurate reading of the good tough books which Oxford places before you, where, in Tennysonian phrase, 'Thought has wedded Fact.'

So again, a man of warm affections and a great love of society is apt perhaps to give his friends too much of his time.

Far be it from me to depreciate friendships, one of the chief blessings of life, or society, one of the great means of education. Still, if we are to get much profit from talking to our contemporaries, the wisdom of past ages, laid up in books, must furnish subjects for our conversation; and whilst I allow that both means of improvement should be carried on together, we must remember that, if we find friends far pleasanter companions than books, we have to watch ourselves lest they take up an undue share of our time.

People say—you say yourself—that your last year at Rugby was crowned with rather more success than your exertions merited: make up the purchase-money of that success in your first term at Oxford. Show your gratitude for laurels gained with less work than usual, then, by even more work than usual now. No doubt, it is hard to set oneself down to work often distasteful, when there are a thousand opposing attractions and influences about us; it requires a great effort of the will, the conquest of the lower by the higher nature within us.

But here is more of Tennyson for you—

> He knows a baseness in his blood
> At such strange war with something good;
> He may not do the thing he would.

And again—

> He seems to hear a heavenly Friend,
> And through thick veils to apprehend
> A labour working to an end.

Or rather, this is not Tennyson, but pure Christianity received and put into poetry by him. Let me therefore turn to the fountain-head at once, and finish this lengthy epistle by reminding you that, whether we are fighting against open sin, or merely against laziness and the love of pleasing ourselves in minor things, these words are true: 'The good that I would I do not: but the evil which I would not, that I do. . . . . O wretched man that I am, who shall deliver me from the body of this death? I thank God, through Jesus Christ our Lord.' So may you be led to carry on in Him all your work and all your relaxation, and then will neither interfere with the other, but both will combine to make your three years at Oxford the beginning of an active, a useful, a Christian manhood.

To a Friend.

Glengariffe, July 1856.

The whole visit impressed me very much, not in the least in the way of inclining me to turn Puseyite, but in strengthening my feeling that amongst us, who regard ourselves as taking a more liberal view, there is far too little of real devotion and earnest Christian faith. This impression has been increased by my finding Arnold's life on the table at F——; I took it up casually, and read on and on with deepening interest, and conviction that too many of Arnold's disciples are unlike their teacher in that which was the central point and main principle in his whole life—a practical belief in Christ, and conduct founded distinctly upon it. I am far from wishing that we should follow him into all his peculiar theories and their consequences, exclusion of Jews from Parliament, for instance, which, though they may be all connected in strict logic, take too little account of the friction of actual facts, and at all events should not be adopted without other consequences of his views, which are allowed to be impracticable. But I think that we stray far from him in our own personal principles of conduct. He talks of feeling 'a rush of love to God,' of being conscious of no greater desire than to conform his life to Christ's pattern, and so on. Now if we are unlike him in these things, I do not think that this arises merely from our own imperfections and sinfulness, which would be a different question, but I doubt whether we really act upon his principle at all; we are conscious, no doubt, of a desire to be good and true, but do we shape our desire in a Christian way, and connect it with the faith in Father and Redeemer, without which experience proves that it only produces half its effects? . . . For myself I often feel the danger very acutely, and not least with reference to our Marlborough boys, lest in trying to make them intellectually vigorous, I am too careless in making them Christians. And undoubtedly this fear, coupled with other reasons which we have often discussed, makes me hesitate very much about tampering with chapel until we can see our way to put the service or the boys' daily prayers on a footing entirely satisfactory as regards the main object for which we assemble them for common worship. It has also made me sympathise more with ——'s views about behaviour at such times, and without wishing to dragoon them into a forced and false appearance of devotion I certainly desire to teach them quietly their duty in this matter. Well, I have wandered far from Glengariffe, and touched, I fear, on the very borders of 'shop.' But you, I am sure, will excuse this outpouring—sympathise at least with parts of it—and think that I may express to an intimate friend what has been very much in my heart, without supposing that I am turning Tory or High Churchman.

No doubt to reconcile modern thought with Christian faith may be a hard matter of practice, but it is only a repetition of the problem which other ages have successfully solved, and by way of beginning the solution let us hold fast to Christian love and all Christian virtue.

To a former Pupil.

I am very sorry that you should be troubled with any doubts of the kind which you mention, because I know that they are often very distressing, and beg that you will never apologise for writing to me on that or any other subject which disturbs you, since to help you is, in my opinion, a simple duty.

Assuming that your taste for a clergyman's life and work has not altered, I cannot see anything in what you say which should make you change your wish to be one. There have been 'doubts thrown on different parts of the Bible' from the days of Celsus and Porphyry to the present hour, but it does not follow that these doubts are well founded, and there is no more reason, because another person tells you that he disbelieves this or that, why you should renounce your belief in it too, than why he should accept the whole Bible because you profess your belief in it all. Doubts are thrown on a great many good things besides the Bible. Some people extenuate falsehood, drunkenness, and other gross vices; but it does not follow that they really are excusable because those persons say so. The question is one of evidence and reasoning, and each particular assertion must be tested separately. However, if you want my opinion on the general question I will give it you; of course I cannot give it in particulars without knowing what the special assertions are.

The Bible, though an inspired revelation of God's will, is written by human authors, preserved by human keepers, handed down from one generation to another by human means.

Hence questions may arise and be lawfully entertained, as to the authenticity of this or that portion of it; and the human element in it is subject to the laws of human criticism.

Research, scholarship, increase of knowledge, have undoubtedly modified men's views of it in some points. To take an obvious instance, it is now almost universally allowed that the passage 1 John v. 7 was not in the original text of the epistle, and has been interpolated accidentally. Again, the Bible was supposed to contain an infallible system of natural science. The Pope once declared that it was inconsistent with Scripture to believe that the world went round the sun.

Latterly, men have begun to see that the Bible was not intended to teach us natural philosophy, but was a record of God's will sent to guide us to heaven and make us His faithful servants. On scientific points they have felt that the sacred writers had not received a divine revelation, but used the natural language of their age. Other instances might be given in which criticism has been exercised on the Bible; and when exercised in an humble and loving spirit this criticism has only served to bring out more fully its true character, and to enable men to understand it more correctly, and apply it more practically to the guidance of their lives.

There has also been a great deal of wild, unhallowed, careless speculation, one theory set up one year to be knocked down the next, and sceptics have been battling more against each other than against the Bible. But take my word for it no true criticism has touched the great facts that the Bible is a continuous authoritative revelation of God's dealings with man, that the Old Testament records the preparation for that redemption which is described in the New, and that the New contains a true account of the life and death of God's own Son for us, of the doctrines which He taught, and the moral precepts which He would have us obey, and of the foundation of His Church, by the divinely chosen and divinely inspired Apostles. Out of this record you are required to find spiritual life for yourself, and to instruct the people committed to you if you take orders, and I am quite sure that by God's help you need have no difficulty in doing either.

At present, all that you have to do is to live as a faithful Christian, to lay a good foundation of general knowledge and thought, and to look forward humbly and hopefully to serving God as a minister of His Church, which surely is a very great privilege and blessing. If when the time for ordination approaches you find that there is anything in the subscriptions required which you cannot accept, then, much as I should regret it, groundless as I believe the objections to be, strong as I think the reasons for ordination, I certainly would not advise you to disobey your conscience, though I should think your conscience misguided. But these enquiries need not trouble you yet: you are at this moment called not to be a clergyman, but a Christian—a Christian student laying that basis of secular learning and practical sense on which a sound theology must be built. Hence I quite agree with your father's advice not to argue on such points; your belief in Christianity I trust is founded on reasons which no argument can touch, and for separate questions about this or that part of Scripture you have neither time nor knowledge. Meantime listen to this. You know that —— has been very ill here, almost dying. I went to him daily all last week, reading to him a few verses and a prayer. He was not, I suppose, a very religious boy when at school, but the simple words of the Bible and the Prayer-book seemed to soothe him in his pain and touch his heart with a divine power; and is not this more to the purpose in reference to a clergyman's work, than questions of manuscripts, various readings and intellectual evidences, which, though not unimportant in themselves, cannot lie at the root of a revelation addressed to the spirit of men by the Spirit of God?

CHAPTER III.

APPOINTMENT TO THE BISHOPRIC OF CALCUTTA — CONSECRATION IN WESTMINSTER ABBEY — RETURN TO MARLBOROUGH — APPOINTMENT OF HIS SUCCESSOR—FAREWELL VISITS—EMBARKATION—LETTERS.

IT was in 1858 that he received the offer of the see of Calcutta. A few words may be given to explain the circumstances. In 1856 his valued friend and former chief, Dr. Tait, had been raised to the see of London. Cotton was appointed to preach his consecration sermon in Whitehall Chapel, and in the following year he became his examining chaplain in connexion with the University of Cambridge, and another of his most intimate friends in connexion with the University of Oxford. Deeply did those weeks at Fulham strengthen the value which each of those two had for their dear associate from Marlborough. The laborious fairness, the alternations of admiration and indignation which the merits and demerits of the candidates called forth, the keen interest which he took in each of them, the sound judgment which he exercised in those trying questions which beset that opening period of a young clergyman's life, whilst they bound him with a yet closer tie to his younger colleague, awakened in the bishop's mind a yet deeper sense of his fitness for a higher post. Accordingly, when the news arrived in England of the death of Bishop Wilson, the Bishop of London determined to use every effort to secure Cotton's appointment to the see of

Calcutta. It was a moment in which more interest attached to the Indian episcopate than at any period since its first establishment. The Indian mutiny was just over. The horrors of the war itself, and the horrors, must we not add, which followed it, are still fresh in the minds of all. Amongst the few who had not been carried away in the excitement of the disastrous tidings from Cawnpore and Lucknow were the Bishop of London and Cotton himself. A sermon is still extant preached on the fast-day of 1857, in which, whilst the prospect of any personal connexion with India was entirely unthought of, Cotton expressed those sentiments of mercy and fairness which made the indiscriminate cries of vengeance in the English press so distasteful to him and which were in thorough accord with the policy which Lord Canning was, almost singlehanded, bent on maintaining in India. The Bishop of London, with all the energy of his character, pressed Cotton's merits on the Government of that day, but, partly from an apprehension lest his modesty should throw some obstacle in the way, without consulting Cotton himself. Meanwhile, from causes unnecessary here to mention, the hope of accomplishing this object had faded away, and the subject was dropped, until the Bishop was suddenly informed that if Cotton would take the post it was still at his disposal. There was not a moment of time to be lost. A change of Government had just taken place, and Mr. Vernon Smith, now Lord Lyveden, who was then the Secretary of State for India, was holding the post only till a new ministry could be formed. The Bishop telegraphed the offer to Marlborough. It was like a thunder-clap to Cotton in the midst of his peaceful labours. The telegram dropped from his hands, and he rushed from the school to his house, and thence hurried up to London. The first person whom he consulted was that friend of many years who has put together these fragments of memoirs.

'What are your reasons for thinking that I ought to take this bishopric?' 'There are two qualifications,' was the answer, 'indispensable to a Bishop of Calcutta, which are possessed by very few, but are possessed by you: one is the power of understanding the old religions of India, the other is the power of dealing fairly and kindly by the different Christian communities. Therefore you must take it.' It was one of those decisive cases in which the mere decision is enough to shake the minds of most. Perhaps in Cotton's case an outside spectator would have been startled and even disappointed to observe how slightly he seemed to be agitated. The calm, disinterested view which on all occasions he would take of his own character and position as of a third person, enabled him in all simplicity to accept the estimate of others concerning himself and to acquiesce in a change in many ways so alien to his habits and feelings. On the following day he saw the Indian Minister, whose brief words dwelt in his memory, as containing in a short compass the extent of his opportunities and responsibilities. 'I believe that in appointing you I have done the best for the interests of India, of the Church of England, and of Christianity.'

He was consecrated in Westminster Abbey on Ascension Day. The sermon was preached by the early College companion by whom, more than any other single person, the whole course of his life had been determined—Dr. Vaughan, then head master of Harrow, by whom he had first been introduced to Arnold. That noble sermon still remains, a record of what was expected, a prediction of what was fulfilled. Those who were present can remember the thrill of sympathy, deepened in after years into a yet more abiding conviction, with which they heard the preacher dwell on the inestimable boon of such a pastor to tne young Englishmen living at Calcutta, to the families suffering from bereavement or disease, to the clergy who would be gathered round him—on the thought, mournful yet inspiring, of the graves of Martyn at Tocat, of Schwartz at Tanjore, of Heber at Trichinopoly—on the consolation, slight yet how full of meaning, 'Friends even in the same land, how little do they see each of the other! when they meet, how little of all that is in their hearts do they tell! how deep a depth lies below, which friend exhausts not to friend, nor brother to brother!' Some there are too, who will recall the words, solemn now as an unconscious prophecy, in which the preacher reminded his hearers that, 'Amidst all the prayers of the Church, she asks not for him a speedy return. Checking the impulses of a natural affection, she rather asks for him that no nearer future may be suffered to become his horizon, but only that more distant of all, the anticipation of which, unlike every other anticipation, is purely invigorating, animating, and satisfying. With his heart in his work, and his hope placed above, he asks of us to-day, not the prayers for a return, but the prayer for success and blessing; for a work that shall abide, and a recompense that shall be permanent.' *

With a sedate tranquillity, unlike the excitement which often follows on such appointments, the new Bishop, after his consecration, finding that he would not sail until autumn, returned quietly to his work at Marlborough, and while at once beginning to prepare himself for his future career by study of the Indian languages, still carried on his intercourse with his pupils to the last moment, as though he were to continue their master and friend.

Meantime a rare tribute of respect and confidence was paid him by those with whom he had acted for the last six years. Instead of the usual process of selection from a number of candidates, his successor was appointed

* 'The Word, the Work, and the Promise,' a consecration sermon preached in Westminster Abbey on Ascension Day, by Charles J. Vaughan, D.D.

avowedly on his recommendation, and he was cheered by seeing his work in England pass into the hands of one of the most cherished of his Rugby friends. Rarely has a successor so entirely entered into his predecessor's labours. Rarely has a predecessor watched with such loving and grateful affection the continuation and improvement of his task in the hands to which he himself had committed it.

The remaining time was spent mostly in farewell visits and necessary business. One short excursion of a few days he made with one of his friends to see the cathedrals of Norwich, Peterborough, and Lincoln. They met for their journey at Ketteringham, near Norwich, at the house of Sir John Boileau, the friend of M. Guizot, who was staying there at the time. M. Guizot was much interested in the sight of the new Bishop, and bade him farewell in words, not the less significant for the foreign idiom in which they were partly couched—'God bless you and your great work! Make peace and good Christians.'

The two friends parted at the London terminus. The agreement was made between them that twice a year, at least, they should on stated days communicate to each other what seemed to each most interesting in the ecclesiastical state of England and of India. It was, in fact, the portion of an elaborate idea, by which the Bishop arranged a systematic correspondence on different subjects with all his English friends.

In some instances it may have dropped through, but in the case just mentioned it was continued with an exactness of date and purpose on either side, and a fulness of information and sympathy from the Indian side which seemed to annihilate the distance of time and space, and only caused the English friend to count the years as they rolled by, which brought nearer and nearer the happy day of the return. In many a desponding hour as to the fate of the Church at home, have those letters brought before him the refreshing thought that in one vast diocese, at least, on the other side of the world, in one great episcopal see, the work of Arnold was carried on in the true faith of Christ; in the true genius of the English State and Church, in the spirit of that text which he had always regarded as his motto, 'In quietness and confidence shall be your strength.'

The Bishop took his last farewell of Marlborough early in September. One of his friends, bound to him by no common ties of gratitude, sat with him late on the last night. They read together the seventeenth chapter of St. John's Gospel, knelt once more in prayer together, and parted. The next morning, the whole school turned out at eight o'clock to cheer him, as he started for Hungerford on the outside of the familiar omnibus. At Southampton, where he embarked on September 25, he was met by the same faithful friend who had preached his consecration sermon. A small gift which he received from him on that day never left him. It was with him at the close. No wonder that when the fatal tidings eight years afterwards reached the shores of England, the scene which recurred to his friends and pupils at Marlborough, as the last expression of thoughts and feelings too deep for words, was that in which the disciples of the departing apostle 'mourned most of all for the words which he spake,* that they should see his face no more.'

From a Friend.

March 1858.

So you are going to India as Bishop of Calcutta! The news took me utterly by surprise, and made me feel at once both very glad and very sorry: at first perhaps more sorry

* 'The Parting at Miletus,' a sermon preached in the chapel of Marlborough College, October 21, 1866, by George Granville Bradley, M.A., Master of Marlborough College.

than glad, for I felt at a glance the risk of the change, and how much *we* must lose—by 'we' meaning myself and all your English friends, Marlborough, England's Church, England's education, and indeed England altogether. However, I am determined to rejoice heartily with you and for you. You have made a great choice, and a great work is before you.

You have also, I think, a favourable season for beginning. Men's minds cannot but be seriously disposed after the terrible events of the last twelve months. The first step towards Christianity in India must be evangelising the English there, purifying English lives, ennobling English conduct—you, I know, will feel this. Yes, it will be a grand work, and I wish you all strength and grace to do it well. In many respects your character seems to me excellently fitted for the work. Let us be full of hope for you. As I write this, I think another name will now be added to my list of Indian correspondents. Yes, certainly we must write to one another, and keep up our friendship while our lives last. It is now of some standing—eight years I reckon: looking back over that time I can trace it distinctly as a peculiar blessing to me. You, I think, were the first person who led me to think seriously at all, and certainly ever since you have been a helper to all my best thoughts and purposes. And I know many others besides me can say the same thing. For all which, and your unceasing kindness and sympathy, may God bless you!

To Rev. W. J. Butler, Vicar of Wantage.

March 6, 1858.

My dear Butler,—Many many thanks for your kind letter and cheering words. I value them very much for old friendship's sake, and because we do not agree in all our opinions; 'truth and bitterness' at once you will say: I trust not, but rather love and charity. I am quite aware that I am not altogether the kind of bishop that you desire to see, but I assure you I go to my diocese with the humble hope that I may be thoroughly in earnest in my work, and impartial and ready to appreciate and encourage Christian goodness wherever

I find it. When one has to try to purify English society in India on the one hand, and to make war on Vishnu, Buddha, and Mahomet on the other, the less that we think of party feuds within Christ's Church the better. Yes, you have triumphed; I am already *half* a doctor: the grace passed on Thursday, and a scarlet hood has arrived.

I suppose that we shall not go till autumn. An earlier departure seems useless, for we cannot go at once, and to start an Indian life in summer is said to be mere folly. I should like to come to Wantage, but will make no promise yet. I have got some books on India, an *aide de camp* from Oxford to take most of my teaching off my hands, and wish to stay here quietly, keep the general government of the school, read and prepare for the unknown but *most* formidable future.

Perhaps I may try to make out a lecture on India, but I will promise nothing at present. Meantime, I am sure you will sometimes pray that God's blessing may be with your old schoolfellow in work which he neither asked for nor desired.

From a former Pupil.

Wednesday, May 12, 1858.

As I cannot come up to see your consecration I shall like to write to you once more, for the last time, before the name by which I have known you for more than sixteen years has ceased to be the beginning of my letters to you. I wish that I could have been at the service to-morrow, but I did not see how I could get away from my work, and perhaps it is as well as it is. I shall be at my ordinary work while you are being consecrated to another and more important part of God's work, and I shall gladly hail the thoughts which this remembrance will bring with it, while I am trying to extract Greek and Latin prose from reluctant boys, as helping me to realise, what it is so easy to hold as an opinion, that my daily work must be made the real hearty service of God if I am ever to serve Him in another way in His own immediate presence. I do not doubt that He will be with you by His spirit to-morrow, and in your new work; and I pray that He will give you richly that love and strength and wise judgment which are

His own most precious blessings to those whom He chooses to be His servants. Our Lord and Saviour, yours and mine, I trust will surely show Himself more clearly to you year by year, and help you to enlarge His kingdom, and by doing His will to know Him perfectly. I do not like to speak of any sorrow that it will be to me to lose you at such a time as this, and so I must turn to the other view and be thankful, as for a most treasured gift, that for all these years your friendship and counsel and help and influence have been near me, and shaped my views of life, and led me to bridge over the chasm between the common and the Christian life. You know that I have sometimes tried to hint at this; and though I am not much in the habit of speaking out strong feelings, for it is better not, yet once for all, before we cease to bear the relation we have borne so long, I should like to say that if Christianity is, or is to be, to me a living principle and not a weary burden, it is to you that I owe it.

To an old Pupil, a Layman, written on the morning of his Consecration.

May 13, 1858. 8.45 A.M.

I will send you the last familiar signature, the last, that is, unless I live to lay down this burthen and spend an old age in England, which I am not sure that I desire—and which, at all events, I can most truly say that I leave cheerfully and confidently in God's hands. A thousand thanks for your letter, which is a great comfort. Let my last presbyteral avowal be a declaration of my conviction that your work, if done in the faith of Christ, is as much His work as mine.

CHAPTER IV.

JOURNAL—FAREWELL TO FRIENDS IN ENGLAND—CAIRO—MAHOMETAN FESTIVALS—BIRTHDAY THOUGHTS—ARRIVAL AT CALCUTTA—INSTALLATION IN THE CATHEDRAL—STATE OF AFFAIRS IN INDIA—POSITION OF THE BISHOP—NATURE OF THE WORK TO BE DONE—LETTERS.

THE best introduction to the Bishop's Indian life is the following extract from his journal, written two days after leaving England:—

September 27, 1858.—I will try now to begin a regular journal of my Indian episcopate. I have kept many diaries and memoranda before of a private character—this possibly may contain some things of more general importance. May all that is in it, whether personal or domestic or public, be written in the love of Jesus Christ, with the great objects to which I have devoted myself constantly before me, in thankfulness to God for past mercies, with the hope and effort after present and future usefulness steadily in view, in dependence on His protection, and with the one desire to consecrate my private and public life to His glory.

Several 'last things' in England were solemn and appropriate. My last sermon was to the Augustinians, the students of a college from which I trust may flow many blessings to India. My last regular Sunday service was in Canterbury Cathedral, the birthplace of English Christianity, and endeared to me privately by the thought of Stanley. My last service of any kind was in Westminster Abbey, where I worshipped in boyhood and where I was consecrated to the office of Bishop. My last visit was to Weybridge, to the grave of dear Conybeare, my closest and in one sense my oldest friend. We were accompanied to the steamer at Southampton by friends and relations of many ages, and representing different classes of valued intimacies and close ties; and though these partings were full of sorrow, yet we separated, not, I trust, as those who have no hope, but in the belief that we are in the hands of a loving Father, whose tenderness has not failed us in time past, and will not fail us in time to come.

In Egypt, that strange connecting link between Europe and Asia, the party made a ten days' halt. It was a break in the outward voyage, resolved upon by the Bishop directly he knew that India was his destined sphere of work. To him the temptation was irresistible to seize perchance this only opportunity in his life to visit the Pyramids; to linger among the many sights of Cairo, the 'Gateway of the East'; to cast a passing glance at two Eastern Churches, the Armenian and the Coptic; and to learn something before reaching India of the outward aspects of Mahometanism. With this latter object in view, the sojourn was well timed. Two sights were witnessed, both most strange to English eyes, both deeply penetrated with the spirit and the fanaticism of Islamism. The one was the presentation to the Pasha of the Mahmel, or sacred canopy, which during the previous year had been placed over the Kaaba at Mecca; the other was the Doseh, the concluding ceremony of the same festival, when a sheykh of great sanctity rides over the bodies of dervishes lying prostrate for the purpose. The first of the sights, picturesque, amusing, oriental in the highest degree; the latter, a wild and extraordinary exhibition of barbarous orgies, were seen to equal advantage through the kindness of some of the English officials at Cairo.

October 29 was the Bishop's birthday. On board the steamer on the Indian Ocean he thus recorded the grave and earnest thoughts which that anniversary, wherever it found him, always evoked:—

How little I thought on its last anniversary where and how this one would be spent; and now what a number of hopes, fears, doubts, and misgivings disturb me in spite of myself. I find it quite impossible on a day like this to avoid unprofitable or worse than unprofitable questionings as to the worth of the task which has been put upon me: whether it was really needful to make so utter a change in my life, to rend asunder so many ties for a future all darkness and uncertainty. Nay, sometimes doubts force themselves upon me as to the reality of the message which I am to deliver, still more as to my own fitness to deliver it in circumstances so wholly new. I trust that all these temptations to distrust and even unbelief will, by God's blessing, be dispelled when work really begins, and that He who called me to the task will help me to perform it. The monotony and want of occupation on board ship doubtless encourage such evil thoughts; perhaps it is better to put them away at once, not to indulge them by dwelling on them even in hopes of conquering them, but to use the simple prayer, *Lord, I believe, help Thou my unbelief*, because I am quite certain of my earnest desire to believe in the greatness of my message and the value of my office, and to try and realise to myself the promise of Habakkuk, repeated by St. Paul and appropriated by Luther, *The just shall live by his faith.* O Lord, grant that as this new year of my life must be one of the most important through which I have passed or shall pass, so it may be most largely blest to me and mine by the help of Thy Holy Spirit, through Jesus Christ our Saviour.

At Galle and Madras brief halts of a day were made. A glimpse of church work at both these places, together with a kind reception from the respective bishops and some of their clergy, formed a fitting introduction to his own diocese. This was reached on November 13, and his journal will best describe an all-important moment in his life.

Saturday, November 13.—At half-past six this morning we were steaming up the Hooghly. The famous approach to Calcutta is rather very pretty than very grand; you pass one handsome villa after another, each standing in a compound green with luxuriant foliage, and at last anchor just opposite Bishop's College, which is a truly academical building, and quite a startling sight in an Indian landscape. As soon as we stopped, people came flocking on board to greet friends and relatives, among them Archdeacon Pratt; and with him I was soon after rowed to the shore of my own diocese in a government boat with a Union Jack flying at the stern. In two carriages left by the late bishop to his successor we all drove along an uninteresting road to the cathedral, opposite to which stood the large and handsome house, which we are to learn to look upon as our Indian home.

May God help us to make it a happy and, as far as we are concerned, a Christian home: may it be a house where He is served and His glory promoted, and His great Name loved and honoured. May He also vouchsafe to accept our humble and hearty thanks for the many mercies which have marked our voyage here, for our freedom from illness and danger, for having brought us safely to this land to which He has called us. Lord help us to dedicate our new life to Thee, and make me a faithful pastor, a guide and a father to Thy children in this land, both to those who know Thee and to those who are in ignorance of Thy love, through Jesus Christ our Lord.

Sunday, November 14.—I was installed this morning in the cathedral at 10 o'clock at the beginning of morning service. The building is too much like a great hall inside; outwardly it is certainly a very pleasant sight from our windows, and will be yet pleasanter when the roof is altered. I like the spire: this and the chimes and the green compound, or close as it really is, bring England back to us continually.

The change in the episcopate of Calcutta occurred at a remarkable crisis. The venerable Daniel Wilson had lived to see India convulsed by a great military rebellion which was not suppressed at the time of his death. His long administration of the See had been marked 'by a zeal which age could not chill, and by an open-handed charity and liberality which have been rarely equalled.' But it will be thought no disparagement to his noble life to say that the last six or eight years were characterised rather by ripened piety than by active church work. During the mutiny he had encouraged others to be courageous in God's name, and then he fell asleep, bequeathing a wide field of labours and responsibilities to his successor. Such of these as appertained to the Church in her missionary character possessed at that time peculiar interest. Amongst the many questions to which the mutiny gave rise, that of missions obtained in England, in 1857, a political prominence such as they had not received since 1813. The evangelisation of India became a conspicuous topic, and some extreme and opposite sentiments on the subject again found utterance. The theory that the presence of missionaries endangered our dominions had still some adherents; the Bible, unfettered and compulsory, was once more a watchword with the large party who have always pleaded zealously, but impulsively, in behalf of India. Calm and moderate views were held by many others no less earnest in the cause, who surveyed thoughtfully the crisis and its difficulties, and urged the need of wisdom no less than of zeal in dealing with them. A deeper sense of Christian duty and responsibility on the part of England towards India was, however, more generally awakened, and practical measures followed upon the discussions that the question excited. Appeals for labourers in that great field of evangelistic work were made with increased urgency; a special fund was opened for Indian missions; missionary studentships were projected at the two universities; missionary studentship associations were formed in some dioceses. The Church at home was thus reviewing her responsibilities and infusing fresh vigour into her Indian mission work, when a new bishop was sent forth 'to quicken the energies and regulate the labours of missionaries of Christ in the East, to build up again from its ruins a Church distressed and desolate and baptized in blood.'* At the moment that Bishop Cotton landed in India, the royal proclamation was sounding the first notes of peace and goodwill through a land over which bitterness and fanaticism were still brooding; the tempest of the great rebellion was dying away in the final campaigns of Oude and Berar; English supremacy was reasserting itself in all parts. Missionaries had resumed their wonted labours, and were restoring the many native Christian settlements which the mutiny had turned into waste places. Strong in the strength of the message they undertook to deliver, and with faith deepened by the trials and the deliverances so lately encountered, they seemed prepared to work on in patient hope and to face with stedfast resolution that aggravated hostility to the Christian's creed which all acknowledged to be one inevitable legacy from the recent conflict between alien races.

Prominently, however, as the evangelistic duties incident to the See of Calcutta were at that time brought forward, the right ordering of the existing Church had an equal claim on the thoughts of its chief pastor. The Europeans and Eurasians forming this Church are found through the length and breadth of the land, in considerable numbers in the large cities, in smaller communities elsewhere, sometimes in almost total isolation in remote districts. They belong to all grades, from the civil and military servants of Government down to the most uncared-for wanderer thrown adrift upon the world. For these several classes, in their temptations, their troubles, their loneliness, the ministrations and ordinances of the Church are urgently required. The obligations to supply them had deepened with every extension of British territory, and had taxed the energies of leaders of the Anglican Church for more than fifty years; but it pro-

* 'Consecration Sermon,' by Rev. Charles J. Vaughan D.D., Westminster Abbey, 1858.

mised to press with more than ordinary weight when, in 1858, English troops were unusually numerous, and English settlers and mechanics were preparing, under the change of policy on the restoration of peace, to seek employment and fortune in India in far larger numbers than heretofore. The resources which the English Church had at command represented in unequal proportions the two principles of State endowment and voluntary aid. The relations which the new Imperial Government assumed towards the ecclesiastical department of the State kept these two principles in view. At no previous time since the creation of an established Church in India had the Supreme Government evinced a more sincere desire to acknowledge the work which the Church had to do, or a greater disposition to strengthen her hands. But it became evident at once, that help would be afforded by the encouragement of voluntary efforts after expansion and development within her borders, rather than by direct increase to the ecclesiastical arm of the Indian service. Early in 1859 the staff of State chaplains was increased by ten; but the numerous European regiments imperatively called for this addition, and the arduous duties of two preceding years had sent home so many chaplains invalided, that the gain was scarcely perceptible. The supply of ministers from other sources was inadequate to the demand, and the dearth of clergy continued to create a standing difficulty in all ecclesiastical arrangements.

Such was the general aspect of the see when it passed into fresh hands at the close of 1858. There was no greater pressure of daily routine work than any one with good business habits and fair physical powers could easily accomplish, even in a tropical climate; no greater questions of ecclesiastical discipline were likely to arise than average tact and judgment could settle. It was the responsibility rather than the toil of the office that weighed most upon the new bishop. He felt from the first, not only that he stood as the chief representative of Christianity to the native races, but that he had also to lead the Church of England in her efforts to provide for the welfare of organised Christian congregations. The needs of these congregations in all their variety and distinctiveness were at once discerned. Their recognition became the key-note of his administration of the see, his whole career being specially marked by the untiring industry with which he negotiated alike with State authorities and with private individuals, the ways and means for promoting the Church's efficiency. Fearlessly and hopefully many English friends had seen him go forth, but it was necessarily a work of time to inspire similar confidence on the scene of his labours. He landed in India with singularly few links either of kindred or friendship to connect him with the country, and he had no name in the ranks of either of the two great Church parties; he was in all senses a stranger among strangers. During many months he was little known; he was engaged in feeling his way quietly and with characteristic reserve. His early sentiments towards India were prompted by thoughtful earnestness rather than by soul-stirring enthusiasm; he realised it as a field for the exercise of a man's highest mental powers; he was prepared to watch with keen intellectual interest the course of every Western influence brought to bear on Eastern minds; he was full of calm and just recognition of the difficulties which surround the moral and spiritual relations of England with her great dependency. The unusual gravity of his countenance at the moment that he set foot on the shores of his diocese, vast in extent, more vast in the variety and complexity of its interests, testified to the solemnity of spirit with which he entered on the work that was awaiting him.

His early occupations included the patient study of two vernacular languages, inspection of schools and missions congregated in and about Calcutta, and intercourse with any who could be sources of information. The following letters will serve to give some early impressions, and to shadow forth the various lines of work with which, as time passed on, he vigorously identified himself.

*To Professor Conington.**

November 18, 1858.

. . . There plainly will be plenty to do. The Bishop is a kind of Minister of Ecclesiastical Affairs, and decides on the stations of all Government chaplains, besides receiving complaints against them, of which there have been three since I came. If he keeps on good terms with the Government, his power over them is much greater than that of an English bishop over his incumbents. Then he is trustee of nearly all the religious, educational, and charitable institutions in the town, including some of a most miscellaneous character; for instance, in one, one of my chief co-trustees is a Mahometan prince.

I am also on the senate of the new Calcutta University, which is to examine for B.A. degrees next March. Then there are, of course, the more purely spiritual functions. I have announced my first ordination for January 25, the day on which I was myself ordained deacon, and my first confirmation for February 2, on which days I and my work will not, I hope, be forgotten by friends in England. Most of the Indian officials with whom I have had short interviews seem to acquiesce in the India Bill, and to hope that it will do good, by making the Indian Minister one of the chief men in the Cabinet; so that they expect always a better ruler than they

* This and other letters in the following pages will now, after Mr. Conington's early death, be read with heightened interest by many who knew the closeness of the intimacy that existed between him and the Bishop. Each possessed a warm and faithful heart, and a friendship built upon a constant interchange of thought about many things, both grave and gay, was neither cooled by time nor weakened by distance. Mr. Conington died in October 1869.

used to get when, as President of the Board of Control, his office was only reckoned one of secondary importance.

The interest and possible magnitude of our work here is, I think, gradually opening upon me: a great impulse was given to this feeling by an interview with a youth who was converted and baptized at eighteen. He was disgusted with Hinduism on two grounds: (1) the crimes of the gods; (2) the degrading prostrations required from his caste (Sudra) by the Brahmins; and the arrogance and rapacity displayed, in consequence, by these authorised priests and teachers. Christianity attracted him, in the first instance, by its moral precepts, and by its tendency to civilise, by overthrowing caste and teaching all men self-respect and independence. Yet he prefers Hinduism to the atheism into which many of the educated young men are rapidly falling. Hinduism operates as some sort of moral check, whereas these unbelievers give full licence to their passions and impulses. The evil often begins by their casting off Hindu observances before they are convinced that they are needless; for instance, many neophytes of the 'Young Bengal' school go and eat their tiffin at hotels, with a lingering feeling that it is wrong, 'whereby their hearts are hardened, and they get to do things which are really bad.' A striking illustration, I thought, of 'Whatsoever is not of faith is sin.'

You will not doubt that I sympathise truly and heartily with your anxieties about the health of your parents, and I am glad that I spent those few hours at Boston, as enabling me to do so more really.

Pray do not think that I am uninterested in comparisons between Eton and Rugby, and in educational matters of other kinds, especially such as are connected with the universities. On the contrary, I feel as to my past schoolmaster life, 'If I forget thee, may my right hand forget her cunning.' . . .

Some crows were enjoying the fragments of a meal which had been eaten in the open air by some officers. An adjutant, a great carrion bird, approached: all the crows dispersed, except one unlucky wight, who ventured to stop and finish his share; the adjutant instantly swallowed the crow whole, who, as he descended into his stomach, was heard to utter a farewell *caw*. This story is chiefly for the benefit of R. B. Smith.

To the Rev. Dr. Stanley.

February 28, 1859.

If you thought of my former work with you during the Fulham ordination, you may imagine how often recollections of you returned to me during my own first ordination. There were five candidates. The chief interest centred in the three natives from the NW. as pastors for native congregations. Their appearance was singular, as they were arrayed entirely in white, always coming shoeless into my presence, and with white turbans. I certainly felt it an impressive moment when I was conducted to my chair within the rails, and the archdeacon advanced up the aisle, with the candidates after him, and presented three heathen-born Hindus, brought down from the very centre of war and anarchy to be ordained ministers of the Gospel of Peace. Soon after the ordination a series of confirmations began, coupled with much school inspecting, and a tour to Krishnagur, Burdwan, and other important places. At the confirmation I hammered through the service in Bengali, but gave my harangues in English, which were interpreted, sentence by sentence, by one of the missionaries present. And now what do I think of the missions? They are very like well-ordered English country parishes, each with its church, parsonage, and schools; cottages neat, people neat and tidy, schools decidedly good. But undoubtedly very little is doing in the way of adding to the converts (at least in the places just visited), though great care is taken to keep the existing converts and their descendants in the right path. Certainly able men are wanted. Few of the missionaries appear to me quite up to the mark of battling with acute Hindu or Mahometan disputants. Some of them are Germans in English orders, and, among many disadvantages, this fact at least has the advantage of introducing more taste and romance into the missions than some of the stricter English puritans would tolerate or appreciate. In two places the singing of the Bengal congregations was quite beautiful, and there was always something picturesque about our reception. I had very interesting interviews with two of the native Christians, whom the Lieutenant-Governor of Bengal has just appointed to be deputy-magistrates. I talked a long time with each about the influences which had led to their conversion, their difficulties, and the prospect of Christianity making way among the educated classes. Undoubtedly the English do not treat these people properly. The two whom I saw were as completely gentlemen as you could desire to see, and were now Government officers in responsible and prominent positions. Yet some of the English functionaries thought it impossible to ask them to dinner, and one spoke of natives in a rude and unkind way in the presence of one of them. I am glad to record that a Rugby man, in the school-house in Arnold's time, and though now a High-Churchman, one who devoutly reverences his memory, has given a banquet on purpose for the deputy-magistrate at his station, and asked all the aristocracy of the place on the occasion.

To Arthur Watson, Esq.

Bishop's Palace, Calcutta, May 1, 1859.

This is a bad time to write to you, for the hot weather is at its height, and therefore very little is going on, so that the materials for a letter are few, while at the same time the power of getting through necessary work is less, and so one's inclination to extra occupation is diminished. Besides the ordinary evils of the hot weather, I am troubled by a development of it called the 'prickly heat,' a sort of rash which does one no real harm; in fact, it is a sign of health; but I certainly find it disagreeable, and very often I desire to spend the whole afternoon on the sofa reading 'Frederic the Great,' which was brought by the penultimate mail, and is now my only light literature.

I have read, not ——'s sermon of which you speak, but a sketch of it in the 'Saturday Review,' and I understand its general purport from having read Comte's 'Catechism,' or at least a good deal of it. Doubtless positivism teaches us some important moral truths, but it is amazing to me how —— can fail to see that Christianity has also taught them for the last eighteen centuries. If anyone really maintained that the Gospel does not tell us to live for others, in the face of our

Lord's declaration, 'Love one another as I have loved you,' or that it makes us indifferent to the true happiness of the world, and the desire of improving it, and doing every duty which we undertake conscientiously and thoroughly, he must be wilfully blind and ignorant. Doubtless some Christians have spoken foolishly about entire separation from the world under all circumstances, and have divided our spiritual altogether from our secular duties, but this is a *παρέκβασις* of Christianity, not Christianity itself, and to remedy it we need not throw away our faith in eternity—our consolation in sorrow, our chief motive power to true holiness. So there should be no dallying with this new religion.

I must end. One word as to the magnificence of the flowering trees here. Imagine great trees rising to the top of the windows in our drawing-room (a first floor not a ground floor room) absolutely laden with huge bunches of orange and scarlet flowers. They are quite gorgeous.

To C. P. Ilbert.

Bishop's Palace, Calcutta, May 22, 1859.

I have not much to say this time, and you must prepare for a stupid letter. The truth is that I am oppressed by a languor and weakness against which I struggle in vain. I am quite well, sleep only too much, and eat and drink as much as is good for me. But all my energies seem melting away, and in writing a sermon or even so commonplace a composition as an address to the Governor-General on the Queen's birthday, I feel as if my power of expressing my thoughts and constructing sentences were gone. The doctor says that it is only the effect of my first hot weather, that I must not be surprised and discouraged, and that I shall come all right soon. We have been getting up some lectures addressed to educated natives, who form the class for whom least is done in the cultivation of the intellect. They are all well trained in English in the Government colleges, and are in some respects unpleasing; but there are points about them which are more hopeful, and at all events they must not be neglected, as they are becoming the most important class in Bengal.

The lectures were designed not to be of a directly missionary character, but to treat on subjects of general interest, regarded from a Christian point of view, and intended to rouse these young Bengalis to the fact that Christianity is not a local or national religion of the West, as Brahminism is of the East, nor, again, a system of outward ceremonies and abstract doctrines, but a principle intended to pervade the whole of human life, all moral speculations and actions.

The programme is as follows:—

Lessons suggested by the Early History of India.

St. Augustine (of Africa).

The Emperor Julian.

The Institutes of Menu (the Hindu lawgiver) and Education.

Dr. Arnold.

Two of them have already taken place, and the success, as far as securing auditors goes, has been complete. The room was crammed by Bengali young men, and just round the lecturer's desk sat a few Europeans. I opened the proceedings on the first night by a brief explanation of the object of the lectures, and then read Arnold's prayer, which I used with you in the sixth, slightly altered and adapted to the occasion, to which I requested the audience to listen, and to join in as far as possible.

Then came the first lecture—hearty, earnest, and well-written, sometimes eloquent, but too generally deficient in historical detail, hardly corresponding to its title, since the lecturer treated exclusively of the Mahometan period, and in its conclusion more directly like a Christian sermon than was expedient. On the following Tuesday, we had Dr. Kay on Augustine—an admirable lecture, extremely interesting, most graceful and touching in its language, and exceedingly well adapted to the Bengalis, who at the end applauded it in a manner which, for their lazy temperaments, may be called vociferous. The scene, as we came out on the first night, of groups of Bengalis in their white garments standing about the steps of the lighted building, discussing the lecture, with the bright clear ivory moonlight of India around them and above them, was one of the most picturesque that I ever saw. One longed to be able to contemplate it with something more than an artistic feeling, and to believe that the lectures might, by God's blessing, take some permanent hold on their hearts and heads. The lectures were the occasion for an absurd piece of caution on the part of a Government official. We had to give them in an inconvenient place, instead of a very convenient one. Lectures are commonly given, on all kinds of miscellaneous subjects, in the theatre of the Medical College, and the principal of the College readily assented to our use of the room. The arrangement, however, was stopped by an official, lest the Government should be mixed up with the missionary work. I certainly thought this refusal unworthy of a sensible man, and it is the only instance which I have seen of that cowardice about Christianity which religious people at home (often unjustly) attribute to the Indian Government.

The natives themselves showed their incapability of appreciating this caution by crowding to the lectures to the amount of some four hundred, and asking with annoyance why they were sent to an out-of-the-way place, instead of going to the Medical College, to which they are accustomed on such occasions. One of them remarked to me that a man must know little of the Bengalis who supposed that the class for whom these lectures were designed shared the blunders of ryots and sepoys, and believed that they were to be made Christians by force.

To Mrs. Arnold.

May 31, 1859.

I little thought when I wrote to you the other day, telling you of the pleasure which we had experienced in Willy's visit to us, that my next letter to you would be so mournfully different. We were greatly shocked a week ago by the news of his death. You will, I doubt not, feel a mournful pleasure in anything which I can tell you about him. We enjoyed his visit greatly. He was particularly lively and agreeable, except when he was positively ill, and we had various intimate talks, reminding me of old days at Rugby. Sometimes these related to various forms of belief and unbelief now prevalent, and he once or twice expressed a desire for some fresh evidence of

Christianity, which should clear away difficulties relating to inspiration. 'But, after all,' he said, 'there was no difficulty greater than to believe that the Sermon on the Mount was not divine.' I was very glad that he had a pleasant interview with Lord Canning. You know that he had written against him in the papers and spoken harshly of him. When Lord Canning heard he was here, he sent for him and consulted him confidentially on various questions relating to education, and Willy returned certainly very favourably impressed with his courtesy, kindness, and desire to do his duty. We parted on February 8, when he went on board the steamer, and we must have left Calcutta at about the same moment: he homewards, we on our tour to Krishnagur and Burdwan. He is, as we humbly trust and believe, the first of the nine children who has gone to his Father, to a truer and a better home than that happy earthly one which he hoped to find with his mother; and certainly, of all the nine, he bore not the fewest traces of his earthly father's character. Everybody who has spoken to me about him regards his death as a real loss to India; for, by his activity and ability in discharging his duties in the Punjâb, he had won himself great credit, so that there were few men of his age who had a higher reputation.

Perhaps the point which most struck me about him (compared with his language in 'Oakfield') was his thorough interest in this country, and keen enjoyment of his work here. One day he said, 'Well, I hope that the Tories are safe in office for three years.' I cried out at this as very unlike his old opinions, and he said, 'Perhaps it is wrong to view everything with reference to India, but really I cannot help it, and as I believe Lord Stanley to be the best man for us now, I wish him to stay in, and therefore the Cabinet.' Both to Lord Canning and to myself he expressed himself strongly in favour of the grant-in-aid system (the despatch of 1854), and urged me to advocate it in my charge to the clergy at my visitation. He always had a Greek Testament on his dressing-table: taking it up casually one day, I saw that on the first page was the date of his wife's death. It would be interesting to you now, and to his children hereafter, to possess this, as it was probably used by him as long as the power to use it was left.

The last day we talked about you, and he took great pleasure in my telling him about my visit to Fox How, and how happy and honoured your life there had appeared to me.

To the Rev. Dr. Vaughan.

August 1859.

Many thanks for your letter, which I answer now, in order to express my regret and annoyance at the manner in which —— was treated about St. Paul's School. I am very sorry that my desire for your intervention has turned out such a signal failure, and only gave you trouble without any corresponding fruit. I have taken an opportunity of expressing my objection to the selection of a treatise on regeneration as a text-book of Church doctrine, and my desire that persons of ——'s sentiments should not be excluded from the diocese. . . . I have written to Mr. —— in much the same strain as my minute to the Governors. Enough of this, which has vexed me a good deal, and, I fear, troubled you. We had our Thanksgiving-day on July 28. It went off, I hope, well. The Governor-General and Council came to the Cathedral in state, and took part in the service drawn up by me, and listened with decorous attention to my discourse. The Thanksgiving-day ended by a great banquet at Government House, where I was struck by the genuine, heart-felt gratitude which Lady Canning expressed. 'I thought it at one time hardly possible,' she said, 'that I should see this day; that the war must have gone on far beyond the time when we should have quitted India.' With this exception nothing has been stirring: the hot weather and rains are always the dead time of the year. We want a Gladstone to restore our finances, and generally a little more vigour and speed of action might be infused into the councils of the State.

CHAPTER V.

PRIMARY CHARGE—DEPARTURE FROM CALCUTTA ON VISITATION—BENARES—PESHAWUR — DHARAMSALA — SIMLA — LIFE AT SIMLA—DEPARTURE FROM SIMLA FOR MUSSOURIE AND NAINEE TAL—BAREILLY—CAMP LIFE IN OUDE—RETURN TO CALCUTTA—THE BISHOP'S WAY OF LIFE WHILE TRAVELLING—HIS WORK ON VISITATION—HIS INTEREST IN SOLDIERS—HIS JOURNALS—EXTRACTS FROM THEM — INTEREST IMPARTED TO THE FIRST VISITATION BY THE RECENT MUTINY — JOURNAL EXTRACTS BEARING UPON IT—LETTERS.

IN SEPTEMBER 1859, the Bishop gave his primary Charge. The weather was very hot and trying, and the visitation in Calcutta was spread over two days. On the first the service consisted of the Litany and a sermon from Dr. Kay, the principal of Bishop's College, and the Holy Communion; on the second day, after morning prayers, the Charge was delivered. It fell into three divisions, and treated of the relations of Government with Native education, of the condition of missionary progress, of the state of the European population, and the demands upon its special ministers. The first of these topics was at that time invested with the highest interest. The connexion of Government with any Christian element in Native education was still a subject for controversy. The Mutiny had revived the question with an agitation and excitement which had not subsided in India in 1859; and many earnest men, besides professed missionaries, were awaiting with anxiety the legislation which was to follow the Queen's proclamation, guaranteeing religious toleration towards all. The state of the native mind could not be a source of satisfactory contemplation to thoughtful observers. While some of the older educated Hindus were intrenching themselves in ancestral orthodoxy, a younger generation was breaking loose from all faith, and scepticism and atheism seemed the only fruits reaped from the seed of Western culture cast upon India. On Christians who desired to read aright the signs of the times, the duty pressed more heavily than ever of claiming that a free course should be granted to the Bible; that, at least, it should be rendered not less accessible to Hindu students than the secular knowledge so freely offered. The Bishop, in surveying this great question, took his stand upon the recent language of the Government. He pointed out that far from being retrogressive, the Secretary of State's Educational despatch of 1859, which was so severely criticised, confirmed that of 1854; that both permitted the presence of the Scriptures in the libraries of Government schools, and that neither placed any restrictions on giving instruction, if voluntarily sought in other hours than those devoted to regular school studies. He was satisfied that, this point once conceded and again ratified, there remained no barrier raised by the rulers of India between the 'seeker after God' and the teacher to whom he might care to turn. To his mind it afforded the one fair and practical escape out of that dilemma, one horn of which was an official ban upon the Bible in Government schools, the other being its compulsory introduction, regardless of the consideration that the teachers must be, for the most part, heathens. On this latter point the Bishop never changed his ground.

'When I consider' (so runs a passage in the Charge, written with all the acute personal feeling which this aspect of the question invariably excited in him) 'how great, whether for good or evil, is the influence of the living voice and the contact of mind with mind, and how disastrous in religious teaching is the effect of the suppressed sneer, the vacant air of indifference, the doubting or hostile comment, I must maintain that it were almost better for a Bengali not to know that the Word of God exists than to hear it explained by one who regards it as an imposture and a delusion.' Such concession or compromise, great as it was, could at best be only partially satisfactory to one who viewed the divorce of religious from secular instruction as unnatural and calamitous at all times and for all races. He acquiesced in it as representing a period of transition, preparatory to that time, only then dimly foreshadowed, when Government, withdrawing from the direct work of education, would limit itself to aiding the efforts of voluntary associations. He accepted it for India as the one onward step then practicable, and he knew that it was capable of indefinite expansion at the hands of secular teachers who were able and really religious men.

As a matter of fact, the principles proclaimed by Government were more liberal than its practice. Orders issued by the late Court of Directors, strangely and needlessly timid, were still unrepealed, and in India official caution evinced such distrust of the voluntary Bible classes in Government buildings, that the Bishop had to make yet again a strenuous and successful appeal in their behalf to the Governor-General. On the whole, however, the educational policy at that time was one to which he could give in his adhesion, and with which he could cooperate hopefully. To make others share this feeling was one aim of the Charge. He brought argument and calm reasoning to bear upon a topic which had often been discussed with prejudice and impatience, and in doing so he occupied that position of a peacemaker which was equally in accordance with his office and his own personal character. The language in which he pleaded for fairness and moderation was too temperate to satisfy some ardent minds; but it won for him, in the early months of his Indian life, much confidence from Government and from many others also, who accepted it at the time, and were content to be guided by it in after years. The necessity for such arbitration has now almost if not wholly disappeared, but in those years it was not so. The susceptibilities of missionaries and their supporters on the one hand, and of Government officials on the other, were at that time easily and quickly alarmed, and incidents were not wanting in the years immediately subsequent to the mutiny to show that the embers of mutual distrust could be quickened into hostility on any misunderstanding or supposed provocation. While irritation, remained the Bishop found his task in seeking to allay it, and in mediating between parties severed far more by mutual misunderstanding than by any antagonism of principles. In the endeavour to raise men's minds to a wider and more impartial contemplation of a much debated subject, he thus summed up a long analysis of it:—

I cannot but express a wish that the word neutrality could be dropped in describing the relations of the British Government to religion. It may be said that a word is not of much consequence; and no doubt some word is necessary to express the facts that the State stands aloof from missionary enterprises, and that, in the language of the Queen's proclamation, 'none shall be in anywise favoured, none molested or disquieted by reason of their religious faith or observances, but that all shall alike enjoy the equal and impartial protection of the law.' But the word neutrality (which is avoided in the proclamation) is liable to perpetual misconstruction, and has received it from certain Madras petitioners. Nor can I ever hear it without thinking of Our Lord's warning, 'He that is not with me is against me.' It is impossible for any thoughtful man to be really indifferent to the contest between two such principles as Christianity and Heathenism. Nor, in truth, can we claim to have been so when we have taken upon ourselves to decide that certain parts of the Hindu system are immoral, and to prohibit them by law. Passing from the word to the principle intended to be expressed by it, there must arise, from the anomaly of a Christian Government ruling over a non-Christian population, a thousand delicate questions, as to the distinction between the private and public capacity of State officers, and as to the acts which are lawful in one character and unlawful in the other. On these multifarious difficulties I cannot enter further than to remind you that we must not be hasty in censuring individual decisions; for the task which our rulers have before them in this matter is one demanding judgment, firmness, and candour in an unusual degree. We must all acknowledge the principle of official non-intervention; coercion and favouritism are alike unchristian; our heathen fellow-subjects have an undeniable right to demand, in simple justice, that no civil or military functionary should use his public position for the purpose of making converts.

On the other hand, it is quite true that the claims of individual liberty and of Christian conscience must be considered by Government as well as the duty of non-interference with the religious belief of their subjects. The distinction will often be so nice that we are bound to abstain from harsh and hasty judgments if the decision is not always in accordance with our own opinion.

A Charge which was characterised as 'over moderate in tone, and, if possible, too impartial in its statements,' could not escape hostile criticism. But concurrence and approval came from other quarters where it was peculiarly valuable. To one home correspondent he wrote :—

I have had a very kind letter from Mr. Venn, of the Church Missionary Society, about my Charge. Of course he does not quite like the part about the Bible in Government Schools, but admits that there is but little difference between his own plan and that which the Government has adopted, and which I defend, and about the rest of the Charge he writes with entire satisfaction. Moreover, the letter is very friendly in its tone, and as he is the person who has done most for, and knows most about, missionary work (except actual missionaries), I do not heed some unfavourable, and, I think, very unfair criticisms which this part of the Charge has called forth.

To another he wrote :—

I have had a very satisfactory and pleasant letter from Captain Eastwick of the Indian Council about my Charge. He says he quite agrees with my remarks on the Santhal schools and the word *neutrality*, and that Sir Charles Wood, in spite of strong opposition, has written out to sanction the university examinations in Butler and Paley. Besides other advantages, I fancy that this will retain Dr. Duff on the senate.

The Bishop passed on from this question of prominent interest and importance to the discussion of evangelistic labours as carried on by missionaries, and of the pastoral agency at work amongst Europeans. At so early a stage of his life in a new country, and with only a limited personal experience of India, he disclaimed the right authoritatively to enunciate opinions or propound theories which wider knowledge might greatly modify. But his survey of the Church's work was comprehensive and suggestive; his views on the broad range that missionary labours ought to take, and on the wide scope afforded by the various classes of English society for the best energies of chaplains, were clearly and impressively expressed. Words, perhaps anxiously looked for, were spoken at last, and were all the more forcible from the long and deliberate thought with which they had been penned. By many in India the Charge was accepted and welcomed as a valuable exponent of the Bishop's mind on various topics. Long afterwards it was said that his wise and temperate language on the subject of the connexion of Government with religious teaching had been the means of laying that vital question to rest. It was no less true that the delivery of this primary Charge constituted, on other grounds also, an epoch in his tenure of the See. From that date he ceased to be a stranger amongst his clergy, who now felt his strength and value as a guide and leader, and discerned how closely he desired to be knit with them in the bonds of common responsibilities and of a common work. The matured thought, conciliatory language, and intrinsic earnestness which characterised the first public utterance of his opinions, cast a light on his character in advance of his personal presence, which the unavoidably ephemeral intercourse with individual clergy during the long visitation about to commence might have failed to afford.

Immediately after the delivery of the Charge, the party in the Palace left Calcutta and entered upon that wandering life which was henceforth to be their lot in India. A month was spent in ascending the Ganges to Benares, and in halts at several of the earliest stations of British India, planted on the banks of that great highway of nature. The home of the travellers during this period was the official barge, kindly lent by the Lieutenant-Governor of Bengal, and towed by a Government steamer. But neither the great comfort nor the comparative coolness of the boat, nor the care of the doctor in charge of the party, could keep illness at bay; and both the Bishop and his chaplain were so prostrated by fever, arising from prolonged sojourn in the damp atmosphere of the river, that even the light duties of the small stations to be visited were often a matter of difficulty. The marvellous size of a tropical river can never fail to be impressive to English eyes. The Bishop wrote of the mighty Ganges: 'It has given me an absolutely new idea such as I never drew from Elbe or Rhine or Tagus or Nile.' But, except for this vast expanse of waters, the Ganges valley is painfully featureless. A dead flat extending for many hundred miles is only broken by the low range of the Rajmahal hills. Its soft and shifting soil, and the absence of stone, forbid the erection of fine buildings near the river, and an unbroken tropical temperature reduces the dress and dwellings of the natives to a dull uniformity. A far more interesting section of the visitation journey opened at Benares, which, from its fine situation and Oriental character, is worthy to be called the gateway of Upper India. Though now left in comparative isolation by its distance from the main line of railway, it then stood forth conspicuously on the Grand Trunk Road, the first in that succession of great cities which, either as thoroughfares of traffic or as monuments of Eastern rule and magnificence, still form centres of Hindu or Mussulman national life through the breadth of the continent up to the frontiers of Affghanistan. From Benares the onward visitation route carried the travellers to Lucknow, Agra, Delhi, and Lahore. The limits of British territory were reached at Peshawur in January 1860. Here the pleasant variety of a family party awaited them, as Sir Sidney Cotton was then commanding the frontier. Right hospitably he received his visitors; he entertained them too, and Lord Canning also (whose vice-regal progress here, as in some other places coincided with that of the Bishop) in a manner highly congenial to himself, by grand displays of the picturesque army of European and native soldiery with which he overawed his Afridi neighbours. Jumrood was visited, an outlying fortress of Peshawur, from which a good view of the mouth of the famous Kyber Pass is obtained. Here some specimens of a wild frontier tribe showed themselves, all, even down to young boys, being armed with weapons significant of 'blood feuds' among themselves, and border forays on the English. From Peshawur the travellers retraced their steps over the dusty plains of the Punjâb with such speed as palanquin travelling at three miles an hour could effect. From Amritsir a divergence to Kangra and Dharamsala brought them for the first time into the midst of grand Himalayan scenery; from Ambala, a little later, the hills were again ascended, and rest and a cool retreat were, early in April 1860, secured at Simla.

During the next six months life flowed on serenely and uneventfully; the Bishop during long quiet days pursued his usual employments with little interruption; he wrote and corresponded for the good of the diocese, and read much for his own edification; he shared regularly with the local chaplain the Sunday ministrations to a lar.e congregation, and one week-day evening service, which was fairly attended. His greatest refreshment was drawn daily at Simla, as at like places in after years, from the beautiful walks and rides among the endless ranges of hills that surround and overhang the station.

Early in October, the rest and refreshment of Simla came to an end, and the party entered upon one of the most fatiguing months they ever encountered. It was still far too hot in the plains to attempt travelling by day, and nine nights out of the month of October were spent in palanquins; and twice during the same period the steep and toilsome ascent of many miles of mountain road had to be performed to bestow visitation on Mussourie and Nainee Tal, and the still more remote hill settlement of Almorah. At length, in the early days of November, Bareilly was reached, a large military cantonment, and a bright and animated native city in the healthy province of Rohilcund. Here a camp provided by Government was awaiting them, and as 'dwellers in tents' they traversed a great part of Oude, reached Benares and the grand Trunk Road in January 1861, and Calcutta shortly afterwards.

These months, the general characteristics of which have thus been briefly sketched, had been chequered by some attacks of illness, but the path of the wanderers had been strewn with many blessings, and few *contretemps* had arisen to hinder progress through the vast extent of country traversed. Many successive days and weeks were unavoidably unsettled and full of change, but the fatigues and distractions of travel never overpowered current business, or interfered with the tenor of the Bishop's industrious life. His love of travelling and long familiarity with it enabled him to find refreshment rather than excitement in all that crossed his path, and through great powers of abstraction, and the method and mental arrangement that pervaded his work at all times, there was not a daylight hour which, when he was in health, was not turned to account. During long weary hours of dâk travelling his love of reading came powerfully to his aid. He was an insatiable reader, and though not an especially rapid one, there were few current works of note falling in with his tastes and occupations, of which he did not, when in India, make himself master. Neither did he fail to recognise and appreciate the 'heaven-born power' of fiction to soothe and refresh in a weary hour. A good novel always had a place among the standard works, papers, and pamphlets with which his carriage or palanquin was filled, its perusal being justified, as he wrote humorously in his diary, by 'a long dâk journey,' or 'a thermometer at 90°.'

The Bishop's work during the first visitation had to some extent a specific character, inasmuch as the ecclesiastical, like the civil and military, machinery of the State had undergone a severe strain under the then recent shock of the mutiny. There was much to adjust and to reorganise to suit the altered condition of stations, and to meet military arrangements, then often temporary and imperfect, for the large European force in the country. Otherwise the business of this tour of inspection was similar to that carried on in succeeding journeys during the next seven years. At almost all places where a halt was made, there were missionary and educational establishments to be inspected; there were the Government chaplains to be visited, and stimulated in their work by counsel or assistance; there were lonely and outlying communities of Christians to be remembered, and, so far as was possible, their spiritual needs supplied. Among the more strictly ministerial avocations of Church services and preaching, ministrations to soldiers held a distinct and prominent place.

The Bishop, from the earliest days of his Indian life, discerned in an English regiment a boundless field for pastoral energy. His sermons addressed to a military congregation were often as close and individual in their application as those which had been preached of old to an audience of school-boys. By Bible classes held during temporary sojourns at hill stations, by visits to the hospitals as he passed from one cantonment to another, he came into personal though temporary contact with the men. He always regarded the absence of candidates from the army for confirmation as one of the greatest blots on a chaplain's work, and in spite of the frequent repetition of this ordinance, he once wrote to an English friend. that he never lost the sense of its deep value, and always prepared to take his part in it with a fresh and living interest. His anxiety for the well-being of soldiers found a more secular channel in his ready sympathy with every effort to multiply reading-rooms and institutes, and to encourage healthful recreation calculated to wean men from vice and disarm a time of peace in a tropical climate of some of its evils.

The marked interest which in his later life he evinced in a profession far removed from his own tastes, received a seal in a paper dated May 1866, and found with his will. In it he expressed his willingness, 'as the son and the father of a soldier,' to be buried in a military cemetery; 'because,' he added, 'some years of my life have now been spent in trying to help chaplains to do their duty to soldiers; moreover the soldier's profession is the best type of the Christian's warfare with sin.'

The Bishop's journals furnished a copious record of his

life while on visitation. As chronicles of events they were often useful for reference, and the fulness and care with which, amidst constant distraction, they were written, were eminently characteristic of one who worked ever calmly and without haste, and whose concentrated attention for any specific purpose seemed ready at a moment's summons. The journals were descriptive rather than reflective, but the latter feature was not wanting, especially when some outward event or circumstance sent the writer inward on himself through its personal application, and suggested the thoughtful comment or aspiration. A few samples gathered out of many pages of manuscript may serve as illustration to the reader of the mind and work of him who wrote them.

Hear, for example, what he has to say on the difficult subject of approaching non-Christian minds with the teaching and doctrines of our religion; it was a subject which naturally was constantly presented to his mind in one aspect or another:—

November 1859.— —— is a convert of a singularly sensitive and speculative turn of mind, the very reverse therefore of certain missionaries, who seem to carry hatred of speculation to a length which must diminish their usefulness in dealing with the subtle minds of the Hindus. An inquirer said to one of them that he was puzzled by the doctrine of Our Lord's Divinity. 'You have nothing to do with such subjects,' was the reply: 'if you wish to be a Christian, you have only to feel and confess your need of forgiveness.' Surely an unwise answer, and opposed to the examples furnished by the New Testament and by early Church history. For certainty many came to Our Lord, and many converts were added to the Church afterwards from other motives than the simple want of forgiveness, although I believe that such a want will always be felt when a person comes to have any spiritual knowledge of Christianity.

. . . .

Dehli, December.—I had to-day another conversation with

Ramchandra. He told me that his non-Christian friends, especially the Hindus, are very kind and civil to him, ask him to their houses, and even to food apart from themselves. The Mahometans occasionally engage with him in argument; their reasons against Christianity being drawn from discrepancies in Scripture, various readings, uncertainty whether the whole Pentateuch was written by Moses. I told him that I could not think that such questions could touch the foundation of any devout acceptance of the Gospel, and that I should have expected, if they had spoken of the Old Testament, they would have argued from certain moral difficulties, such as the extermination of the Canaanites. But this, he answered, is too much in accordance with their own principles to allow them to object to it, though they always quote it, if accused of propagating Mahometanism by the sword. The cases, of course, are not *in pari materie*, but how strange that they should reply by an appeal to Judaism, when Christ expressly disallowed such appeal, and pointed out the new spirit of the Gospel, when He rebuked the Apostles for wishing to imitate Elija's punishment on Ahaziah's messengers. Ramchandra himself was reclaimed from a philosophical deism by reading the New Testament and seeing the devout worship of educated Englishmen—a striking instance of the concurrent evidence of the Gospel and the Church, Christianity and Christendom.

Hear him again, when an incident in his travels suggested an expression of his strong views about tact and discretion in the work of evangelization:—

The American missionaries described a very unsuccessful interview with the Maharajah. They requested an audience in order to present him a Bible, and took with them a native convert whom they had ordained. On seeing him the Maharajah asked who was that native in European dress, and whether he held any office under Government. Matters being explained, he said that such a person must not sit down in his presence, whereupon all the missionaries refused to sit, and presented the Bible. 'What is this?' inquired the Prince, and then expressed his belief that the Shastirs contained all that he wanted, and that he did not wish any Christianity in

Cashmir. Finally he handed it to one of his attendants. I much doubt whether it was desirable to give him the Bible at all. They argue that, even now perhaps, some of his attendants may read it. It is equally or more probable that they will light the fire with it; and this plan of thrusting the Word of God at unbelievers without any preparation certainly exposes it to contemptuous treatment, and is likely to raise a prejudice against the donor and his religion.

On the occasion of visiting a missionary school which he did not think satisfactory, he wrote, in conformity with his cardinal theory about evangelization, that education must go hand in hand with preaching:—

There is a tendency now certainly in the committee of the Church Missionary Society at home, and among some missionaries out here, to depreciate schools in comparison with preaching. Yet surely the great influence which a really kind, earnest, and able missionary must obtain over intelligent scholars, the undoubted improvement in the tone of morality, regard for truth, obedience, and discipline, effected in a well-ordered mission school, strongly asserted by the Peshawur missionaries, the favour which a good school wins for the mission as the source of a great benefit to the city where it is planted, a fact resting on the evidence of the Agra missionaries, and general clearing away of ignorance, folly, and superstition effected by education, are as likely to pave the way for Christ's Spirit as the plan of hurrying from village to village, preaching for a day or two, and not reappearing to deepen and confirm the impression of the visit till a year has passed away, and all that was said is forgotten. The Apostles brought with them two evidences of power and goodness; of the first by their miracles, of the latter by their lives. We should also bring forth, substituting for miracles, now withdrawn from the Church, the fact that knowledge, civilisation, activity, intellectual and material greatness, law, order, discipline, are all in the hands of Christian nations, and in theirs only.

Another extract may afford a glimpse of the Bishop's nature on its lighter side, and reveals him giving, as was his wont, a quaint and odd turn to the ordinary affairs of life. After describing a military service, he proceeds:—

What a comfort it is that I can extemporise with some fluency! I should be sorry so to use the power as to get careless or lazy about writing sermons, but the ability to do it seems absolutely necessary to my present office. This is one of the many good things that I learnt at Marlborough, where it was necessary sometimes to harangue the school at a moment's notice, especially in the early days, when some of them had murdered a dog. . . . . . I have been much pleased to see again my old Rugby friend ——, whom I tried to deter some twenty years ago from going out to India, telling him he was too good to run the risk of being devoured by a tiger, not foreseeing that I should one day share his perils.

It is not perhaps every pen that would describe the simple elements of camp life with such an odd mixture of magniloquence and grotesqueness as the following extract contains:—

The comfort and neatness of our camp makes its construction a work of 'high art.' A large double-poled tent stands in the centre as our living room; in front is the shemianah or canvass 'hall of audience' for the reception of native functionaries who wish to pay their respects, and all around are tents of various grades for ourselves and our suite. Here is a correct list of our *cortége*:—

1 prelate	4 masalchees
1 prelate's wife	10 bheesties
1 prelate's daughter	8 sweepers
1 chaplain	8 sowars
1 doctor	80 sepoys
1 captain of escort	31 dooly bearers
1 nurse	1 moonshee
31 servants	55 kelassies
10 elephants	65 camels
14 horses and ponies	16 bullocks

One cow and her calf, goats, sheep, ducks *ad libitum*, sundry pariah dogs, and one cat never seen, but said to consume all butter, sugar, &c. that disappears unaccountably.

Here is a passage testifying to that sense of grandeur in the Himalayan scenery which was always a source of the deepest enjoyment :—

Kangra, opposite Dharamsala.—The view from the German missionary's house on the hill is an exceedingly grand one. The spectator stands on a hill about 3,000 feet above the sea. Before him, and about 1,000 feet lower, stretches a wide plain, beautifully diversified with rocks, trees, luxuriant crops, and a mountain stream. From this plain rises a range of mountains, the highest peak being 16,000 feet above the sea, the tops of course wholly covered with snow, the lower parts with trees. It may be compared with Mont Blanc from the Flégère, the Iungfrau from the Wengern Alp, and the Orteler Spitz from the Stelvio. But it is in some respects superior to any of these. For, however magnificent Mont Blanc looks, the valley of Chamouni between it and the Flégère is ugly; from the Wengern Alp one cannot (so far as I remember) see the valley at all; and from Stelvio only one Orteler is to be seen, whereas here there is a whole range of Ortelers.

Here is an Easter Day record, very characteristic of one who was always ready to discern aids to religion in external objects or the circumstances of the moment :—

Subathoo, Easter Day 1860.—The congregation here consists mainly of men of the Rifle Brigade. In the evening after prayers, we all repaired to the burial-ground, which I consecrated, giving an address on the combined lessons of the consecration service and of Easter. The situation of the ground is very beautiful, and the sight of the lines of riflemen in their white uniforms, standing amidst the graves on the hill side, with the mountains towering above them, to listen on Easter-day to the hopes of immortality, was inspiriting and impressive.

It was, however, the constant presence of local traces of the then recent Mutiny that imparted to this first visitation tour a distinct interest and character at the time, and stamped it on the memory afterwards. From

Benares, the onward route of the travellers in 1859 lay for a long distance through tracts of country which had witnessed the greatest and most mournful events of the two preceding years. The strong hand of British rule had already, it is true, done much to repair the breaches in the land; but at that time, many roofless churches, ruined bungalows, and desolated missions still remained to tell the tale of war and havoc. Cawnpore had a death-stricken aspect, the Residency at Lucknow was a wilderness of ruins, and Delhi was feeling the weight of stern retribution. There was scarcely a household among the many that received our party with proverbial Anglo-Indian hospitality, which, if spared participation in the actual horrors of that terrible time, had not undergone the discipline of profound alarm and anxiety. Incidents that had marked a convulsion then scarcely subsided, filled the minds of English residents in India; and imminent perils, hair-breadth escapes, or long trials of patient waiting, were a constant and natural theme of conversation. Places too there were, and those not a few, where the silent dead, from their chance and hastily made graves, by the bare wayside, or under a tope of forest trees, or within some garden precinct, spoke yet more eloquently than the living, to the *great fight of afflictions* of those days. Any reminiscênces of that crisis in the history of the British Empire in India must possess an undying interest, and a few journal extracts now to be given will describe the outward aspect of some places which have become famous or have acquired fresh associations since 1857.

November 26.—Soon after 1 P.M we reached Cawnpore, and drove straight to the Lieutenant-Governor's camp, where tents were provided for us. At five we drove out, and were taken by Dr. Bird to the fatal well and Wheeler's intrenchments. He is well fitted to be our cicerone, having come into Cawnpore from Lucknow with Sir John Colin in November 1857.

All traces have vanished of the house in which the massacre took place; but in a wide expanse of sand, with a few palm trees and two European houses near, is the mouth of the well, completely bricked up, rising about a foot from the ground, and surrounded by a wooden fence. On one side is the well-known cross put up by the men of the 32nd under Moore's auspices; on the other, a plain horizontal gravestone with a cross carved upon it, and the two texts from Joel ii. 17:—*Spare thy people, O Lord, and give not thine heritage to reproach, that the heathen should rule over them: wherefore should they say, among the people, Where is their God?* 21. *Fear not, O land; be glad and rejoice; for the Lord will do great things.* This was put up by a non-commissioned officer of the Bengal Artillery to the women and children belonging to his corps. On the upright cross to the memory of those belonging to the 32nd, the motto is, *I believe in the resurrection of the body.* Surely these are among the most melancholy memorials in the world: there are some in Paris which speak of tales as tragical, but it is most solemn and striking to think that the historical scenes of these NW. Provinces are of events which occurred only two years ago, whereas most of the notable places which I have ever visited before are associated with doings or sufferings not greater or sadder than these, and of which the impression is blunted because they are removed from us by long years or even centuries. Hence, perhaps, I never was more moved by any place than by this Cawnpore well. The remains of Wheeler's intrenchments are about a mile and a half further on. Traces of the ditch which surrounded the garrison are still visible, but the rampart has altogether vanished. Within the ditch are the ruins of a barrack which was occupied till the mutineers set it on fire, and the well still remains in which the dead were buried secretly at night, by parties who stole out at the peril of their lives, to perform the last rites to their comrades. We left Wheeler's intrenchments wondering how any defence at all could have been made in an open plain, with no protection but a ditch and parapet, over which, as some one said, a buggy might have been driven, and which actually was overleapt on horseback by Lieutenant Bolton, who escaped from the massacres of Oude to meet his death by treachery at Cawnpore.

Sunday, November 27.—I have said nothing about the general appearance of Cawnpore. In desolation it surpasses any station which we have yet seen. It is of great length, five miles from the civil lines to cantonments, the camp where we are being pitched about half-way between them. A long straight road leads through the station, bordered by a treeless waste of sand, which in the rains is said to be green and pleasant, but now is absolutely devoid of a trace of grass. On each side are houses, some still in ruins, some restored, with compounds round them. There are also the remains of the theatre and assembly rooms burnt by the Gwalior Contingent; Christ Church also nearly destroyed by them, but now in the course of rapid restoration, and intended to be the church of the civilians. All this long range of European buildings is between the Ganges and the city, the minarets and pagodas of which are seen through the trees. Everything at present looks miserable and depressed, and even the residents seem specially to dislike the place, as if the curse of the Nana still blighted it. On the other hand, there is the memory of Henry Martyn to hallow it; while the thoroughly solid and substantial masonry of the Ganges Canal, which terminates here, and the handsome new railway station, hold out a prospect of future material prosperity. I preached twice in St. John's Chapel, a 'cutcha' building of a very inconvenient description near Wheeler's intrenchments, soon, I hope, to be superseded by the Memorial Church, which is actually to occupy their site, and to be the place of worship for the military.

November 28.—At 1 to-day we quitted Cawnpore, crossed the Ganges by a somewhat rickety bridge of boats just where the canal joins the river, and then found ourselves in Oude, on the road which, two years ago, was the scene of such hopes and fears, anxieties, disappointments, noble deeds, and unflinching resolution. I had heard so much of its ugliness that I was agreeably surprised at the number of fine trees which diversified it. It was quite dark when we reached Lucknow (about half-past 8 P.M.), where we found the Chief

Commissioner's house placed at our entire disposal. He is out on his winter's tour, but Colonel Barrow and Charles Currie, the latter once my pupil at Rugby, and now Secretary to the Oude Government, act as our hosts, and live in a bungalow hard by.

Tuesday, November 29.—The house in which we are, comfortable, two-storied, thatched. commanding a beautiful view, and surrounded by a large garden, was once the abode of an Oude Begum; then, after the annexation, it was handed over to Major Banks, and under the name of 'Banks House' it frequently occurs in accounts of the siege, having been occupied by the rebels, who placed here a powerful battery, taken from them after the final capture of the city.

This evening, Colonel Barrow, who commanded the cavalry when Havelock relieved the Residency garrison in September '57, and was shut up with the rest till Sir Colin arrived in November, took us a drive through the town to give us a general notion of the whole scene of these great events and the principal points connected with them. First, he made us mount to the top of the house, and look down on Lucknow. The view is strikingly beautiful: from a great mass of trees there rise in every direction domes and minarets, mosques and palaces, giving the impression of a really splendid Eastern city. This is a little dispelled when you descend into it, from the fact that the large buildings have in them so much plaster and chunam, and that the style is often bad, a mixture of the French chateau with the mosque of Mohammed Ali at Cairo. The whole splendour of Lucknow is modern: before Warren Hastings' time, Fyzabad was the capital of Oude. Still the mosques and palaces are very large and very numerous, and the whole effect is really fine. We see the city now in its transition state. Enormous spaces are wholly without buildings, long narrow native streets and bazaars have been cleared away, and broad roads are run straight through it. By the side of these, English-built bazaars, in good Oriental style, are rising, which will probably make the future Lucknow far superior to the past. Indeed, I am surprised that Heber says so little about the beauty of the place, so that perhaps in his time the squalid native houses choked up the great public buildings. We passed at night through the many courts of the huge Kaiser Bagh, a great palace as big as Versailles.

Just opposite the palace is a small monument surmounted by a cross, marking the spot where Sir Mountstuart Jackson and his fellow-prisoners in the Kaiser Bagh were murdered.

Next we passed the ruins of the Residency itself; the iron bridge over the Goomty, across which the troops retreated from the disasters at Chinhut, the Muchie Bhawn, the Imambara, all destined to be familiar names in future Indian history. There are now three forts: the principal one is of great size and strength, and will certainly prove a tougher morsel than the Residency, which is itself now protected by huge ramparts, rather different from the narrow ditch and puny parapet which defended it during the siege.

Wednesday, November 30.—This morning, S—— and I, accompanied and lionized by Colonel Barrow, had a deeply interesting walk round the Residency. He fully explained to us the scenes of the events. At present, the Bailey guard gate, a tower and fragments of the Residency itself, the shell of the banqueting hall (used as a hospital during the siege), part of Dr. Fayrer's house, and the foundations of Mr. Gubbins', are the chief remains, together with the whole of the Begum Koti, which alone, as a Mahometan building, the mutineers spared after we left the place. Of the church very little more than the foundations is left; the burial-ground is full of monuments (including one to Neill), and it is sad to see how ugly and tasteless most of them are. None is yet erected to Sir Henry Lawrence. The site of every battery was pointed out, and never was any historical scene more completely realised to me before.

Tuesday, December 6.—We left Lucknow at half-past 8, after a very pleasant and interesting visit. Our last sight was an impressive one, Havelock's grave at the Alumbagh, where we stopped on our way. A large slab, destined, I suppose to receive a monument, under a mango tree, marks the spot where he lies, and a piece of metal fastened to the tree bears his name. I trust that the tomb to be erected to the gravest and sternest and most puritan of Indian heroes will be simpler and in better taste than the hideous erections which deform the burial-ground of the Residency. We reached Cawnpore about 5, and went to stay with Sir John Inglis, now general of the district.

Wednesday, December 7.—This house is well placed on a high bank immediately over the Ganges, with plenty of sand in the middle of the river, and Oude opposite. Just here the station of Cawnpore is less ugly than elsewhere, for the ground is broken and wooded. Burn and I walked this morning to the fatal spot called Suttee Chonder Ghât, where the victims of the Nana's shameless falsehood embarked in the boats, and were massacred by the cowards who had been unable by fair fighting to conquer such a force in such a fortress as Wheeler's intrenchments. A bungalow with a pretty garden stands just above the ghât, and on the right of this garden is the road by which our countrymen came down to the boats from the higher ground above, congratulating each other, as I have been told, on deliverance from the intrenchments, and the approaching comforts of Allahabad.

Friday, December 9.—Sir John Inglis showed me three interesting relics of the siege; two letters addressed to him by Outram and Havelock, announcing the one immediate, the other speedy relief. Havelock tells him never to surrender, rather to perish sword in hand. Both are written on small scraps of paper; the important words in Greek characters; but as Havelock had forgotten how to make a Λ, he has written Lucknow, Lυκνω, so like its English appearance, that a sharp native would have read it. Both were brought to him in quills secreted about the persons of the bearers. The third relic was the order book, beginning with Sir Henry Lawrence's orders, and ending with the triumphant acknowledgment by Sir Colin of the glorious defence and 'unparalleled feat of arms' by which Havelock and Outram had accomplished the relief. It contains Sir Henry's last orders, announcing that 'it has pleased God that Sir Henry Lawrence should be severely wounded,' and appointing Major Banks, Major Anderson, and Colonel Inglis to the supreme authority in their respective departments. It contains, too, the *coup d'état* by which, on Banks' death, Inglis ordered that 'the office of

Chief Commissioner should remain vacant,' and so overthrew the civil power. The book is so valuable that the Government will not allow Sir John to keep it, but after he has had it copied, the original is to be preserved among the records of British India.

Tuesday, December 27.—This morning we reached Delhi. The Jumna was again crossed by a bridge of boats. We drove under the grand red walls of the palace, passed out of the city through the Cashmere Gate, so famous in the history of the siege, and entered the compound of the Commissioner, who had kindly promised to receive us. In the evening we went to see the palace. Like all the present city of Delhi, it was built by Shahjehan; indeed, Shahjehanabad was the official name for the town in all royal documents. Its exterior wall, with great bastions and the serrated Mahometan parapet, is, if anything, finer, and certainly higher than the wall of the fort at Agra. The entrance is through a lofty gateway, and through similar gateways we passed to the interior of the palace, which has been greatly injured from its recent conversion into a barrack by our troops, red arcades round the courts whitewashed on sanitary grounds, and some beautiful marble railings wholly removed. Moreover, the exterior arches of the famous Diwan-i-Khass, celebrated in 'Lalla Rookh' and elsewhere, are bricked up, a great deal of the inlaid work (which is the same as in the Taj) picked out, and the crystal throne packed up, and *en route* to England, so that we have pretty well completed the work which Nadir Shah began when he plucked away the silver roof. The inscription about the Paradise on earth still remains. The arches here are of marble, not quite so white as that of Agra, and the style differs in two respects from the buildings there; the columns are more solid and massive, and there is a great deal of gilding. The Diwan-i-Amm was filled with soldiers' beds, and whitewashed. We saw other very pretty parts of the palace, baths with floors beautifully inlaid (now officers quarters), and a small Moti Musjid of white marble, with the same differences from Agra as I noticed in the Diwan-i-Khass, only here the domes were covered with copper gilt, all of which has been pulled off by natives and prize agents. The great building furnishes altogether a remarkable commentary on fallen grandeur; and it is striking to look back upon it through the real splendours of Shahjehan and Aurungzib, the violated majesty of their successors, the desolation caused by Nadir Shah, and the follies of the later protected Moguls, down to the imbecility or wickedness (whichever it was) of Shah Bahadoor, the present exile of Rangoon, and the murderous crimes which brought to a richly merited end even the nominal rule of Tamerlane's house.

Wednesday, December 28.—We drove out this morning on the now famous heights, behind which our small besieging force was encamped. They begin from the Jumna, and then, stretching away from Delhi, gradually rise into the Arivalli hills in Méwar and Jodpur, and reach the height of 5,000 feet. There they are comparatively insignificant, though they are sufficient to give diversity to the wide plain, and to have been the means of the capture of Delhi. It was really strange, as we stood on them and looked over the boundless expanse of plain on the one side, and the walled and battlemented city on the other, to remember that both were in possession of the enemy, and yet that they could not prevent a handful of Englishmen from occupying these heights, and so taking the town. Surely, the fact is a proof that at present the Hindus are not fit to be an independent nation. The most interesting point is the Flagstaff tower where the fugitives spent the whole of the weary May 11, while they saw the townspeople flinging the bodies of their friends and relations into the ditch below, and whence they fled at night to Kurnaal. Several other places were shown us by Mr. Brandreth as having been the scenes of hard fighting, and at a place called the Sammi house the heights dip down to the plain, and round this point the mutineers used to creep through the rocks and shrubs with which the heights abound, and appear suddenly in our camp. As we looked over Delhi we could see the bridge of boats, across which fresh bodies of auxiliaries were frequently pouring into the city; the arrival of any new force being always a warning to the English to expect a fresh assault. To call this the siege of Delhi is almost a misnomer; we were as much besieged as besiegers: it was an obstinate occupation of the heights on one side of Delhi, ending by a successful assault through the breach by the Cashmere Gate. In the evening we saw the last scene of this great drama, for we visited the tomb of Humayun, Abkar's father, the asylum in which the king and princes took refuge when the city was stormed. The tomb itself is a large building of red stone in the style with which we are now familiar, and with a very fine and spacious terrace. Near it live two princes of the royal family, distant cousins of Shah Bahadoor, who came out from their retreat to see Mr. Brandreth. One of them was the very person who took to the king the message from Hodson that, if he would surrender, his life should be spared, and he showed us the exact spot in one of the recesses of the octagon where the old man was lying on a bed, and received the promise. This prince has a weak but not unpleasing face, and was dressed in a long black gown, and glittering turban: in his hand was a rosary of black beads, as he had just been worshipping at the tomb of Nizam-ud-din, a Mussulman saint, which we also visited, and where there is abundance of beautiful work in white marble, and also a mosque of the time of the Toghlak kings, older than any which we have yet seen, and very grand and impressive in its arches and other features. The domes are low and flat. The whole district on this side of Delhi is covered with the ruins of former capitals; with mosques, tombs, serais, houses, and a large fort bearing considerable traces of former grandeur. The comparison is obvious with the environs of Cairo.

Tuesday, January 3.—We went out this morning through the Chandni Chouk, said to be the finest native street in India: but not so in my opinion, for it has no merit but width, being devoid of picturesque architecture. Thence we went to the Jumma Musjid, a very grand mosque indeed, raised on a terrace approached by four noble flights of steps, which lead into a spacious courtyard. Three sides of this are surrounded by a most graceful open cloister, the fourth is occupied by the mosque, surmounted by three white marble cupolas. The whole building is of red sandstone, relieved by white marbles. From the roof is a fine view of Delhi, the palace being the most conspicuous and imposing object; but the whole city and its environs are eminently picturesque. No prayers are now offered in the mosque, but I think that in justice it should be restored to the Mahometans. It was theirs, built by the emperor of their faith, and endowed with their property. The only excuse for their making it a college or a Christian cathedral (to neither of which purposes it could be appropriated without utterly spoiling it) is that the Delhi Mussulmen deserve a merited punishment for their murderous rebellion. But have they not had enough in the following? (1) The shadow of the house of Timour blotted out; (2) All their personal property confiscated by prize agents; (3) Exclusion from the city for two years; (4) Necessity of building fresh houses outside the walls; (5) Diminution of their number by at least one-third; (6) Destruction of many of their houses, and serious injury to all. Justice is surely satisfied, and may now permit or rather require the restoration of the Musjid.

Shahjehanpore, Sunday, November 11, 1860.—This morning I consecrated St. Mary's Church, scene of the awful tragedy of May 31, 1857, when the mutineers rushed upon the congregation in the middle of service, murdered Mr. Ricketts, the magistrate, just as he was escaping through the vestry door, and six others in the immediate neighbourhood, including Mr. M'Callum, then minister of the station under the Additional Clergy Society. The seven bodies were afterwards buried in a tope of trees which surrounds the church, and I hope that soon a proper monument will be placed there. The rest of the fugitives were very coldly received by the Rajah of Powayn (who, I am sorry to say, got off with a reprimand from Lord Canning, in consequence of good service done by some of his family), and sent on by him to Mohumdee, where they were joined by my old pupil Thomason, then Deputy Commissioner of Mohumdee, and on June 5 all marched towards Aurungabad.

Thursday, November 15.—A very short march this morning, and we forded the Goomtee exactly as the sun was rising. For some way on each side of the river trees cease, and we passed over waste grass land. Almost the first tree (a neem) on the left bank of the river in a wide plain of grass and corn fields, one mile from Aurungabad, marks the scene of the massacre of the Shahjehanpore fugitives. We visited it in the evening, accompanied by the tehsildar of Mohumdee, who is escorting us through his district, and a zemindar of the place named Ashik Ali, descendant of an old princely family, the Nawabs of Aurungabad. He actually saw the massacre, and, after the mutineers had dispersed, buried the bodies. There were twenty-two men, five women, and four children killed. The number of Sepoys was about two thousand. One party had followed them from Mohumdee, and they were met by the Seetapore mutineers at the Goomtee. There the Sepoys held a consultation, told the Europeans that they might go on where they liked, but almost immediately followed them, and forced them to halt at the tree under which they had retreated for shelter from the rays of a midday sun. The Sepoys surrounded them, except on one side, keeping at the distance of about 100 yards, and then began shooting them down; the tree still bearing traces of the musket-balls. The last who were killed were two children, who during the whole time showed no signs of terror, or attempted either to run away or to beg for mercy. Ashik Ali knew Thomason well as the Assistant Commissioner, and showed me exactly where he fell. How little I thought when I looked over his copies, and scolded him for his false concords at Rugby, that I should ever stand on a spot so mournfully connected with him! Happily his character and tendencies were such, that I believe him to have been ready to face without shrinking even so sudden and terrible a death. The bodies were buried in two graves; the men in an old dry well, the women and children in a pit close by. The tree is to be enclosed and connected by a wall with the two graves, which are also to be walled in and marked by a monument, now on its way from England.

Seetapore, Saturday, November 17.—The Seetapore mutiny was on June 3. The 41st Native Infantry and two irregular regiments mutinied and murdered their officers, and the military police posted round Mr. Christian's house immediately followed their example, and fired on the inmates. Mr. Christian and several others were killed on the spot, and some as they were crossing the Sureyam, which flows by the compound, while Sir

Mountstuart Jackson, one of his sisters, and some others, found refuge with Rajah Lonee Singh of Mithowlee, who afterwards gave them up to the Lucknow soldiery and now labours as a transported convict in the Andamans. It was a party sent by Mr. Christian from Seetapore to escort the Shahjehanpore fugitives which joined the Sepoys at Mohumdee on June 4, and with them murdered the victims under the neem-tree of Aurungabad.

Sunday, November 18.—This morning I consecrated the new and still unfinished church by the name of All Souls, intending thereby to remind those who worship in it of the sufferings and deaths of their Christian brethren, former inhabitants of Seetapore.

Friday, November 23.—A long march this morning into Lucknow. We are longing to see again the place which we had so much enjoyed last year, and S—— and I had intended to enter it triumphantly on our elephant; but at Marioun the two chaplains met us with the Commissioner's carriage, to which we transferred ourselves, and drove through the ruins of the old cantonments. Then appeared, separated from us by the Goomtee, various distant minarets, the crumbling tower of the Residency, the great earthworks round the Muchie Bhawm, the Chatr Munzil, the old iron bridge, the tombs of Ghazi-ud-din with their fine domes; and then we crossed the bridge of boats opposite the Kaiser Bagh, and found a completely new order of things established, a garden being laid out in front of the palace, round the cross marking the scene of Sir Mountstuart Jackson's murder, which cross, now standing in a great open space, is certainly small and insignificant. Then came the new bazaar—building last year, finished now—with gay purdahs of different colours, such as I have seen in market-places in Italy; then the new church, and a large public garden called after Wingfield, enclosed by a light pretty balustrade, and entered by a rather flimsy gateway topped with plaster females and urns; after which we entered the Martinière compound, and found our camp pitched.

Saturday, November 24.—I consecrated the civil service church by the name of Christ Church. By a remarkable coincidence, to-day is the anniversary of Havelock's death. Surely a great mercy, and therefore a great responsibility, that in exactly three years from that time our power should be wholly re-established, Lucknow restored and beautified, and the Christian congregation assembled in perfect peace to worship God in their new church. It is to be filled with memorials of the victims of the Mutiny: the four Gothic tablets in the aisle are reserved for Lawrence, Havelock, Neill, and a general memorial of those who fell in the Residency. The interior of the church is really good: it is cruciform, has side aisles, and a roof of successful woodwork. Externally, the building is too much squeezed together, and too high for its length.

To Rev. G. G. Bradley, Master of Marlborough College.

Simla, April 1860.

Hurrah! we are here at last—a great boon after our long wanderings. The rest and homelike feeling are most delightful, though it is hard to feel altogether at home when we are told that we are living 'on the *Thibet* road.' However, here we are in a comfortable house, with a glorious mountain view before us, with no need to start to-morrow, either in jonpon, dooly, dâk ghari, or camel carriage. The visitation, though undoubtedly attended by a good deal of fatigue and physical discomfort, has been of the highest interest, and not, I hope, without its use. Moreover, we are all in sound health, indeed I am much better than before it, though I have serious doubts whether an *old* bishop could accomplish it. With the missionaries I have been agreeably surprised. Spite of some heresies in the charge, they received me everywhere with real cordiality, listened attentively to my entreaties that they would not neglect their schools for the more exciting work of preaching in bazaars, and many of them are not only devoted Christians, but sensible and practical in their work to a degree which I had not expected. One whom I ordained priest (a high wrangler at Cambridge) is a really superior man, and passed as good an examination as I have ever seen either as chaplain or as bishop, while Burn, who saw a good deal of him in private, was still more struck with him. His school is the best of the missionary schools and the only one which could compare in secular knowledge with the Government colleges. I regretted, however, that some of the missionaries study the Revelation more than the Koran and Shasters, or rather, perhaps I should say (since the Revelation itself is a most profitable study) Elliott's 'Horæ Apocalypticæ,' Cumming's 'Great Tribulation,' and similar works. 'What does your lordship think about the theory that the Affghans are the ten tribes? What has your lordship heard about the flocking of the Jews to Palestine?' In the former case I could tell them that a rigid Presbyterian missionary at Peshawur had assured me that they were *not*; but I longed to exhort them to dismiss all speculations as to the Millennium, and devote themselves to a thorough investigation of the Vedanta philosophy, or of the doctrines either of Mahomet or of Nanuk. But these millennial speculations, *and on the part of some only* an inordinate belief in the efficacy of galloping from village to village, and 'making the proclamation' to the unprepared and ignorant heathen, were the only exceptions to much really edifying intercourse, and the sight of a great deal of self-denying and practical piety, from which I am sure that I have great need to take a lesson. I was also much interested and pleased in many places with the soldiers. Schools are flourishing in nearly all the military stations, in which you see grizzled heroes of Delhi and Lucknow working out vulgar fractions or copying dictation, 'On Linden, when the sun was low,' &c. In most regiments there is a nucleus of really religious men. They build, often for themselves, with the help of officers, and the grant of a site from Government, neat little chapels in which they can retire from the crowded barracks for private prayer, and where the chaplain can assemble a Bible-class or hold a short week-day service. I went to three of these, and preached or expounded to most attentive bodies of listeners. Though I do not agree with all Hedley Vicars's views of religion, yet it is a remarkable instance of real goodness that his regiment, the 97th, which was at Banda when I was there, is one of the best and steadiest of the service, and that a large number of them attended the Communion when I administered it after consecrating the church, and also meet for daily prayers with a very modest and sensible

Scripture reader, with whom I had a long interview. It really seems as if it may be said of Vicars that 'he being dead yet speaketh.' Much has been laid against the English rule in India, and undoubtedly there is a great deal that ought to have been otherwise; but is it not remarkable that within two years of the height of the Mutiny we travelled from Calcutta to Peshawur, through days and nights, along by-roads, and I may sometimes say *no* roads, without an alarm of any kind, and that everywhere there is perfect order and security? This at least is something to set against our shortcomings, and is a strong contrast to the Mahometan rule. Everywhere, too, I see symptoms that we are mending our ways, and the prosperity of the country is rapidly increasing. The submontane part of the Punjâb is like a continuous garden, 'the valleys standing so thick with corn that they seem to laugh and sing.'

. . . .

It is most true that the present age has need of anxiety in its belief, but perhaps the extremity of the danger is the real security. Tennyson said to you what I have often thought, and what I told poor Willy Arnold in almost our last interview, that the question was not so much of Christianity as of man's immortality. There seems to me no resting-place between Christianity and Positivism; and as to the latter, I can only say, first, that Comte's *religious* system seems to me rather a subject for laughter than serious discussion, and, next, that he bears unconscious testimony to the truths which he denies when he finds it necessary to provide such an extraordinary support for our religious feelings as his catechism. He testifies to the reality of these religious feelings and longings, which to my mind point indubitably to a God, and, given a God and immortality, then I think that a Revelation is almost a necessary consequence. I am sure (pardon a little confession, not desirable generally) that whenever doubts and difficulties come into my mind, they always take an immoral, or at least *un*moral, tone. It is not 'Did Christ really rise from the dead?' but 'Why should I think that duty and immortality are realities? What is the use of troubling myself about all this? Why should not I take my ease, and live an idle dignified life of indulgence and literary leisure? Let us eat and drink, for to-morrow we die.' Hence, to me at least, scepticism and temptation to selfish wickedness are identical.

To H. R. Tomkinson, Esq.

July 1860.

Have you read Mansel's 'Bamptons'? I cannot condemn the book, spite of Maurice's attack upon it. Indeed, I think that there may be much help in it from theological difficulties which now perplex people, though I question some things, especially the remarks on morality. But he shows well the inextricable confusions into which we are plunged when we attempt to reduce the infinite to the laws and conditions of the finite, and to argue that God cannot do this, or that something else is contrary to His nature. I have not yet so studied the book as to form a decided opinion, but certainly after reading it, I issued an order the other day to the clergy to use the prayer for rain with a much clearer conscience and livelier faith than I should have done had I been fresh from a course of Buckle or Mill.

Meantime rain has come. There was serious alarm last week at the delay of the periodical rains: grain rose enormously in price, and old Indians looked back with a groan to the horrors of the great famine in 1837, and seriously anticipated their renewal. It is believed that the weather has changed in time: prices are falling, and there are again hopes of a sufficient harvest. All the North-west Provinces were suffering under a similar drought. The rains, though most needful, are very disagreeable, even here: clouds float through the windows into our very drawing-room, we have fires blazing everywhere, and Burn feels it very much and has a great deal of fever about him. I, who suffered from the protracted hot weather, am much better just now, and am going to preach again to-morrow, after an unusually long silence. . . .

To the Rev. Krishna Mohun Banerjea, Professor in Bishop's College.

August 1860.

I have had such hard work lately from Mr. Burn's illness that I have only just been able to read through the proof-sheets which you kindly sent me of your projected dialogues. But I can now tell you that I have read them, and with great pleasure and interest. As a proof of it, I may say that I lay down on the sofa with them and did not stir till I had finished the fifty-sixth page.

It is exactly the book which I desire to see emanate from Bishop's College, and above all from a clergyman of Bengali race. I do not quite see for what class they are especially designed, though I think that there are three classes for whom they will be especially useful. First, for your own unconverted countrymen of the higher orders, only that for them they should, I suppose, be published in Bengali. I hope that you are going to do this. Next, for European missionaries, that they may know better the state of feeling and opinion which they have to encounter; and, thirdly, for the educated English both here and in England, as giving them a good picture of the wants and difficulties of mission work in India. Only for the third and possibly for the second class a little more explanation is required. I should recommend you to prefix to the dialogues a short introduction as free from arguments or disputed points as possible, and merely giving a popular sketch of the history of Hindu religion and philosophy. Doubtless this is intended to be given at length, but gradually, and is even begun in the second dialogue; but I think that an ἰδιώτης might be deterred from reading your book by encountering at once such phrases as 'kali,' 'satya yugà,' and 'mahápralaya,' and five or six pages are all that would be needed to enable him to enter into it with pleasure. I do not see why the edition should be tentative: as far as I have read I cannot perceive any objection to immediate publication.

What has become of the translations of the Psalms by you and Dr. Kay? I heard some English missionaries object to your part of it as being ill adapted to the language and comprehension of the Bengal peasantry. Probably you can judge of this better than your critics, and it may be difficult to translate into a vernacular familiar to them, without lowering the dignity and poetical grandeur of the Psalms. Certainly, much of our English Bible and Prayer Book must be unintelligible to the English peasantry, and it is perhaps impossible to bring theological language down to them; for, indeed, we ought rather to raise them by moral and mental culture to the capacity of appreciating it. But it may be well to tell you that the objection has been made, if you have not heard it before, *valeat quantum.*

The following extract is from a letter to the Rev. Henry Venn, containing a review of the Church Missionary Society's missions in the North-west Provinces and Punjâb:—

September 1860.

. . . From Kotgur we have just returned. Kotgur is the most unsatisfactory mission, perhaps the only unsatisfactory one of our Society, that I have seen. The place no doubt is very small and the people very ignorant, but the school is bad; still worse is the branch school at Muttiana, two marches from Kotgur, where I found fourteen boys reading St. Luke's Gospel with a heathen teacher, who seemed very inefficient and complained of their constantly running away. Neither was the secular knowledge worth much either at Muttiana or Kotgur.

. . . .

This is the chief part of what I have to say about existing missions; but there is one other district of the Punjab to the wants and claims of which I desire to call your attention. Ferozepore is the centre of a large Sikh population, is itself an important place, and is wholly unoccupied by missionaries. As Simla would be an additional starting-point to Kangra for operations among the hillmen, so might Ferozepore be an additional starting-point to Umritsur for operations among the Sikhs; each would strengthen the other in both cases. Then, besides Mooltan, of which I cannot speak from experience, we should have the missionaries at Peshawur, with a branch mission at Attock, devoting themselves to the Affghan Mussulmans, Urdu and Pushtoo languages, the study of the Koran and Mahometan superstitions; the missionaries at Umritsur and Ferozepore devoted to the Sikhs, the Urdu, Hindi, and Punjab dialects, and the Grunth and religion of Nanuk and Govind; and the missionaries at Simla and Kangra to the Hindi with its mountain peculiarities, and the simpler work intellectually, but no less difficult spiritually, of preaching to the hill people, and training their children. In this way the Church of England would be more worthily represented in the Punjab than it is now at present. I feel a little (I trust harmless and Christian) jealousy of the American Presbyterians who are working at Rawal Pindee, Sealkote, Lahore, Loodiana, Umballa, Kupperthala, Murree, Subathoo, and are talking of other plans also. In this way, too, I think that our labour and strength would be divided and concentrated on definite objects.

To Mrs. Arnold.

Kotgur, near Simla, September 1860.

. . . The place from which I am now writing is about fifty miles from Simla, on the Thibet Road, and therefore quite in the interior of the mountain land. We came here partly because it is a mission station which wants a good deal of organising and stirring up, partly to get a little more knowledge of the Himalayas, and health from their breezes before we go down again into the plains. I have often tried to compare this Himalayan scenery with that of other mountain countries; but the result has been an increased conviction of the proverbial odiousness of comparisons, and a determination to enjoy what is before me without hankering after the unattainable. Doubtless one may miss here the lakes of Italy, the glacier scenery of the Bernese Oberland, and the peculiar repose, freshness, and mountain streams of Westmoreland. But nowhere have I seen such foliage and vegetation; the forests are of a grandeur and solemnity which remind me of the effect of a great cathedral, and from any height the enormous scale of the green landscape, the vast ranges of hill-sides clothed in verdure and rich cultivation, the lines of mountain rising one behind another and terminating with the distant snow, give you the impression of a 'mountain *country*' far more than any other scenery, and realise the fact that you are in the loftiest mountain range in the world. On Saturday morning we went up Hawathoo, 11,000 feet high, in this country of course a mere dwarf, but famous for its beautiful view. In the Alps at this height we should have been in the midst of ice and bare rock: here we sat down to a breakfast of coffee and mutton chops! on a greensward covered with potentillas and other flowers unknown to us, but some like anemones and others like China asters, with oaks and pines all around us and the ruins of an old Ghoorka fort to lean our backs against. The lichens and ferns are of great beauty, and the trunks of trees are clothed with the Virginia creeper, which now has turned red, just as we have seen it against an old English manor house or a college in Oxford or Cambridge.

We are all, thank God, quite well. We were somewhat knocked up with the long winter travel, which was prolonged a little too far into the hot weather, as we did not reach Simla and rest till April 11. So each of us has had a touch of illness, but in every case this has passed away, and we are all as well and strong just now as we were in England. As I get older, and since my duties have become more and more solemn, I have learned to value increasingly one of the many lessons which I learned from your husband, to be grateful not for health only, but for occasional illness also, as a warning that the night cometh when no man can work. My chaplain had a real fever, and was the only one who kept his bed, but that we are both really well you may gather from the fact that we *walked* up Hawathoo, 1,800 feet above the level of our halt the previous night, before breakfast without fatigue.

CHAPTER VI.

QUESTION OF OPENING EPISCOPAL CHURCHES FOR PRESBYTERIAN WORSHIP STATE OF RELIGIOUS FEELING IN THE PUNJAB—APPLICATIONS FOR THE USE OF CHURCHES CONSECRATED TO THE WORSHIP OF THE CHURCH OF ENGLAND — CORRESPONDENCE ON THE SUBJECT WITH GOVERNMENT CHAPLAINS — RELATIONS WITH THE CHAPLAINS — EFFORTS TO IMPROVE THE ECCLESIASTICAL SERVICE—LETTERS TO CHAPLAINS.

In 1860 the formidable ecclesiastical question arose of lending Government churches for Presbyterian worship. Owing to the Mutiny the number of Highland regiments in the country had been increased, and in many stations there was no place of worship for Presbyterians. The subject came first before the Bishop in 1859 through an application from a Punjâb chaplain for authority to permit Scotch service to be held in his church. The Bishop took legal advice and gave his sanction. Subsequently a second case occured at Mhow, and the similar necessity raised the same questions in Madras. The authorities in that Presidency addressed themselves directly to the Home Government; and the Secretary of State, by the advice of Dr. Lushington and with the concurrence of the Archbishop of Canterbury, sent out instructions that under suitable regulations the churches should be available for the worship of the Scotch regiments. It was the receipt of these instructions, and the submission of them to the Bishop for his sanction of their application within the Diocese of Calcutta, that first brought him and the Government of India into correspondence. In the face of high legal authority, it would have been a difficult and ungracious act for the Bishop to withhold his consent. When the law was tolerant and elastic, he did not care to make the Church narrow and illiberal; neither could any common sense view gainsay the emergency of the case. One apparent means for meeting it, viz., that of building more Scotch places of worship, was of course not lost sight of. The Bishop once brought forward the suggestion at an early stage of the official correspondence, but he never renewed it. It was certain that the Government would not consent to multiply churches for a few Highland regiments, whose detention at any given station, or in India at all, might be of short duration. Persistence in the recommendation of impracticable measures would have endangered influence with the authorities—an imprudence which the Bishop was not likely to commit. If therefore the use of existing buildings should be refused, no refuge from the open air parade service during the extreme heats or excessive rains of India would be available for large bodies of troops, while other means of grace and opportunities for religious exercises among the men would be lamentably crippled and impeded. On the other hand, the Church of England had to be protected; the feelings, even the prejudices, of ministers of the Church of England had to be considered. The Bishop was well aware that, however much reason and law might favour the concession, it would be a novelty in the English Church, and as such be deemed by many Churchmen an innovation on her special rights. He knew that some of his clergy would share this feeling, and that many others with whom ecclesiastical objections might have less weight would yet look upon any interference with the exclusive possession of their churches as a grave inconvenience and hindrance in their pastoral work. He discerned from the outset many practical obstructions to the smooth working of the arrangement, arising partly from local circumstances, and partly from the limitations imposed by a relentless tropical sun upon all public worship to which troops have to march. While accepting therefore the necessities of the case, and yielding his consent to the proposed loan of the sacred buildings with the liberality of spirit with which he viewed the question, he from the first directed his efforts towards restricting the concession within the narrow limits of the military exigencies, and securing such stringency in the regulations to be laid down as should dispel any notion that the churches were to become common property between the two communions.

At one moment in the long negotiations that went on, there was a marked inclination on the part of Government to claim for the Scotch parade service, under certain circumstances, a prior right to the use of the church. The Bishop at once took alarm and sent in a strong remonstrance. The following extracts from it are subjoined because they exhibit the main point that was at issue and show how steadily he declaimed against any settlement of it which should involve a suspension of the Church of England services:—

To the Viceroy in Council.

Simla, June 25, 1860.

I certainly should strongly deprecate any arrangement by which the morning or evening service of the Church of England should be given up, in order to leave time for Presbyterian worship. I think that such an arrangement would be unjust, offensive to many members of the English Church, and (as far as I know) it has never been requested or supposed possible by any of the Presbyterians themselves, who have only asked for the use of our churches when not required for the performance of English service.

I think that it would be unjust for two reasons: (1) The churches have been consecrated, and whatsoever be the legal effect of consecration, undoubtedly, in the memorial presented to the bishop (to which the local government signifies its assent), the request made is, that he will 'consecrate the said church for celebration of Divine service therein according to the rites and ceremonies of the United Church of England and Ireland,' and in the decree of consecration the bishop repeats this phrase. Hence I infer that the primary use of the building must be for the Church of England, that this must not give place to any other, and that no other can be celebrated in it without the consent of the bishop. (2) It must be remembered that, though these churches have been built in a great measure at the expense of the Government, whose liberality in this matter I thankfully acknowledge, yet they have been largely aided by private subscriptions from members of the Church of England. At least fifty-two churches in the diocese, in which the English service is performed, have been aided by grants from the Calcutta Church Building Fund (besides missionary churches, which of course I do not take into account), and many churches have been mainly built by the personal exertions and unfailing liberality of my predecessor. I am sure that this would not have been done had it been supposed that Scotch service would ever be substituted for our own.

. . . .

In some cases such an order would deprive half a regiment of the service of the English Church altogether. *Ex. gr.* at Ferozepore and Rawal Pindee the churches are so small that one wing has to be marched to church in the morning and the other in the evening. If one of these times is to be given up to the Church of Scotland (which might happen, if two regiments, one of Highlanders, were stationed at a place where the church is small), half the Episcopalians will not have their own worship at all.

I do not quite agree with your Excellency's remark, that unless either sunrise or sunset were always conceded, a favour would be granted on paper which was of no practical benefit to the recipients, and which would therefore only serve to provoke disappointment—I think that while we steadily maintain the principle, that the service according to the rites of the English Church must be performed twice every Sunday, the amount of concession to the Scotch Church is still considerable.

I would remark that it shows a considerable progress in catholicity of feeling that the Archbishop of Canterbury, the Bishop of Calcutta, and the chief legal functionary of the Church of England should all agree that Presbyterian service may be performed, without sacrifice of principle, in buildings consecrated by Episcopalian forms. Certainly some years ago, in Bishop Middleton's time for example, this would not have been the case.

. . . .

In some stations where there are two churches at no great distance, such as Peshawur, Sealkote, Lucknow, I have little doubt that the wishes of the Government can be carried out, and that the use of a church may be granted, for the morning or evening, without interruption to the Presbyterian minister.

Or again, where there is a very small Episcopalian community, who would naturally go to church in carriages, and a Scotch regiment, which would be marched to church, I should think that the English evening service might be at some hour in the afternoon before the sun goes down; and the parade service for the Presbyterian troops at sunset.

I therefore earnestly hope that your Excellency, maintaining the principle that these buildings are designed for the service of the Church of England, and placed under the care of the English chaplain, acting under the authority of the bishop, will simply direct that they shall be used where it is possible for the service of the Church of Scotland, particular cases being referred to the bishop (whose consent in every case is necessary, according to Dr. Lushington's opinion), who may fix the time for the English service; and therefore decide whether the particular hour of sunrise or sunset is available for the Scotch. The fact that I agreed to permit Presbyterian service in an English church, before Dr. Lushington's opinion or the wishes of Her Majesty's Government were known, will at least show that I should be desirous to exercise this power in a liberal and conciliatory spirit.

The above letter practically closed the correspondence, for the Government accepted its arguments and framed the official notice of the arrangement in conformity with them.

It will readily be believed that this boon was welcomed by Presbyterians as in the highest degree gracious and conciliatory. Indeed the sudden and keen appreciation of Anglican places of worship expressed by the Scotch Church introduced an element almost of amusement into a matter in itself harassing and beset with difficulty. But the views of some Churchmen were different, and hostile criticism, chiefly from England, was passed upon the Bishop. This act of legislation was one of the earliest ecclesiastical measures of wide and general interest with which his tenure of the see brought him into contact, and it was through the medium afforded by his line of action on this occasion that much of his future administration was scanned. Threats of withholding help from church-building and other diocesan funds, and even from general missionary objects, were expressions of the feeling which interpreted the transaction as an innovation upon Church of England rights openly countenanced by the Bishop. The case was judged from an English point of view. The anomalies which intrude into all ecclesiastical arrangements beyond England were overlooked, and no credit was allowed to the Bishop for his scrupulous care that an act of friendly assistance to a sister Church should involve no slight or hurt to the Anglican Liturgy. Local circumstances and necessities were dimly apprehended by, or appeared insignificant to those afar off, though they had to be duly estimated by him on whom rested the responsibility of a decision which was certain to excite bitterness of feeling on one side or the other. There was no precedent, in India at least, to guide this decision; there was no obligation that could aid the Bishop's judgment, except the moral one of choosing the liberal path which the law had left open. His powers were purely permissive and discretionary, and the doubt and perplexity frequently involved in the exercise of such powers cannot be denied. Probably some who so reproachfully deprecated the loan of Anglican places of worship would have paused before committing themselves to a refusal which in India would simply have brought obloquy on the Church of England. On the other hand, many who marvelled that the Bishop should have felt a moment's hesitation would, in face of the circumstances with which he had to deal, have shared his anxiety to guard an unusual privilege with a cordon of restrictions. For it has now to be told how quickly this first concession begot a desire for more, and how soon the Bishop was called upon to deal with requests for the opening of the church doors to other bodies of Christians. Applications for thus extending the loan of the churches beyond what either the Bishop or the Government intended, were connected with a religious movement of some strength at that time in the Punjâb. From the earliest days of its administration as a British province, many of the leading officials had been deeply religious men. Under the friendly shelter of their rule American Presbyterian missionaries advanced from Loodianah and established themselves firmly and influentially in many places. On the other hand, Church of England mission work was only slenderly represented, chaplains were few in number, the presence of a bishop was almost unknown; hence the earnest Christian life that animated Englishmen in the Punjâb was but slightly leavened with loyalty to the Church. Persons of different communions were bound together by religious feelings running deep and strong, and by the single desire to be preachers of righteousness to the civil and military communities around. Indian houses are not large; few could supply rooms fit for large religious gatherings, and thus to lay and clerical leaders in spiritual things, ready to sink outward differences in united and informal worship, the order to lend the churches for Scotch service sounded as a boon available for themselves also. To such applications there was but one answer to give. When the Bishop supported the State in meeting the temporary and accidental exigencies of large congregations of another State Church, he desired to magnify the Church over which he presided by an act of catholic and large-hearted sympathy but he disclaimed both the wish and the power to lower her distinctive teaching and position by opening the doors of the consecrated buildings to a promiscuous worship in which the services of the Prayer Book would find no place. He felt compelled to refuse the use of the churches, but at the same time he felt and expressed sympathy with the movement which had called forth the request. Though he often regretted that the spirit that was abroad was more sectarian than catholic, he could thank God for any agency which boldly and powerfully confronted vice and godlessness everywhere, and especially among soldiers. He once said of an officer in India whom he greatly respected, 'I think Colonel —— most edifying on the campaign of Affghanistan, but singularly the reverse on Baptismal Regeneration.' It was thus with his usual weapon of quiet humour that he entered a protest against a narrowness of doctrine from which he utterly dissented. The existence of the movement stimulated his efforts to make the Church more influential through her appointed ministers, but he sought rather to guide than to repress it, and never came forward prominently except where, as in the matter of the churches, he was asked to authorise what was against all Church order. The subject occasioned much correspondence with several chaplains, and some letters are annexed as giving an insight into a movement which within a limited circle had many of the features of a strong religious revival:—

To a Chaplain.

1860.

I should be very sorry if I were to appear to undervalue the good understanding which exists between you and Mr.——, or to place any discouragement in the way of your cordial co-operation in all good works in your station. But I do not think that the proposal of a united service, in which you shall both take part, is consistent with my circular or with the principles and practice of the English Church, and it would open embarrassing questions which are much better left quiet. What I have tried to lay down in my circular to the clergy is this, that to lend our buildings, when necessity requires, to the chaplain of the Church of Scotland is a friendly act to a sister Church, but that it is not to be mixed up with any questions as to the ministrations in our own congregations, which are to remain as at present. The fact therefore that my letter makes it lawful for Mr.——to assemble the Presbyterian troops in your church and preach to them does not empower him to take part in the services of the English Church. It is true that in your absence he kindly consented to read our liturgy to the Episcopalian troops, but this again is quite a different case. According to the custom in India, when the English chaplain is unavoidably absent, the service (with certain exceptions) is read by a layman, and if it may be read by a layman, then *à fortiori* by a Presbyterian clergyman. But the proposal that you should unite with a Presbyterian clergyman in a common service involves the whole question of the intercommunion of the Scotch and English Churches, which I, as an individual bishop, am not competent to decide by my sole authority. It cannot be justified by any plea of necessity, it would to some extent stultify my prohibition of prayer-meetings in churches, as contained in the later paragraphs of my circular, it would excite many remonstrances and much disapprobation at home and indeed in India; and therefore, with every good wish to the Scotch Church, and the fullest appreciation of Mr.——'s kind and liberal feeling in his dealings with you, I must beg that, when you are at——, our services may be conducted solely by yourself or by some other clergyman of the Church of England.

To a Chaplain.

1860.

. . . Considering the amount of godlessness and careless living which prevails, especially in the army, I could not speak of a revival as you do, as I often think that something extraordinary is required to awaken nominal Christians from the sleep of death. That a revival generally involves many questionable features, and would require careful watching, I quite allow; but if it produces permanent moral improvement its origin is known by its fruits. . . . The best counsel I can give you is to do all that you can to unite your flock closely to yourself by unwearied activity, and by seeking so to build them up in Christian holiness that they shall not need nor desire the more exciting ministrations which you deprecate.

To a Chaplain.

1860.

I altogether approve of the clerical meetings. Interchange of thought, experience, and knowledge is one of the great wants of the Indian clergy arising from geographical causes, and I am sure that wherever it can be obtained it should be sought. Of course the only point which requires watching is the union with ministers of another Church. And I certainly do not envy you the Calvinism which your next subject suggests, for the older I grow and the more I read, the more I dislike that system, not only from the untenable theory, but from its practical evils. Most wisely said Butler, 'though it were admitted that this opinion of necessity were speculatively true, yet with regard to practice it is as it were false.' I have, however, no fear of your yielding the distinctive character of the English Church in your intercourse with your brethren of another, though I own that one or two of the clergy seem to me to think that the way to stop the spread of dissent is to give up every point in which we differ from dissent. But you will not forget that the motto should be comprehension without compromise, and that conciliation and brotherly love are possible without the abandonment of principle. The calm and, candid discussion of the meaning and application of Scripture between persons who agree in its divine authority is a clear gain.

To a Chaplain.

1861.

I very much regret the embarrassing position in which you are placed by the conduct of the soldiers about whom you write to me; I had heard of them before as well-intentioned and pious men, but unhappily self-righteous and self-confident.

No doubt that they should include a self-appointed administration of the Holy Communion in their prayer-meetings, and decline to partake of that ordinance according to the order of the Church, is grievously inconsistent with Scriptural principle and precedent, and an unchristian act of schism in the strictest sense. But on full consideration I cannot recommend you to interfere with them by any means except private influence. It would be unwise now to deprive them of the use of the room, as they would be made more self-righteous than they are by fancying themselves martyrs, and would probably find other places for their irregular services. By trying to attach them to yourself through kindness, by showing them the excellence and necessity of the Christian ministry, by your own zealous fulfilment of its obligations, and by taking any opportunity which may occur of quietly pointing out to any of them in private the dangerous, unpractical, and unscriptural character of this system, you may hope gradually to win them over, but certainly you will not do so by any other means.

The above letters deal with a specific matter, but they touch indirectly upon the Bishop's general relations with the chaplains, and it will not therefore be out of place to add a few words on this subject. He found on arriving in India, an active and zealous body of clergy. Many were accepting with cheerfulness labours by no means light, and some were exposed to much personal inconvenience and discomfort through imperfect or uncertain military arrangements. The Bishop used to say that during the Mutiny every class had its heroes, that of the clergy being no exception. Some of their number had fallen victims to the enemy or to sickness; many others, while serving with troops in the open field, or in the beleaguered garrison, or ministering to feeble women and children shut up in some chance place of refuge, had been tried in the balances of peril and privations, and had not been found wanting. Jennings, Polehampton, Harris, are now added to honoured names in the Indian ecclesiastical service. They have entered into their rest, while many still remain who toiled and suffered during that same trial-time, but were spared to resume their wonted labours in a time of peace, among civilians and Eurasians, or with compact masses of English soldiers. The Bishop's personal interest in this particular spiritual charge has already been alluded to, and he rejoiced with thankful joy over many bright examples of chaplains wisely guiding the strong, but often peculiar, religious instincts characteristic of the serious-minded soldier, or using with energy and perseverance such opportunities of laying hold of the careless and godless as might be afforded by voluntary church services, and careful preparation for confirmation; or by the ministrations in hospitals, which at times become of overwhelming magnitude and importance.

To a worthy discharge of pastoral duties such as these, the Bishop knew well that freedom and independence were more effective incentives than the keen supervision of military authorities, powerfully as this may operate as a security against laxity or indifference in the discharge of ministerial functions among troops. Hence, much of his work in behalf of the clergy was directed towards strengthening the hands, and vindicating the pastoral position of those who were appointed to military stations. Through official representations made from time to time, he obtained for them a more recognised footing in regimental schools, more control over such church services as were voluntary and independent of the regular parade service, and the removal of some obstacles which stood between soldiers and a free attendance at the Holy Communion.

The clergy in general were much isolated, especially those whose field of labours lay among civilians. It was a necessary but not wholly beneficial condition of things. If the vast distances between station and station made theological controversy difficult, the same cause was a hindrance to that mutual intercourse which for pastoral and practical work would have been a pure gain. To help them in difficulties, and indicate their line of action on doubtful points, Bishop Wilson had drawn up a useful manual of directions. This was their chief guide in a service so centralised that everything, from controverted ecclesiastical points down to the sale of grass in a church compound, goes up to Government. But no text-book of advice or instructions could meet every case of collision provoked by over-sensitiveness and struggles for prerogative. Feuds between chaplains and the military authorities, and sometimes between one chaplain and another, constituted the real ecclesiastical troubles of the See of Calcutta, and called for an exercise of judicial functions on paltry and personal points which was exceedingly distasteful and irksome to the Bishop. It became necessary to speak or to write unpalatable words, liable, perhaps, to be misunderstood; but his aim was always to meet such cases with fairness and kindness, and to give due weight to every extenuating circumstance. On one occasion an annoying affair was under discussion with a friend who assumed that the Bishop would handle it severely; he replied, 'Amongst my titles the one I like the best is "Father in God," and I desire never to forget it when I have to censure any of the clergy.' Yet more thoughtfully and solemnly he wrote on another occasion to a correspondent: 'I hear that Mr. —— is dead. His was a very troubled life, and as his faults seemed to arise a good deal from physical temperament, he has at last found rest. My relations to him had more than once been so unpleasing that it is a matter of thankfulness to me that we parted friends, and that, after his last illness began, I had opportunities of seeing and helping him. It is painful to think of separating in anger from one who will be seen no more till we meet at the Judgment.'

The Bishop's efforts for an improvement of the ecclesiastical service in outward things can only be cursorily noticed, though they were spread over the whole of his Indian life. Strongly deprecating anything which tended to make secular motives take the place of zeal, he still maintained that men worked at an unfair disadvantage with their fellow-men when fixed for the best part of life in a service which, though respectably paid, offered no preferment, except that of one archdeaconry, and bestowed rewards only in such exceptional times as the Mutiny for long and faithful labours. He frequently made representations to Government respecting the dead level of the service, and his own difficulty in providing for the spiritual wants of large and important stations, appointments to which, though nominally a testimony to the value of a chaplain's services, were in reality, from the heavy expenses attached to them, a fine upon his income. One great measure of improvement was that of a revision of the rules about pensions, and will be referred to hereafter. Time and perseverance, and, it must in all justice be added, the favourable attention accorded by Government, brought about also some other advantages. A few parsonage-houses were built; an increase of salary was granted at some of the larger and more expensive stations; by the revival of an old rule, free passages were allowed on board troop-ships between England and India; the substitution of fixed promotion to a higher salary at the end of ten years for an uncertain rise depending on vacancies among the senior chaplains, was granted by the Secretary of State. All these were real boons to the ecclesiastical service. The suggestion of them did not in every case originate with the Bishop, but he was the only medium of negotiations in which State considerations and private interests were mutually confronted, and which, therefore, often needed cautious and temperate management. One distinct position which he maintained for himself was that of standing between the ruling powers and a body of clergy who, from their limited numbers and comparative isolation, have but a slight collective voice or influence in a country to which many give most loyal and faithful service. The peculiarities in their public position deepened the Bishop's sense of responsibility towards them, while a vast capacity of sympathy, though hidden under an undemonstrative manner, with private troubles and anxieties incidental to a land of exile and a perilous climate, led him to keep their interests always in view, and to exert influence at all times to assist and befriend them.

Letters to Chaplains.

1860.

I am much obliged to you for your letter and interesting information which you give about your work at ——. Most heartily do I sympathise with your feeling that personal growth in holiness often seems too much for our own strength, and the duty of labouring for others becomes a depressing burden. But I do not know that I can give you any further advice than such as is obvious.

It is quite certain that if we neglect our work for others, our own souls suffer from it; that the two duties are inextricably interwoven, and that by praying to God for grace to fulfil the one, we are at the same time promoting the other.

I should not feel too anxious, were I you, about the expression and outward exhibition of religious feeling in my flock. Perhaps from being reserved myself, I have always acted on the belief that the great thing to care for is the evidence of the life. If the Lord's Table is neglected, if in ordinary society gossip and calumny are prevalent, if any of your flock are leading self-indulgent and godless lives, then you have great need for anxiety, watchfulness, and intervention. But the expression of religious conviction in conversation often depends on a person's natural temperament.

Doubtless you should contend against a low and worldly tone, and language implying indifference to duty or the absence of Christian faith and hope. But, in general, I think that you must exercise a Christian influence by being yourself a pattern of diligence and good works, by mixing with your parishioners in a kind and friendly way, and showing, rather indirectly by quiet influence, that the life of every Christian must be bound up with obedience and love to Jesus Christ, than by bringing such truths prominently forward in ordinary conversation.

1860.

It is my hope to be at —— in the course of December, and to have the pleasure of making your acquaintance. I shall be ready then to hold a confirmation and perform any other necessary episcopal offices, and I send you the notice of confirmation which should be read to your congregation.

Your charge, I suppose, is almost purely military, and doubtless you are prepared for difficulties and disappointments in dealing with soldiers, especially in India, where climate, want of occupation, and often a necessary suspension of church ordinances from the illness or absence of the clergy, conduce to indolence and forgetfulness of God. But, from my observation during my visitation, I feel sure that a slow but steady improvement is going on in the army, and that the services of a devoted chaplain are gratefully appreciated.

I earnestly hope that you will find this to be the case in your own special sphere of duty, and that you will begin it in a hopeful and cheerful spirit, which is generally one necessary condition of success. It is my earnest prayer that God's blessing may rest upon your labours, and that you may be the means of imparting to many comfort, encouragement, and the true knowledge of our Lord and Saviour Jesus Christ.

1862.

I notice in your returns that the Holy Communion has been administered at —— only on Easter Day and Whit Sunday. I think that it should unquestionably be administered every month. Doubtless it is much to be regretted that the number of communicants should be so lamentably few as seven, but I am sure rare administration tends to diminish the number. People cannot think that to be the central ordinance of the Christian religion of which they are only invited to partake three times a year. You ought to make it the chief effort of your ministry to restore your people to a proper sense of their duty in this matter. If they wilfully disobey Christ in one of His plainest commands, and throw away a great and precious privilege, I do not see how they can expect His blessing to keep them from sin. Sermons on the subject, and the monthly administration, seem to me two obvious remedies for so great an evil as habitual neglect of the Lord's Supper.

I cannot help expressing my regret at a letter which I saw on the subject of your desire to be a honorary magistrate, in which it was said that you complained that you had too little to do. It was sent to me when the Lieutenant-Governor asked my consent to your appointment. Doubtless —— is not a station affording so much scope for work as Benares or Meerut, but I should have thought that sufficient work might be found. The acquisition of the language might facilitate a little missionary work, the study of theology has an obvious bearing on the composition of sermons. It has struck me that you may desire to be moved from —— to a place where there is more room for activity, and that such a change may be good for you. There is always a fear of our vegetating if we stay too long in a quiet place.

1862.

I have read your letter with great interest. I need hardly say that I warmly approve of the plan of soldiers' clubs, and fully appreciate the exertions which you have made and the interest which you feel in the welfare of your men. . . . I pass on to details and to the questions which you put to me about amusements, and the approbation which you desire that I should give to your sanction of theatricals. I do not give an opinion on the subject hastily. I know that it is generally considered as a matter of course that clergymen should disapprove of play-acting, and that military chaplains should refuse all sanction to military theatricals. But this fact would only incline me to form my opinion the more carefully, lest I should follow a popular cry without consideration. Nor have I formed it without talking on different occasions to more than one chaplain well acquainted with military stations, so as to correct my own want of experience. And the result is, that I agree with the opinion most common among my brethren, and could never, were I a military chaplain myself, give my sanction to theatrical amusements among my soldiers. The reasons which influence me are such as these :—

It is quite certain that the pieces likely to be acted are generally of a coarse and vulgar character, and very questionable morality. They would be the ordinary farces of the present day, and no one, I suppose, can pretend that they are in any way improving. It is vain to say that the chaplain can control the selection of the pieces ; the officers and men would never consent to too strict a censorship ; and if the chaplain attempted to exercise one, his object in sanctioning the theatre would fail, for the theatre would cease to be attractive.

Again, theatrical amusements are exceedingly exciting and absorbing. When they are going on those engaged in them think and talk of nothing else, and there is an end of serious occupation or devotional feeling. I have seen something of this on a small and carefully-guarded scale, having been myself educated at Westminster, where plays were performed by the boys, and where certainly the results were questionable, in spite of many safeguards and circumstances which would not exist among grown men. It may add force to this argument when I say that it is strongly felt by Mr. Norman, who is so often mentioned by the speakers at your meetings as a great authority in soldiers' clubs, and is the founder of the one which has acquired the widest popularity. He not only would have nothing to do with the theatre, but hoped that the Outram Institute would draw men from it ; nor are theatricals allowed in connection with the similar institution at Fort William.

I am told by persons of experience that, as a fact, the theatre is looked upon in a regiment as injurious to the progress of Christian feeling and conduct among the men. When a soldier determines to amend his course of life he always turns away from it. To be much given to the theatre is regarded as a sign that a man is careless about the highest things. . . .

You defend theatres in your speech by citing the proverb, 'Out of two evils choose the least.' I should be inclined to reply by another saying, not less commonly quoted, but sanctioned by higher authority, 'Shall we do evil that good may come ?'

Your programme includes many safe amusements : concerts, lectures, reading-rooms, cricket, bowls, gymnastics, are all not only innocent, but positively desirable. Bagatelle, which you unjustly class with theatricals, and similar games seem to me quite harmless in the army, where gambling is strictly prohibited by military regulations. Of course it must be a condition that there should not be an approach to playing for money ; but that, I believe, will be cared for by others, so that you will be relieved from supervision in that respect.

1863.

You ask me whether it is lawful at a small out-station to celebrate the Communion when only one person remains to partake of it.

I answer with a good deal of hesitation. Undoubtedly, it is not only intended by the Church, but regarded as a point of great importance, that the Lord's Supper should be strictly a communion, at which '*we being many* should be all partakers of one bread.' And therefore a clergyman should, as a general rule, certainly not administer to one person only. Still I cannot overlook the fact, that at——, where there is only one communicant, the whole congregation only amounts to five ; that of these, four may be hindered from coming by youth, by not having been confirmed, nor being 'ready and desirous' to be so, or other causes ; and that the Lord's Supper is doubtless a special privilege and blessing to a person living in so remote a place and in so small a society. The existing state of things too in India was one never contemplated by the framers of our

Liturgy. Hence, judging from the analogy of their own directions in the last Rubric to the Communion of the Sick, I think a clergyman justified in such a case as that of —— in communicating with one person only.

1863.

. . . . I quite admit that during the rains the service for the troops can neither be in the open air nor in the church of ——. *If therefore there is positively no other building in the cantonment which can be used except the theatre,* I must perforce assent to such a humiliation of our Church service. But I have the greatest possible dislike to the proposal. The associations of the place will, I should fear, be fatal to any feeling of reverence on the part of the men. I always deprecated the services in the London theatres, but I should think that all the evils of such services would be doubled and trebled in the case of a soldiers' theatre, when the very same persons assembled to worship in it on Sunday have perhaps been acting some ridiculous farce in it on Saturday. I therefore give my consent if it is a matter of absolute necessity. And if you are really reduced to preach in such a place, I hope that you will exert yourself to the utmost of your power to make the service solemn and devotional.

I do not think that you can refuse baptism to the adult soldier on account of his occasional deflections from the right path, if he seems to you humbly and heartily to desire it. Of course you must speak to him very seriously about the guilt and peril of inconsistency, and you must watch him well after his baptism, especially with reference to attendance at the Lord's Supper. But, unless you think him insincere in his desire for baptism, or to be plainly actuated by worldly motives, or to be ignorant of the fundamentals of Christianity, he has, I think, a moral right to the sacrament of initiation into Christ's Church.

1863.

You are not justified, by the law of our Church, in reading the burial service over an unbaptized child. For though it is true, as you say, that Canon XVIII. only mentions one out of the three exceptions prescribed by the Rubric (probably from not considering that the body of an unbaptized person would be brought to the church or churchyard at all), yet if ever a canon appears to conflict with the Rubric, you are bound to obey the Rubric and not the canon. For the Rubric is part of the Prayer Book, and therefore was made the law of England by the Act of Uniformity, and is included in the promise which you made at your ordination. But you have made no promise to obey the canons, except the thirty-sixth; many of them are inapplicable to the present time, many are habitually violated, and it is generally understood that they are only binding on the clergy in so far as they are enforced by their diocesans, who must judge how far each canon can and ought to be enforced or not. But the claim of the Rubric upon you is altogether closer and more binding than this.

Thus far I give you my official answer to your letter, which is briefly that you were wrong in reading the service over an unbaptized child, and must not do so should a like case occur again. If, as you were informed, a chaplain did so on another occasion, he acted wrongly. But I do not blame you, being in doubt, for deciding in favour of the kinder course, and giving the dead and the parents the benefit of your doubt.

I know that this necessity of refusing the burial service to an unbaptized child is often a trouble to a kind-hearted clergyman, called to sympathise with parents in time of affliction. If, indeed, the baptism was omitted through carelessness or indifference, then the want of the burial service is a proper rebuke to those who, having undervalued the benefit of a Christian ordinance in health and happiness, cannot claim the consolation of one in sorrow. But if, as in the case which you mention, a very young infant dies suddenly, without previous sickness, then the want of such comfort is no doubt a hardship. I have known of a clergyman who in such a case has accompanied the body to the grave, and there read to the parents some passages of Scripture, and prayed with them, not using any of the prayers in the burial service. I do not know that I have any right to authorise such a proceeding—certainly not to order it. But it is nowhere forbidden; and if any one of my clergy, in such a case as I have described, were to adopt it, I certainly should not interfere with him or censure him. But the use of the burial service I have no right even to permit.

1864.

. . . . By all means administer the Lord's Supper to the Presbyterian, if he is willing to receive it according to our forms, and you know of no moral impediment. I am quite convinced, on historical grounds, that the Rubric ordering that it should not be administered to unconfirmed persons was only intended as an internal code of discipline in our own Church, and not designed to exclude from communion Christians of other Churches. I have no time to go fully into my reasons for this opinion, which was given to me when I was a young man, by one who had very great knowledge both of history and divinity. One reason only may be mentioned. William III. and the early Hanoverian kings, and other foreign Protestants resident in England before them, had never been confirmed, but surely cannot have been excluded from the holy communion.

As to rebuking a person of advanced age who is living in sin, or has sinned openly without repentance—first be very careful as to your facts. Be quite sure that you do not act on mere rumour, and so bring a false charge. Nothing is so likely to turn a wavering person in a wrong direction as the sense that he is treated with injustice or accused without reason. But if your facts are, unhappily, clear, then I cannot advise you to shrink from the duty of remonstrating with the culprit. Only, as a young man, you must do so humbly, affectionately, and discreetly; as one who is weak and prone to sin, you must do so gently and thoughtfully, considering 'thyself lest thou also be tempted.' Doubtless, John the Baptist is the great preacher of repentance, and so far is the model of all who deliver the same message; but in taking him as your pattern, you must consider the vast difference between yourself and him, and while you follow him in principle you will assume a tone of far less authority than his.

It is to me a matter of sincere thankfulness if you have found in my charge any help in perplexity and support in your work.

1866.

I certainly think that there ought to be a sermon when the holy communion is administered—first, because the communion service is the only one in which a sermon is positively ordered; secondly, because the occasion is one of peculiar solemnity, and it may be hoped that a few words of Christian exhortation, earnestly spoken at such a time, would be peculiarly impressive; thirdly, because unhappily the proportion of communicants to non-communicants in a military congregation is so small that, for the sake of a very few, you deprive the vast majority of a means of edification.

To the first of these reasons I imagine no answer can be returned. To the second you will object to the length of the service. You propose to meet the difficulty of the third by requesting non-communicants to remain and witness the administration.

With regard then to the second, I do not wish the sermons on such occasions to be long. A few sentences on the nature of the sacrament, which some are neglecting, and of which others are going to partake, a short practical exposition of the epistle or gospel which have just been read, or something in the style of Dean Goodwin of Ely's admirable 'Short Sermons preached before the administration of the Lord's Supper,' would satisfy all that I require, and be probably more impressive than a long formal essay.

As to the third, the practical difficulties are great. Without the concurrence of the officers, the thing must be a failure; and even if they consent to remain, it is hard to force the soldiers to do so; while if they are not forced, it is very unlikely that they will stay of their own accord. But even if they do, I doubt whether it is desirable to encourage them to stay; that is to say, it may, I think, be very right to urge a man who is kept from the Lord's Supper by ignorance of its nature to remain and see for himself how simple and yet how impressive a rite it is, and it is quite possible that the actual sight of what is done may remove prejudices and turn him into a communicant. But to effect this desirable end, one stay in church during the administration of the holy communion would generally, I suppose, be sufficient. I am not ignorant of the distinction which is made by some modern writers on the subject between the 'representation' and 'partaking' of Christ's sacrifice, nor of the other arguments which are used to justify the habitual presence of non-communicants. But I am entirely unconvinced by them. It seems to be, both from the New Testament and the Prayer Book, that the essence of the whole benefit is in the eating and drinking; the habitual substitution of mere presence at the communion for partaking of it would lead to dangerous error, and be hardly in accordance with the spirit of the last clause of Article XXVIII.

CHAPTER VII.

RETURN TO CALCUTTA—DEPARTURE OF DOMESTIC CHAPLAIN FOR ENGLAND —THE BISHOP'S DEPARTURE FOR ASSAM—LETTERS IN 1861—VISITATION OF BURMAH AND THE STRAITS — LIFE ON BOARD SHIP — MISGIVINGS ON THE GREAT EXTENT OF THE DIOCESE OF CALCUTTA—RANGOON—BUDDHISM —DEATH OF LADY CANNING—MOULMEIN—MISSION SCHOOL—BURMESE SYSTEM OF NATIONAL EDUCATION—RETURN TO CALCUTTA—DEPARTURE OF LORD CANNING.

IN February 1861 the Bishop's party were reassembled in Bishop's Palace, after an absence of eighteen months. Life in Calcutta brought a return to more settled occupations, and to pleasant social intercourse with a large English community. The Government also went through the hot weather with its servants; and there was in those days no migration of Court and Council to the hills, reducing Calcutta to the dulness of a Mofussil town. Many large and small parties at Government House broke the weight of the trying hot season, and one scene of historical interest was the durbar in which Lord Canning received the thanks of the talookdars of Oude for the privileges it had been his special policy to restore to them. The event of chief importance to the Bishop personally was the departure for England in July, through failing health, of his chaplain, Thomas Harris Burn. The parting was the rending of another tie with England and the past. Their adoption together of a wholly new work had sealed the confidence and friendship of fifteen earlier years, and the Bishop felt that the separation in 1861 would cause a blank in his life which could never be wholly filled. It was practically a resignation of the office, for Mr. Burn returned to India in 1862 to resume it only during one visitation journey and a few more months. When, in 1864, he was released from long and painful illness, the Bishop mourned the loss not only to himself of a tried and trusted friend, but to the whole diocese of one who was a bright example to the service he had adopted, by his high sense of ministerial duty towards both Europeans and natives, by the energy with which he quickly mastered the language sufficiently for much practical usefulness, and by many excellent gifts of head and heart which led him to spend and be spent for India.

Just as this vacancy in the domestic chaplaincy occurred, the Bishop was preparing for an official voyage of two months up the Brahmaputra. Looking round for a companion and helper on this fresh pilgrimage, he sought and found one in Archdeacon Pratt, whom he had long learnt to look upon as a real friend and coadjutor, and this, their first journey together was full of interest and profit. The Archdeacon was an excellent travelling companion. He was calm, imperturbable, and cheerful under difficulties as was the Bishop himself; seldom overpowered by the languor incident to a region of extreme tropical humidity, and so full of varied knowledge that he was as much an authority on curious points of physical geography, raised by the vast water system of Assam, as on the station needs or mission schools that came under review.

The annexed letters belong to the year 1861 :—

To Professor Shairp.

Palace, Calcutta, April 9, 1861.

This is not a letter, but a mere bit of friendly chat: not a regular constitutional round by the Dunchurch Road and Bilton, or the Holbrooke Grange fields and Aganippe, but a simple stroll after second lesson to our homes and a little beyond perhaps, or a turn round the close after chapel on Sunday. I write partly to introduce to you the 'Calcutta Christian Intelligencer,' a monthly publication, which, having sunk to the lowest depths of dulness and debt, is now endeavouring to struggle into a new life under the auspices of Burn, who has become its editor. Its objects are explained in an article written by me in the February number entitled 'Ourselves.' As long as it exists (which may cease to be the case unless the sale can overtake the debt) I hope to send it you as a present monthly, as it will record most of my public and official proceedings. If you could ever be induced to furnish an article, a scrap of poetry, a brief review, religious reflections, a short memoir—anything pertaining more or less directly to theology, whether practical or scientific, you would edify the Indian *clerus*, and place us under deep obligations.

Your letter, just received, gave me extreme pleasure, as your communications always do. There are few persons with whom I generally agree more thoroughly, owing to the mixture of religious enthusiasm, firm faith, and thoughtful reflection which distinguishes your Christianity, arising perhaps from an Oxonian manhood grafted on a presbyterian boyhood. I cannot answer it now—to-day is mail-day; but in answer to your question as to what work in life can best be taken up in the time not absorbed by the professorship, I answer that books to strengthen the faith and deepen the Christian convictions of young men seem to me the chief want of the age in England.

We are all, thank God, very well, though the hot weather is upon us with all its fury. I rejoice that you are complete professor.

To C. M. Bull, Esq.

Dibroghur in Upper Assam, September 3, 1861.

As I wrote to you last from Simla, and now date from the banks of the Brahmaputra, you must think that my whole life is spent in wandering about India, a supposition, however, which is not quite correct, for last year I had six very happy months undisturbed at that place, and this year have spent six more in my own home at Calcutta. It seems odd to call Calcutta *home*; yet, besides the fact that no home can be homeless which contains wife and child, I feel more and more that it would be ungrateful to refuse to it that name of endearment, considering the multiplied comforts and advantages which mitigate its heat and its exile. . . .

Though travelling now in the full state of a government steamer, I find considerable discomforts arising from the occasionally frightful heat, and the absence, in these recently established and imperfectly provided stations, of those means and appliances whereby in Calcutta we make our houses cool in the hottest weather. Yesterday the thermometer was at 94°, and the blinds by which the sun was nominally excluded were far less serviceable than good calico blinds, such as you have in any well-provided English house. The result is that one can do nothing. Before the heat of the day began I had a confirmation, and at sunset consecrated a burial-ground, but during the interval was absolutely useless, lying on my bed fanning myself. So that the ice, and punkahs, and other instruments of coolness in the more civilised parts of India, are not luxuries, as they would be in England, but means of doing work efficiently. Even as a tour the present one is not of first-rate interest; the two chief objects for observation being some extremely grand river scenery, and the gradual transformation of a wild jungly valley, 400 miles long, into one huge tea plantation, to which change Assam is submitting, apparently with most successful results to tea-planters, tea-drinkers, and Assamese labourers.

With regard to India, the point which chiefly troubles me as bishop, and should, I think, cause most anxiety to all its well-wishers just now, is the result of the constantly increasing influx of European settlers and their relation to the natives. . . And there are unquestionably three points on the side of the settlers worthy of much condemnation—(1) the calumnies of their newspapers; (2) the claim which they set up to be the public and people of India, wholly forgetting the unquestionably prior and wider rights of Hindus; (3) the commercial spirit of magnifying capital and its claims above all other considerations. Nothing would, I think, be more disastrous than a parliament or council in which they would be the preponderating element, since they would be a mere oligarchy of race without any responsibility, such as presses upon the official class, and we all know from history what is the course which such an oligarchy usually runs. Hence, though not given to admire arbitrary government, and sufficiently detesting the present French *régime*, I am very glad that the new constitution with which Sir C. Wood is favouring India is of a somewhat despotic character, though in truth India cannot be despotically governed, if the English Parliament does its duty. . . .

My educational work is not wholly over; besides certain schools and colleges whereof I am visitor, I have been elected on the syndicate, or governing committee, of the Calcutta University, which is really now the most efficient agent in educating the Hindus, and there I sit monthly with the Advocate-General, Dr. Duff, the Free Kirk missionary, a physician, and a native (a son of Ram Mohun Roy); a curious 'Hebdomadal Board,' is it not? I think that we do some good, and we are as harmonious as if we were canons of Durham, dividing our money, and banded to resist a radical commission. Kindest regards to your father and mother.

To Professor Conington.

Palace, Calcutta, October 1861.

Your letters are always very interesting, and I can say without flattering that I never receive one without great pleasure. The last reached me as I was voyaging up the Brahmaputra on a two months' visitation of the remote and somewhat uninteresting province of Assam, and most agreeably recalled my thoughts from its opium-eating inhabitants to Oxford and English interests. I confess that such matters still occupy a very foremost place in my mind, more so perhaps than they ought to do, considering the work assigned to me here. But I cannot help it, and it would be affectation to say that I view India with the absorbing interest felt in it by Martyn or Corrie or my immediate predecessor. Not that I at all dislike my work, or that I am not interested in it. On the contrary, the work itself I like very much: it is not oppressive, it gives me plenty to think about, I throw into it willingly such energies as

I have, and as long as God mercifully preserves my health, I have no cause for regret except the want of Edward and some English friends. But then, when it comes to India, I feel certain drawbacks. Thus, as to the missionary work, I am only concerned in it occasionally, and as it were indirectly, while the evangelisation of the country to such an extent as to bring me into more constant connection with it is very distant, hardly reserved for my episcopate unless there were to be some special interposition of God's providence. Again, the politics of India are not of a kind to interest, but rather to disgust me. At present, the great subject of newspaper controversy is the rivalry between the governmental or official classes, and the mercantile community of settlers, planters, and other persons who come here to make their fortunes. . . . I do not deny that there are excellent men among them, some who are true Christians and would gladly make the natives Christians also. But even these come here simply for purposes of trade, and undoubtedly their views for the future of India are largely coloured, not merely by commercial but by personal considerations. . . . Among civilians, I see often a real interest in the natives, and a desire to improve them for their own sake. But then the civilians, like all the rest of the Anglo-Indian world, are always looking forward to going home, and regard England as their country; so that the utmost that one ever sees, excepting in a few devoted missionaries, is a readiness, perhaps an earnest desire, to do good to India during the time of sojourn in it. Thirdly, constitutional changes, such as those lately announced, are only alterations in the way of nominating counsellors and disposing of patronage or working the details of Government, and these are certainly not matters of high interest. The change which is likely ultimately to lead to the most important results is Lord Canning's last order, which permits the sale of waste land and the redemption of the land tax, so as to introduce into the country a class of real landlords holding the fee simple of their estates. . . . On one part of my duties of life, I have come, I think, to a pretty clear opinion—the nature of my reading. I do not consider that I should be doing my best for the Indian Church in its present aspect, so much more European than native, by spending my time in trying to make myself an Oriental scholar. Two living languages, Hindustani and Bengali, of which I already know something, I wish to keep always on hand, alternately, as work calls me to the NW. Provinces or keeps me in Bengal. For I think it desirable to be able to ordain, confirm, and perform, other services in the native congregations in their own tongues, and to be able to talk a little to them. And I always hope to keep up and improve my acquaintance with Indian history and such studies as will enable me to feel an interest in the people. But to learn Sanscrit or Arabic, and to read Vedas and Upanishads or Koran and Mahometan literature in the original languages, would consume immense time without corresponding fruit. My business is to influence and help the clergy, to be a *Christian* theologian, to do my best to spread in the country true views of Christianity, to interest people by freshness and sound matter in my sermons. Hence I hope to make Divinity my chief study, and therefore I have resumed Hebrew and read divers books of Scriptural criticism: the last being Elliott's 'Horæ Apocalypticæ,' by which, however, I remain unconvinced, though the learning of the book is great, and it is written by a good man. . . .

To the Bishop of Adelaide, South Australia.

Palace, Calcutta, October 28, 1861.

I was absent from Calcutta on my first visitation of Assam when your letter arrived with the kind contributions of your diocese to the Famine Relief Fund, for which I return my best thanks. The famine is, by God's mercy, over, and has been succeeded by a bountiful harvest. But its effects of course remain, and among these there is none more melancholy than the great number of orphan children. Orphanages have been set up by both of our missionary societies, where these children will be trained up as Christians under the care of clergymen. The most important is that of the Christian Missionary Society at Agra, but that has been so largely aided by the committee of the Famine Relief Fund that I have thought it needless to help it further with the Australian money. I have therefore divided this between two other orphanages of more recent origin, which are more dependent on private contributions: that of the Society for Propagating the Gospel at Cawnpore, and that of the Christian Missionary Society at Umritsur in the Punjab, and I trust that this appropriation of the money will meet the wishes of yourself and of those who have kindly given it. It may add some interest to the appropriation of the money sent from Adelaide, if you know that at my first Ordination I admitted to deacon's orders two Hindustanis who had been saved from the last great famine (1837–8), and trained up in a missionary orphanage.

In the cold weather of 1861, the primary visitation was resumed through the British settlements, along the seaboard of Burmah and the Malay Peninsula, down to the gate of Chinese waters at Singapore. The routine work was of the usual kind. There were the scattered civil and military congregations to be visited, the latter involving a voyage of two hundred miles up the Irrawaddi to the frontier garrison of Thyetmyo; there were churches to be consecrated; seamen in gaols and hospitals to be visited; schools and missions to be inspected, and ecclesiastical matters generally to be inquired into, and set in order. The expedition was entirely by sea. So much official care was always taken to facilitate travelling and diminish fatigue, that the Bishop used to be occasionally disturbed by an amount of comfort and consideration which certainly helped to promote the external dignity of the great Eastern See. On this occasion, however, a humble pilot-brig was appointed by Government to the temporary service; and its quarters were so limited, that the small deck had to do duty as the Bishop's study, the child's playroom, the general sitting and eating-room for everybody. Many days passed pleasantly when a favourable wind speeded the vessel and tempered the heat, but calms not storms were the drawback of the voyage; and when the ship lay motionless in the midst of the Bay of Bengal, or mocked hopes of progress by drifting a few miles with the current, the Bishop secretly registered a vow that he would not go forth again except under steam. 'Certainly,' he wrote from the deck of the 'Mutlah,' 'a sailing-vessel is an undesirable mode of conveyance. That one's morality should be seriously influenced by the points of the compass, and depend on the force of the wind, is in itself humiliating. Yet it really requires an effort to receive with perfect cheerfulness the announcement that in the course of twenty-four hours we have advanced eighteen miles, or receded half a degree of latitude. . . . The uniformity of the life, too, gets wearisome, although it gives me ample time for reading. I read Hebrew and Bengali, and get through sundry books of an historical and theological character. In the evening, after tea, we sit on deck in the balmy night air, and I read aloud Helps or Macaulay on week-days, Trench on the "Seven Churches" on Sundays. . . . I must add a word of admiring criticism on Goldwin Smith's "Lectures," and of thankfulness that a layman of unquestioned ability and mark should stand up in the University in direct opposition to an atheistic school of writers, and really put forth utterances in defence of Christianity more forcible than those of almost any one among its modern apologists.'

The tour itself was full of novelty. Much beautiful scenery and the glorious vegetation of the tropics; the fresh aspect of outward things in countries whose inhabitants are complete aliens from Hindus in race, language, customs, and religion; a glimpse of wild savage life among the Andamanese, watched and overawed by the diminutive British settlement on Ross Island, two miles long and less than one in width—were all in their turn sources of keen interest and enjoyment. Buddhism was the social and religious feature of special prominence. Buried in India in mouldering sculpture, it is in the more remote East the powerful living faith of millions; and as such the Bishop made its external aspect and characteristics his study, so far as brief opportunities and much other work permitted. The spurious Buddhism of the Malay Peninsula puzzled him much, and his discomfiture was complete when, in a Joss-house at Malacca, he wholly failed to discover, by the most energetic inquiries, whether the hideous many-armed idol before him, designated as Fo, was identical in the minds of the placid Chinamen around with the Buddha or Gotama of the Burmese. He ended, however, a four months' visitation with an uncomfortable sense of the whole territory being an unnatural excrescence on the see of Calcutta, and full of responsibility, which it was beyond the power of an Indian bishop adequately to discharge. The inspection of a handful of widely separated European settlements absorbed time ill spared from India; total ignorance of either the Burmese, Chinese, or Malay languages was an embarrassment, and in paying a graceful tribute to the Vicar-Apostolic of Pegu, Bishop Bigandet, as a learned Orientalist, the Bishop gave expression to his own feelings, that the Burmah missions needed at their head some one who would make Buddhist literature and philosophy a special object of research and study.

The missions, then in their infancy, needed both fostering care and organization. The Bishop was compelled to devote an unusually large amount of time to the settlement of local matters, which were producing not only confusion but discord; and he was convinced that the missions required a more frequent and more personal supervision than he or the Calcutta Secretary could bestow upon them. Such points of difficulty and incongruity were those which made the diocese of Calcutta really unmanageable. Within the limits of North India the Bishop's work was sufficiently varied and extensive; but a thread of connexion ran through it, and he could feel that his mind was comparatively master of it; the same kind of work, carried on under the different conditions of practically foreign countries, assumed a totally new aspect, and claimed a different and special line of thought and knowledge. Outward diversity overpowered the inward harmony between the two, and there remained the sense of impotence in the presence of distinct duty, which was vexatious and depressing. The Bishop was at that time ready to give in his adhesion to any plan whereby he might abdicate, in favour of some other bishop, all episcopal jurisdiction to the east of the Bay of Bengal. Meantime, so long as he was unrelieved, his responsibility for these territories continued; and one occupation of the tedious return voyage to India was the writing of a letter to the London Secretary of the Propagation Society, to describe their two missions just visited, and to recommend them to the attention and vigorous support of the parent Society, as each presenting some hopeful points. Through that at Moulmein, the Church of England was making her first aggression upon the religion of Burmah. The Singapore mission was directed chiefly to the Chinese, who form in that city a fluctuating population of many thousands, of whom many are constantly returning to their own country. By God's blessing on evangelistic efforts, a Chinaman may now and again perhaps carry back with him some better possessions than his expert handicraft and his neat box of tools.

Rangoon and Moulmein were the two chief centres of Buddhism and Burmese national life, visited during this tour, and journal extracts will be limited to notices of these two places.

EXTRACTS FROM JOURNAL.

Rangoon.—In the evening we drove to see the great pagoda. Taken altogether, with its various dependent buildings, it is one of the most grotesque, fantastic, and striking sights that I ever beheld. From the bottom of the hill to the platform the ascent is by a steep succession of steps, under a wooden roof supported by thick posts, generally coloured red. The platform is of immense extent, with the gilt pagoda in the centre, surmounted by the sacred *htee*, or umbrella—a solid mass of brickwork, but containing, it is said, in its interior various precious relics, including eight of Gotama's hairs, and even some memorials of preceding Buddhas. Round it are a vast number of smaller pagodas, each with its *htee* ; tall red flagstaffs with streamers floating from them; lofty trees; covered wooden buildings elaborately carved, with countless niches, each containing a colossal sitting statue of Gotama, always with the same mild feminine semi-Tartar features (the Rajpoot princes from whom he sprang are said to have had Mongolian blood in their veins), and with a robe over him—generally gilt, sometimes black.

The pagoda itself, as containing a relic, is the object of worship, and the prayers are in a manner addressed to Gotama; not that he can hear them, or is conscious of the wants of his adorers—for he has attained *nirwana*, and is therefore in no intelligible sense existent—but by a law of nature the fact of worshipping him leads to births in happy conditions hereafter, and ultimately to *nirwana*. Hence Buddhists may be said to adore Gotama's memory; and this is one of the numerous facts in which Buddhism is an anticipation of Comte's religion, and deprives that monstrous invention of even the merit of originality. In their atheism, their denial of a future state continuing through eternity, their adoration of the unconscious dead, the exclusively educational work of the priests, and the inexorable supremacy of law, both systems are identical; they have also one good point in common—the unfailing certainty with which wrong leads the wrongdoer into suffering—though in this Gotama is superior to Comte, because by the doctrine of *metempsychosis* he provides a manner in which punishment may follow crime, whereas I do not see how a wicked Comtist would practically be deterred from sin by any such belief, since in this life it is at least not visibly and obviously the case. Comte's devices of punishing a bad man's memory, and dishonouring his carcase, by exclusion from a consecrated grove surrounding the Temple of Humanity, are of course too ridiculous to be of any avail against the present pleasures of vice and self-indulgence. There is no doubt that the Buddhist doctrines are very superior to the Hindu, and that so far Gotama was a real reformer; but as I looked on one of his devotees praying to the unconscious and annihilated Buddha, I was, I trust, thankful for the revelation of a High Priest who can be touched with the feeling of our infirmities, and for the promise that He would be with us always, even to the end of the world.

. . . .

December 6.—To-day I went off to see one of the most encouraging sights in the East—the American Baptist Mission to the Karens. These people generally live up in the hills, but they have villages near Rangoon, and there is an institution for their education at Kemmendine, about three miles from the town, prettily situated in a grassy dale under fine trees. There is a chapel of brick and plaster, but all the other buildings are of wood, perched up on posts in the usual Burmese fashion. They consist of a missionary's house, a school, and a number of cottages for students, close together, almost like sets of rooms in a college, opening out upon a raised verandah, and each divided into two rooms, with a garden behind.

The institution is under the care of Dr. and Mrs. Binney, from Massachusetts, who seem both thoroughly absorbed in the work, the wife (like our own Mrs. Smith at Benares) quite as much so as the husband. He has about fifty Karen youths, all not only professing Christianity, but pledged to pastoral and missionary work among their countrymen; and the nineteen most advanced of these were brought to me for examination. They are, I think, fairer than the natives of India generally; of course, with broad Tartar features, but most of them of a pleasing and intelligent appearance, dressed like the Burmese. They knew no English, but Dr. Binney interpreted; they certainly answered remarkably well to a somewhat stiff examination in scripture. Their other studies are the grammar of their own language, arithmetic, and geography. It was a most cheering sight, and it is a still more cheering thought to remember that these fifty are only the advance guard of 30,000 Karen Christians, and that the number is constantly increasing; so that there is every reason to hope that the whole nation will become Christian. They give every evidence of sincerity, contributing most largely to the support of the missions, and, according to the testimony of Colonel Phayre, are most conscientious in abstinence from all excess in drink, in observance of Sunday, and other Christian duties. Not only should the sight make us thank God and take courage, but teach us also many lessons as to the persons to whom missions may be sent with the best prospect of success, and the manner of working them. For instance, here are two sufficiently obvious. Vigorous attempts should be directed to the conversion of all the mountain tribes of India, and every effort should be made to develope the native pastorate.

. . . .

December 10.—We have been deeply shocked by the news of Lady Canning's death from jungle fever, caught in her journey from Darjeeling. I can imagine no one more admirably suited for such a position as hers, in grace, quiet dignity, varied accomplishments, kindness, winning manner, and, above all, in high principle and Christian example, nor any one more entirely uninjured or unsophisticated by a Court life and the manifold dangers of wealth and high station.

I think her character a proof of the truth of the Lord's words, that it is possible for a rich man to enter into the kingdom of heaven. Among the pleasures and refreshments of my Indian life, I shall always reckon my opportunities of a quiet talk with her during a dinner or morning visit to Government House. It is sad to think that as she has so faithfully shared all her husband's anxieties during the last eventful six years, she is not to share the rich reward of honour and gratitude soon to be paid in England to services now universally recognised and appreciated. Yet this is but a human and earthly way of viewing the matter, and it is better to dwell on the belief that, as she must have resisted and conquered abundant temptation, she now inherits the blessing promised to him that overcometh.

. . . .

Christmas Day, 1861. At the very earliest dawn this morning the Government steamer 'Nemesis,' which had been instructed by the Moulmein Commissioner to look out for us, and help us up the river, entered it from a monthly voyage to the Andamans and south ports of Tenasserim; the captain being possibly made eager to return, not only by the desire of helping the Bishop, but also by the wish to eat his Christmas dinner on shore. The steamer hove to and received us all on board, and leaving poor Captain Hodge and his officers to follow as tide and wind would permit, we began a rapid voyage to Moulmein. As we went up, the scenery became really beautiful—far the most striking that we have seen since we left Calcutta. Both the Martaban (right) and Tenasserim (left) banks of the river are beautifully wooded, and the latter, upon which Moulmein stands, rises up steep from the water. In front of us were some precipitous limestone rocks, which emerge suddenly from the plain, and behind them the long range of mountains which stretch from the Himalayas to Singapore, through Burmah, Siam, and the Malay Peninsula. As a foreground we had the broad river, and presently the varied shipping of Moulmein, with Burmese ships and Chinese junks, gaily gilt and painted, and the European and American vessels dressed out with flags in honour of Christmas Day. A brighter inauguration of the festival I do not remember ever to have experienced. Arrived off the main wharf at 10.30, the captain hurried us on shore, and himself ordered a tikka ghari for us; at 10.50 we were in the vestry; and at 11, I amazed the unconscious Moulmeinians by appearing in full robes in church. . . .

Monday, December 30.—I breakfasted at the Society for the Promotion of the Gospel Mission, and afterwards began the grand business of the day—viz. a public examination and prize-giving at the mission school, at which I was to take the chair. Of the excellence of the school, and entire success of the public exhibition, there can be no doubt. Established only two years ago, it now numbers 270 boys, the great majority being Burmans, a few Chinese and Europeans, or semi-Europeans. The buildings are excellent; there is a capital schoolroom and dining-room, with tank for bathing, and various gymnastic appliances, given in great measure by the munificence of——. The sight of the assembled boys, or rather the whole examination scene, was of almost romantic interest. Nothing could exceed the picturesque variety of the bright colours of their pustos and turbans, sometimes relieved by the dark dress of an English boy, and the blue jacket and trousers of a Chinese. They were examined for about two and a-half hours in the Bible, geography, English and Burmese reading and arithmetic, and answered remarkably well. They showed their English writing, and sang sundry hymns, chants, and even an anthem, with one or two rounds or catches, certainly with harsh voices, but in capital time and tune. The curriculum is lower than in a good Bengal school, as may be expected, considering the recent origin of this; but all that is done is well and thoroughly done; and it is quite plain that if there is some discord between the managers, there is also a large outlay of zeal, ability, and enthusiasm in behalf of the school.

So much as to the education which we English are trying to give the Burmans; but it must not be forgotten that they have a national system of education of their own that all poongyies are bound to teach, and do teach, and that every Burman gentleman spends some time under them in a kyoung, just as an English gentleman goes to college. Moreover, as in every village there is a kyoung, every boy, gentle or simple, has gratuitous teaching offered to him. But as to the character of the education, I could not obtain anything like a unanimous opinion. Government officers generally, with some exceptions, said that every male in Burmah can read, write, and do a simple sum. Missionaries universally affirm that they often read very badly—so ill as hardly to be intelligible—and do not themselves understand what they are reading. All agree that, as soon as Burmese education gets beyond mere reading, it plunges into the grossest absurdities; as Buddhist cosmogony, geography, and astronomy exceed even the Brahminical form of those sciences in folly. The chief characteristic of the systems taught by Gotama's disciples is, that they delight in the most inconceivable numbers, durations of time, and extensions of space, which transcend all human powers of memory, and almost of imagination, but which are gravely set down in figures; while beings twelve miles high are of quite ordinary occurrence, and some personages measure 800 miles from eyebrow to eyebrow, and 19,200 miles from the elbow to the tip of the finger. The size and shape of the world and heavenly bodies are all minutely described in the most absurd fashion, the whole being placed under the sanction of religion, and resting on 'scriptural authority.' Hence no one questions the necessity of teaching the Burmese Western science, and therefore the English language as the introduction to it. Thus the mission school in Moulmein is universally popular among the Europeans, and, strange to say, the Burmese priests themselves seem to regard it with no jealousy, while the number of pupils is constantly increasing. Neither could I get a unanimous verdict about the moral character of the poongyies, though on the whole the evidence is favourable. They are very rarely indeed brought before a magistrate for any offence, and there seems no reason to suspect them, as a class, of violating their vow of continence; though to keep it is rendered less difficult than it might be from their power of renouncing the priesthood and marrying whenever they please. On the other hand, their scholars are said to be given to foul vices. The poongyies do not practise asceticism at all; they still keep to the rule of mendicancy, but receive such ample and handsome presents that this causes them no self-denial. I saw nothing of that vacant, half-idiotic expression of countenance which the Bishop of Victoria attributes to the Buddhist priests of China; and it is generally admitted that the Burmese priesthood are respected by the laity. My impression, on the whole, is that they are a fair average set of priests, doing nothing to raise their countrymen and turn Burmah into a real nation, nor particularly active or self-denying or learned, but maintaining a decent exterior and conversation, according to their lights. That the existence, rapid spread, and deeply-seated influence of Buddhism are phenomena most deserving of study and attention, was known to me beforehand, and certainly all that I have seen, heard, and read since I came to these parts has fully confirmed the impression. By his destruction of caste Gotama showed himself a real social reformer, and the good effects of his teaching are visible here in Burmah after he has been dead 2,400 years. The great moral defect of the system which he taught is its almost exclusive inculcation, or at least extravagant exaltation, of the passive virtues; its great spiritual weakness is the entire omission of a personal God, or any living and conscious Saviour.

. . . .

Calcutta, February 24.—At half-past 7 we landed at Lushington's Ghât, and thankfully and joyfully breakfasted in our own house. Thank God for all His mercies, through Jesus Christ. We return indeed with sad remembrances of the mournful events, public and private, which have marked the tour, and especially of one who went out with us but has not come back again. Yet I hope that it is a sign that I am getting more devoted to my Indian life and work. I am thoroughly glad to find myself again in Calcutta, and in the midst of its people, its duties, its interests, its refreshments. May God give me grace to use my increased familiarity with them for His glory, and for fulfilling the office and ministry to which He has called me.

The preceding extract summed up the record of events during four months' absence from Calcutta. Lady Canning and the Prince Consort had passed away. He who had gone forth in November and returned no more, was the Bishop's temporary domestic chaplain, the Rev. J. Rofe. He left Calcutta ill, in hopes that the sea voyage might arrest an acute attack of dysentery; but he grew worse, was ordered to England from Rangoon, and died before reaching India. Though young in years and in the service, he was full of promise in all ways, and especially as a preacher. His short career amply justified the mode of his appointment; for he had been nominated by St. John's, Cambridge, when Lord Stanley, as Secretary for India, placed two chaplaincies at the disposal of that College and of Trinity. A long succession of public and private losses was mournfully completed when, almost immediately after the return to Calcutta, Mr. Ritchie, the legal member of Council and Vice-Chancellor of the University, was called, through one of the sudden and rapid illnesses of India, from his life of goodness and usefulness and from a large circle of friends. Early in March the Bishop consecrated the cemetery in the Barrackpore gardens, where Lady Canning was buried. As the sun of a hot Indian day was setting, the ceremony was simply and quietly performed over the solitary tomb and circumjacent ground, henceforth to be set apart, as the petition for consecration declared, for the families of the Governor-Generals of India. When all was concluded, Lord Canning kindly greeted the few who were present: he turned to the Bishop and said, 'I think the ground is large enough to justify consecration,' and then walked away slowly and alone to the desolate house hard by.

Almost immediately afterwards the scene changed to State ceremonies and formalities, attending the retirement of one Viceroy and the reception of another; addresses were presented and replied to, and large parties were gathered each evening at Government House. 'On the 18th of March,' in the Bishop's words, 'the dignitaries of Church and State assembled at Government House, shook hands with Lord Canning, and then hastened to Prinsep's Ghât, where the Governor-General's barge was moored. Lord Canning came down to the river in state, got on board the barge, thence to the "Sunamucki," the flat which was to be towed by the steamer "Celerity" to Kedgeree, where the "Feroze" was waiting to convey him to Suez. There was a considerable crowd at the Ghât; a good English cheer was heard, and a very bad native imitation of it; the ships were dressed with flags, the guns boomed from the fort, hats and handkerchiefs were waved as the steamer began to move; and last, but not least, in the way of adding splendour to the scene, the great red sun was blazing away in its evening majesty, just about to sink below the horizon, and lighting up with-golden fire the waters of the Hooghly. So departed one of the most conscientious and upright of Indian Governors, and one who, more than any of his predecessors, has been tried by a combination of public anxiety and private sorrow.

CHAPTER VIII.

ANGLO-INDIAN EDUCATION—SCHOOLS IN CALCUTTA—EURASIANS—DEFICIENCY OF MEANS OF EDUCATION IN NORTH INDIA—THE BISHOP'S EFFORTS TO INCREASE IT—CONNEXION OF THE MOVEMENT WITH THE DAY OF THANKSGIVING—GENERAL PLAN OF EDUCATION SUBMITTED TO THE GOVERNMENT—MINUTE OF THE GOVERNOR-GENERAL—MEMORIAL SCHOOL AT SIMLA—SELECTION AND POSITION OF THE HEAD MASTER—SCHOOL PAYMENTS—CREATION OF A DIOCESAN BOARD OF EDUCATION.

IT may be well at this point to suspend the chronological order of events in order to narrate with continuity the earlier steps in that development of Anglo-Indian education which distinguished the sixth Episcopate of Calcutta. The time was not unfavourable for the attempt. The subject had attracted some attention before the Mutiny; its revival on the restoration of peace was likely to command sympathy and support, apart from the special interest which it derived from the proposal to connect the first fresh steps in the movement with the day of public thanksgiving. To the Bishop, personally, the work was congenial. It was the first that he made entirely his own, it was a link between his past life and the present, and supplied in a distant land an outward expression to that spirit of loyalty to the memory of his life's chief teacher, which prompted him on one occasion to write, 'Whenever a large school is governed on enlightened Christian principles, its masters will reverence the great man who in our day first showed such government to be possible. In whatever part of the world Englishmen are thinking, planning, working, struggling, conquering, there some of

Arnold's pupils, and the pupils of schools carried on in Arnold's spirit, will be found foremost in the battle of life.' In Calcutta, in 1859, there was no deficiency in the supply of English and Christian education; schools had become as numerous as the churches. Even in the self-enriching days of early English rule, the foundation and liberal endowment of the Free School, Doveton College, and Martinière, testified to a sense of responsibility on the part of the Government or of private individuals towards the forlorn semi-Asiatic children around. The Church, though in a depressed condition in those days, put forth efforts in the same direction, represented by St. James's School, due to Bishop Turner, and the High School, since known as St. Paul's School, founded after long delays and with great difficulty by Archdeacon Corrie, who may be called the forerunner of Bishop Cotton in the matter of Eurasian education. Other schools were added from time to time as the Eurasian population increased, through the exertions of English residents in the Presidency city.

The Bishop, either as visitor or as a member of the governing body of many of these institutions, necessarily came into contact with their working system. From his earliest occupation of the see, his advice on all points of school management was sought; his active personal interest was cordially welcomed; and the directors of one flourishing seminary, containing Church of England boys, but under strong Free Kirk influences, were not afraid to ask him to succeed Dr. Duff as its visitor. The standard of instruction in these schools was not lower than that of middle and national schools in England, and the religious influence they imparted was often deep and enduring; but their general system and training, carried on at a disadvantage in a debilitating climate, was not as a rule robust enough, physically or mentally, to invigorate feeble and inert Eurasians. These half-castes, forming a numerous and distinct class throughout India, have many grades of respectability amongst themselves, but, as a body, they have never secured any solid or profitable social position.

Possessing very little ambition or capacity for self-help, they have been outstripped in the race of life by pure Anglo-Saxon energy, while the almost heathen degradation into which the lowest class sometimes sinks has been overlooked by the fervour of missionary zeal directed exclusively to the natives. The presence of this race in its full proportions was unknown to the Bishop until he reached India, and in his first charge in reference to a chaplain's work, he thus spoke of it with all the force of a fresh and strong impression:—

. . . I imagined Calcutta to be a large city, occupied by European officials and merchants; with the soldiers in the fort and sailors by the river side, but with no poverty, strictly so-called, except among the natives, who would of course be cut off from us by barriers of language, religion, and caste. . . . I need not say that such anticipations have been entirely falsified by the reality; there can be no city where, from the strange mingling of inhabitants, of English and East Indians, descendants of the old Portuguese settlers or of the slaves whom they imported, of traders from all parts of the world, the Church's work is more imperative or more difficult. For, in dealing with these classes, the clergy have to encounter faults and peculiarities to which in England they are unaccustomed. From early marriages and frequent deaths, they find families in strange and unnatural relations; widows who have hardly ceased to be girls, step-mothers charged with the care of their husband's children before they are well able to take care of themselves. Many are the hindrances too which an Indian sun and an enervating climate interpose between us and the energetic discharge of our duties; but we know that our high calling must carry us through these and even greater difficulties, that we must never forget that the same voice which said to Saul 'Why persecutest thou me?' will say to any one of us, 'Why neglectest thou me?' if through indifference those for whom Christ has died are left in misery and ignorance.

In the North-West Provinces the demand for education was to some extent met by a good school at Lucknow, on the same foundation as the Martinière in Calcutta, and by one or two private schools in the hills, dependent on the life and health of the proprietor, and therefore possessing only a precarious tenure of existence. Eastern Bengal, Assam, and the Punjâb were unprovided with any middle-class education, except what the convents afforded for girls.* The quota of children contributed by each British station might be small, but the aggregate was constituting a whole generation deteriorating physically, and growing up in a state of deplorable ignorance and neglect. A project for establishing two schools in the Punjâb to meet the wants of that province had been started early in 1857. Like many other good works which flourish only in peaceful times, it fell prostrate before the great tempest of the Mutiny. On the Bishop's arrival in India, the scheme and some money collected for it were placed in his hands, and became the nucleus of a fresh and more extensive undertaking. His first step was to obtain statistics as to the extent of educational destitution, and his own conjectures on the subject were abundantly confirmed by the general testimony rendered by the officials of Northern India.

Such testimony came from Commissioners, Deputy-Commissioners, Directors of Public Instruction, and others whose work brought them constantly into contact with the heterogeneous elements of Anglo-Indian life. A few extracts from replies to the Bishop's inquiries are subjoined, as touching on distinct evils, for which it was hoped that a more organized education might be one remedial measure.

* The Lawrence Asylums at Sunawar and Murree, being intended exclusively for the children of English soldiers, cannot be included among the schools available for Anglo-Indians generally.

. . . At present for want of some institution like that now in contemplation, many children are being educated by Roman Catholics, not because their parents are hostile to our Church, but from the absolute dearth of schools conducted on Protestant principles, and at a moderate cost.

. . . .

. . .. As the seat of one of the local Governments, Allahabad has drawn to itself a miscellaneous homeless Christian population, whom the rebellion has rendered dependent on Government and on charity. Amongst these are widows and orphans of mixed blood, often speaking only Hindustani, and though nominally professing Christianity, so ignorant of its first principles as to be utterly unable to teach their children. Many cases have come under my notice in which whole families of children are utterly uninstructed, growing up in the city among Mahometans and idolaters, and learning all that is bad.

. . . .

. . . Knowing that such a school is the crying want of India, as far as the clerks and that class of society are concerned, I warmly second the Bishop's project myself, and hope that he may be able to establish a good school on the hills, to the support of which I shall gladly contribute. There are several clerks here with families. Their children are growing up. They can never hope to send them to England, and I do not know to what schools they can send them in India. They would be glad enough to send them if a good cheap school were established; but men of this class are unable to assist in carrying out such a project. As regards the rates of schooling, ten rupees per mensem should be the lowest, and thirty rupees per mensem the highest.

. . . .

. . . I am extremely happy to hear of the movement which the Bishop is making to establish good schools for the children of European parents. That the want is a real one is apparent to all who have had much opportunity of being acquainted with boys brought up in this country. I confidently hope and believe that his Lordship's efforts will be largely responded to. Certainly few objects can be more worthy of the support of all Christian residents in India, and well-wishers of the country.

Whilst so many direct efforts are made for Christianizing and improving the people around us, it is too often forgotten how enormously important, with reference to this work, is the indirect or unconscious influence of the resident Christian population, more powerful, perhaps—or rather, *certainly*—one way or other, than all the missionary labours in the country. And thus for the sake of those around us, as well as for our own, whilst we urgently need, for the present generation, a large increase to the spiritual agency at work among the adult Christian residents, both the present and succeeding generations, Christian and heathen, will, under the blessing of God, reap the benefit of such schools as his Lordship has proposed.

The following extract is from a letter from Sir Charles Trevelyan to the Bishop, which, though written at a later date in the course of the educational movement, indicates his sympathy with the principle which lay at the root of that movement.

. . . We owe a great duty to our countrymen and their offspring who are scattered over the face of this great country in a manner which makes them peculiarly dependent upon the combined action of their more fortunate Christian and English brethren, in all that relates to the upholding and improvement of their moral and intellectual condition. Without such combined and well-sustained action, the Christian minority inevitably becomes absorbed in character and manners in the Hindu and Mahometan majority, and that portion of the Christian community which is in most habitual intercourse with the natives, becomes a scandal and a stumbling-block in the way of their conversion. Example is better than precept; and although no means of instruction are to be neglected, I am of opinion that more can be done for the religious improvement of the natives by exhibiting Christianity to them in all its blessed practical fruits than by any amount of direct didactic teaching.

The Bishop's investigations were primarily made in behalf of neglected Eurasians; but with quick discernment, while still only imperfectly acquainted with India, he detected the further demand for education created by Europeans of the non-official class whom railroads and other commercial enterprise drew to the country in increasing numbers very shortly after the suppression of the Mutiny. The thought of future generations of English settlers growing up with no Christian education to redeem commercial life from its hardness and selfishness was appalling to him; 'he saw that if there could be one thing fatal to the spread of Christianity, it was the sight of a generation of unchristian, uncared-for Englishmen, springing up in the midst of a heathen population. He felt that, if there could be one thing subversive of our Indian empire, it was the spectacle of a generation of natives highly educated, and trained in missionary and Government schools, side by side with an increasing population of ignorant and degraded Europeans.'*

In the words of his earliest manifesto on this subject, 'he hoped that a sound physical, intellectual, and religious education might, under God's blessing, not only benefit children likely to remain permanently in the land, but might also, indirectly, tend to remove the barriers of prejudice and misunderstanding which separate the races to whom India is now a common country.'

The scheme, in general outline, by which the Bishop proposed to roll away this great reproach, to avert this great evil, from British India, contemplated (1) the establishment of a system of education, physically and intellectually vigorous, suited to the requirements of commercial life, or the army, or of the Calcutta University, with religious teaching in conformity with the Church of England, modified by a conscience clause for dissenters; (2) the foundation of a school or schools in the healthy heights of the Himalayas, in which such

* 'The late Bishop of Calcutta.' *Macmillan's Magazine*, December 1866.

education should be carried on with the best chance of success to the sickly and feeble children of the plains; (3) endowment funds to impart permanence and stability to new institutions.

The foundations of extended Anglo-Indian education were laid in the thanksgiving service for the restoration of peace on July 28, 1859. The offertories of that day were to be devoted to the establishment of the first hill school, with a chapel in which its memorial character should be recorded. Other forms of memorial had been thought of: a large and imposing church in the Upper Provinces was proposed; a general subscription for missions was at one time contemplated. The Bishop preferred to associate so solemn and peculiar an occasion with the principle which was the mainspring of his work in India, that missionary success was miserably hindered and delayed so long as European life in India was not elevated, purified, Christianised. His sermon in the Cathedral had for its text the latter part of Romans xii. 21; for its title, *the Christian victory over evil.* He recurred with thankfulness to a policy at once calm and just, which had prevailed over the din of passionate invective; to the heroic endurance and unshaken faith which had met the trials of one most mournful year; he dwelt upon the restoration of supremacy and security, as an overwhelming responsibility cast upon England; he exhorted all to be stirred by recollections of the past, by thankfulness for the present, by hopes for the future, by the memory of the brave and good who had gone, to live more truly by faith in Jesus Christ and to confess Him more plainly before all men; he pleaded for the work that day begun as one means to the great end of guiding professing Christians to make their Christianity a reality in a heathen land. The Church of England collections throughout the diocese amounted to nearly Rs. 35,000 (3,500*l.*). Of this sum 1,500*l.* formed the Cathedral offertory, 1,100*l.* being contributed by the Viceroy and Lady Canning.

From that day the work went on steadily, though slowly, after the manner of all things in India, and 1860 was far advanced before it passed from the stage of preliminary discussion to that of official correspondence. In August of that year the Bishop submitted a definite and comprehensive scheme to Government, comprising three objects; viz. the completion of the Memorial School which the Thanksgiving collections had started; the establishment eventually of similar institutions in other parts of the Himalayas; and schools in the plains to supplement, at a lower rate, those in the hills. The Viceroy's reply was dated October 29, 1860; and out of a long State paper, the following extracts are selected to show the position of Government towards the movement.

Extract from a Minute by the Governor-General in Council, dated October 29, 1860.

. . . .

3. If measures for educating the children of the fast increasing European and semi-European community are not promptly and vigorously encouraged and aided by the Government, we shall soon find ourselves embarrassed, in all large towns and stations, with a floating population of Indianized English, and Eurasians loosely brought up and exhibiting most of the worst qualities of both races. I can hardly imagine a more profitless, unmanageable community than one so composed. It might be long before it would grow to be what could be called a class dangerous to the State; but a very few years will make it, if neglected, a glaring reproach to the Government, and to the faith which it will, however ignorant and vicious, nominally profess. On the other hand, if cared for betimes, it will become a source of strength to British rule, and of usefulness to India.

. . . .

6 But the Government of India cannot undertake to provide education for either Europeans or Eurasians. It has

other things to do, and it would not do that work well: the missionaries cannot do it; their task lies with those who are not Christians: to wait till private enterprise shall supply schools of the kind required, will be to wait indefinitely. Therefore, the case seems to be exactly one in which a system such as has been proposed by the Metropolitan of India may fitly be encouraged, and liberally aided by the Government. It may be hoped that it will be supported by the British public in India and in England; but the principle of self-support should be carefully kept in view, to the fullest extent to which it may be attainable.

. . . .

10. The scheme proposed by the Bishop of Calcutta is, so far as it goes, a thoroughly sound and practicable one. I say, so far as it goes, because it does not profess to supply the wants of those Christian children who are not of the Church of England, and because, even as regards children who are of that Church, or whose parents are willing to accept for them the teaching of the Church of England, it will not, as I understand, put education within the reach of the poorer of them until those whose families are more at ease shall have been provided with it.

11. His Lordship contemplates the establishment in the plains of schools of a humbler and cheaper class than those in the hills; but it is proposed that the former shall be day-schools only, and that they shall be treated as a future and subsidiary step in the scheme.

12. I am strongly of opinion that schools in the plains should be provided as soon, at least, as schools in the hills. The expense of education at a hill-station must, at the lowest, be beyond the means of a vast number of Eurasian families settled in the plains. . . . The error into which we are most likely to fall, is that of constructing a scheme above the reach of those whom it is most necessary to benefit; and this being so, we ought not to begin to construct from the top only.

. . . .

15. As to the form and extent of the aid to be given by the Government of India, I recommend that, to the sum collected from private subscriptions, as a building and endowment fund,

an equal sum be added by the Government; that, from the opening of each school, it should receive a grant in aid to the fullest extent allowed by the rules; that if the school be built where ground is at the disposal of Government, the ground be given.

. . . .

18. I have said that the scheme does not profess to supply the wants of Christian children not of the Church of England. I did not mean to impute thereby any fault to the scheme. It is right and prudent that in this case nothing more should be aimed at than to meet those wants.

. . . .

20. The schools now contemplated are not charitable institutions; they are designed for the use of a class, the families composing which can supply abundance of scholars of the Church of England, and which, for the most part, would not willingly pay for the teaching of a school which was not essentially of that Church. I have no doubt that the attempt to accommodate such schools to the teaching of children of all Churches would lead to its failure.

. . . .

23. I have written of schools to be established in Bengal only, because the Bishop's scheme applies only to Bengal and the Himalayas. But if a scheme similar to that should be originated in Madras and Bombay, I recommend that the Government take the same part in supporting and executing it. I do not, however, think it advisable that such a scheme should emanate from the Government.

This memorable Minute, confirmed by the Secretary of State, renewed the charter of Anglo-Indian education. Such a charter already existed in the terms of the Educational Despatch of 1854. From many causes, this despatch, which now reads like a legacy from the East India Company to India, had remained all but a dead letter in respect of English Christian education. Some influential and guiding mind was needed to claim the aid it liberally offered, and to give to such aid the extensive development which the country urgently required. It seemed as though the instrument for the work were found when, in the providence of God, Bishop Cotton filled the see of Calcutta. The Government, having thus ratified the scheme in its general principles, took up the position of spectators, and only came forward prominently when grants of land or funds came under discussion. They gave the Bishop's project the dignity of an imperial question, and left him unfettered to work it out. A circular was issued to the clergy as the year closed, with a view to getting subscriptions, and shortly afterwards matters of detail connected with the Memorial School began to claim attention. Simla was selected as the locality, and Government solved the difficulty of a suitable site by making over the ground of a recently-abandoned cantonment at Jutog, four miles out of the station. The Bishop, far away himself, put local business into the hands of a temporary committee, consisting of the Rev. Julian Robinson, chaplain of Simla, and some other residents. With the former, and with officials of the Public Works Department, he carried on for months a brisk correspondence, and was always deeply sensible of the efficient aid they rendered to the undertaking while still in its infancy. After many vexatious delays, the Bishop could write, in 1862, that subscriptions and the grant in aid from Government amounted to 120,000 rupees (12,000*l.*), part of which he hoped to reserve as the nucleus of an endowment, the rest being available for the purchase or erection of buildings and for heavy preliminary expenses. He was ready also with a head-master, negotiations having been concluded with the Rev. S. Slater. Mr. Slater was at that time in England, but much of his former life had been spent in India and in posts connected with education. His position was a point of great importance with the Bishop, who characteristically refused to entrust the school to the permanent council of ex-officio and elected

Governors, until he had installed its first head on his own terms. It was not one of the least benefits conferred by him on education in India, that in the school which he founded, and intended to be a model as to constitution for other schools, he put the head-master in his right place, made him autocratic and independent, and left him to stand or fall by his own merits.

The rate of the school payments was a matter very difficult of adjustment. Many deprecated the naming of a figure which might prove too high for slenderly-paid clerks to meet. The Bishop, on the other hand, dreaded future insolvency, if the popularity of the school should decrease; and he was ready for a sharp contest to prevent an undertaking, intended to be national and permanent, from becoming at any future time a disastrous failure financially. All inquiries had led him to believe that the North-West Provinces and the Punjâb could supply boys foı one hill school at a charge of thirty to thirty-five rupees per month. He looked forward to a gradual growth of nominations and scholarships to ease the school fees in some cases; but the material fabric and an endowment fund being secured by subscriptions, he strenuously advocated the self-supporting principle as that which should be maintained to meet ordinary current expenses. 'When the buildings are complete,' he once wrote, 'when more boys are admitted, when more money comes in, it will, I hope, be possible to reduce the terms. Meantime there could be no surer way of securing the failure of the school, than by starting with terms that would involve it in debt.' This fundamental principle which he desired to enforce was in the end adopted, though the actual figure originally named was subsequently changed, when the numbers in the school made it possible to reduce the terms from thirty-five to twenty-eight rupees monthly. The annexed letter will show how strongly he felt and wrote on a point which occasioned more serious diversity of opinion than any other connected with the school.

To the Rev. Julian Robinson.

June 18, 1862.

I am very much obliged to you for your long and carefully considered letter of the 2nd inst.

. . . .

With regard to the terms, though I know that your local knowledge and Captain ——'s is far greater than mine, yet I venture to oppose to it my own disagreeable experience of a very similar case, which leads me to dread, almost above all things, the mistake of placing terms too low. Marlborough was started under the most promising auspices, under the patronage of the archbishop of the province and bishop of the diocese; with a committee consisting partly of peers and privy-councillors, partly of practical men of business; with a large capital subscribed, an admirable site, and a great prestige of popularity. The council fixed the terms at a rate which would not pay, trusting to future development and the liberality of the English public. The result was a series of embarrassments, from which, towards the end of my mastership, the first prospect of deliverance dawned upon the school. I know how great was the odium excited by raising the terms, how disheartening all the pecuniary troubles were to the masters, how near the school was to actual dissolution. Now, it seems to me plain that the terms which you propose will involve the future authorities of Jutog in these same miseries and dangers. I am quite prepared to admit that the policy of my former letter sacrificed the present too much to the future; excuse me if I think that the policy of your letter sacrifices the future altogether to the present. The subscribed capital will vanish in educating one generation. Nor do I see any reason for such very low terms. You say that we shall, if we announce them, be 'deluged' with applications. But a deluge is not wanted as long as we can only accommodate forty boys, and a moderate shower is all that will be of any use to us. . . . I am sure you will excuse me for mentioning one caution very necessary in the present aspect of affairs. We have to deal with public money, and there is always a tendency to regard this as less sacred than private funds, because no individual is specially injured by prodigality. I hope, therefore, that it will not be forgotten that the sum which we possess is exceedingly small to carry out a design which is, as you say, to be a real benefit to India, and therefore that the strictest economy will be used in applying it. I am sure that, unless this is remembered, the scheme now so promising will be a disastrous failure.

'The first boy joined the school on March 16, 1863. Next day three more came.'* In these words of unadorned simplicity, the first start of the Simla school stands recorded for the benefit of posterity. Long before the year closed, the number reached thirty-five, being as many as the limited space would accommodate. To meet the applications for admission, which continued throughout 1863, more dormitories were shortly added. Early in 1864 the premises at Jutog took in sixty-five boys—the utmost number they could receive—and the pupils in the school continued at this figure until the locality of the school was changed, as will be mentioned in the right place.

Thus, by the opening of the Memorial School, one stage in the Bishop's extensive undertaking was reached, with no greater deviation from the original plan than a commencement on a smaller scale as regarded extent of buildings and number of boys than the Bishop at first contemplated. The account here given of the undertaking can yield no adequate conception of the amount of time and correspondence and patience which its prosecution demanded. It must suffice to say that it was entirely incorporated in the rest of the Bishop's work: wherever visitations led him, the concerns of the hill schools travelled also; every detail respecting their foundation and organization was referred to him, and it was often from remote parts of the diocese that he had to decide on points continually arising. Whatever other matters pressed for attention, there was always in the background the heavy care of an important

* Account of the Foundation of Bishop's School, Simla, published under authority of the Governors, December 1869.

work being in hand, for which he was personally responsible, and of which, with God's blessing, he must be the directing, controlling, and animating mind. He knew that if he flagged, others would flag; subscriptions would languish, the public would become impatient. There was much help; none greater than that rendered by Archdeacon Pratt, who threw himself cordially into the project, and worked, thought, and pleaded for it unceasingly, and eventually became chief treasurer and auditor of complicated accounts. But there were deep anxieties likewise. Under these the Bishop's calm temperament, and trustful rather than buoyant or sanguine faith, upheld him, while the confidence ripening year by year in his judgment and practical power upheld others.

Meantime the circular to the clergy, issued at the end of 1860, had called forth not only subscriptions for the Simla school, but a great increase of activity in the cause of education generally. Many chaplains in the plains were making efforts to establish local day-schools, and thus to create a fresh link between themselves and their flocks. The difficulty of starting these lowland schools with a sound organization and with some prospect of stability hastened, in 1863, the creation of a Board of Education. This Board thus became a fresh nucleus of diocesan work, and proposed to help schools founded in accordance with its rules by grants in aid towards buildings or towards the outfits and passage-money of teachers from England. It undertook likewise to sketch curricula of study and procure school-books, and, in short, to be what all work in India imperatively needs, a fixed centre for operations widely scattered, and liable, from fluctuations in society, to be feebly sustained. As a good omen of future success, it happened that the treasury of the new Board opened with a windfall in the shape of 12,000 rupees (1,200*l.*), the gift of a private person. This benefactor—repeating, in modern phraseology, the hope expressed, in his will in

1800, by the queer old Anglo-Indian Frenchman, General Claude Martin, 'that Government or the Supreme Courts will devise the best institution for the public good, as I am little able to make any arrangements'—entrusted a sum to the Supreme Government of 1863 for churches and schools in the three Presidencies. Lord Elgin, who was then viceroy, granted the Bishop's application for the moiety of the Bengal share, in behalf of the Diocesan Board of Education, as the prospective foster-parent of many schools.

This educational sketch may fitly close with a letter to a chaplain. It is one out of many to which the planting of small schools gave rise, and has also an interest because it indicates that in these lowland day-schools, where the chaplain and the parents come in close proximity, occasional difficulties arose to disturb what was otherwise the singularly smooth course, theologically, of the whole movement.

To a Chaplain.

October 1862.

. . . .

With regard to your troubles from persons not belonging to our Church, I was aware that you had experienced some, from a paragraph in the 'Friend of India,' and I will shortly state my opinion upon the chief of them, which I understand to be your rule that all children attending your day-school should also attend your Sunday-school. I do not claim any right to interfere in the matter, for though the 'Friend' calls your school 'the Bishop's School,' I do not see exactly on what grounds he gives it that title, except that I am considered generally to have given an impulse to the duty of educating poor Europeans and Eurasians. Perhaps, too, as I lately commented on the alleged want of Church of England instruction for Church of England children in your school, you will be surprised to hear that I do not altogether sympathise with your rule, which is now called in question. But I do not see any inconsistency between my opinions on these two points.

Ever since I took up the question of educating the poorer classes of Christians in India, I have desired that the Church of England should act on one principle in regard to it. All persons, whether belonging to the Church or not, should be invited into its schools, on the condition of joining in daily prayers, and receiving scriptural instruction from English churchmen. But the peculiar formulas of our Church were not to be pressed on those whose parents objected to their learning them. This is obviously implied in paragraph 12 of my Pastoral about the Simla school, dated Christmas Eve, 1860, has since been expressly stated by me in answer to a letter of inquiry from another chaplain, and is the principle adopted by the new Madras Board of Education, in a paper just issued by them, and in which my statement or letter above mentioned is quoted as an authority. It has also been affirmed by yourself in your letter just received.

The question is, therefore, whether the compulsory attendance at the Sunday-school is or is not in accordance with this principle. Now I think that you would clearly violate it, if you were to compel all the children of your school to attend the English church on Sunday, instead of allowing the children of Presbyterians to attend the Presbyterian service. And if so, it seems to follow that the children should be free during the whole of Sunday to receive such religious instruction as their parents choose, or to receive none at all on that day, except such as they receive from their attendance at service. If parents like to have their children at home all Sunday (except during church-time), I think that they ought to be encouraged rather than otherwise, on grounds wholly independent of the religious question. We cannot too strongly encourage the ties of family and love of home, and I never have thought Sunday-schools desirable in an ideal state of things; only good because many homes are unhappily irreligious, and many children are unable to receive instruction on any other day.

I quite feel the force of the argument that you are naturally more anxious about the spiritual than the secular teaching, and that you therefore desire to have all your flock around you on Sunday, in order to speak to them on the most important of all subjects. But doubtless your religious instruction is not limited to Sunday: you probably have some scriptural reading or teaching daily; and if, therefore, you were to take those opportunities of setting Christian truth before all your scholars, and to reserve Sunday chiefly for the explanation of the formularies of our Church, excusing, therefore, Presbyterians from attendance, you would, I think, fully carry out the principles which I have laid down as most desirable under the actual circumstances of India.

In writing this, I beg you to believe that I only write as an adviser, for I must again repeat that, in the present circumstances of the school, I do not see that I have any right to interfere in its management; and, besides, I speak with diffidence, from being but imperfectly acquainted with the local circumstances of the case. Undoubtedly I should think the establishment of a rival Presbyterian school at —— a great evil, and I believe that the real influence of our own Church is strengthened by securing to itself the secular and scriptural instruction of all Christians, far more than by any other plan of operations. But I can truly say that, apart from all such considerations, I attach very great weight to the other argument which I have mentioned—the great importance of leaving Sunday as free as possible for the unrestrained intercourse of parents and children; giving, of course, all opportunities of religious instruction on that day to those who desire it, and therefore keeping up the Sunday-school for voluntary attendants.

CHAPTER IX.

DARJEELING—SUGGESTIONS TO THE S. P. G. SOCIETY—THE ADDITIONAL CLERGY SOCIETY—ADVICE TO THE COMMITTEE—DIFFICULTIES CONNECTED WITH THE USE OF THE BURIAL SERVICE—COMMUNICATIONS WITH GOVERNMENT ON THE SUBJECT—THE ENJOYMENT OF HIMALAYAN SCENERY—LETTERS—VISITATION OF THE CENTRAL PROVINCES—DIFFICULTIES IN TRAVELLING—THE BISHOP'S JOURNAL LETTERS—CONSECRATION OF THE MEMORIAL WELL AT CAWNPORE—AGRA—LETTER TO GOVERNMENT ON ECCLESIASTICAL AFFAIRS IN THE CENTRAL PROVINCES.

THE hot months of 1862, from April to November, were spent at Darjeeling, in the Eastern Himalayas—the most beautiful, the most rainy, and in some respects the least civilised of hill-stations. Once more settled for a time, the Bishop as usual took in hand some definite branches of business, in order to deal with them more in detail than was possible among the distractions of travelling. He had at this time much at heart an extension of the Propagation Society's work in the north-east of India. Reference has already been made to his desire that the Moulmein and Singapore missions should be maintained with vigour; but these only formed integral portions of a larger scheme for bringing within the range of the Society's operations an immense extent of territory peculiarly destitute of pastoral care, and therefore lying open to any missionary body that would *go up and possess the land.* He lived to witness only a very partial accomplishment of his wishes; but his letters on this occasion, as on others when similar objects were in view, remain as records of the method and arrangement which pervaded his programmes of evangelistic work, and of the clear principle that prompted all his suggestions or recommendations to the parent Societies. The scope of the particular extension urged on the Propagation Society in 1862 will be seen by the following extract from a letter to the Calcutta Secretary.

. . . I need hardly repeat at any length the arguments which I have all along used, and with which the Calcutta Committee fully coincided, for the adoption of Tezpore by the Society. These were the high character and devoted piety of Mr. ——, the existence of a church and mission buildings, the local interest in the mission, very real but needing support from the change of officials in Assam, the promising beginning already made, the nucleus of converts and schools, and above all the neighbourhood of hill tribes free from caste, to whom I am most anxious that the Gospel should be preached; while the example of the Karens and of Chota Nagpore makes me hopeful that under God's blessing the results may be great. To these I will now add that the adoption of Tezpore would form part of a much larger scheme which has gradually been forming in my mind from the experience of recent visitation tours. . . .

I am very anxious that the Society for Promoting the Gospel should gradually extend its operations systematically through the north-east and east parts of the diocese, including East Bengal, Assam, the hill tribes on the frontier, Burmah, and so down to Singapore. The Church of England is in all ways, whether we consider mission work or the ministry to Europeans, poorly and insufficiently represented there. The territory is an immense one, and can of course only be slowly and gradually occupied. But the hope that it may be occupied by a connected chain of missionary posts is not chimerical, for the Church Missionary Society has a series of missions stretching at no very long intervals in a north-west direction from Calcutta to Peshawur and Mooltan. Just so then let the Society for Promoting the Gospel extend itself from Calcutta to Tezpore to the north, and Singapore to the south.

The field would be of varied and hopeful interest. In Bengal, Burmah, and the Straits, the Society is already to a certain extent planted. It would have to deal with several great cities, many tribes in various degrees of civilisation, wholly free from the trammels of caste, Hindus, Buddhists, Malays, and Chinese.

In thus proposing a rough division of the diocese between the two Church Societies, I do not mean at all to suspend operations in those more westerly cities where the Propagation Society already has missions. Calcutta and its neighbourhood, Delhi, Cawnpore, Patna, and Roorkee must be carefully maintained and fostered, and will afford full occupation for students of Bishop's College, and others who may be versed in the Urdu, Hindi, and Bengali languages.

But with obvious and legitimate exceptions such as these, I should like to see the Propagation Society established in real force in the east of the diocese, and the attention of young men from St. Augustine's, or other missionaries who may be sent out from England, mainly turned to that field of action. And I think that the multiplication of clergy in that direction might hasten the division of the diocese, and probably suggest a better division than has hitherto been proposed.

Besides thus administering a stimulant to missionary work, the Bishop entered also upon a warm and protracted correspondence with the committee of the Additional Clergy Society in Calcutta. This Society was established by Bishop Wilson in 1843, to provide pastors for small stations for which no chaplain could be spared, and whose residents, frequently to some extent of the non-official class, were willing to bear a portion of the expense. The Society had been well supported by voluntary contributions, and possessed substantial endowment and reserve funds; the East Indian Railway Company had evinced a ready willingness to assist in the maintenance of ministers supplied through its agency for their European employés; and as relieving charges upon the public revenue for pastoral objects, it was always favourably recognised and liberally assisted by Government. But at the end of nineteen years the auxiliary clergy in the diocese numbered only eight: the Society was becoming unpopular, and its energies appeared crushed under a weight of rigid rules and traditions at a time when the disproportion between the demand for clergy and their supply was increasingly manifest and was becoming a more constant source of anxiety to the Bishop. Sometimes, when on visitation in remote districts, he came across some Government servant of a lower grade destitute even of a Bible, and with literally nothing but the remembrance of Christianity between himself and the heathenism on all sides of him. More frequently he encountered small European and Eurasian communities dependent for all Christian ordinances on the rare visits of a distant chaplain; and of these, many were willing and anxious to help in obtaining a resident minister, if the means for doing so were facilitated. In order to meet these varied needs, the Bishop's great desire was to multiply a staff of pastors, who, combining zeal with activity, would fix their head quarters at small stations, look upon a whole district as their parish, make light of palanquin journeys of fifty or a hundred miles, and itinerate regularly through a large extent of country, so that no Christian family should be left long without the services of the Church, nor solitary tea and indigo planters be abandoned to a careless, and sometimes worse than careless, life without the 'word in season' of counsel or warning. The Additional Clergy Society, in theory the agency available for supplying such ministers, had practically become almost stationary in its operations, and was disposed to draw a hard and fast line in two directions. It disclaimed any obligation to take up a station where from the number of Government servants a chaplain ought to be employed, and it imposed conditions in the matter of building a parsonage-house, too heavy to be fulfilled by congregations which were neither large nor rich. When the Bishop vigorously took in hand, in 1862, the inert condition of the Society, some half-dozen stations were illustrating one or other of these obstacles to the conclusion of arrangements for the supply of a minister, and conspicuous among them was Port Blair, the mid-ocean British settlement in the Andamans. The committee were vigorous and firm in their defence, pleading the rules of their constitution and their responsibilities in the dispensing of public funds. The Bishop assailed no fundamental principles. The point of his objection was a want of elasticity in the rules framed on those principles, which took no account of the extremely varied circumstances of Indian stations, so apparent to himself in constantly passing through the country. He contended energetically that while the committee took credit for prudence and caution, many Christian communities were, in the terse phrase used many years before by Bishop Middleton, 'virtually excommunicated;' he expressed his own strong conviction that increased activity on the part of the Society would be met by a corresponding increase of goodwill and of subscriptions on the part of the public; he entreated them to rise to the emergency and to exchange a policy of mere stability for one of more expansion and usefulness. Especially he combated the old traditionary notion, so fatal to all vitality within the Church, of looking to Government only for the supply of all the spiritual necessities of Christians in India. 'There can be no doubt,' he wrote during this correspondence, 'that Government is very liberal to the Indian Church; compared with any colonial Church, our revenues and advantages are very great: I think therefore that the members of the Church are bound to extend its operations and act with Government in every possible way, and certainly to respond readily to openings for additional usefulness which are offered to them. I can only re-state the opinion expressed in my former letter, that we should go hand in hand with

Government in supplying the spiritual wants of stations, whether mainly occupied by Government servants or not, all over the diocese.'

Some compromise and a relaxation of rules to a certain extent were in the course of time proposed and gladly accepted by the Bishop, to whom such serious divergence of opinion on matters of great practical importance was utterly repugnant. The following letter marks a more pacific stage in the controversy:—

To the Archdeacon.

August 1862.

I think that the sub-committee of the Additional Clergy Society yield a good deal, and I am not prepared to say that I wish them *practically* to yield more—certainly not at present. Only I should like the committee when they meet on September 9 to take one undeniable principle into account. It is troublesome, and in the end useless, especially considering the constitution of our Society, to hamper ourselves with restrictions—such, I mean, as that the committee's contribution to the parsonage-house shall not exceed a certain fixed sum. Any sum distinctly named is sure to be a source of divided opinion in the committee, and will be liable to perpetual alteration, according as the liberal party or the opponents of liberal contributions have a majority in the councils of the Society. Hence I urge the wording of the rule in some more general manner, *e.g.* 'that where a station satisfies the committee that the cost of a house is beyond its means, the committee shall be at liberty to make on certain conditions such a money grant towards its purchase or erection as shall appear reasonable.' The committee will thus be left unfettered to act upon its own discretion in dealing with the varied circumstances under which applications for the clergy of the Society are made. I always think that the standing rules ought to lay down essential principles, and that wide liberty within these principles should be allowed to the executive. Surely this is a lesson to be learnt from the fate of college and university statutes as enacted by our ancestors.

Peaceful words were substantiated by helpful deeds, for the Bishop's first act on obtaining an instalment of increased liberality on the part of the Society, was to write to the five stations which he was labouring to get at once occupied, urging a renewal of negotiations on the improved basis, and offering in each case a donation of 10*l.* to help to erect the inevitable parsonage-house. Under rules thus modified, and with the increased grant in aid, which on the Bishop's application Government consented to give conditionally upon the Society's extending its work, some few stations were speedily supplied with pastors. A year later the obstacle to further progress lay not in the rules or the funds of the Society, but in the difficulty of finding men for a branch of work which was not endowed with the attractions of the missionary calling or with financial advantages equal to that of the State chaplain. With a view to increasing the small pecuniary value of the service, a successful appeal was subsequently made to Government for a grant towards the establishment of retiring pensions. A body of referees in England kindly undertook to interest themselves in the matter, and efforts to procure ministers on the Society's terms were so far successful that the Bishop could write in 1864, that 'he *was thankful to say* the work of the secretary had become very laborious through the extension of the Society's operations.' The employment of twenty clergy in 1866 formed the best justification of his remonstrance with the Society in 1862.

The Bishop was at this time also engaged in a troublesome correspondence with Government on a case in which the admitted difficulties of the Burial Service were aggravated by being brought into relation with the different discipline of the Romish and Protestant Churches. A Roman Catholic soldier died of delirium tremens, and was in consequence refused burial by his priest. The commanding officer then applied to the Protestant chaplain in conformity with an Order of Council promulgated by Lord Dalhousie, which enjoins Christian burial in all cases except those specified in the rubric, even though refused by a Catholic priest. The chaplain also refused, on the ground that, as a Protestant, he could not read the Burial Service over a Roman Catholic; and the funeral was therefore conducted by an officer. The case went before the military authorities, and was by them forwarded to the Bishop, the latter step being equivalent to a demand for episcopal censure on a recalcitrant member of the clergy. Meantime the chaplain had himself reported the affair to the Bishop, mentioning in his statement that excessive drinking was the cause of death. The Bishop was thus placed at a disadvantage in taking cognisance of the case, since it contained an important feature which did not appear in the representation originally made to the secular authorities. To refuse censure would be to lend apparent sanction to the violation of a Government Order held to be based on the law of England; to administer it would be doing violence to his sympathy with the scruples felt by very many of the clergy against the indiscriminate performance of the Burial Service, scruples to which he deemed that the case under consideration imparted unusual force. He wrote his views at great length to the supreme Government. As a summary of them, a letter in a similar strain to a private correspondent is annexed, from which it will be seen that he approached the subject on its theological rather than its legal side :—

To Archdeacon Pratt.

Darjeeling, June 1862.

I send you a correspondence which stirs up the difficult question of the burial of Romanists by Protestant chaplains. My opinion, as at present advised, is as follows :—I never will support a clergyman generally in refusing Christian burial to a Romanist or a Protestant dissenter. I consider that the English Church has defined the essence of Baptism to consist of the use of water in the name of the Trinity, and by that I interpret the rubric of the Burial Service and Canon sixty-eight. It is true there are objections to this view and anomalies in it, but not equal to the anomalies and objections on the other side. I consider therefore that Mr. ——, by resting his refusal on the fact that the man was a Romanist, has done but scant justice to his case. But when we come to the case of a Romanist to whom his own pastor has refused burial, matters wear a different aspect. For if the literal interpretation of the rubric is pressed, we may reply that the framers of the rubric did not contemplate the toleration of Romish priests at all; that if the Government appoint Roman Catholic chaplains they ought to accept Roman Catholic discipline, according to which, apparently, a priest may grant or withhold any religious office at his pleasure; that it is hard, absolutely to prevent the Protestant chaplain from interfering in any way with the Roman Catholic soldier in his lifetime, and yet to compel him to give him Christian burial when his authorised pastor says that he does not deserve it; that the ceremony is quite unmeaning, for we do not suppose that it benefits the dead, while of the living the Romanists despise and ridicule it, the Protestants ought to be shocked by it; and that such a rule degrades the Church of England, both in the eyes of its own members and of dissenters. Moreover, I am inclined to admit Mr. ——'s argument that the Order of December 21, 1855, violates that of November 10, 1815. On the other hand, it cannot be denied that there are difficulties. I suppose that in England the minister of a parish would be compelled to bury a Roman Catholic refused burial on moral grounds by his priest. From the arbitrary power claimed by the priests, the refusal to bury a Romanist might arise from other than moral causes. I can see only two possible solutions: cancel Lord Dalhousie's order, accept the Roman Catholic discipline as well as the priesthood, and determine that when the priest refuses burial no service shall be performed unless the chaplain chooses to do it; or retain the order, but let there be an understanding that every such case is to stand on its own merits, and be dealt with by the bishop. He could then inquire if the chaplain declined to bury on any other ground than the simple fact of Romanism, and deal with it accordingly.

The Government, in replying, discussed the matter as lying entirely under the jurisdiction, not of the Church, but of the State. They maintained that the Order in Council of 1855, making Christian burial the privilege of all Christians, whether Romanists or Protestants, was based on English ecclesiastical law, and could not therefore be set aside or cancelled; they intimated that the Bishop's view was erroneous, and that in his proposed lenient admonition to the chaplain he insufficiently recognised the gravity of the offence.

The Bishop returned to the charge, and changing his position from moral to legal ground, he questioned the correctness of the assumption that the canon law, stated to be the foundation on which the enactment of 1855 rested, was, in the case under discussion, binding on Indian chaplains, being rather, as he conceived, connected with the parochial system at home. With this doubt strongly on his mind, he requested that the Advocate-General's opinion might be taken with especial reference to the 68th Canon. This was done, and judgment was given in favour of the Government. The Advocate-General laid down that the right of all Christians to receive Christian burial, except in the cases specified in the rubric, rested on English ecclesiastical law, no excommunication being valid, except that pronounced by a competent court. He also gave his opinion that, far from the 68th Canon being inapplicable to the circumstances of India, it was impossible for a Government chaplain with no rights in the soil or surface of the station burial-ground to claim exemption from its obligations. The matter then dropped; Government were content with an assertion of the law, and the Bishop limited his warning and censure four months after the occurrence to the theological rather than the moral scruples of the chaplain. The contest, indeed, if pursued still further, could have had no decisive result, for a door of complete retreat from the infliction of any penalty on the offender remained open for the Bishop through his inability to hold a Consistory Court. Before leaving England he had been legally advised never to attempt the process, the machinery for doing so being imperfect in India. As far as the case was suffered to proceed, it must be admitted that the Bishop lost it. It remains on record as a testimony to his strong sympathy with clergy compelled to use the Burial Service under all circumstances. The issue of the contest was, however, from the first doubtful, and sympathy with moral scruples seemed for the moment to weaken the judgment of one who was usually peculiarly sagacious in discerning how far the Church could assert her independence without risk of collision with the numerous State enactments which constitute both her guardians and her checks in India. Through the legal decision that was given, the principle in the English Church of mercy rather than sacrifice was vindicated; but a striking illustration was also supplied of ecclesiastical difficulties in the diocese of Calcutta. It was in reference to another troublesome matter in some respects akin to the one here noticed, that the Bishop once wrote: 'I cannot help being amused at the truly Erastian aspect of these cases, which are an undeniable testimony to the connexion between Church and State, being generally a jumble of some particular Canon, the Anglican view of the doctrines in the Prayer Book, the Queen's regulations for the army, and the status of an Indian chaplain in a military station.'

The ecclesiastical matters touched upon in the preceding pages, and others of a like kind, though not demanding a separate notice, tended in a greater or a less degree to disturb the tranquillity which was generally one chief feature of residence in the hills. Amidst the vexations and annoyances to which they gave rise, the Bishop turned to outward nature as a great source of solace and relief. In striking contrast to the disquietude engendered by the divergence or even collision of opinions which marked the considerations of some ecclesiastical or official questions of the time, the soothing yet inspiring influences of scenery full of variety and beauty were always at hand, and made themselves powerfully felt. Wearied within his study by the perplexities of harassing business, the Bishop had only to pass into the verandah to draw refreshment from the sight of mountain ranges lining the horizon on every side and crowned by Kunchinjinga, which, rearing its enormous snow-clad mass at a distance of less than fifty miles, seemed but a stone's throw from the eye. This great monarch among mountains was too often veiled by the mists belonging to a region of heavy and protracted rainfall; still its near presence brought a sense of repose and solemnity overpowering the turmoil of life's cares, and long periods of 'dim eclipse' served to throw into more grand relief clear and radiant mornings when every height glistened in the early sun, or nights of almost unearthly beauty, when all nature was illuminated by the light cast from that huge breast of snow bathed in the golden moonlight of India. The matchless grandeur of the Himalayas became a source of deeper enjoyment to the Bishop year by year. The 'gigantic rampart of eternal snow' was quite a passion with him: every fine view of it seemed to stir the depths of his soul. His near sight debarred him from observing or studying nature except in her large and grand forms, and beyond a keen interest in physical geography he was quite devoid of scientific tastes. But the imaginative side of his character had been quickened from early boyhood by intellectual culture, by much travelling, and by his intuitive sense of all that was really beautiful either in nature or in art; he thus seemed to have been receiving a life-long preparation for the high and pure enjoyments imparted to his later years by scenery of unsurpassed sublimity and on a scale truly colossal. During temporary residences in the hills he seldom went out for walk or ride without binoculars in his pocket, that no view near or remote might be lost to him. He never, however, rested content with a vague and confused impression of what was around him; the mental order and arrangement for which he was conspicuous were brought to bear on the points of difference in all the snow-cooled settlements which break the yoke of a tropical climate from Assam to the north-west frontier. Each peculiar type of scenery in these places to which visitations successively led him; the marked varieties of outline and sweep in the great mountain chains; above all, some grand peak towering from the midst of a near or distant range, were clearly pictured on his mind and noted on 'the tablets of his memory.' Mont Blanc and Monte Rosa had been cherished and familiar names in past years; no less familiar to him in India became Kunchinjinga and Nundidevi, Gungutri and Jumnutri, and the far-away Pir Punjal.

In the journal extract that follows, and in the first of the annexed letters, his pen writes eloquently on the many natural attractions of Darjeeling, and on the grandness of one great panoramic view within easy reach of the station.

Extract from Journal.

June 1862.—There is no doubt of the extreme beauty of this place. At first the weather was detestable (almost ceaseless rain) and we saw nothing. But after a while matters got brighter, and on Monday morning, April 21, we saw for the first time the great view of the snowy range. It is magnificent, the finest that I have seen, occupying one-half of the horizon and rising on each side in a series of steps as it were from the nearer hills on the west and east up to the peak of Kunchinjinga, which is exactly in front of our windows, forty-five miles distant, and is more than 28,000 feet high. It is finer than the view of Nundidevi and its comrades from Almora, because there the different peaks rise separately from behind the near range, while here it is all one grand continuous sweep from Nepal to Bhotan. Nor are other attractions wanting to Darjeeling besides this glorious but seldom-revealed prospect. The green and wooded hills are most picturesquely ranged in three main branches, with deep khuds at the bottom of each.

There are not so many sweeps of mountain, range behind range, as at Simla, but the foliage is richer and more diversified, the grass more continuous and English in its appearance, and the views more concentrated and regular. Next to the snowy range, the most characteristic beauty of the place consists in the number and variety of orchids, air plants, and epiphytes which clothe the trees in the khuds; gorgeous bunches of purple, yellow, and white, such as would be the glory of an English hothouse, are brought up by coolies. Tree ferns too grow, though very inferior to those of Penang: and the trees are generally draped and festooned with creepers. A favourite short walk is round the church hill, or to the top of it, where is a ruined Buddhist monastery, and from which is obtained a glorious view of the snow, with a nearer panorama of the green hills dotted with the white bungalows of the station.

. . . .

From a sketch of a tour into the interior, printed privately by Captain W. S. Sherwill, and from Hooker on the Sikkim Himalayas, I find that Darjeeling clearly means 'place of holiness,' for dorje is a sceptre, as I said, but it is the sceptre borne by a lama, the sceptre of the priesthood; and that this is its special sense in reference to Darjeeling, and not either a regal sceptre or lightning (which it also means, the sceptre being like forked lightning), seems proved by the existence of the ruined lamaserai on the top of Darjeeling hill. Kunchinjinga is Thibetan; kon=snow, chin=covered, jing=coequal or coeval, and hence Kunchinjinga, the 'covered with eternal snow.' Its height is said to be 28,177 feet. Moreover, I find that the name Mount Everest, bestowed upon the great peak in Nepal, which measurements have shown to be the highest known mountain in the world, is somewhat justified by the doubt entertained whether it is exactly identical with the peak called by the Nepalese, Deodanga, a name which, signifying 'God's hill,' is quite sublime, if its connexion with really the highest mountain could be proved.

. . . .

To his Son.

Darjeeling, Whit-Monday, June 9, 1862.

. . . And now I have two requests to make of you, one very easy of accomplishment, the other more difficult.

1. *Do take care that we have a school list of this Midsummer and of all future half-years as long as you are at Rugby.* It would help us much more to realise your progress if we saw your place every half-year.

2. I wish that, all being well, you would make a real effort to get out at Christmas. I always used to hate quarter promotions, as sources of a quarter's idleness and hinderers of a half-year's prize. So pray get out of the line of them if you can, unless indeed you could get out in October, in which case I will accept another quarter promotion thankfully for the sake of your more rapid advancement. But I shall be satisfied with Christmas, and this I earnestly desire. I should think that you would find the 'Phœnissæ' hard, and I never take much pleasure in Euripides, though he is now and then pathetic. At present, however, I suppose that you will be more occupied with the observation of cæsuras and constructions than with the woes of Jocasta or frenzy of the two brothers.

Well, having now delivered myself of my thoughts on Rugby and your duties there, I return to the Himalayas, and proceed to describe a most active frisk which your father took this morning, and which showed, I think, extraordinary juvenility in a person whom the 'Burmese Times' described as 'our venerable Metropolitan.' We have lately had a most unexpected burst of quite glorious weather, at a time of year when we should naturally look for a deluge of rain. About six miles from Darjeeling is a mountain called Senchal, nearly 9,000 feet high, the plateau at the top being occupied by barracks, but above this rises a conical hill to the height of some 400 feet, from which we heard that there is a wonderful view. Unsuccessful attempts had already been made to see it. At last, yesterday we thought that during this halcyon weather a great effort must be made. So this morning I was up before five, saw that the sky was fair, and at half-past five was on the back of Sir John, accompanied by Aunty on Scarecrow, and Mr. Mayne on Snowdrop (a perfectly black steed). The road first ascends the high hill of Jallapahar, then descends it to a meeting of mountains called the Saddle, then ascends Senchal through a magnificent forest, and the desired cone is at the end of the Senchal parade-ground.

Off we set, and so safe do I feel on Sir John, that though I never did and never can take kindly to riding, or think it other than a necessary bore in these regions, yet I actually cantered and trotted along with the rest of the party, who are all thorough equestrians, and even ventured to career at full tilt along the parade-ground in full view of her Majesty's 38th, just emerging from their beds. At the foot of the cone we dismounted, and had a steep climb along a slippery path through jungle, and were wholly breathless when we reached the top at 6.55, exactly 1 hour and 25 minutes after quitting the house, which, considering the precipitous nature of part of the road, I consider was a great triumph, at least for me. Most splendidly were we rewarded. The view is of enormous extent and almost unequalled grandeur. It is a complete panorama. Beginning from the north-west, we saw the Singalela hills, steep, black, craggy, snowless, from 10,000 to 12,000 feet high, which divide us from Nepal. Above them rose three conical hill-tops, perfectly white, of which the central is Mount Everest, the highest mountain in the world. Proceeding towards the north, another group of Nepal snow mountains appeared above the Singalela. Due north of us rose our own beloved Kunchinjinga, second of earthly mountains, just forty-five miles from us, of course to us infinitely grander than Everest, since we saw all its snow and part even of its unsnowed side, as there was no Singalela to hide it. Kunchinjinga is in Sikkim and Thibet. Then came a long line of snowy peaks and ridges, stretching away east through Bhotan, including one about which the Lepchas, a tribe in Sikkim, have a tradition resembling the resting of the ark on Ararat, for to this hill, Tendong by name, they say that the only two human beings who escaped the deluge retreated. The hills gradually vanished from our view, and below them we saw the valley of Assam. Southwards, a great line of hills called the Mahaldaram Range, projected from Senchal, forming the watershed which divides the waters which flow into the Brahmaputra from those which seek the Ganges. This terminated with Kursiong, and then sank into the Terai and the plain of Bengal, which lay stretched before us in apparently infinite expansion, diversified by jungle and river courses. The rest of the view to the west was filled up by Senchal hill and its barracks, Jallapahar, and Darjeeling, which seemed to unite itself to the Singalela. We saw fine flourishing English settlements, Darjeeling, Jallapahar, Senchal, Kursiong, and Hopetown, and, strange to say, no native town, a sign that the motto 'Ex Oriente Lux' is now reversed, and that Europe is giving back its light to Asia. But only conceive the wonderful nature of the view, the hundreds of miles which were stretched before us of Nepal, Sikkim, perhaps Thibet, Bhotan, Assam, Bengal; the two highest mountains in the world, and a host of others higher than any Andes or Alps. I regard the sight as one of the noteworthy moments of my life; and the whole party shared my enthusiasm. My next desire is to bring your mother up, which I hope may be accomplished, all being well, by going up overnight and sleeping. But it can hardly be yet, as this fine weather must cease, I should think, at once.

We went down a little more leisurely but not lazily. Just as I was descending on our house I heard nine strike and the prayer bell ring, and about five minutes after nine I was dismounting. Your aunt rode into the compound just before me, and it was so pleasant as I was turning in to hear Ursula's ringing voice shrieking out, 'Well, Aunty, have you brought papa back?' . . .

To Godfrey Lushington, Esq.

July 1862.

. . . There are matters of great interest in your letter touching the present position of the English Church, and of religious belief in England. Into these I will not enter at length, partly because I have not yet read your father's judgments, which are of importance in discussing the former, partly for the reason that I gave at the beginning of this letter, that after a morning spent in writing a sermon and two practical essay-like letters to Government on soldiers' institutes and chaplains' allowances, I really need recreation in writing to an old friend rather than a yet more abstruse disquisition. I will only express my grief that one characteristic of our present *jeunesse dorée* is an entire want of positive conviction, not only on minor matters, such as the authorship of the second epistle of St. Peter, but on matters of primary and essential importance, whether spiritual, such as the reality of revelation, or practical, such as the way in which people should be educated. And this absence of positive conviction seems to me a most formidable evil, and fatal to all true greatness and usefulness. I cannot but think that a person who suffers from it is, to a great degree, responsible for it, though some of the blame rests with —— and others of various schools, and, alas! partly with myself, so far as I have failed to influence anyone in a right, or have influenced them in a wrong direction. I think also that the youth of the present day are given to speak sneeringly, unfairly, and almost profanely about creeds and articles, without having really examined the subject. With these observations against one party in the present disputes, I turn from a sad and wearying subject, conscious, however, that there is plenty to be said against other parties also.

We are happily all well and enjoying ourselves in a place of glorious walks and rides. Your goddaughter both rides a pony and learns a hymn; and, as old Dr. Wordsworth used to say to us in Trinity Chapel when he praised or quoted his brother's poems, 'false delicacy shall not prevent me from' telling you that she is a most charming little girl, and a constant source of delight both to her mother and to me.

. . .

To the Rev. J. N. Simpkinson.

Darjeeling, 1862.

Again, as in 1860, we spend our summer in the Himalayas, but this time nearer to their eastern than their western extremity. Darjeeling is a small British station hemmed in between the three semi-barbarous states of Nepal, Sikkim, and Bhotan. . . . Our chief human beings are Lepchas, said to be the aborigines of these mountains: fair in complexion, wholly beardless, with long hair twisted in tails down their backs, so that it is hard to distinguish men and women, Buddhists after a sort, filthily dirty, not dainty in their food, inasmuch as they eat cats and snakes, and performing their devotions by the singular process of twisting round and round small brass cylinders on a wooden handle, each revolution being a prayer. Our English neighbours are, for the most part, devoted to tea, not to drinking it, but to planting it, for which purpose the lower slopes of the hills are being rapidly cleared of jungle, and the produce of the plantations is exceedingly good. The speculation is said already to answer very well, and if the natives of India generally become a tea-drinking race, it will be exceedingly lucrative for many years. Great numbers of people are crowding into the business, and the result must be to make India more of a colony than it has been, but I trust that we shall not be altogether Yankeeised or Australianised. The existence of this class makes me exceedingly anxious to push education in India, and I am happy to say there is some prospect of my Simla school coming into operation next year.

As to English theology and Church, I cannot throw much light upon them from Hindustan, and I shrink from writing about them more than is needful, as many of their aspects are now distressing and exciting. The Lushington judgment, I should think, would be a discouragement to prosecutors, for if it closes some doors it opens some wider than ever, and those the very doors through which persons are now most eager to press. But I invite you to write on such subjects *ad libitum*, for one of my chief distresses here is that I have no one with whom I can freely interchange opinions on matters which require full consideration. An able theologian in the diocese, with whom I once made an attempt to talk, seemed so shocked and horrified at the bare mention of 'Essays and Reviews,' that I found it useless to continue the subject. At the same time I cannot deny that the horror excited by the book in the minds of really pious men who know Greek and Hebrew, and are therefore capable of forming opinions, is a strong condemnation of the reckless manner in which that unfortunate work was pitchforked into the world. . . .

To his Son.

. . . . We hope that the next mail will bring us some account of your confirmation. It certainly would have been a great happiness and interest to me to have laid hands on you myself, but I should not have thought it right for a matter of personal feeling to delay your right to receive the Holy Communion, and perhaps so throw your preparation into the charge of some far less efficient teacher than those who have conducted it at Rugby. I wish that you would read over my three Confirmation addresses at the end of my Marlborough Sermons, and also a sermon called 'Outward and Inward Changes,' (p. 97). They contain all that I should have been able to say to you on the subject. Now I can only commit you in very earnest prayer to God's blessing, and I trust that you feel that you are not only called to a thoughtful life of duty, but also specially to a *Christian* life, that is, to the belief that in all temptations and troubles you must seek help and comfort from the Lord Jesus Christ. I hope that you, my own darling, will have grace to see that a life of duty and a Christian life are in truth inseparably connected; and when I speak of doing your duty in Christ's strength, of course you understand that this strength is to be obtained by habits of prayer. To begin these habits steadily, and to persevere in them through the changes and chances of life, should be the chief lesson which you have learned from your Confirmation and from sharing the Body and Blood of the Saviour who died for you. May God bless you, dearest, and give you wisdom to think of these things while you are yet young, and before habits are formed which hinder good intentions from coming to maturity. One of the pleasantest parts of dealing with boys used to be that the work with them was *hopeful.*

To the Rev. Dr. Stanley.

Darjeeling, September 9, 1862.

I need hardly say that I have often thought of you with true sympathy as I heard of the trials and interests and enjoyments of the last months. With regard to the sorest of the first of these I could not write to you at the time, not knowing where or when a letter might reach you, but I sent a few lines to your sister, not forgetting that she was suffering like yourself. I repeat now what I said to her, that, during that agitating year 1858, when I was whirled about between hopes, fears, excitements, sorrows, new duties, new scenes, and new interests, your mother's brave words and affectionate sympathy had no small share in strengthening me for the work which God had given me to do. . . .

I have myself, as you will have heard, had to bear my part in some melancholy duties this year, though I was away at the worst time, when Lady Canning died, and the funeral was performed by the archdeacon. But as soon as I returned to Calcutta, Lord Canning wrote me a note to ask me to come to him, and we had a long interview in his dreary-looking sitting-room at Government House, with its rows of cupboards and red boxes, and white unornamented walls. He began to speak of her, but could not go on, and fell back sobbing in his chair. Considering that his manner was chiefly marked by a cold and stern dignity, I never saw before a stronger instance of the heart asserting its absolute supremacy. . . . Next day he wrote me a note to thank me for having written to him at the time of his loss, and said that he had found it impossible to do so when I was with him. A week afterwards I went down to him at Barrackpore (where he spent every Sunday after her death), and consecrated the new cemetery which he has constructed in the park 'for such Governors-General of India and their families as shall die in India,' and which is almost as lovely from its situation and foliage as the Protestant burial-ground at Lisbon.

'Three days after this I was sitting opposite to him at the entertainment which he gave in the marble hall at Government House to welcome Lord Elgin; three days more and I received his parting shake of the hand, and accompanied him to the steamer, which was to take him down the Hooghly; four months more and I read the mournful telegram announcing that he too was gone. He was a very mirror of honour and integrity, the pattern, as far as I could see, of a just, high-minded, unselfish, and fearless statesman; kind too and considerate for others, *a terror to evil doers, but a praise to them that do well*, without any personal bias or any ill feeling against those who had opposed him. . . . Lord Elgin has shown that he does not prefer popularity to duty by rejecting a numerously signed and clamorous petition for the pardon of an unhappy European soldier, sentenced to death for shooting a native. The man was no doubt greatly to be pitied, but could not have been pardoned if the principle of equal justice between the dominant and subject races was to be maintained.

To a Director of Public Instruction.

1862.

. . . I have read the 'Friend of India's' remarks on figs and thistles, and as I have not on former occasions agreed with his criticisms on your department, so neither do I now. I am particularly glad of your assurance that the normal schools of which he speaks with such interest are really efficient institutions, and I am thankful that you regard the new place as 'moderately hopeful.' I need hardly add that I wish it all success.

I do not, however, quite agree with your general remarks either as to the evangelisation or education of a country. The view that the former must descend from the higher to the lower orders is hardly borne out by history. Certainly it was not the case with the first preaching of the Gospel, as we may gather from the Acts, and are distinctly informed by St. Paul. The Reformation, too, took a strong hold on the common people generally before it reached the nobles.

In Henry VIII.'s time the middle and lower classes were reading the Bible and being burnt for heresy while the king was still denouncing Luther, and but for the conjugal necessities of Henry, and political necessities of Elizabeth, the English Reformation might probably have been postponed till the time of Charles I. The only facts in your favour, as it seems to me, are the conversion of the northern nations at the fall of the Roman empire, and these are apparent rather than real, because they were brought about not by the influence of the upper classes of each race, but by the will of its king or leader, and after all they were scarcely conversions in the strict sense of the term. As to education, if the upper classes of India were Christian, I should then believe that it would penetrate by a legitimate development from above to below, because there would be in them a new moral and spiritual principle which would make them anxious to impart to others the benefits which they have themselves received. But as it is, while they are fettered by caste, by pride, by selfishness, I do not see any prospect of this, and so I think that the duty of educating the masses falls upon us English, as having at once the power, as being the dominant race, and having, or being bound to have, the will, from possessing the Gospel.

Nor do I think that the consideration of the number of rupees per mensem to which education admits a man need enter into the question. If, as I have always been told by Long, Banerjea, and others of the missionary clergy, the people do already flock in considerable numbers to the schools of the Gurus, surely by training the Gurus we shall almost force them by the laws of nature to improve the instruction which they give, for no one who possesses a right knowledge of facts would (without some strong personal motive) deliberately impart a false view of them. No professing teacher who has learned how to teach would abstain from teaching properly according to what he has learned. We certainly do not want for the Bengal peasantry the standard of the first Examination in Arts any more than we expect the English peasantry to pass the Little Go, but we do want to make a beginning of national education for the masses in India as we have done at home; and if the normal schools are well looked after, I cannot see why the scheme which you are now starting should be barren of happy results.

In November 1862, the Bishop left the hills for the Central Provinces. On the banks of the Ganges, he met his old friend and chaplain T. H. Burn, who had just arrived from England with a fresh instalment of health, again to be exhausted in an Indian climate before two years were over. But the pleasure, though short-lived, was great to the Bishop. In his journal he wrote: 'Restoration to Burn is indeed a cause of the most abundant joy, and I thank God for it as a real comfort and help to me in my many needs and frequent perplexities.' The Central Provinces, the latest political division of British India, had been formed through the amalgamation of the province of Nagpore, annexed by Lord Dalhousie, with the Saugor and Nerbudda territories. In 1862 an exceedingly vigorous local government was rapidly establishing order and security; civilisation was slowly following; but ecclesiastical arrangements were in a peculiarly crude and incomplete state. The presence of chaplains from the Presidency of Madras at Kamptee and Seetabuldee, the two chief stations in Nagpore, was an anomaly and source of confusion. Scarcely a church was to be seen except the fine modern one at Seetabuldee, and numerous communities of Europeans, connected either with Government or the Great Central Railway, then in course of construction, were springing up, with a very inadequate supply of pastors. The whole region presented an unbroken soil for the Additional Clergy Society, whose labours the Bishop had so recently been stimulating. The Bishop's route lay through Benares, Mirzapore, and Jubbulpore, to Nagpore, where Christmas was spent. Thence, in due time, he reached the Nerbudda river, and, crossing it, passed through Holkar's territories, to visit the remote stations of Mhow and Indore, and finally, by way of Saugor, Jhansi, and Gwalior, regained the North-West Provinces and the land of railways, which seemed like life from the dead after a protracted experience of jungle travels.

For this final section of the primary visitation presented throughout its course a sample of the same primitiveness of arrangements and barrenness of comforts for travellers which still linger in many parts of our Eastern empire, recalling the general aspect of British India within the memory of the present generation, and reminding the Indian bishop of these days that, amidst all the alleviations of his exile, he has occasionally to encounter on a small scale the loneliness, difficulties, and privations which fell to the daily lot of Heber, in his almost exploring journies in search of a few scattered clergy. As far as Nagpore the Bishop's progress was tolerably smooth, but from that point the toils of the tour fairly set in. The distances to be traversed were far less formidable from length than from the lack of resources for speedy locomotion in a region just roused from the semi-barbarous stagnation of native rule. During many days and nights doolies (a lighter sort of palanquin) formed the chief homes of the Bishop, the chaplain, and the doctor. Occasionally the way lay simply through jungle. Tigers—happily unseen—were constantly heard of, and at one mountain ghât or pass, haunted by a man-eater, a whole village turned out with blazing torches as an escort through the perilous defile. Much help was afforded both in British territory and in the small native States, and tended to mitigate, though it could not avert, the annoyances arising from execrable roads, from the want of the usual staging bungalows, and the paucity of palanquin-bearers. Not much room, however, was left for the external adjuncts of a dignified position when comforts were few, when the commissariat supplies were scanty and precarious, or when for a night journey the capacious side of an elephant was accepted as a satisfactory exchange for the dusty doolie. But the kind welcome that awaited the travellers at every halt on their way, and the evident comfort and pleasure derived from

Christian ordinances by those for whom their celebration was only a casual privilege, were the best reward for fatigue and discomforts. A visitation extending over three years and a half had served to reveal the needs of Christians sprinkled over the vast area of Northern India. Its completion left the Bishop with the conviction profoundly impressed on his mind that, amidst all the varied work of the diocese, no duty lay more prominently in his path, or was more entirely a personal responsibility, than that of providing the helps and ministrations of the Church for scattered sheep in the wilderness, in order that, as he once wrote, 'no one should be allowed to feel himself neglected or forgotten.'

This visitation journey was all but the only one which I did not share with my husband. The following extracts from an unbroken succession of letters addressed to myself will afford a sketch of his life between December 1862 and February 1863:—

Benares, November 1862.

. . . I have seen again here ——, and cannot but think that a man of such eminence wastes his time by spending three hours a day in teaching geography to the first class of a mission girls' school, while he might be the most effective of native pastors and evangelists. He is, I suppose, more or less the victim of irresolution, arising from the convulsive effects of a change of creed on a man of such deep feelings and subtle intellect, like the many now in England who are kept from a life of real usefulness by over-speculation on unsolved and insoluble difficulties. When I see all these missionaries and their wives at work, wholly given up to the endeavour to promote the highest welfare of these Hindus, I feel that here is one great branch of the true evidence to the reality of Christianity, and to many of its doctrines, such as conversion, the difference between the Church and the world, spiritual holiness and self-sacrifice. The other branch is the New Testament itself, the life of Our Lord and the moral teaching of His apostles. So we come to Coleridge's conclusions, that the two proofs of the truth of the Gospel are Christianity and Christendom. And against these proofs F. Newman and Theodore Parker and Comte thunder in vain.

Jubbulpore, December 11, 1862.

. . . At Maihor my opinion of native princes was raised. Soon after breakfast, a present of fruits, sugar, and sweetmeats arrived from the rajah, with a request that he might be allowed to visit us. As we had admired the picturesque fortress and city, we expressed our desire to visit him at his palace. This is situated at the end of the long street of the city, which is walled with towers, like one of the Punjab towns. It is a regular castle, which we enter through gates covered like porcupines with projecting iron points. Within them is a very pretty garden and shrubbery, thickly planted with orange trees, whose bright fruit glittered in the sun as they did at Seville in 1850. The actual abode of the rajah is a picturesque old house in the middle of this shrubbery, with a court in the middle, enclosed with two rows of colonnades of genuine old Hindu architecture, elaborately carved and ornamented.

After the rajah's officials had lionized us over the house, we were placed on three chairs, and presently his highness entered and occupied the fourth. Unlike his toothless neighbour at Nagode, he is a handsome manly boy of nineteen, attired in his shooting costume—a brocaded jacket, white trousers, and a cap of red and gold bordered with fur. He has been educated for two years in the Government College at Agra, where he was taught by Charles Pearson; but now, wearying of the society of Government professors, and preferring that of leopards and tigers—one of which he has lately shot—he has returned to his ancestral home. He spoke English fairly, and though he showed a little of the usual Hindu curiosity by some personal questions, yet there was so much grace and dignity about him, that he interested and pleased us. But, alas! though he looks promising now, his future can hardly be a bright one, since there is no one near to improve or elevate him, and his life must, one fears, be an old story of self-indulgence and superstition. In such a case, I think shooting a most profitable occupation.

Seoni, December 18, 1862.

. . . On Tuesday morning we quitted Jubbulpore. I shall not describe all the petty vexations of the journey, but confine myself to the speech with which an overseer of the road dismissed us just at sunset one day:—'You will not find, right rev. sir (*sic*), that the travelling is very convenient. There are four or five tigers between this and Seoni, the road is very bad and full of rocks, the bearers are very weak and can scarcely carry at all, and the dâk bungalows have no roof.' However, here we are, not having encountered any tigers, nor any rocks absolutely impassable; but the other two parts of his prediction were true enough, for though we have been here seven hours, some very important luggage is still behind, and we are lodged in the office of the electric telegraph, the dâk bungalow being in the state which he described. The air is fresh and cold, as we are 2,500 feet above the sea. If you look at the map which I gave you, you will see that the Vindhya range pushes out branches called the Khyonne and Deva Hills, and Seoni is on the tableland formed by the latter. We have ascended two passes since we left Jubbulpore, which itself is raised far above the valley of the Ganges by the Kuttra Pass, which we ascended on the day after leaving Mirzapore. These hills form a watershed, and we have crossed rivers flowing respectively to the two seas—on Tuesday the Nerbudda, which runs into the Indian Ocean; and this morning the Wyngunga, which is in fact the main stream of the Godavery, and reaches the Bay of Bengal.

Hoshungabad, December 31, 1862.

. . . . On this last day of the year I write to you with a thankful remembrance of its many mercies. Thank God for our continued health and strength, for the child's satisfactory growth in all ways, for the return of Burn, for definite progress about the Simla school, for the impetus given to some diocesan work, for many family blessings in England. The sorrows that have most troubled me are the public deaths which India has this year had to mourn, and the undeniable growth of the difficulties connected with Scripture and Church questions, which continue without any opposition, or solution, or attempt at rectification with which I can thoroughly sympathise. A true Christian prophet is sorely needed. May God raise up among us those who are fitted to strengthen the bulwarks of His Church!

Panibijwara, Sunday, January 4, 1863.

In my last letter I did not tell you all my cause for disquietude; for Burn, having imprudently walked too long in the morning after the sun was up, and then found no more wholesome breakfast than a cup of hermetical soup, seemed to be fast becoming quite ill: happily, however, the arrival of some tea from the railway sahib refreshed him, and a moderate repast of cold chicken so restored him that he started at night much as usual. I went to call on the railway sahib to thank him for his tea, and found that he was overflowing with desires of hospitality, which he made good by sending to the tent, unknown to me, a huge hamper of provisions, so that a day which began with famine ended with feasting. I was greatly amused with the conversation of the tehsildar (a village functionary) who accompanied me to the sahib's house, followed, of course, by an immense tag-rag from the town. His whole mind and that of all his attendants seemed set on the glorification of Seoni, which is a very clean town, of exceedingly pretty architecture. This they assured me was the only genuine Seoni, the other Seoni through which we had passed being a spurious, imperfect Seoni; the one Seoni Chipara, the other Choti Seoni. Their Seoni was the centre of wealth and enlightenment; here the railway would come, here was a school, here the bunniahs (grain-factors) were men of fabulous riches. They even seemed offended at my supposition that tigers were rare in these parts. On the contrary, they assured me they abounded; only last week an inhabitant had been devoured; I was quite mistaken in supposing that they could produce fewer tigers than their neighbours. We left this paradise at night, and on the morning of January 2 reached a civil station of recent origin called Hurda. The next day a carriage drawn by trotting bullocks conveyed us to the bank of the Nerbudda, which we crossed in boats, and then took to our doolies, which had been sent on over night. We were now in the territories of Holkar, and after travelling for nine miles came to Khattaganu. Here we found that the Maharajah Holkar had despatched ten sowars to escort us through his dominions—wild-looking horsemen, quite unlike those in English territory, dressed in white, with red turbans, bare legs, and slippers, and each carrying a spear ten feet long. Under their protection we trusted ourselves at nightfall to the unknown men and perils of this foreign State; but hitherto we have found the people even more civil and attentive than in our own provinces. We reached this place at eight this morning, and here the far-reaching forethought of an English official had caused a tent to be pitched, so we are spending our Sunday in quiet and comfort, though in a complete jungle and with no other outward reminder of religion except, alas! the tomtoming and horn-blowing from a Hindu temple. We have, however, just had a short service, with a sermon of Archer Butler's—eloquent and argumentative, but somewhat abstruse. The jungle wherein our tent is pitched absolutely swarms with doves and peacocks.

Saugor, January 22.

. . . . At 8 A.M. yesterday we were passing through the city and beneath the frowning walls of the fort of Saugor. We are now again in British territory, having re-entered the Central Provinces, and certainly the cleanliness and good repair of Saugor is a pleasing contrast to the frouziness and ruined condition of Bhilsa, Garripoor, and other cities under native rule. To-day the fort has been visited, which rises above the lake and commands the city. There is a fine extent of wall with picturesque round towers, but the walls are said to be weak and incapable of standing a siege. Here in 1857–58, all the residents of Saugor, three hundred in number, including the present chaplain and his family, were shut up for six months, for fear of the Gwalior contingent, till they were relieved by Sir Hugh Rose. The true way of realising to oneself what the mutiny was in its daily bearing on all English life in India, over and above its more conspicuous horrors, such as the events of Cawnpore, Lucknow, and Delhi, is to open one's ears to little facts narrated by persons who have gone through such a period. Thus, said ——, the only accommodation allowed during these six months for himself, wife, and five children, for all purposes, day and night, except that they dined, when it did not rain, under a tree, was half a small verandah, in which they were separated from the occupants of the other half by a purdah or curtain.

Lullutpore, January 28.

. . . . We left Saugor two days ago, and have quitted the Central Provinces and are again in the familiar regions of the North-West. The country is all stones and rocks, and as ugly as need be. The news from Peshawur is very sad. French, who is the life and soul of the Derajât mission, is prostrate with jungle-fever, and, though recovering, must go to England immediately; and poor Roger Clark, the younger brother of the Clarks with whom we breakfasted at that old Mussulman's house in the city, has died of dysentery. He was only twenty-eight, and this loss, coming after that of Tuting, is not only a great blow to the work in those distant regions, but it makes one seriously anxious about the safety of Peshawur for European life—a fact hard to realise when one remembers that glorious girdle of mountains which encircles it. You recollect how seriously it has been visited twice since we came to India by cholera. I should think it very likely that the city is unsafe from defective drainage and Eastern dirt, and that the missionaries ought never to sleep there, which I fancy they have been doing. I have written about this to Robert Clark, who is now absolutely alone, where a few months ago there were four missionaries, all apparently in strong health. When these events occur I sometimes reproach myself for not thinking more about the missionaries; for my daily administration and routine duties bring me into such far closer personal contact with the chaplains, that I am apt to forget the other division of my clergy; and yet there is no body of men more worthy of all thought and sympathy.

Cawnpore, February 11, 1863.

. . . . At 5.30 P.M. to-day came off the grand ceremonial. On the whole I think that it may be pronounced successful. There were very few hitches—none of importance—the scene was undoubtedly most picturesque, and the service solemn. The assemblage was august: the Viceroy and Vice-queen, with all their attendants; Sir Hugh Rose and his Staff; Wingfield and his Court from Oudh; all the chief authorities from Lucknow, Allahabad, Futtehpore; the Archdeacon and nine other clergy, and finally some thousand soldiers—the 46th, some troops of the Bays, and a battery of artillery. Thornhill having conducted Lord Elgin to the steps of the monument, I advanced with the Archdeacon, Burn, and Stamper to its foot, and Thornhill read the memorial signed by the Viceroy, 'in the name of the Christian subjects of Her Majesty Queen Victoria.' The chant then began, first round the interior of the monument, then across to the larger burial-ground, where are the two original crosses, and then to the smaller one. The service then proceeded as usual, Psalm xc. being sung. After this the troops were all moved up as close to the steps as possible without pressing too much on the other people, and then, with the Viceroy on one side and the Archdeacon on the other, I delivered my harangue. I confess that at first my heart beat fast and I was quite nervous; for the spectacle was very impressive, the audience numerous and critical, and, with nothing whatever to help or prompt or remind me of what I had determined to say, I entertained some fear of breaking down. In truth, the few first sentences actually spoken were more or less different from those which I had arranged. But at last I warmed with the sight and the subject, forgot bystanders, went on with fluency and no embarrassment, keeping very faithfully but not slavishly to the address which I had prepared. The prayers which followed were read by Stamper, and then came the hymn and blessing. People seemed pleased, and some very much impressed by the solemnity. The change which has come over Cawnpore is wonderful. From a howling wilderness it has become an attractive and pretty station. Christ Church, now the property of the Society for the Propagation of the Gospel, rises with its handsome tower from the midst of a well-arranged compound, and, above all, sixty acres of land in the middle of the station have become a garden full of shrubs, flowers, and grass-plots, which are kept green even here by copious irrigation from the canal. In the middle of this garden the ground has been raised so as to form a mound, and on the top of this mound is the

Gothic octagon screen surrounding the fatal well and the scene of the ceremony just described. The screen and covering of the well are of stone, most beautifully carved, the whole of the details being due to the taste and untiring care of Mr. Thornhill, who has been here for the last three months superintending the erection of the monument. A vine-leaf and passion-flower ornament which runs round the screen inside is of especial delicacy and finish, and of a truthfulness which would satisfy Ruskin. The graves of the soldiers and others who died when Cawnpore was reoccupied by Sir Colin Campbell, at the end of 1857, are in two groups, each enclosed by a very tasteful iron railing, and planted with shrubs. The two original crosses, the spontaneous and most interesting memorials of the soldiers themselves, are carefully preserved and included in the larger of these two inclosed burial-grounds. Of the whole arrangement I can say, what very seldom can be said of modern artistic efforts, that I should not wish a single detail altered in any way. The essentially Christian character of the Cawnpore memorials is most satisfactory, and it is fortunate that the persons who, publicly or privately, were most concerned in their erection were Colonel Yule, Thornhill, and Lady Canning. They might have been as ugly and paganlike as the building at Jhansi.

Agra, February 18.

. . . . I began this Ash Wednesday by service at St. Paul's Church, which is now finished, the spire having been one of the works on which the sufferers from the famine were employed. But for the absurd stumpiness of the chancel, it would be one of the best churches in India. In the afternoon the Archdeacon and I went over to Secundra, which in 1859 was a mass of ruins, but now is completely restored: church, mission buildings, and Christian village all built up again; printing press in full operation, and about three hundred children clothed, taught, and rescued from starvation. Indeed, fifty girls recently admitted were rescued from something more than starvation. Who shall say that such labours of love are not the proper work of missionaries? The city of Agra is surrounded at this time by a belt of green from the young wheat and other crops, which cuts it off from the brown desolation of the surrounding country. In driving about to-day we have greatly admired the pains taken to improve as well as to restore Agra since the Mutiny; the good roads, well watered and planted, the very pretty new gardens, the ornamental railing which encloses the compounds of the public buildings, the general look of comfort, neatness, and elegance which pervades the English station, the pains taken to keep in repair and beauty all the glorious buildings of the native city. On the whole, I consider that Agra, with all these secular attractions, the memory of Akbar and its other historical associations, its four Church of England churches, its vigorous mission, extensive Orphanage, and flourishing Missionary College, is the brightest jewel in the mitre of Calcutta. I have also accomplished my great desire of a state visit to the Begum of Bhopal, who received us in her Durbar tent, Major Hutchinson doing the honours. She is a most pleasant-looking old lady, chatty, with a clearly marked sense of humour, and signs of a firm will tempered by kindness and good nature. Her attire was not beautiful; red pantaloons dotted with gold spangles, a tunic of blue and silver, and a shabby old brown cloak thrown over her shoulders to keep all together. She had no head-dress, but her hair was tugged violently backwards and gathered into a dishevelled top-knot. I believe that Lady Canning gave her a handsome head-dress as a hint to improve this part of her costume, but in vain. She displayed her star of India, her present just received from Lord Elgin, and finally her grand-daughter, a child of four years old, named Sultan Jehann Begum, who, when first introduced, whined and whimpered at the sight of strangers, but was coaxed by her grandmother into displaying her accomplishments, which consist mainly in a knowledge of English as abstracted from the most singular spelling-book I ever saw. I promised to send her one more advanced. I then complimented the old lady on the state of her territory, the beauty of her city, and the excellence of her sowars, with which I had been provided in passing through her dominions. She presented me with a nuzzer of five gold mohurs, which she earnestly requested me to bestow on some charitable object, and I told her I should give them to the Simla school, and so departed.

Shortly after the return to Calcutta the time came round for writing the annual official letter addressed to the Viceroy in Council, which undertakes to give a *résumé* of ecclesiastical work during the year, with statistics of the diocese, and to call attention to its special needs. The Bishop made use of the opportunity in 1863 to bring under the notice of Government some ecclesiastical inconvenience in the Central Provinces which had just been visited. These provinces, when made into a separate local government, had been annexed to the Presidency of Bengal. The Nagpore division, however, being on the confines of the Madras Presidency, had been viewed as belonging ecclesiastically to the Bishop of Madras, and two of his chaplains were posted at the seat of the local government, doing duty at the large civil and military stations of Kamptee and Seetabuldee. The Chief Commissioner found the inconvenience of having a double episcopal jurisdiction within the length and breadth of his territory, and applied to the Bishop of Calcutta to have more uniformity introduced. This opened the question as to which see was legally responsible for Nagpore, and it was referred to the Advocate-General. He looked up the matter, and found that the Acts of Parliament creating the dioceses of Madras and Bombay had declared them to be conterminous with their respective presidencies, leaving by inference all the rest of India to the Metropolitan See. Under this view the Bishop of Calcutta appeared to become responsible for ecclesiastical matters in many large and small native States which, though really in no diocese at all, contain a quota of European officials either civil or military. It was legislation more honoured in the breach than the observance, for bishops of Madras had long visited Christian congregations in Berar and Mysore, and in Nagpore, where, as has been said, their chaplains were established. Similarly the Rajpootana States had been tacitly recognised as under the episcopal jurisdiction of Bombay. The opinion of the Advocate-General left no doubt that the province of Nagpore, on its annexation to the Bengal Presidency, had passed to the Northern See. Bishop Cotton therefore accepted it as an integral portion of his diocese, visited it in 1862, and then reported to the Supreme Government on the points which called for re-arrangement in the Central Provinces. In the first place, he represented the anomaly and inconvenience of Madras chaplains serving in the diocese of Calcutta, but not holding his licence; and urging his inability to remedy this evil by supplying the stations of Nagpore from the limited number of chaplains allotted to Bengal, he renewed the frequent but often fruitless request for an increase of the State Establishment. In the next place, he desired, with regard to these regions, a revision of the ecclesiastical map. The fatigue and loss of time incurred in journeys to reach the detached and remote stations of Mhow and Indore, had led him to contemplate, as an obvious and feasible improvement, the transfer to the Bishop of Bombay of the Christian congregations in certain native territories which lie in close promixity to his diocese, and, in one direction, intersect it. Vagueness about jurisdiction and eccentricities in boundaries offended the Bishop's innate love of symmetry and of a clear and distinct field of labour, just as incongruities in his position as Bishop of Burmah had the year before disturbed all his notions of homogeneous and connected work. A remedy for the evils of Central India was more accessible than for those of Burmah. By an Act of William the Fourth's reign, passed doubtless with a view to future needs or territorial changes in British India, the Sovereign in Council had power to alter and assign the limits of the Indian Sees. The purport, therefore, of the Bishop's representation to Government was to urge that by a formal and authoritative declaration, Mysore and Berar should be declared to be henceforth attached to the diocese of Madras, Rajpootana and Baroda to that of Bombay, and that to the latter should also be ceded Malwa and Scindia's territories, with other small native States known as the Central Indian Agency. An order of the Queen in Council assigning these ecclesiastical boundaries on a geographical rather than a political principle would thus have sufficed to reduce within more manageable limits at its south-western extremity the huge northern diocese which Lord Dalhousie's annexations had doubled. But the Bishop's representations made in 1863 and renewed in 1864 bore no fruit. The whole subject was postponed by the Indian or Home Governments to a more convenient day—a day which will probably not dawn until the dream of another Indian See shall become a reality, or until some point of ecclesiastical discipline shall arise to enforce a more precise definition of the territories and jurisdiction of the Indian bishops.

CHAPTER X.

REVIEW OF THE CHARGE OF 1863—METROPOLITICAL VISITATION—MADRAS—BOMBAY—COLOMBO—TINNEVELLY—THE SYRIAN CHURCH—LETTERS.

IN September 1863 the time came round for the delivery of another charge as the opening act of a second visitation, which was to be at once diocesan and metropolitan. The charge was widely read in England, with as deep an interest as that which attended its delivery in India. Much was expected from one of so genial a character, such wide and hearty sympathies, so keen yet calm an insight into all that came under his cognisance. Nor were these expectations disappointed, except in some perhaps who looked chiefly for originality of views, or the disclosure of some new means of access to the Indian mind, and who forgot, what the Bishop himself could never forget, that the one thing above all else required in such a charge was help and counsel for his clergy in their daily duties, and amidst their actual perplexities and trials; counsel to be given by one who, though standing at their head, chose rather to place himself by their side, sharing their labours, entering into their difficulties, and patiently endeavouring to attain their point of view, before he offered advice which thus alone could be made at once acceptable and effective. After noticing with thankfulness the marvellous progress made in five years towards repairing the effects of the Mutiny, he passed on to consider, first of all, 'the perils, hopes, and duties of the Church in India.'

The subject was approached from the vantage-ground of accumulated experience and extended knowledge. When the Bishop delivered his primary charge in 1859, he had been only a few months in the country, and it was from impressions and observation chiefly limited to Calcutta that he touched upon points affecting the welfare of the Church in a diocese extending from Peshawur to Singapore. But it was otherwise in 1863. During four years of constant travel he had fully realised the spiritual needs of a large English army; he had made (as passages in this memoir constantly indicate) the moral and spiritual needs of European and Eurasian middle-class life, the pastoral care of the isolated English home in a foreign land, objects of peculiarly personal charge and responsibility. Just as the collections for the poor Christians in Judea took such hold of St. Paul's mind during some two years of his ministry that they claimed a foremost place in his Epistles even when treating of the sublimest doctrines of the faith, so with Bishop Cotton no prominence seemed too great to give to this paramount object of the Church's attention and duty. A close analysis of his counsels and exhortations on this occasion would be superfluous, since the subject rises so constantly to the surface in journals and letters. It will suffice to say that, postponing for the moment the discussion of missionary operations and of those great theological topics which, as a bishop, he felt it to be at that crisis an imperative duty to discuss, he directed the attention of his hearers, first of all, to the European portion of the Church in India; to a review of what had been accomplished; to notices of work then in progress, or to suggestions for work still needing to be undertaken; while with renewed emphasis he gave utterance to the hope that, as Bishop Wilson's episcopate had been distinguished by the increase of churches, so his might be distinguished by the increase of schools and of other kindred channels through which the restraining and elevating influence of the Gospel might flow.

Turning next to the prospects of missionary labour, he dwelt with mixed feelings of regret and hopefulness on the well-known fact that it was chiefly among the lowest castes, and, still more, among the aboriginal tribes of India, that Christianity had made, or was likely to make, substantial progress. Seeing, however, in the success already granted in such quarters a plain indication of the Divine will, he urged persevering exertion in the same direction, commending especially to the Church Missionary Society a new field of labour opening among the Gonds of Central India, and to the Society for the Propagation of the Gospel a similar field among the Cachari aborigines of Assam, and the hill-tribes above the Brahmaputra; while more universally he looked to the instruction and improvement of the ryots, and to the extension of female education throughout India, as the most hopeful agency for promoting the ultimate evangelisation of the country.

Of the immediate prospects disclosing themselves for the reception of Christianity among the upper and more cultivated classes of Hindus, he spoke with greater hesitation, appearing, it may almost be said, to be himself attracted rather towards the Mahometans, whose closer approach to Christianity he pointed out, and the neglect of whom, in the general work of missions, he earnestly deprecated. To those friends at home who looked to him with confident trust, as one specially qualified to win his way with thoughtful and educated Hindus, and who had formed, perhaps, too high an estimate of the prevalence and nature of the doctrine of the Brahmo Somaj, this part of the charge may have been somewhat disappointing. It was not to any want of sympathy with the cultivated classes, or to any disparagement of the importance of the movements at work amongst them, that scantiness of specific and successful efforts in their behalf could be attributed. The Bishop's attitude towards educated Bengalis, amongst whom adherents of the Brahmo Somaj form only a limited party, was, like the whole of his public life, in truthful harmony with his own character. His calm temperament withheld him from strongly pronounced demonstrations of sympathy with intellectual progress which, in its religious aspect, reflected much of the latitude of modern thought. He desired to be the guide of those who in humility and sincerity were finding their way to the gospel of salvation rather than to be known as welcoming with enthusiasm every mental phase in men who, while breaking with heathenism, were content to stop far short of Christianity. He regarded the actual state of things around him as one of transition, out of which, he was well assured, would come at last a general recognition and acceptance of Christian truth. But the merely negative and destructive period must first be brought to an end. He was too sadly impressed with the self-sufficiency, the merely deistical belief, and worst of all (as their own confessions showed), the licentious morals of 'young Bengal,' to welcome the abandonment of Hinduism, unaccompanied with the sense of sin or consciousness of the need of a Redeemer, as any positive approach to Christianity. Even in 1863, however, he saw signs of a better day at hand; and it was with a confidence which brightened as he looked forward that he exhorted the Church of Christ, while waiting patiently for the coming opportunity, to use all efforts meanwhile 'to surround the educated classes of India with the power of Christian evidence, Christian example, and Christian influence.' Penetrated himself in early manhood with convictions decidedly evangelical, Bishop Cotton ever retained substantially the same basis of religious sentiment under the broader system of theology which his maturer judgment approved; the devout personal element deepening indeed and strengthening with the growth of his character, as he drew nearer and nearer to the sad and sudden end. Hence, it went to his heart to see how English influences over the native mind, and the spirit of inquiry which had been stimulated by the beneficence of English rule, and by the glories of European civilisation, were neutralised, or even perverted—wilfully perverted in their spiritual aspect—by the endeavour of philosophical writers at home to turn aside the stream of conversion from Christian channels. And, like his friend Dr. Duff, to whose memory he paid in this charge a touching and eloquent tribute, he determined that, whatever else his work in India might be, it should at least be distinctively and resolutely Christian.

The duty, therefore, to which he felt himself most imperatively called was to keep alive and kindle to a brighter lustre the beacon of Christian example in India itself; to elevate the condition of existing converts, and to clear away the mutual prejudices which too often obscured their relations with their European brothers; while, for the further abatement of the darkness resting on the land, whether as regarded the supply of fresh missionaries for the purpose, or the proof to be held up to the Indian mind of the nature and effects of our holy faith, he felt that the hopes of the future must still mainly rest on Christian England. It was with these objects ever present, if not uppermost, in his thoughts that he turned to review the state of things at home, (1) as they affected the National Church, and (2) the Church at large.

In the National Church, after remarking with sorrow the growing disinclination of young men of ability to enter into holy orders, he noticed with much regret (as one cause among many) the dissatisfaction very widely expressed with the existing formularies of the Prayer Book. In this matter, like his friend Dr. Vaughan, he firmly deprecated change. Though willing to consent to such an alteration in the terms of subscription as was soon afterwards carried into effect, and desiring also a revision of the Lectionary (such as is now accomplished), and still more of the canons, he feared to see concession carried further. Reviewing the objections urged against the baptismal, the burial, and the ordination services, and against the recital of the Athanasian Creed, he pronounced, in every case, after a candid consideration, against the necessity for change, with the one exception of the burial service. In this case, the scandals incident to the indiscriminate use of the office were brought into special prominence in India, where an Anglican chaplain might find himself compelled to read it over some Roman Catholic soldier whom the Romish priest had judged unworthy of the rites of sepulture as prescribed by his own Church.* Here, accordingly, especially after the admissions which have been made by the bishops themselves in Parliament, he recommended that the service as it now stands should be reserved for communicants only, while for others a shorter and less explicit form should be drawn up. In all the other cases he urged that the explanations offered of obnoxious expressions by thoughtful and approved divines ought to be accepted as sufficient, though he would gladly have seen such explanations embodied also in declaratory rubrics. Whether such rubrics, lying wholly in the Prayer Book, while the expressions objected to were persistently enforced, would either conciliate Dissenters or satisfy remonstrant Churchmen, will probably be doubted, and more than doubted, by all except those who are already content. But, even on the score of expediency, the question of a revision of the formularies is undeniably a very difficult one; and on the higher ground of truth and consistency, and agreement with Scripture, Bishop Cotton's remarks deserve the respectful attention of all right-minded men. Very remarkable, too, is the testi-

* See ch. ix. p. 187.

mony which his Indian experience enabled him to offer to the merits of the Prayer Book: so suitable did he find it, and so acceptable also to the native congregations in his diocese; while the same experience confirmed him no less in his approval both of the baptismal service and tended to diminish his sympathy with those who assail and condemn the dogmatism of the Athanasian Creed. The repugnance felt by some to the strong language of the former could not but be modified, he felt, in a country where every Christian must be conscious of the wide difference subsisting between the heathens around and those who, however careless and inconsistent in life, were yet recognised members of Christ's body, the Church; while, with regard to the latter, he pointed out how errors which we are apt to regard as things of the past are in full activity even yet in the East, under the influence of Oriental systems of religion and philosophy—'and we may well pause before we expunge from the records of our Church an ancient protest against the application of these tendencies to Christianity;' a protest which will be needed again 'whenever the educated classes of India generally embrace the Gospel.'

Lastly, passing on to the 'hopes, perils, and duties of the Catholic Church,' he fixed his attention chiefly on the great questions of the nature of inspiration, and the mutual relations of the various parts of Scripture; questions which, then as now, were agitating Christendom, and which had been stirred, more especially in England, since his departure by the publication of 'Essays and Reviews,' and of the works of the Bishop of Natal.

With these high and momentous questions no mind was more prepared than his to deal in a devout yet fearless spirit; and few were so capable of doing it. Acknowledging, on one hand, the irresistible claims of reason in matters of critical investigation, and firmly believing that such investigation, fairly pursued, would but confirm the conclusions of faith, he unhesitatingly pointed out that the patent facts of various readings in the sacred text, of discrepancies in statement between the sacred writers, and of altered or irreconcilable quotations in the New Testament of passages from the Old, necessarily refuted the theory of a plenary verbal inspiration: a theory which is nowhere advanced by Scripture itself; while the Vedas and the Koran, in significant contrast, do actually make such a claim for their contents. On the other hand, he still more earnestly maintained that the acceptance of the Gospel as a revelation from God imposes necessarily and at once upon every sincere believer a submission of the understanding and judgment to the Divine voice, involving the acknowledgment of a special inspiration accorded to the sacred records, and setting limits to the province of criticism in dealing with them. What those limits exactly are he was far from thinking himself competent to define, though some guiding landmarks seemed to him unquestionably evident. Indeed, he did not consider a precise definition as either attainable or desirable, regarding it rather as part of each man's moral probation to order his steps with reverent care upon that holy ground. For himself, he feared chiefly to err on the side of presumption; and in this spirit he suggested to his clergy some of the principles which he strove habitually to keep in view. Thus, while he readily admitted that 'on matters of natural phenomena the writers of Scripture speak according to appearances and not in language scientifically correct,' and while he would not refuse to believe with Bishop Ellicott that men inspired to communicate moral and spiritual truth might in matters of narrative be liable to 'such incompleteness and such imperfections as belong to the highest form of purely truthful human testimony,' he still reserved the right of expecting that on many controverted points a maturer science and a deeper historical research might yet come round to confirm the statements of the Bible.

The moral difficulties in Jewish history were fully solved, he was persuaded, by the principle, everywhere perceptible, and in some places plainly avowed in Scripture, that God deals with the conscience according as it is able to bear His precepts, and that thus accordingly He had disciplined the chosen people, 'not forcing on them a standard of morality which they could not have appreciated, but raising them far above every contemporary nation,' while also leading them onwards and ever onwards, through many imperfections, to the light which was to be unveiled in Christ.

Above all he protested, with the loyalty of a devout trust that knew no bounds, against any hypothesis which could impugn the perfect wisdom and sufficiency and the transparent veracity of Christ himself. Whatever train of human reasoning seemed to lead to such a result, that he required every Christian unhesitatingly to reject, waiting in faith, if need be, for the further knowledge which would justify the decision. Hence, he strongly condemned 'the reckless speculations to which a new impulse had been lately given by the Bishop of Natal.' With respect to the Pentateuch itself, he was ready to admit, if necessary, the composite nature of its authorship, and its obligations possibly to patriarchal records preceding it, and to the hand of Ezra in its final redaction; but his whole soul revolted from the thought that it owed its existence to Samuel, or some later writer. Such a theory in his judgment not only imputed the crime of forgery to those holy men, but controverted the authority of Christ Himself, who had definitely owned and appealed to both Moses and his writings, and with that, overturned the very foundations of our faith. And, though willing and ready to believe that such disastrous consequences were not contemplated by Bishop Colenso himself, and uniformly showing this spirit of charitable trust, in a subsequent correspondence with some of the Bishop's apologists, and again with Dr. Rowland Williams, who had written to complain of some expressions in the appendix to the charge, he yet would not depart a hair's-breadth from the position he had maintained, nor even qualify the stern rebuke which he pronounced on those whom he considered to have failed in deference to the Divine authority of Christ.

Nor would he admit the too depreciatory estimate formed, as he thought, by others of the Old Testament in its relation to Christians. That part of Scripture he regarded as retaining still its divinely-appointed office of 'a schoolmaster to bring us to Christ'—an office which he believed it to possess, not for a time only, but in perpetuity; not for the Jews only, but for the whole human race. In connexion with this subject there is one passage of his charge so striking and important that it must be quoted at length:—

It is a remarkable proof of the world-wide power of Scripture, that points which are felt as difficulties by one class or generation are seen to be of the highest importance by other sections of the great human family. I have lately been struck by two instances of this. No parts of the scriptural records have been more severely criticised than the Mosaic cosmogony and the doctrine of sacrifice. One of the best known papers in the volume of 'Essays and Reviews' undertook the refutation of the former; and more than one vain attempt has been made to show that the latter has no connection with Our Lord's death, and no part in the Christian scheme. Such are the opinions of students who have grown up in habits of thought exclusively European. We bring the Gospel to India; we persuade a few thoughtful men to accept Christ as their Saviour, and we find that these very parts of Scripture strike home to their hearts as full of instruction. In a lecture delivered in London, Professor Gannendro Mohun

Tajore thus speaks:—'Cosmogony forms the essential basis of all religious development, as far as we are able to collect. Hence the vast importance which must necessarily be attached to the Mosaic cosmogony, notwithstanding the many and perhaps everlasting disputes which may be raised against it. The Hindu cosmogony is the mythical development of the historical realism of the Mosaic; and the absence of the notion of a personal and living God in all false religions, and its conservation in Judaism . . . . forms the most remarkable feature in the religious history of mankind.' And the Rev. Krishna Mohun Banerjea sees in Christ's sacrifice the explanation of a remarkable feature in the religion of his countrymen. 'We find,' he says, 'that, in the inscrutable wisdom of God, there could be no remission of sin apart from sacrifice, that Christ was revealed in the primitive age of the world as the great sacrifice for the sins of men, and that immolation of animals was ordained as typical of that rite. . . . While the ceremonial performance of the rite was kept up probably everywhere, its object and intention were gradually forgotten. . . . The zeal and assiduity with which it was maintained in our country is accounted for by its transmission from age to age as a primitive practice; but the inability of our ancestors to give the least intelligent explanation of the rite, and the want of any information in the oldest of the Vedas on its connection with the celestial fruits of which it was believed to be productive, are enigmas which can only be understood by the light of the Biblical history.' Miracles furnish another instance of the same kind. If there are some scientific minds which cling so closely to the conception of law that they are unwilling to imagine any interruption to it, there always have been other minds to which miraculous agency seems an essential part of the evidence of Christianity, proving that the Gospel was the work not only of infinite goodness, but of infinite power. Surely, then, God's wisdom is vindicated by the provision made for the spiritual needs of all His children. At great turning-points in the world's history miracles have proclaimed His especial presence, but in the ordinary course of events His fatherly care has been manifested in the unbroken supremacy of those wise and merciful laws which His providence has impressed upon His creation. All these facts show that the Bible contains a universal revelation, and confirms the truth of Bacon's words, that 'the Scriptures, being written to the thoughts of men, and to the succession of all ages, with a foresight of all heresies, contradictions, and differing estates of the Church . . . have in themselves infinite springs and streams of doctrine to water the Church in every part.'

The charge concluded with an earnest exhortation to the clergy to trust and to put forth in their ministry the full power of the Gospel—an exhortation singularly impressive in the mouth of one whose Christian energy had been so largely manifested, and who showed so habitually, even in the most unguarded moments of social intercourse, how truly he himself lived by the principles which he inculcated.

Very shortly after the delivery of the charge the visitation of the other Indian dioceses commenced. The right of the Bishop of Calcutta to make this visitation as Metropolitan dated from the time when the sees of Bombay and Madras were created. Bishop Wilson had encountered some difficulty in getting this right recognised by the Indian Government or by the Court of Directors; but he firmly upheld it, appealed to his letters-patent, finally overcame the financial and other objections raised against the quinquennial visitation, established the precedent, and the formal official sanction is now given as a matter of course. As complete isolation with respect to his special work is the portion of every Indian bishop, the advantage of an occasional interchange of opinions and experiences with those sharing the same office and responsibilities can hardly be gainsaid. This was the view of the approaching tour taken by the Metropolitan in 1863, mingling with bright anticipations of the rich and varied interests inseparable from extensive Indian travel. Intending to go forth, as he said, more as a learner than a teacher, he determined to leave episcopal duties, as far as possible, behind him; and to effect this, he caused to be withdrawn, under legal sanction, from the mandate announcing his visitation a strange clause suspending each suffragan from exercising the functions of his office while the Metropolitan was in his diocese. The following letter is a link between Calcutta and the southern presidency:—

To Professor Conington.

Steamer 'Nemesis,' Bay of Bengal, between Calcutta and Madras, November 11, 1863.

It is impossible to be actually on board a Peninsular and Oriental steamer, in the midst of passengers bound for England, without some longing thoughts of home, old friends, and Edward. There is much to remind us of England in the habits of the ship: Englishmen waiting on us at dinner instead of Mussulman khidmatgars, luggage directed to Southampton, and a hundred minutiæ of like kind. I complete the στοργή by sitting down to write to you.

Yet, though I certainly should like to come home and see you all, I am sure that none of you will feel otherwise than glad that we both like India better and better; that there are many schemes of usefulness afloat, which I should be reluctant to abandon or leave uncared for, even for a time, in their present nascent condition; and that I doubt whether it would be right to come home just now, except from the pressure of illness, or other dire necessity. It seemed possible two months ago that such pressure might actually arise, for I was visited, as you may have heard, by a sudden and severe attack of acute dysentery. But, by God's mercy, my recovery was rapid and complete, and I feel now as well as if I had never been ill.

From my opening sentence you will have discovered that our usual winter tour is begun. This time, the diocese being finished, I am on the 'metropolitan' visitation to Madras, Bombay, and Colombo; Stuart, secretary to the Church Missionary Society, acting as my chaplain in Burn's place.

I look forward with much pleasure to seeing Gell at Madras, and he is to accompany us to Bombay, as is also his chaplain, W. S. Smith, formerly, as you may remember, head prefect at Marlborough, and now Fellow of Trinity College, Cambridge.

One of the chief interests of the last two months in Calcutta has been the proposal for a memorial of the services of Dr. Duff, a Free Kirk missionary of great eminence, who, after more than thirty years' efficient service of a remarkable and original character, is now leaving India, with broken health. His great merit consisted in the stand which he made against atheistic education, and the Christian turn which he gave to the intellectual movement which of late has agitated the mind of young Bengal. Three meetings of mingled Churchmen and Dissenters were held at the palace on the subject, and two rival schemes proposed: one, a hall and library for the Bible Society; the other a lecture-hall to be placed near the Presidency College, and new University buildings, in which lectures should be given, and meetings held on Christian subjects and others of a cognate character. The first would have been mainly for the use of Europeans, and planted in the European quarter; the other for the use of Europeanised natives, and planted in the native quarter. Opinions were divided, not according to the tenets of Church and Dissent, but according to the affirmation or negation of the Arnoldian principle of doing secular things in a Christian way, and sanctifying by the presence of Christ's Spirit all intellectual and other earthly occupation. I dislike nicknames, and still more any savour of self-complacency; but I do think that the discussion illustrated the distinction between narrowness and breadth, and that on the side of the latter were not only all persons of really cultivated minds and extensive Indian knowledge, but also quite as great an amount of earnest Christianity as among the supporters of the narrower view. Some could imagine no missionary work or really Christian influence except such as consists in printing, publishing, and distributing the Bible; and all these were for a Bible house in the European quarter. But others stoutly argued that to treat general subjects from a Christian point of view, to promote good and benevolent works, to show that the Church is now as ever in the van of civilisation, is a more direct continuation of Duff's work than the other, and more likely to influence the educated Hindu. Happily this view prevailed, chiefly through the energy of Sir Charles Trevelyan; and a committee, with me for its chairman, was named to carry out the scheme of a lecture-hall in the native city. . . . . .

I have written and delivered my second charge, and it will, I hope, reach you in a mail or two. It has also to be delivered at Madras, Bombay, and Colombo, *mutatis mutandis.* It took me a long time and a deal of work to write it, and already I see divers defects in it. It is of an eclectic character, and will not thoroughly satisfy High Churchmen, Evangelicals, or Liberals: each will pick plenty of holes in it. I will not anticipate or deprecate your criticisms by any further remarks or explanations.

The first halt was at Madras, under the hospitable roof of its bishop, then only recently settled in his Indian field of labour. A week was spent in constant and varied occupation. The charge was again delivered, and sermons were preached. There was much cordial intercourse with the clergy, and much profitable inspection of schools and institutions which have long had a firm root in the Southern diocese. The Bishop brought with him the scheme just started in Calcutta for a national memorial to Dr. Duff, and procured for it, at an influential meeting, with Bishop Gell as chairman, an acceptance and sympathy at once ready and liberal, and free from all presidency narrowness or jealousy.

In order to bring about a much-desired conference between the three Indian prelates, the Bishop of Madras consented to visit the northern parts of his diocese by way of Bombay. A double episcopal party, therefore, quitted Madras on November 20, and took the railway to Beipore, on the western coast. Here a Government steamer, busy on various official errands, was in readiness, and became the private yacht for the voyage up to Bombay. The steamer put into Honore, in North Canara, and the party landed for a three days' excursion to the Gerseppa Falls, where all were much refreshed by grand scenery, by rest and holiday among rocks and jungle, and by the fresh air of hills 2,000 feet above the sea. The 'Dalhousie,' obeying episcopal commands, anchored yet again for a day, to enable the travellers to see in ruined buildings and fine but empty churches the ghost of what the great ecclesiastical city of Goa once was. Bombay was in due time reached, and to it was devoted what the Bishop could speak of in his journal, as a most interesting, enjoyable, and, as he trusted, not wholly profitless fortnight.

A succession of varied occupations filled up the hours from early to late of many hot and trying days. The inspection of schools entered largely into the programme of engagements, for they are in Bombay numerous and flourishing, and interesting from being supported and encouraged as much by the natives as by Christian societies, and directed to a great extent to the education of both sexes. Time was economised during the shorter sojourn of the Bishop of Madras to bring the three prelates into frequent conference, a practical result of which was the issue of pastorals to clergy and laity on the oft-repeated tale of India's wants, and England's duties towards her. As a relief to graver business, expeditions to Elephanta and Karli were organised by the Governor, Sir Bartle Frere, whose kindness tended, no less than the unflagging hospitality of the Bishop of Bombay and Mrs. Harding, to make the visit to the second city in British India an entire success. A notice of this visit to Bombay would be incomplete without allusion to Dr. Wilson, the Free Kirk missionary, who, leading native education there, as Dr. Duff has done in Calcutta, is also well versed in Oriental learning, and is a fountain of information on subjects connected with surrounding races and religions. Greatly to the Bishop's satisfaction, Dr. Wilson accompanied the expedition to the caves of Karli (to be noticed in a subsequent letter), and, by his extensive knowledge on a difficult subject, turned the sculpture of the grand rock-cut temple into a legible page of remote Indian history. Of these two, whose paths in life thus for a moment crossed, one has entered into his rest; to the other it has been accorded to reach the fortieth anniversary of his arrival in India, and to receive a public recognition of his sustained and enlightened labours for the spread of knowledge and of truth. The editor of an Indian periodical closes with the following true and kind words a notice of the event:—'The present writer well remembers the keen delight with which our late Bishop on his visit to Bombay explored the stores of information that Dr. Wilson had at his command. The sympathy between these two remarkable men was of no ordinary kind. They seemed to coalesce at once as kindred spirits, distinguished alike by intellectual vigour and by high moral purpose and philanthropic aims.'

The mail steamer landed the Bishop's party in Ceylon late in December. Christmas was spent at Colombo with the Bishop and Mrs. Claughton; New Year's Day at Kandy, in the spacious country house of the Governor, surrounded by its beautiful tropical garden. From Colombo, they sailed across the chopping waters of the Gulf of Manaar and landed at Tuticorin, in a southern corner of the great continent of India. This place was the starting point for a tour through the Christian districts of Tinnevelly, to which the Bishop had long looked forward as a valued privilege of his metropolitanship. Dr. Caldwell, of the Propagation Society, met the travellers on their landing, and was their most kind guide and escort during the ensuing fortnight. The Tinnevelly missions are now so famous that a few words of brief and general description will suffice. The missions and Christian settlements are chiefly congregated in the southern portions of the province, and are spread over an undulating district of red sand. Vegetation is mainly limited to Palmyra palms, their cultivators being Shánárs (Palmyra-climbers), who draw from them their food and their wealth. Hence a rich man's worldly substance is computed not by the number of his acres of ground, but by the number of his trees. It is the business of the industrious Shánár to ascend some fifty trees, many of these being ninety feet in height, twice a day during eight months of the year, to extract the saccharine fluid by an incision into the flower-stalks, underneath the crown of fan-shaped leaves. Fresh from the tree this saccharine juice forms the family breakfast; boiled into a hard black mass, the midday meal; and by its sale, rice and curry (the staple Indian dinner) are procured. These Shánárs are an aboriginal tribe; and it is from a devil worship, partially overlaid with superstitions and caste prejudices derived from their Hindu conquerors, that Christianity has reclaimed them. Schwartz, Jänicke, Satyanáden, Rhenius, are honoured names in the small band of Lutherans who first sowed the seed which has brought forth an hundredfold. The Church of England now owns the missions, and her two great societies are, by labour carried on in close proximity, and in entire co-operation, adding yearly to a federation of 50,000 native Christians, isolated and compact within itself through low social standing and by peculiarities in geographical position and industrial pursuits. Nine missionary stations and centres of Christianised rural life were visited. At each in turn the travellers were received with a kind and cordial welcome from the missionaries, and a very noisy, though not less hearty, one from the native Christians, who escorted them into their village, and again at their departure, with a deafening clang of bells and gongs.

At each station there were Church services to be held, the Bishop's sermon being translated clause by clause to the Tamil congregation by the local missionary; there were addresses to be received from catechists, schoolmasters and village headmen: there were piles of sugar-candy to be accepted, if not consumed.

From the province of Tinnevelly, the Bishop's party passed to the kingdom of Travancore, and made straight for the Syrian Church. Their way led through the 'back-waters'—strips of inland sea lining the coast like Venetian lagunes. Up these they passed in small narrow row-boats, and on January 25 they reached the beautiful station of Cottyam, as rich as Ceylon in tropical scenery and vegetation. Cottyam is the head-quarters of the Church missions of Travancore, and is also one of the centres of the Syrian Church. This withered branch of Christ's Holy Catholic Church has always had a powerful attraction for leaders of the Anglican Church in India, the bishops of the latter having included it in their 'visitations' as much as if their letters-patent enjoined the duty. Claudius Buchanan, in his researches among other bodies of Christians, drew the Syrians out of the silence and seclusion of long years, and made a beginning in the great work of turning their scarce manuscripts into print. The first Protestant bishop of British India examined their doctrines and their archives with the profound interest of a scholar, and his immediate successor corresponded with the Metran or Metropolitan of his day. It is easy to imagine the zeal and enthusiasm with which the fervid prelate, Daniel Wilson, after witnessing the celebration of mass, preached to the assembled congregation on Evangelical truth. But the permission to Protestants to preach to the Syrians was subsequently withdrawn. Their relations towards the Church Missionary Society, which at the time of Bishop Wilson's first visit were in a critical state, became shortly afterwards entirely hostile. A college, shared by both

Churches, and intended to be the passage of the Syrians to ordination, was a fruitful source of discord. At Bishop Wilson's second visit, some years later, the property had been divided, the building was made over to the Syrians, and the rupture was complete. The two communions are now more friendly in their mutual relations, but each retains its independence. 'A gentle hand and a master mind' would seem especially needed for the maintenance of salutary influence over a Church which survived the crushing persecutions of the Inquisition of Goa, and which numbers on its muster-roll of bishops, men like the Metropolitan Mar Dionysius, who, sixty years ago, with that same spirit of independence that has flashed in more modern utterances of Eastern patriarchs, replied to the overtures of Buchanan, 'I would sacrifice much for union: only let me not be called upon to compromise anything of the dignity and purity of our Church.' With the Metran in office in 1864 Bishop Cotton had no personal intercourse, for he was absent; but the Cathanars, or priests, with their usual courtesy and willingness to receive if not to follow counsels, asked if he was really the successor of 'Bishop Daniel,' and requested him to address their congregation: 'so I spoke to them,' to quote a passage of the journal, 'a few words on the need of Christian unity, and the deep importance of the points on which the Syrian and English Churches are agreed, which I briefly enumerated, ending with an exhortation that, as to those on which we differ, we should pray that the Holy Spirit may guide us into all truth.' There were indications in 1864 of slight progress and reformation. The Metran then in office permitted the Syrians to be students in the new college, built since the quarrel by the Church Missionary Society, and was developing other liberal tendencies. Still, while the Church reposes tranquilly on its connexion with Antioch, and on the due observance of a formal ritual, and does little for the spread of light and knowledge within its borders or for the evangelisation of the heathen without, its aspect is rather that of an ancient ecclesiastical relic than of a living member of Christ's Body. The Syrian Church has been so fully described in the memoirs of Bishop Middleton and Bishop Wilson, that it will be sufficient to subjoin the following brief notice of points which were made the subject of special inquiry during the short stay at Cottyam here recorded.

EXTRACTS FROM JOURNAL.

January 1864.—. . . I had some conversation with Marcus, an old and infirm Cathanar, and with Philippus, a younger one, through an interpreter, and abundance of talk with the Church Missionary Society's missionary, Mr. Baker, and with George Matthan, who was ordained deacon in his national church, and in spite of his secession to ours, in consequence of the unscriptural practices and stagnant condition of the Cathanars, retains a very kindly feeling to his brethren after the flesh. How the Church ceased to be Nestorian, and to what degree it is now exactly Eutychian, are points on which I could not get satisfactory information. George Matthan thought that when the Portuguese tried to force Romanism on the Syrians, they sought aid from Antioch, and thence obtained Jacobite bishops; but they have had Nestorian bishops since that day, for Marcus showed me the grave of one of them in front of the altar of his church. I was told that, during the service of consecration of the bread and wine, the specially Jacobite form of doctrine is stated—'One very Emanuel, who cannot be divided into two natures.' At present, in the ordination service the Cathanars are made to anathematise both Nestorius and Eutyches, for there seems to be some slight difference between the Jacobite and Eutychian dogma. . . .

The font, which is near the entrance of the church, is large enough to immerse an infant, but not an adult. If an adult is baptized, water is poured so completely over him that he is practically immersed in it. He stands by the font, and nearly its whole contents are emptied upon him, and flow down over the floor of the church. There are a good many ceremonies besides the simple baptism—the exorcism of evil spirits; the chrism; the breathing upon the water by the priest; a strange plan of mixing warm and cold water, with the assertion that 'John mixed water for baptism, and Christ sanctified it, went down into it, and was baptized;' and an investiture of the baptized person with a girdle and crown, of which the latter is removed by the priest seven days after the baptism, with a prayer that the child may receive instead of it a crown of glory. The doctrine of regeneration in baptism is strongly stated, and the personification of the infant by the sponsor, to which Simpkinson so vehemently objects, is found in the Syrian service.

'Those that are at variance with each other shall not communicate until they be reconciled' (from the Syrian canons, cf. our Rubric).

The administration of the Holy Communion to the laity in both kinds is expressly enjoined by the canons, but 'if that be impossible [why ?], the priest shall dip the body in the cup, held by the deacon, and then administer it.'

Buying, selling, and travelling (except for urgent necessary affairs, or on the compulsion of Government) are forbidden on Sunday. Rest on Saturday is forbidden as Jewish.

Metrans are buried under or close to the altar; priests in the body of the church; laymen outside the church. The Syrians (at least of Cottyam) are apt to treat irreverently the remains of the dead; they bury a corpse in a grave which has been previously occupied, throwing the bones which they find in it into a great pit overgrown with weeds and nettles in the corner of the churchyard. I find that they offer prayers both to and for the dead; but as to the latter kind of prayers, their doctrine is very much less objectionable than that of purgatory, as they only maintain that the final state of each soul is not always decided till the day of judgment, and that meantime it is possible that the prayers of the Church may prevail with God to pardon at the last those in whose behalf they are offered. They do not profess to know much about the present condition of the departed, but believe that they are affected by the memory of their past lives, their general abode being an unknown region called Paradise, though some who have lived very wickedly are already in hell, from which, however, it is possible that prayer may rescue them. . . . . .

The Syrians would, but for Church schisms, acknowledge five patriarchates: Rome (to which they would allow precedency if they were in communion with it), Alexandria, Constantinople, instead of Ephesus, Antioch, and Jerusalem or Cæsarea (the two being united like Bath and Wells). To these was added a patriarch of Seleucia and Ctesiphon for Arabia and Persia. The chief of the Abyssinian Church is not to be allowed to make himself a patriarch, but is a metropolitan under Alexandria. Metropolitans are under patriarchs, and consecrated by them. The Metrans are to ordain, at the entrance to the chancel, widows as deaconesses. . . . . .

They hold part of the Apocrypha—Tobit, Maccabees, and, I suppose, Wisdom—to be canonical. Philippus was anxious that I should get him a copy of the Book of Maccabees, which he did not possess. They include Clement's Epistles in the New Testament. . . . . .

Besides Nestorius and Eutyches, they anathematise in the ordination service all heathens, Jews, astrologers, Leo, the Synod of Chalcedon, Paul of Samosata, Julian the Apostate, Arius, together with (convenient vagueness) 'all whom the Syrian Church anathematises;' and to these the late Metran expressly added Luther, but his name has been removed by order of Mar Athanasius, the present Metran. After the kiss of peace in the Sunday service, there is a long commemoration of departed saints, including James the Lord's brother, Ignatius, Clement, Athanasius, Basil, Gregory, Dioscoros, Cyril (who is styled 'a lofty and true wall, and the professor who openly acknowledged the manhood of the Son of God'), James Baradæus (from whom, I believe, they are called Jacobites), Ephraim, and Simeon Stylites. . . . . .

Practical corruptions seem considerable, and their general condition ignorant and somewhat degraded, certainly from the level of Christianity, though not, I rejoice to think, to the level of heathenism; for they are described as a quiet, industrious, and at least fairly respectable generation, while their houses, to judge by one which I entered, are very neat and clean. Spite of the quarrel with the Church Missionary

Society, which arose mainly, I am assured, from the desire of some of the Syrians in the late Metran's time to finger the property of the college, the neighbourhood of the English Church is plainly improving the Syrians; and the present Metran, Athanasius, who was not at Cottyam during our visit, is a reformer. He does not hinder his people, nor even his deacons, from pursuing their studies in our college; he has encouraged the Cathanars to give the cup to the laity, the practice having generally been to give the wafer dipped in the wine; he has ordered them to say the prayers as far as possible in Malayalim, and even to preach, though they have a difficulty in obeying this order, as none of them have been trained or accustomed to do so. Unhappily, he does not seem to carry much weight personally.

Nor is there much help to be hoped for from Antioch, where the Church is sunk in superstitious bigotry, and whence a prelate named Curilos has lately been sent to check and watch the reforming tendencies of Athanasius.

To the Dean of Westminster.

St. Thomas's College, Colombo, Ceylon, January 4, 1864.

. . . I cannot say with what pleasure I think of you as ruling the noblest and grandest of our English churches—the one to which, in historical and religious interest, even Canterbury must yield; the one in which I worshipped as a boy, was confirmed, and was consecrated to the great work of my life; the one which (more even than St. Paul's) brings you into influential contact with London society, and gives you opportunities of leavening with good its frivolity and selfishness.

Do you remember that in 1858 you and I drank tea together in Dean Trench's drawing-room? I wonder whether in 1868, when, if alive, I shall be entitled to furlough, we shall drink tea together in Dean Stanley's drawing-room. As to the school of Westminster, in which, spite of other influences, I still feel considerable interest, I see only two courses open by which it can be made worthy of its great name, and restored to usefulness. Either make it a great day school for the city of Westminster, retaining boarders in the college, and others who like to come, or move it bodily to some pleasing country retreat, and make it a rival to Eton, Harrow, and Rugby. Its connexion with the Abbey may be retained through yourself, and by bringing the boys up once a year to a great service and other public display at election-time. There is no *tertium quid*, except to leave it a comparatively insignificant institution with 120 boys. I shall be curious to hear your judgment on the play. The four selected for representation (Andria, Eunuchus, Phormio, Adelphi) seem in any case indefensible. . . .

Most earnestly, too, do I hope that God's blessing will be on you as a husband, as well as in your work as dean, though, doubtless, Lord Elgin's premature death throws a shadow of melancholy over this part of your new life.

All India has been impressed by the really magnanimous calmness with which Lord Elgin waited for the fatal hour in full certainty that it was at hand; the thoughtfulness with which he gave such directions that the public service might not suffer, and that his widow might travel home in comfort; and which seemed the fitting end of a life spent not on his own amusement or enjoyment, but in the service of his country. The chaplain of Dharmsala wrote to me in admiration of the peaceful composure and reverent devotion with which he received the Sacrament, in entire consciousness that it was his last communion. . . .

There has been so much to say about you and yours, that it seems rather a bathos to descend to my own personal movements. This year the visitation has been metropolitan, and began on the birthday of your prince and of my daughter.

Out of the objects which the tour has presented to us, I shall, *more tuo*, select three for a few concluding remarks. These shall be—(1) Goa, (2) Karli, (3) the Dalada Temple at Kandy.

(1.) Goa is a very pretty place as far as scenery is concerned, and the visit to it was made singularly pleasant by the courtesy of the Portuguese Governor, and the attractive qualities of his aide-de-camp, Dom Genge de Mello, whom he deputed to escort us and show us all the sights. But he who has just read Buchanan's description, and expects to see it realised, will be disappointed with Goa. Much that Buchanan describes has vanished for ever. The convents are all suppressed; the monks are driven away; a few nuns (about eleven) survive in the Abbey of St. Monica, but no novices are admitted. The great Augustinian convent is a ruin. Of the Inquisition buildings nothing can be seen but the foundations cropping up from the dense jungle. The Viceregal Palace is pulled down, and both Viceroy and Archbishop have transferred themselves to healthier regions, the one at New Goa, the other at Rabendar. Three churches of importance alone remain—the cathedral, St. Cajetan, and the Church of the Bom Jesus—all are large, some beautiful. The second of them is attached to a Theatine convent, where some cells have been thrown together, and turned into a set of rooms for the Governor, who usually spends Holy Week there. The third church contains Xavier's tomb, and therefore all the remaining interest of Goa. The shrine is adorned by four fine bas-reliefs in bronze, representing Xavier preaching, baptizing, persecuted and dying; and on the top of the shrine, which is very lofty, rests the coffin of solid silver containing his body. Just outside the chapel is a portrait of him, said to be perfectly authentic, and representing a face of marvellous pathos and devotion. I confess, however, that while he deserves the title of the Apostle of India for his energy, self-sacrifice, and piety, I consider his whole method thoroughly wrong, its results in India and Ceylon most deplorable, and that the aspect of the native Christians at Goa and elsewhere shows that Romanism has had a fair trial at the conversion of India, and has entirely failed. Let us only hope and pray that Protestantism may do better. The one bright example of a flourishing and industrious settlement of native Romanists is at Bettia, near Nepaul, and with it neither Xavier nor the priests of Goa had anything to do.

(2.) Karli took us back to a yet earlier form of worship, the cave being, it is believed, one of the earliest efforts of Buddhism. It is really magnificent. Having sufficiently admired the surrounding landscape, you stand at the richly-carved entrance of a vast excavation, hollowed into a shape resembling the choir of a great Gothic cathedral, divided into three aisles by two rows of columns, with fantastic capitals composed of elephants and their riders, ending in a semicircular apse, which is filled up (as the east end of a Christian church is by its altar) by a *daghoba*, a bell-shaped structure covering a relic of Buddha or one of his saints. Hard by the great cave, by climbing up the rock, you come to a *vihara*, or monastery, with the monks' cells arranged in rows, all excavated from the rock, and a common room in front with a stone ledge, on which doubtless they sat and taught their disciples. On the other side of the cave, also excavated from the rock, is an apartment for the lodgment of pilgrims. The whole is attributed, on evidence fairly satisfactory, to the time of Asoka, the great patron of Buddhism, about 200 B.C. It is one of the most striking of Indian sights, and illustrates and is illustrated by the Bhilsa topes, which I saw and imperfectly described to you last year.

(3.) From Buddhism prostrate and extinct in India, we passed to the temple of the Dalada, and there saw it alive and rampant in Ceylon. Max Müller will have taught you to recognise *dens* and ὀδοὺς in *dalada*, and to perceive that this temple contains Sakya's tooth, the most sacred of Buddhist relics. A promise was given that we should see the tooth itself; but when we reached Kandy we were told that the keeper of the key had gone away—perhaps a civil excuse for not showing what they are very reluctant to show. However, I did not care much for the tooth itself, which is, I was assured, merely a long piece of discoloured ivory, unquestionably part of an elephant's tusk. We were carefully admitted to see all the paraphernalia which surround it. The Temple itself is small and rather tawdry with red and yellow paint; the chapel in which the tooth is enshrined is so minute that we could hardly squeeze our party into it. In front of the shrine is a silver table, covered with flowers offered by the faithful. The tooth is guarded by a large iron cage, secured by many locks, within which is a silver gilt shrine in the daghoba (the tope of Bhilsa, the pagoda of Burmah), richly adorned with jewels, and doubtless both pretty and gorgeous. Within this daghoba are six others, each decreasing in size, and within the seventh lies the tooth. Candles burned before it and about it; the smell of the flowers was exactly like the odour of incense, and the resemblance of the whole to the chapel and shrine enclosing a Roman Catholic relic was most striking. In another chapel hard by are some costly images of Buddha, of rock crystal; and at no great distance is a colossal image of him, thirty-six feet long, lying down, with his head resting on his hand, supposed to be in the act of receiving *nirvána.*

To the Rev. G. G. Bradley.

Cape Comorin, January 21, 1864.

We have just finished a fortnight's most interesting visitation of the Tinnevelly missions. I can assure you that I have been deeply impressed with the reality and thoroughgoing character of the whole business: and I entreat you never to believe any insinuations against missionary work in India, or to scruple to plead, or allow to be pleaded, in your chapel, the cause of either the Society for the Propagation of the Gospel or the Church Missionary Society. All the English humbug, the petty rivalries between the two societies, the nonsense which one hears from a wandering 'deputation,' vanish in this land where the real work is going on, and the actual contest is waged between Christ and Belial. In Tinnevelly, the two societies work hand in hand, their districts interlace; and we were escorted continually by a Society for the Propagation of the Gospel missionary into the domain of a Church Missionary Society man, some five miles distant from his own, and met altogether for family prayers, a cheerful breakfast, a pleasant practical talk about parochial and evangelistic plans, a joint inspection of schools and church, and other parochial institutions. The whole country is now mapped out into regular Christian districts, each furnished with a substantial church, parsonage, and schools in its central village, and with small prayer-houses in the minor hamlets. A thoroughly good simple vernacular education is given all over the country, and there are four efficient training schools—two for schoolmasters, one for catechists, and one for mistresses. In one of these, and also in a large central school at Palamcotta, the capital of the province, English is taught; in the others instruction is given through the medium of Tamil. And to one of these training-schools (for masters) is attached a regular play-ground and gymnastic apparatus, where I witnessed cricket being played, and poles climbed by tawny Indian Christians with light white garments wrapped round their middles; and where, at Christmas, there had been athletic games worthy of Marlborough, including flat races, high jumps, sack races, and every kind of exhibition of muscular Christianity. In every parish there are short services morning and evening, which all attend when not hindered by house or field-work; and bible-classes of men and women, systematically taught, some of which I examined, and found the women most intelligent and correct in their answering. Compare this, I entreat you, with the condition of women in a zenana! Industry, order, cleanliness, domestic purity, improvement in worldly circumstances, are all conspicuous among the Tinnevelly Christians, and if they are still somewhat given to prevarications and untruthfulness, yet we must remember that this is the national vice of India, and that Christianity can no more eradicate it *all at once*, than it eradicated by a sudden blow impurity from Corinth or Ephesus, or worldly selfishness from the higher and drunkenness from the lower ranks of English society. Most of the converts are *Shanars*, a caste corresponding to our small farmers, and chiefly occupied in the culture and climbing of the palmyra tree, from which they extract sugar; some are Pariahs. But the leaven is spreading upwards, and I myself had a conversation with two inquirers of the caste next to the Brahmans, who seemed to me at once intelligent, humble, and earnest in their Christian aspirations. As to the temporal results of the Gospel in these parts, one person told me that society is getting turned upside down, and instead of the Shanars being in debt to the Brahmans, the Brahmans are now borrowing money from the Shanars. Altogether, I do not think that anyone can go through the Tinnevelly missions without being the better for it; and I feel that my own faith in the Gospel has been strengthened by the journey, and by the actual sight of what Christianity can do. 'I have heard of Thee by the hearing of the ear, but now mine eye seeth Thee.'

. . . .

To his Son.

Ootacamund, February 6, 1864.

We are deeply thankful for the improved accounts of your health. The banquet and charades of Christmas Eve would have furnished sufficient proofs of recovery, without the addition of the cracked table and cascade of port wine. Your restoration is indeed a great mercy, and I rejoiced to read in one of your letters that you were ready to acknowledge by whose hand this mercy had been sent.

We have had very hard travelling of late, and have, I think, deserved a brief rest on the hills, up at Ootacamund. The Nilgherries are a projection from the Ghâts, the grand range of mountains which run north and south from Bombay to Cape Comorin, and the name means *Blue Mountains*, since the part of the Ghâts against which they abut are of a most lovely blue tint, especially near sunset—such a tint as Turner should have perpetuated on canvas. We had breakfast and luncheon at Coonoor, the first station on the hills, and afterwards had a most toilsome ascent in bullock carriages to Ootacamund, twelve miles further, which we did not reach till 10 P.M. We found rooms secured for us in a most comfortable hotel, and slept like tops. The place has many great attractions. It is a little more than 7,000 feet high, and therefore delightfully cool, in fact, in the mornings and evenings piercingly cold; and it is situated in a kind of basin of table land surrounded by hills, so that it is possible to drive about in carriages, the only difficulty being that the horse is an animal as nearly unknown in the 'benighted' Presidency of Madras as it was to the American Indians when the Spaniards landed on their coast, and were imagined to form part of the animals on which they rode. Hence horse-carriages are outrageously dear, and bullock-carriages are used instead. The flowers are most luxurious: in wild flowers, indeed, I see nothing to match Darjeeling, with its glorious orchids and air plants; but of English garden and semi-greenhouse plants—roses, geraniums, heliotropes, verbenas, and the like—the profusion is quite wonderful, the roads being bordered by whole hedges of them. The great inferiority to the Himalayan stations is in the want of a snowy range. The

Nilgherries rise scarcely 500 feet higher than Ootacamund, and their tops are mere green mounds. Hence a person who remembers the magnificence of Gungutri or Kunchinjinga feels something like contempt when an Ootacamundian, in a voice of triumphant self-complacency, points to a snub-nosed hill as 'Dodabetta, the highest peak in South India.' Of course, the Nilgherries, as seen from the plains of India, are fine mountains enough, but from Ootacamund, which is nearly at their top, their elevation is but paltry. We have been to visit a wild hill tribe here called the Todas, the aborigines of the Nilgherries, who live in houses like inverted boats, made of bamboo and rattan, about seven feet high, and perhaps eleven long and six wide, wholly without windows or chimneys, and with no approach but through a door about eighteen inches square. They were rather good-looking and friendly folk, with long black hair, and raiment very scanty for such a climate, and invited us to enter their dwellings. This your mother declined to do, but Mr. Stuart and I crawled in on our hands and knees, but were nearly blinded by the smoke of a wood fire which blazed in the house, and by a kind of perpetual miracle does not envelop it and its inhabitants in the flames. Their food is rice and milk, their property bullocks. They had a temple shaped like their houses, but would not allow us to enter it. Combining the useful with the spiritual, they store away in it their *ghee* and other provisions. Except the Andamanese, they are the wildest people that I ever saw. Ursula was not with us on this occasion, but was so excited by our description that we must, I think, take her to see our Toda friends.

To Professor Conington.

Ootacamund, Nilgherry Hills, February 10, 1864.

Since I wrote to you last, I find that the fears and anxieties which you expressed in your letter to me have turned out only too well founded, and that you have been deprived of the affection and support of your brother. I saw a pleasing little notice of him quoted in the 'Friend of India' from the 'Spectator,' which gave me the first intimation that he was actually taken from you, and since that the sad news has been repeated from many quarters. You know me too well to doubt that my thoughts were with you, even amidst the multifarious interests and distractions of a rapid visitation tour. You have been much tried lately by family losses and illnesses, but it is not hard to discern in them an element of mercy and fatherly love, so far as they directly affect you. A man of books and thought in the midst of the most intellectual society of an intellectual and sceptical age requires to be reminded practically that he needs something higher than intellect to rest upon, and that 'whether there be knowledge, it shall vanish away.' And, of course, a word like this, which might be spoken to any active-minded man at Oxford, has a very real and definite application when spoken by me to you, remembering, as we must, all our letters and many conversations on such subjects, and the doubts, difficulties, and temptations by which we have been both troubled in different degrees and manners. I feel myself, at the sight of death and trouble, how utterly powerless are the nostrums of Congreve, or Newman, or Colenso; how certainly there is no rest for us except in Christ. May you, my dear old friend, find there abundant rest, and be enabled to believe with your whole heart that 'thy brother shall rise again.'

Our tour, just beginning when I wrote to you last, is now verging to its close. We are resting for ten days in this delightful and bracing climate, till we must descend upon hot Madras in time for the next Peninsular and Oriental steamer to Calcutta. We both look forward to our return there with hope and pleasure, and are both getting really to like India. Once I remember comparing my feelings towards the diocese and India with those entertained by Arnold to Rugby school and Rugby town, the diocesan work being my plant, and India my pot. I now formally recall that comparison, and declare that I like the pot as well as the plant.

To Mrs. Tomkinson.

Coonoor, Nilgherry Mountains, February 17, 1864.

I have formed a habit, a praiseworthy one I think, of writing to you a letter of pure chit-chat at the end of each cold weather tour. I am sure that it is good occasionally to write on absolutely general and public topics, and to banish difficulties, uncertainties, private concerns altogether, just as it is desirable to vary the real work of life by seeing fine scenery, or by reading a number of the 'Small House at Allington.'

I consider that this has been the most interesting and noteworthy of all our tours, except, perhaps, the first, from Calcutta to Simla, in 1859-60, when everything was new. The recollections of that journey are most delightful, but the one now ending is only second to it. As to races and religions, we have seen Parsees at Bombay worshipping the setting sun, and exposing their dead on high towers to vultures; we have recalled the past greatness of Buddhism in the magnificent cave at Karli, and witnessed its present apathy and degeneracy in the priests and worshippers of Kandy, who gather round the temple where Buddha's tooth is enshrined; we have visited Syrians at Cottyam, anathematising Nestorians and the Council of Chalcedon, and repeating the Nicene Creed without the words acknowledging the double procession; white Jews at Cochin, some with blue eyes and light hair, boasting of the perfect purity of their Hebrew blood, like St. Paul to the Philippians, but without the accompanying confession that 'What things were given to him these he counted loss for Christ;' black Jews in the same place, probably either Hindu converts to Judaism, or illegitimate descendants of the white Jews, not, as some have vainly imagined, fugitives from Pharaoh Necho, or I know not what other Egyptian king; castes and races on the west coast, including two royal families, in which, owing to the horrid custom of polyandry, the inheritance, and even the rajahship, passes to the sister's son, as the only one certainly inheriting the family blood; and lastly, a mountain race in these hills called the Todas, exacting tribute, as lords of the soil, from certain Hindu folk who fled up here from the persecution of the Mahometans, and worshipping in a manner which would gratify the Comtists as a purely industrial form of religion, since it consists entirely in churning butter. To this enumeration of races and religions I must thankfully add one which deserves a paragraph to itself, the Christianised peasantry of Tinnevelly and Travancore, a most encouraging and edifying sight. The parochial system is carried out much more thoroughly than in England; my only fear is that it is too thorough, that the people are kept too much in a state of drill, and that enough play is not allowed for national and individual characteristics. However, the whole aspect of things is most cheering. Of the intelligent knowledge, and orderly, industrious, and religious habits of our fellow-Christians in the extreme south of India there can be no doubt.

Descriptions of scenery are always tiresome and vapid, unless undertaken by a Kingsley, a Ruskin, or (let me add from old boyish recollections) a Mrs. Radcliffe, so I shall only enumerate a few of the most striking places and views we have seen:—The Falls of Gerseppa, with the ghât leading up to them; the Goa River; the views from Elephanta towards the Bombay harbour, and from the heights above Bombay towards Elephanta; the magnificent view of mountains and valleys from Khandala at the top of the Bhore Ghât on the Bombay Railway; the road from Galle to Colombo, with its sea, rocks, and groves of cocoa-nuts; Kandy; Cottyam; some peeps along the backwater which, like a series of Venetian lagoons, forms the watery highway through Travancore and Cochin; the view from the top of Dodabetta, highest of the Nilgherries, and several views about Coonoor down the pass, and over the plains at the foot, though Charlotte need not think that the Nilgherries, with all their beauty, can compare to her own Himalayas, from the absence of the glorious snowy peaks piercing the blue sky, or tinted with the colours of sunrise and sunset, which are perhaps the most sublime of earthly sights. There was also great interest in seeing the character of the whole west coast of India from the sea from Bombay southwards, including the grand chain of the West Ghâts, from which the Nilgherries and some other groups of hills are projections; and especially in standing on the very extremity of India at Cape Comorin, looking over the waste of waters on which Phœnicians, Greeks, Arabs, Portuguese successively struggled to India, and to see how the huge continent manages at last to get itself finished. Cape Comorin, however, in itself is not a fine object; it is the last expiring effort, and a very puny one, of the great convulsion which upheaved the Ghâts. To make up for this, it is surrounded with a number of legends about Shiva and his wife Parvati, and to bathe in the waters near it is a very effective way of getting rid of one's sins. We did so, but I do not know that I have been morally much the better for it since, though doubtless, after a night's journey, I was physically invigorated, and, therefore, on an old (but probably transient) view of P.'s, that virtue and vice depend mainly on atmospheric and climatic influences, I perhaps shared the benefits which the worshippers of Shiva derive from the lustration. While standing on the Cape, S. and I recalled the day, just four years ago, when, hoisted on an elephant, and reading a very amusing letter from the said P., we approached Jamrood, the north-west extremity of India, and looked down upon the Khyber Pass. Between these two extremities we have seen and done a great deal; would that the doings were at all in proportion to the opportunities given to us, and the countless mercies for which we have so much reason to be thankful in our Indian life. As to work, there has been a suspension of confirmations and clerical business, but perhaps rather more abundance than usual of preaching and haranguing. The charge was delivered with parched throat four times. Spurgeon-like, I preached in Tinnevelly eleven times in a fortnight; and the practice there of presenting an address to the metropolitan in each Christian settlement, led to interminable minor harangues. Still, on the whole, there was an agreeable sensation of being a visitor, a learner, and an inquirer, rather than an official teacher and decider of controversies, which is necessarily my position when on a diocesan visitation.

To Rev. H. Venn.

March 1864.

. . . It is needless for me to speak about Tinnevelly. The evidence of reality and thoroughness in the work was even more striking than I had expected, and I have nowhere seen more reverence and attention in church, or listened to more hearty and devout congregational singing and responses. There is only one subject on which I think it necessary to write, because it is one on which opinions seem still in some degree divided, though the tendency is, I think, inclining to the view which I am going to advocate.

I am strongly convinced that the time has come when the study of English should be more encouraged than it has been among our converts. Of course I do not advocate its introduction in the ordinary village schools, any more than I should wish to have Latin taught in the national schools of England; but I do wish it made a part of the training of catechists and schoolmasters, for the following reasons:—

In the first place, without English a man cannot obtain that efficient theological training which a teacher at least ought to have received. It is true that some of our standard works in English theology are translated, but we all know that a translation is not equal to the original, and some of the so-called translations are mere epitomes and abstracts. Now all who have had to do with the Universities must remember how cramping and unsatisfactory is the use of cram books and abridgments, which the inferior tutors at Oxford and Cambridge substitute for the original works of our great authors, that so they may push their pupils through their examinations with the minimum of trouble and also of profit.

But, again, the study of English is spreading further and further among the heathen. We must not allow the Christians to be inferior to them in knowledge, and in the power of taking a good social position. The influence of the native Christians ought to be such as gradually to leaven all society.

Again, there is a great and increasing desire among the Christians to learn English; I am quite sure that to put any hindrance in their way chafes them with a sense of unkindness and injustice, and leads to those evils which were justly deplored in the report of the Punjab Missionary Conference.

I do not overlook the arguments which are urged in favour of an exclusively vernacular training. It is said that a knowledge of English, being exceptional, makes a young man conceited, gives him European tastes, and produces in him indifference to his countrymen. But first, in proportion as the knowledge becomes less exceptional, these evil results will diminish. Next, this is only arguing against the use of a privilege by its abuse, which is seldom satisfactory. If the knowledge of English confers substantial intellectual benefits on its recipient, we may trust that God's grace will ward off any moral dangers which may follow. The more Christian and prayerful the student is, the less likely is he to be vain or unpatriotic.

Also, it is said that our trained students, by knowing English, are tempted away from mission work to some lucrative secular employment. This will not be the case with those who are most remarkable for piety and devotion; as to the rest, it may at least be hoped that their Christianity will to some extent influence the heathens who are their fellow-members in the professions which they adopt. In any case the argument cuts two ways. If we are reluctant to part with some of our schoolmasters, we should be glad to provide secular employment for others who turn out, for any reason, inefficient teachers; but if they do not know English this cannot be done. They cannot be provided for in a Government office, for example, where they might be useful, and we are saddled with them for life.

There is, however, an argument against teaching English to those who are to be masters in vernacular schools, which undoubtedly deserves attention. It is said that unless they are trained in the vernacular they will not be familiar with technical terms in various branches of learning, such as arithmetic and geography, and, above all, that they will not know thoroughly the vernacular text of Holy Scripture, and therefore will not be efficient teachers of a village school, where the vernacular is all-important. But this evil will be entirely met by adopting the suggestion of Mr. Spratt, a missionary who seemed to me no less remarkable for thoughtfulness and sound sense than for earnest piety, and whose training institution for masters at Palamcottah is admirably conducted. He proposes to give the ordinary lessons to his pupils through the medium of the vernacular, but to teach English as a foreign language for two hours a day, so that it would occupy the same place in his training college which Latin and Greek take in an English school. This plan seems to me quite to meet the difficulty, and at the same time materially to diminish some of the objections mentioned above. . . . .

Let me, in conclusion, thank you for sending me various educational documents, and keeping me informed of all that is going on in England on that subject. Sir Charles Trevelyan is disposed to be most useful in forwarding education here, and would take a much more active part in it than he does if he were less overworked and absorbed in his budget and other financial duties.

But we never had a Government more disposed to give free course to missionary education than we have now. The latest proof of their friendship (though but a trifling one) is the readiness with which they have assented to my request that your secretary, Mr. Stuart, might be made a member of the university senate.

To Rev. F. Farrar.

Bishop's Palace, March 1864.

I was very glad to get your letter, which broke in agreeably upon the fatigue and excitement of the longest, most varied, and most interesting tour that I have yet taken. From such a whirl of exciting and novel objects it was well for me to be recalled by home letters to the no less pressing interests of England. Among those referring not to private but to public anxieties, yours, with its dissertation on present theological controversies, caused me at least as much thought as any, especially from your repeating the sentiment which is very commonly expressed now-a-days, that we are 'on the eve of a new reformation.' I candidly own that it is a maxim with which I have no sympathy, and which I do not clearly understand. That there is at present a great theological agitation going on is of course clear. That people who have long tried to scoff down all the current doubts and difficulties, and obstinately oppose even the consideration of them, are severely to be condemned, is also clear. Moreover, if I could fancy that by reformation you meant constant improvement, growth in knowledge, piety, wisdom, and good works, I should trust that we are not on the eve but in the very midst of a new reformation, since I never believe that the Church of Christ is to stagnate and to refuse to admit and assimilate to its own system new discoveries, new forms of prayer and praise, in accordance with new wants and new projects of evangelising the world and turning its kingdoms into the kingdoms of the Lord. But I imagine that by a new reformation is merely meant a general belief in these current biblical speculations, and that its apostles are to be Rénan, and others in our own land. If so, I really cannot see a single feature in which their writings and preachings resemble those of the men who are usually called reformers. Their speculations undoubtedly tend to Deism (Rénan's somewhat further), to the denial of a supernatural revelation, to the reduction of Our Lord to the level of Plato, Buddha, and Mahomet, though morally doubtless their superior, and *perhaps* more fully enlightened than they by the Spirit of God. Luther and Melancthon restored Our Lord to the dignity which St. Paul and St. John believed Him to hold, and which had been tampered with by the Romish addition of other mediators to His all-sufficient intercession. The reformation of the modern reformers is a denial of primitive and apostolic truth; that of Luther was a restoration of it. Again, the matters about which people now interest themselves are purely intellectual: those for which our fathers fought and suffered were spiritual and moral. Compare, in mere importance to the world, a creed of which the leading article is that Samuel forged the Pentateuch, with that which was mainly concerned with our justification in the sight of God. What an *articulus stantis aut cadentis ecclesiæ* is the question whether Jeremiah palmed off the book of Deuteronomy or King Josiah. If the difficulty about the six days of Creation is insoluble, what difference does it make to the *moral* condition of mankind, unless, indeed, it can be proved that the world has no personal Creator, in which case doubtless our religion will be more nearly akin to that of the Puranas than to that of the Gospel? And this is just what a little provokes me in that talk of a new reformation. If it is meant that we are to cease to be Christians, that the Nicene Creed is about to be disproved, and if with it the writings of St. Paul and St. John are shown to be either forgeries or insanities, then I quite understand that we are to have a reformation with a vengeance, though

I should be unable to give that name to the change which is coming upon us. But if the meaning of the term is that we are to hold our ears perpetually open to a long-continued utterance of German hypotheses, then I must beg to retreat partly behind the mantle of Sir George Cornewall Lewis, who has, I think, dealt a deadly blow to such conjectural criticism, and partly behind the bulwark of practical work and humble efforts to improve spiritually and morally, which rest, as I believe, wholly and exclusively on that faith in God as revealed to us in Christ which Rénan consciously and designedly, Colenso unconsciously and undesignedly, and other writers through presumptuous dogmatism and the love of vituperation, are, in my opinion, labouring to undermine. . . . .

With regard to your work on the mixed origin of the human race, if, as you say, you can *disprove from Scripture* the fact of our common descent from Adam and Eve, then I cannot see that by publishing the book you will run counter to the current flow of thought among your brethren of the clergy. Rather you will fall in with it, by basing the facts of history on a scriptural foundation, and by clearing away false inferences from the Old Testament. What is objected to, and I think justly, is the practice of Colenso, and others of that school, of absolutely ignoring and vilipending the authority of Our Lord and the Apostles, or the express statements of other parts of Scripture, for the sake of some baseless or half-formed conjecture, or some alleged scientific discovery imperfectly ascertained, and of which the full bearings are not known. If you can prove both by Scripture and by science that we have not all the same parentage, then even Archdeacon Pratt himself can only welcome you as a coadjutor and ally. After all, this view has been propounded, I believe, in the 'Genesis of the Earth and Man,' which, whether convincing or not, for I never read it, has certainly not exposed its author to martyrdom or any minor persecution.

*To the Most Rev. Mar Athanasius, Bishop and Metran.**

1864.

I regret very much that I had no opportunity of seeing you during my visit to Travancore. There were many subjects on which I should have desired to confer with you, as some of my predecessors have done with your predecessors. I was much pleased with my short intercourse with your Cathanars and people, and desire to thank them, through you, for the kindness and respect with which they received me.

It is my earnest prayer that God may prosper all wise and Christian endeavours for the improvement of the venerable Syrian Church in Travancore, in which I feel the deepest interest, and with which our English Church has many bonds of connexion. This is not the time or occasion for discussing the points of doctrine on which our Churches differ; but I may perhaps be allowed to mention some of the practical agencies by which, through the grace of God's Holy Spirit, the Church of England has flourished and acquired much influence among the people, and by which doubtless the Syrian Church, through the same all-powerful guidance, will recover its primitive importance and purity. The first is the example of high principle, blameless living, unselfish devotion to Christ's flock, and laborious activity on the part of all who exercise spiritual authority; the next is the circulation of the Holy Bible among the people, and their intelligent acquaintance with its contents; the third is the diffusion of education, both theological and secular, among the clergy, including of course the careful preparation of candidates for holy orders; the fourth is preaching; and the last which I will mention is the celebration of Divine service in the vernacular language of the people. I doubt not that all these subjects have engaged your attention, and I heard with thankfulness at Cottyam that you had shown a special interest in the last two of them. I heartily hope that you will succeed in your efforts to teach all your Cathanars how to preach, and that you will be able gradually to substitute Malayalim for

* This letter was in answer to one from the Metran, expressing hi regret at his absence from Cottyam during the Bishop's visit.

Syriac in the public prayers and reading of Scripture, as priests and people get accustomed to the change. I respectfully commend to your watchful care the other means of improvement also which I have ventured to bring before you, being quite sure that such practical reforms furnish a firm basis for doctrinal reforms. I value your Church, as one which retains, like our own, many primitive customs and principles, while it repudiates the usurpations and innovations of the Papacy ; and if the best elements in the spirit of the Reformation could be added to the best in the spirit of antiquity, I see no reason why your clergy should not stand side by side with ours as powerful agents in the blessed work of winning India to Christ. Such sentiments have been expressed by former Bishops of Calcutta, and I trust that we shall not always be disappointed. Perhaps the happy day, when we can fully act together, is reserved for our successors rather than ourselves, but it is our duty to labour and pray for it. Meantime I am sure that both the English Metropolitan of India, and the Metran of the Syrian Church have noble fields of Christian usefulness before them, which must one day become a common field, if only they have grace to exert themselves in proportion to the several opportunities which God has given to each in abundant measure.

With the fervent hope that God's Spirit may pour out His grace and blessing on your clergy and people, I remain, &c.

CHAPTER XI.

RETURN TO CALCUTTA—MEETING WITH SIR JOHN LAWRENCE—WORK FOR EUROPEANS—TITLE DEEDS OF THE SIMLA SCHOOL—INTERCOURSE WITH NATIVES—CALCUTTA UNIVERSITY—VISITS TO LUTHERAN MISSION AT RANCHI—CATHEDRAL LECTURES TO HINDUS—THE BISHOP'S RELATIONS WITH MISSIONARY SOCIETIES—HIS PERSONAL RELATIONS WITH MISSIONARIES—SYMPATHY WITH THEIR DIFFICULTIES—DISPOSITION TOWARDS INQUIRERS ABOUT CHRISTIANITY—HIS VIEWS ON NATIVE EDUCATION AS ADMINISTERED BY MISSIONARIES—GROWTH OF FEELING ON THE SUBJECT AMONG MISSIONARIES—LIBERALITY OF VIEWS ON THE PART OF THE STATE—LIMITED AMOUNT OF MISSIONARY SUCCESS—AFFAIRS OF BISHOP'S COLLEGE—LETTERS TO THE SECRETARY OF THE PROPAGATION SOCIETY.

ON reaching Calcutta, in March 1864, the Bishop had the great satisfaction of meeting Sir John Lawrence, whose recent installation in his high office had been hailed both by natives and Europeans as an event full of hope and promise for India. The new Viceroy was already vigorously at work, investigating official departments with the practised eye of one to whom all grades of State duty were familiar. At their first interview, the Bishop found him buried in papers, with neck-tie discarded, and with attire generally in accordance more with comfort than conventionality. 'Excuse my dress, it's very hot,' said the Viceroy, with the true distaste of a denizen of the Punjâb to the hot-house climate of Bengal, and then plunged at once into a series of inquiries about the Christians in South India. The Bishop was soon engaged again in the usual routine work of a residence in Calcutta. It was in this year that the first stone was laid by the Viceroy of a new Seaman's Home.

A pastor also was provided to minister exclusively to the low Eurasian population of the city; his stipend being paid by the voluntary contributions from the surrounding Church of England congregations. Both these undertakings were steps towards that provision for the moral and spiritual needs of Anglo-Indians which was an ever-present subject of the Bishop's solicitude. A specific stage in another great work for the rising generation of this same class, is recorded in a brief recapitulatory notice of occupations during these weeks:—

'One of my pleasantest public acts has been putting my signature to a deed sealed with the episcopal seal, founding and declaring the statutes of "the Bishop's School," near Simla, as the new institution is called by a kind of popular acclamation; so I trust that now I have done something permanently for the good of the diocese, and I pray that He through whose mercy it has been accomplished may grant to it His blessing, and make it a home of godliness and good learning.'

The distinguishing feature, however, of the Bishop's residence in Calcutta of 1864 was his intercourse with natives, both Christian and non-Christian. His health was, by the blessing of God, sustained during several months of great heat, and no illness arose to impede the execution of distinct work, with which, as was his wont, he desired to stamp a distinct period of time. The kind recognition which has been so freely granted to the Bishop's friendly advances towards the native community is the more valuable because they were necessarily imperfect and occasional. From this point of view, as from many others, an Indian bishop's position is one of isolation. Unlike civilians whose official duties bring them into daily contact with natives of many grades, he has no such link to turn to account. Moreover the bishop can never represent religious neutrality. Though strictly a servant of the State, he will always be looked upon as the head and leader of a proselytising Church, without possessing that passport to toleration which the professed missionary holds as he exhibits his self-denying life in the eyes of multitudes, and goes freely in and out amongst them. In the common course of daily life the bishop's path seldom crosses that of the educated Hindu. The gulf is great between those who are within the pale of the Church and those still outside it. A chief pastor directing his care and attention mainly to the former may easily miss, during long years, those points of contact with the latter which do not readily reveal themselves but must be sought for and even created. One leading principle of the Bishop's Indian life was that the Christian Church must labour either directly or indirectly to exert an influence over the native mind equal to that which was so widely and powerfully exercised through secular education. To this work he exhorted and stimulated others; to it he personally devoted such time and opportunities as were available during his brief and intermittent sojourns in a city which was the chief seat of intellectual activity among natives. Through the University he found one of the desired links with the educated classes. He was always on the Syndicate, and in 1864 acted for the vice-chancellor during his absence, and was president of the Faculty of Arts. He thus obtained a distinct voice in the direction of the studies of the place, and it may therefore be well to insert here a notice of the University and of his relations with it, which has been contributed by Professor Cowell, formerly Principal of the Sanscrit College in Calcutta, and now Professor of Sanscrit at Cambridge.

Bishop Cotton arrived in Bengal when a great experiment had been just commenced by the founding, in 1857, of the Calcutta University. Ever since the memorable despatch of 1835, by which Lord W. Bentinck established the principle that the study of English literature and Western science should henceforth supersede the exclusive devotion to Sanscrit and Arabic, with their obsolete systems of science and philosophy, English has become the staple of the education given in the Government higher schools and colleges; and the native students have abundantly proved, by their enthusiastic appreciation of English literature, how wise the change was which was thus introduced. A new era then began for India. No longer secluded in its own world of ideas, no longer isolated from the rest of mankind, the Hindu began to awake from the torpor of ages to a new activity and interest. We are just beginning in our day to see the effects of this mighty movement; but it needs little foresight to prophesy that the superstitions which have so long brooded over the national mind will be gradually dispelled, and the nation will regain that conscious activity which once raised it to a foremost place among the creative races of the earth. The press is now busy in every native language; native newspapers are issuing in every great city; a vernacular literature is slowly springing up which will gradually transform mere spoken dialects into cultivated instruments of thought; and everywhere in India (to quote Lord Bacon's words in the 'Novum Organon') we hear on all sides, as in a mine, the sounds of new explorations and onward progress. The rise of the Bráhmo Somáj, and its rapid extension in the great cities, the native agitation for female education and for the remarriage of infant widows, are proofs how the leaven of English education is working in the national mind; and perhaps no country in the world at the present time, offers such an exciting spectacle as India, to the philanthropist and the philosopher.

Bishop Cotton, on his arrival in Calcutta in 1858, found the university already established, two entrance examinations had been held, and in 1858 the first examination for a B.A. degree, in which two Hindu students from the Presidency College passed with success. The numbers have year by year steadily increased; in April 1857, 244 candidates presented themselves for examination, of whom 115 passed in the first, and 47 in the second division; while in 1864, 1,396 candidates presented themselves, of whom 143 passed in the first, and 559 in the second division. In the Entrance Examinations in December 1869, 1,730 candidates presented themselves, of whom 817 passed ;—178 in the first division, 440 in the second, and 199 in the third. At the first Examination in Arts (corresponding to the Previous Examination at Cambridge), 520 candidates presented themselves, of whom 225 passed ;—23 in the first division, 81 in the second, and 121 in the third. At the B.A. Examination in January 1870, there were 210 candidates, of whom 98 passed ;—16 in the first division, 46 in the second, and 36 in the third. Such a movement as this is almost unparalleled in history, and even our railroads and telegraphs, however vast their effects, are less important in their influence on the social and moral condition of the Hindus.

Bishop Cotton from the first took the deepest interest in the University and the progress of education which it so successfully stimulated. When in Calcutta he was continually a member of the Syndicate or ruling body, and he always took the warmest interest in the various questions connected with the working out of the scheme, especially in the selection of books for the examinations. Thus one of his suggestions was that in every B.A. examination some one of Bacon's great works should be one of the text-books in English, and consequently the first or second book of the 'Advancement of Learning,' or the first book of the translation of the 'Novum Organon,' became a recognized portion of the student's course. The Hindu mind is naturally dreamy and imaginative; it loves literature intensely, but chiefly for its poetical or rhetorical beauty; and such books as these are the very diet which it needs to brace its intellectual fibre. The study of Bacon opens a new world to the Hindu student, he learns to widen his interests and deepen his mental sympathies, and the charms of fiction and poetry no longer exclusively engross him as his eyes open to the 'fairy tales of science and the long result of time.'

But the Bishop could not be blind to the grand defect in all Government education—the necessary exclusion of all Christian teaching. Few will hesitate to concede that, in the peculiar position which we hold in India, this exclusion was an unavoidable condition of a Government scheme of education. The grants in aid are freely given to any missionary school which trains its students to reach a certain standard; the junior scholarships are open to all the students in the university entrance examination, and are simply prizes for which the students of Government or private institutions are equally eligible, and similarly the senior scholarships are equally open as prizes for the first public examination. But in the Government schools and colleges religion is excluded; and though the teacher is left free in his private capacity to exercise what moral influence he may possess, his lips are necessarily closed in the class-room, and there secular knowledge can alone be taught.

In 1862 a very interesting discussion was raised in the Faculty of Arts of the Calcutta University by a proposal of the Rev. Dr. Duff, that the professorships of Law, Medicine, Civil Engineering, Sanscrit, and Arabic, now attached to the Presidency, Medical, Civil Engineering, and Sanscrit Colleges, and the Madrisah, should be converted into University professorships, open to duly qualified students of all affiliated institutions; and that new professorships should be founded of Physical Science, Natural Philosophy, and Paideutics. The proposition was rejected except so far as regards the professorships of Physical Science and Natural Philosophy; but the minority appended some vigorous protests, and the following is an extract from that written by the Bishop:—

'The present Government scheme of education in India can, in my opinion, only be accepted as one of transition. It is liable to the four great objections, that it is incapable of educating the whole man, from its necessary omission of the religious element; that it is a system of thorough centralisation; that, in proportion to the numbers who benefit by it, it is enormously expensive; and that it does not encourage private efforts. Considering the peculiarity of our position in India—a Christian Government ruling over a nation which is not Christian, and called upon to *initiate* a scheme for the education of the people—I think that the State was not only justified in acting as it has done, but even bound to do so; I think, however, that it is also bound to hasten (as far as can be safely done) the substitution of a system not exposed to these objections, and, therefore, to adopt all such prudent measures as are likely to assist institutions founded or maintained by private munificence, and gradually to retire from the position of actual instructor of the people, and retain only the function of aiding, promoting, inspecting, and rewarding education. This I conceive to be the footing prescribed to us by the Educational Despatch of 1854.'

These views were afterwards expanded into a paper, published in the 'Calcutta Christian Intelligencer' for June 1862. He there remarked :—

'As to the non-religious character of Government education we are not among those who think that this can be avoided. Something, no doubt, may be done by voluntary Bible classes out of school hours, and we have always deeply regretted the needless interference of our late Lieut.-Governor with their extension by his (as we think quite unauthorised) insertion of the fatal condition that they must be excluded not only from the school hours but from the school buildings. Still, if that condition were cancelled, it is not likely that many of these classes would be formed, and we cannot think that it would be either just or expedient for Government to introduce the Bible into their schools any further than by sanctioning these classes. Bible reading or teaching conducted by heathens, we utterly abominate. All that we ask from Government in reference to the present system is to take the greatest care that persons of high moral character are appointed to educational offices, and we readily acknowledge that this has generally been the case.'

The following extract is interesting in more points than one, where the Bishop sketches the way in which one or two university professorships would benefit the general cause of education :—

'Thus material pecuniary aid will be given at once to all the colleges, governmental and non-governmental alike, but especially the latter, which cannot afford, depending as they do on small endowments, or voluntary contributions, or the payments of scholars, to maintain first-rate men as teachers of the various distinct branches in which instruction should be given to members of a university. Thus, too, teaching power would be saved, for as it is probable that but few students from each college would seek this special and additional instruction, the same teacher would be available for all. Thus, too, the way would be prepared for gradually separating the details of education from State management (except as far as inspection is concerned), since the quality of the instruction given to the students of the non-governmental colleges would be improved. Thus, finally, encouragement would be given to individuals and societies, to natives and Europeans, to establish schools and colleges, since the cost of doing so would be diminished, and the chief difficulty, that of supplying adequate training for the abler and more advanced students, would be removed. For example, it is clear that the Church of England does not take at all an adequate part in the education of the native youth of Calcutta. Either of the great societies of that Church might, we imagine, set up a college in some part of the city, without interfering at all with the other educational institutions which already exist there. Or if not in Calcutta, then at least such a college might be instituted in Howrah, whence the railway steamer would daily convey the selected students to hear the Professor's lectures at the University.'

These concluding words of the Bishop's did not fall in vain. The Cathedral Mission College was established by the Church Missionary Society in 1865, 'chiefly,' it is said in the notice of it in the 'University Calendar,' 'at the instance of the late Bishop Cotton, who, in his last charge, delivered in 1863, expressed his earnest desire to see a Missionary College established in connexion with the Church of England, in which native undergraduates might be educated up to the B.A. standard under purely Christian influences.'

Calcutta at the present time presents the nearest parallel which the Christian Church has ever seen to what Alexandria was in the second and third centuries; and it is such men as Bishop Cotton who seem the prepared instruments to turn the restless and wayward activity of such periods into healthy channels. In an eminent degree he united clear views of truth with a large-hearted sympathy for an inquirer's difficulties; and we may be sure that there was a special work to be done when he was called to a position for which his previous life and character so peculiarly qualified him, and that, unexpected and sudden as was his removal, it was not until that appointed work was done.

In the hot month of April a journey of three hundred miles was undertaken in order to visit the mission in Chota Nagpore, a district of hill country north-west of Calcutta. A Lutheran mission had been at work for twenty years among aboriginal tribes bearing different names, but all grouped together by Hindus under the contemptuous designation of 'Kòls,' i.e. 'pigs.' As usual, the introduction of Christianity among a population free from the trammels of caste had been attended with marked success, and a colony of 6,000 Christians settled in Ranchi, the chief town, and among surrounding villages, was fast making the district of Chota Nagpore the Tinnevelly of North India. But work spiritually so flourishing was in a deplorable condition financially. The mission had been started in the first instance by Pastor Gossner, of Berlin, and was in connexion with two parent committees in that city. The divided councils which prevailed in these committees call for no notice here; it is sufficient to mention the unfortunate results which ensued to their missionaries by the reduction of the salaries already, even on a German computation of requirements, miserably small, and by the stoppage of funds for the maintenance and extension of the schools. The local mission had two staunch friends in the Commissioner of Chota Nagpore and the chaplain of Hazareebagh, the nearest European station. It was at their solicitation that the Bishop, with Archdeacon Pratt for his companion, undertook a pilgrimage to investigate the condition of the missionaries, and to devise, if possible, some remedy for their troubles. The heat and fatigue of the journey were fully repaid by the extreme interest of the visit. It revealed a native Church on a scale without a parallel in North India, strong in discipline, compact in organization, and numbering its converts annually by many hundreds. It was a hope-inspiring pledge of what all India may one day be; and even in its purely external aspect the spectacle of an impressive Western ritual blending with the daily life of rustic and obscure Eastern tribes was one of rare and picturesque interest. The Bishop at once rose to the full appreciation of all that was unfolded before him. True to himself, it must be added, he could not avoid detecting a humorous feature in his somewhat ambiguous position at the moment. Indeed, it is doubtful whether he did not cherish for his own amusement the secret suspicion that at first the good Lutherans were not quite at ease about a friendly intervention from a prelate who 'might possibly seize them by the aid of the secular arm, and compel them to swallow the Thirty-Nine Articles on the spot.' How misplaced was even a transient alarm in the presence of one who, desiring unity, was yet absolutely tolerant of differences; who, truly believing that his own Church set forth the more perfect way, knew nothing of ecclesiastical annexations where the Gospel of Christ was having free course and was glorified!

The journal may now describe the animated and impressive scenes in the Christian settlement of Ranchi on Saturday and Sunday, April 23 and 24, 1864:—

. . . . Attached to the mission is a large serai, built for the reception of the native Christians, who come in for the Holy Communion, and on other special occasions, from distances of forty and fifty miles, and here rest on the Saturday and Sunday nights, each receiving from the mission a mat to sleep on and some firewood to cook food. There we found about two thousand assembled, some without and some within the serai, who gathered round us, bowing and stretching forward their hands; but instead of saying *Salám* they all said *Yesu sa hay*, 'Jesus be with you,' which the missionaries have taught them to substitute for *Rám Rám* and other heathen salutations. Meantime the school children and others walked in procession singing to the church, a solid and tasteful stone building with a rather heavy tower, needing a spire to relieve it. Within, it consists of a nave and side aisles, with a clerestory, and a chancel terminating in a polygonal apse, raised considerably above the nave, and connected with it by a flight of steps. In the middle of the chancel is the Communion table, with a large cross worked upon the cover, and near it the font, full of water. We took our seats near the chancel to witness the baptism of one hundred and forty-three converts and children, of whom the former have been long under instruction, and are admitted to baptism on being able to understand and to repeat the Creed and Commandments, with portions of the Lutheran *Kleine Katechismus*, and showing, both by adequate testimony and a probationary residence at Ranchi, that their moral character is good. The church was soon crammed full of natives; F. Batsch, in a full-sleeved black gown and bands, stood in front of the Communion table, and summoned the elders of the Christian congregation, in number about sixty, to gather round him in the chancel and on the steps; the candidates were placed in front, and the choir sang very sweetly the *Kyrie Eleison* and a hymn, a converted Brahman, now named William Luther, playing the harmonium. The candidates were addressed, questioned, prayed for, repeated the Creed and some of the Commandments, and were then summoned to ascend the steps, where each was baptized with the words (in Hindi):—'I baptize thee into the death + of Christ, in the name of the Father, + and of the Son, + and of the Holy Ghost. + Amen.' At each of the words marked + the minister poured a handful of water on the head of the baptized person. After a convenient number had been baptized, he signed each with the cross on the forehead, and then sent them down the steps to be replaced by a fresh set of candidates. While this was going on, the choir sang the *Te Deum*, and the effect of that grand verse, '*The holy Church throughout all the world doth acknowledge Thee,*' sung just as these people reclaimed from savagery were received into the love and care of Jesus Christ, was quite sublime. None of the great 'functions' of St. Peter, with Pio Nono and all his incense and peacock's feathers, could excel in conception or in impressive solemnity the scene in the crowded church, the white-robed candidates thronging the steps, the minister baptizing in the midst, and the choir chanting out the triumphant hymn of Ambrose and Augustine.

Sunday, April 24.—Our host's servants call me the *Mahaguru* (great teacher), and certainly they must think that I work my disciples pretty severely, for to-day we went four times to church. We had our regular morning and afternoon English services. Both were held in the Lutheran church, cordially lent to the English whenever a clergyman is here, so that I cannot see why a home newspaper should have made such a caterwauling about my consenting to lend English churches in military stations to Presbyterian chaplains, when Scotch regiments need such aid. Between the two English services was interposed the ordinary morning service of the natives; it was very liturgical in its character, including hymns, the *Kyrie*, a confession repeated by the whole congregation kneeling, the Nicene Creed, and the regular Epistle and Gospel for the fourth Sunday after Easter, of which the latter was read from the pulpit and then expounded by F. Batsch. When he had finished, he told them that it was an occasion of great joy to them that the 'spiritual father of all India' (so this non-episcopal Protestant styled me) had come to visit them, and that I had consented to address to them a few words of counsel. So he came down from the pulpit and stood by me on the top of the steps of the chancel, whence I delivered an exhortation to godliness and good works, dwelling greatly on truthfulness, as I find that the Christians here, as in Tinnevelly, are not free from the heathen vice of prevarication when examined in a court of justice. This F. Batsch translated into Hindi, after which I read the Lord's Prayer in that language and gave the blessing. There were about twelve hundred native Christians in church; the rest were gathered outside. In the evening we again were present at the service, when the Lord's Supper was administered to six hundred communicants. There, too, the forms resembled our own; there was an address, a confession, and an absolution; Our Lord's words were repeated as a consecration, then the *Ter Sanctus* was sung by the choir, the communicants went up the steps and knelt all round the table, and received the elements, which were given them with words nearly resembling those which we use. All these services have been deeply interesting and impressive; the character of the Christian families for purity stands very high; drunkenness, a great vice of the Kòls, is very greatly checked among them, and the officials speak thoroughly well of them in all respects but the one I have mentioned, and even that charge they qualify with the remark that very few of them come into court, and that those who do are generally the worst section of them, often unbaptized, but calling themselves Christians because they are inquirers.

Discussions with the missionaries occupied the rest of the Bishop's time during his three days' sojourn at Ranchi. At the end of the first long conference he propounded four possible courses for their consideration: (1) that a great effort should be made to interest India in the work; (2) that a letter should be written by him to the Gossner Committee in Berlin, representing the great merits and the great needs of the local mission; (3) that they should join the other committee and merge the Gossner Committee in it, (4) (with the reservation that he came not to proselytise or build on another man's foundation) that the negotiations which Pastor Gossner had begun should be resumed for the absorption of the mission by the Church Missionary Society. At a later conference it was decided that the second of these suggestions should be adopted at once, and the fourth held in reserve, the senior missionary declaring that he should have no difficulty in submitting to re-ordination and conforming to the English Church, and also giving satisfactory replies to the Bishop's inquiry, how a change of ritual or of Church organisation would be received by the native Christians. On reaching Calcutta, the Bishop's first care was to redeem his promise, and write to the secretary of the Gossner Committee in Berlin. The main purport of his letter was to intreat that the impoverished condition of the mission might receive immediate attention, and he hinted indirectly at the remedy for present difficulties which was afforded by the well-known wish of its founder for its incorporation into the English Church. He wrote also, at the same time, to

Mr. Venn to prepare him for a possible, but not probable, overture from Berlin. It is needless to add how earnestly he represented that the proposal, if made, should be accepted, as opening a mission field white already to harvest, and one also which would be in geographical connexion with the work then recently taken up by the Church Missionary Society among the Santhal tribes in the neighbouring hills.*

Refreshed and encouraged by the sight of this living peasant church among the hills, the Bishop descended upon Calcutta, to make a fresh effort to meet the doubts and difficulties of restless Bengali minds, to water with a rill from the fountains of Christian truth the dreary wastes of a cold scepticism or a creedless morality. Six lectures 'On the Need, Evidences, and Difficulties of a Supernatural Revelation' represented this effort. They were delivered in the nave of the cathedral by the Bishop, Archdeacon Pratt, and two missionaries of either society. The Bishop, with his usual moderation, spoke of the lectures as an attempt to place, in a simple and unpretending way, the arguments for Christianity before Eastern inquirers troubled through doubts suggested by Western unbelievers. It was, however, an impressive sight; a sight realising an aspiration of Bishop Wilson's on his foundation of the cathedral; a sight full of hope for the future, when a congregation of non-Christian Bengalis voluntarily assembled in the metropolitan church of India to listen to the grounds of the Christian's hopes,

* These letters remained without any results, and the later history of the mission is briefly this: It continued to exist for five years, chiefly through help collected in India, but the breach between the missionaries and the Berlin Committee grew wider. Charges brought against the former were examined and refuted by an auxiliary committee in Calcutta. But the connexion with Berlin was finally severed, and the missionaries had to give up all the property, church, schools, dwelling-houses, &c. Union with the Church of England was again sought as a remedy, and in 1869 the Chota Nagpore mission was absorbed into the Propagation Society.

and to be urged to accept the Christian's faith as the one answer to spiritual cravings. The Bishop opened his lecture with the quotation of a passage in which Ernest Rénan, in his 'Vie de Jésus,' acknowledges Christianity as an historical fact, and its founder as a pure and holy teacher. In addressing an audience conversant with modern writings, he thus far admitted the common ground of agreement between himself and the able and attractive French writer; but only to show how short could be their way together, how widely their paths diverged, when he went on to set forth the need of a supernatural intervention which should raise mankind from the depths of misery, and to claim for the instrument of this intervention a Divine origin. The *à priori* probability of a supernatural exercise of Divine power and love to reclaim a sin-laden world, which philosophical systems had failed to purify, was always with the Bishop an argument of irresistible force for Christianity as a Divine revelation. From this starting-point, he dwelt upon the infamies of the world at the time of the Christian æra, and the inability of current philosophical systems to furnish remedies capable of regenerating the mass of moral corruption. But he followed more faithfully the bent of his own mind when he passed from the outward to the inward evidences of the truths he sought to recommend; when, turning aside from historical facts, or the arguments of reason, he placed the heart and conscience above the intellect, and urged with persuasive earnestness his own deep conviction that Christianity alone, accepted as a system divinely and supernaturally given, can achieve peace and order in the world or within the individual soul. Willing and ready he always was to give to intellectual arguments their full weight, and to sympathise with intellectual difficulties, however little they disturbed the serenity of his own faith. But as a minister of Christ, he cared rather, in addressing non-Christian hearers so abundantly nourished with intellectual food, to set the momentous subject before them on its evangelical side, to claim the Christian revelation as the one supreme and ultimate satisfaction amidst the moral conflicts and the spiritual yearnings to which the universal conscience of mankind bears witness. To the Brahmos (the philosophical sect of which his audience was mainly composed) he pointed out the deficiency in their religious system, so far as it borrowed from Christianity its ethics, its hopes, its forms of prayer, but refused the confession of a Divine Saviour, as the only Mediator between God and man, the sure refuge for the sin-laden soul. Courteously recognising in this leading sect an intellectual and moral effort to rise out of the abyss of Hindu degradation, he disputed its assumption to rival Christianity as a regenerating element, or its power to do more for the spiritual elevation of India than Greek and Roman philosophers had done for the heathen world. To Eastern hearers, whom he addressed as 'guests in his own cathedral,' he quoted the struggles of Augustine, in order to utter the earnest hope that they too might be led through a 'tangled thicket' of deistical or pantheistical guesswork to the highway of the Christian revelation, and at length find repose like Augustine in the blessed conviction, 'O Lord, Thou madest us for Thyself, and our heart is restless till it find rest in Thee.'

I had at that time gone for a few months to England. The letters which I received from the Bishop described each lecture, as week by week a similar audience gathered in the cathedral, and the following extract has some points of special interest:—

June 1864.

. . . On Monday some of the natives who heard my lecture on the previous Friday were invited to come and demand my explanations and discuss any difficulties arising from it. It was rumoured that many were to appear, and accordingly we mustered strong on the Christian side; but after all only four came, and of these two were Christians; the other two were —— and Keshub Chunder Sen, a well-known leader of the Brahmo Somáj. The latter was thus quite outnumbered; but we treated him very courteously, and gave him full scope for expressing his convictions, which he did in a remarkably simple, earnest, and pleasing way His account of the reasons for which he believed in God, prayer, and the spiritual life generally, without revelation, was interesting and reasonable; but he entirely broke down in some of his arguments, partly from an insufficient education, partly from the Hindu indifference to facts and history. Thus he seemed surprised at our maintaining that the idea of a Church, which he said that the Brahmos hold tenaciously, was altogether Christian, and borrowed by his sect from the New Testament, saying that he thought it had existed everywhere, apart from revelation; and he avowed that his chief difficulty in believing the Scriptures was that he could see no connexion between facts and morals. He even said that, assuming the fact of Christ's resurrection to be demonstrably proved, he did not see that it need influence our belief or practice, further than as a kind of illustration of the immortality of the soul. We had tea, sandwiches and ice, all which he eat without scruple, and the whole party attended prayers in the chapel. . . . On Friday the second lecture came off, by Banerjea. The attendance was about the same as before, and the lecture was exceedingly interesting and successful, admirable as an English composition and most telling and impressive as an argumentative exhortation. This praise chiefly applies to the second portion; the first was merely a kind of Paleian sketch of evidences, but the second part brought the subject home to India by copious references to Hindu religion and philosophy, showing how the necessity of a revelation had been felt by the old Rishis, and how many faint shadows of the truth appear in their writings. The allusions to 'our ancestors,' 'our nation,' 'our Rishis,' &c., quite recalled to my mind the thought of St. Paul preaching to the Jews. Some of the applications of Scripture, too, were most forcible, and Stanley would have been delighted to hear the opening of the Epistle to the Hebrews adduced to show that there were fragments of revelation in the Vedas.

Immediately after the delivery of the lectures at the cathedral, the Bishop and his company of lecturers repeated them in the Free Kirk Institution, at the request of Dr. Duff's successor in the Free Church mission. An audience of 250 in the cathedral rose to 800 in the hall belonging to the Scotch Mission, which, from being situated in the native quarter of the city, had a great advantage over the remote English church in point of locality. The Bishop followed up this movement in a different direction, by giving a short course of sermons on the moral and social effects of Christianity to the usual European congregation on Wednesday evenings at the cathedral. The attendance was good, and in writing to me about them he remarked, 'I am sure the sermons have been popular: a vain-glorious assertion you will say; but I am so thankful for the success of any attempt to throw life into the cathedral services.'

By intercourse such as that described in the preceding pages, the Bishop came occasionally into personal contact with non-Christians; but his work was to aid and guide missionary thought, rather than to share missionary labours. As president of the local committees in Calcutta, he maintained official connexion with the two great societies, the 'two arms of the Church of England' labouring for the conversion of India. The transaction of business with these committees was always a source of interest to himself; and harmony and good-understanding were never endangered by any disregard on his part of the twofold relation in which he stood towards the work that they administered. As bishop of the diocese, he confirmed the native Christians, took cognisance of points strictly ecclesiastical, and ordained and licensed missionaries; but he never swerved from the decision at which he arrived quite early in his tenure of the see, of declining to ordain a missionary except on the title of a presentation by one society or the other, and he disclaimed, as a general rule, any control over details of management beyond that which his vote as a member of a committee gave him. This theory of his position was maintained quite as much in the interests of the parent societies as of himself. The bent of his own mind was so utterly opposed to all loose and irregular action for the furtherance of the great cause at stake, that it was always his sincere desire and, so to speak, his friendly policy, to uphold the distinct position occupied by the Church Missionary and Propagation Societies, and to vindicate a compact and organised system, such as they represented, as the only effectual means of grappling with the false religions of an empire. Moreover, he felt so keenly the responsibility involved in the *care of the Churches* among professing Christians, that he experienced a sense of personal relief in sharing the supervision of the Church in her missionary character with two powerful agencies practically representing the zeal and sympathy of the Church of England. The following letter bears testimony to his appreciation of the two societies, and it also exhibits the distrust with which he invariably met the aspirations of volunteers for a difficult and arduous work, whose zeal might be praiseworthy, but was often not according to knowledge :—

1861.

. . . . My chief object in writing is to answer your application for employment in the diocese, and the conditions which you annex to it. I own that I do not like these conditions. I should be the last person to undervalue independence of action, or to desire unduly to fetter it, and I fully agree with the opinion that government by a bishop is more in accordance with Church order, and likely to be more successful than government by a society. But it appears to me that the Propagation Society really, in theory as well as in practice, and the Church Missionary Society, as at present administered, at least practically, do place their missionaries, in all theological and ecclesiastical relations, under the sole control of the bishop; indeed, I may say, in all relations except those of temporal and pecuniary character, in which it is, on all accounts, much better that he should only interfere as president of a managing committee, and not in his episcopal character, with which they have no necessary connexion. During your diaconate, I should think it contrary to Church order, and otherwise inexpedient, to give you the sole charge of any mission; and after your second ordination, it would probably be necessary for you to learn to act in union with some colleagues, certainly in connexion with some general system. I do not think that a person who would be unable to do so would be likely to submit very readily to a bishop who should think himself called upon to interfere with his proceedings. Indeed, I might have given a briefer answer without entering into all this reasoning. The thing which you ask is, as you have put it, impracticable. I have no means of employing clergymen in this diocese except in connexion with some society or with Government, or at least with some person or persons associated with myself in the administration of trust funds. But if I had merely stated this, and left you with this answer, I should not have expressed my feeling, that a mere impatience of control is not Christian independence, but a snare against which we ought to guard; that the system of the English Church, and certainly of the Propagation Society, which, I think, faithfully represents it, does provide for the combined subordination and independent action of the clergy, in a manner which ought, in my opinion, to satisfy any thoughtful Christian that he would have full scope for his activity and originality, within such limits as must be imposed, if we are to have any order or discipline at all. I must therefore reply to your letter, that, under present circumstances, I could only ordain you in connexion with the Propagation Society (I assume that its constitution is more akin to your own feelings than that of the Church Missionary); that, in afterwards appointing you to a station, I should do my best to meet your wishes and idiosyncrasies, and that I should be very glad to see your zeal and self-denial, your earnest Christian faith, and intellectual ability, enlisted in the service of our Church; and that I shall think it a subject of real regret if any restlessness or dislike of control, or other questionable feeling, should prevent you from devoting yourself to that high and holy calling to which God's providence seems to have been hitherto directing you.

Beyond the limits, however, of well-defined relations with the societies, there lay ample scope for the far-reaching personal influence of the chief pastor. By regular correspondence the home secretaries were kept in full possession of the condition of their affairs in North India. Existing missions were, as to their strength or their weakness, freely criticised; new ones were suggested, and their adoption recommended by arguments of a practical kind; new fields of labour were mapped out, always on some definite principle, whereby each society, while abandoning no footing already gained, might, in a time of profound peace, systematically extend its borders. It was, of course, far more easy to suggest than to get what was suggested carried out. It remained an abiding source of vexation and disappointment to the Bishop, that through the vast territories of Eastern Bengal and Assam, Church work among the heathen continued to be represented by only one small mission.

Opportunities for personal intercourse with widely-separated missions were necessarily few and of brief duration; but they were always turned to some practical account, and they tended much to strengthen the relations of mutual regard and confidence which sprang up in very early days between the Bishop and several of the principal missionaries. One bond of union between them was his sincere sympathy with their difficulties. Though many of these, of a mere external character, have been diminished by the more open recognition yielded in recent years to the cause of missions generally, the individual missionary still often pursues his labours under the discouragement of indifference on the part of those whose sympathy and support would be much valued. A sense of this stimulated the Bishop constantly, when on visitation, to excite interest in the local mission among the residents of the adjoining station, and to commend it to their friendly sympathy; and the same feeling could impart to his occasional sermons on missionary subjects a vividness of application and almost picturesque freshness of style, contrasting strongly with the insipid and conventional handling with which the theme is often treated. Other and more perplexing difficulties, those namely which beset the guidance of men's souls from the darkness of heathenism to the light of the Gospel, must increase with the increase of education. They draw largely upon the intellectual resources of missionaries, and the Bishop earnestly desired that they should be recognised as reasonable and inevitable difficulties, and be met not only with the zeal, but with the sympathy and large-hearted wisdom of which St. Paul is the great apostolic model. Had he been called to the work of an actual missionary, he would have entered upon the conflict with the bigotry or puerile superstition in which millions in India are still enshrouded, with the recognition of some common ground even amidst overwhelming differences; he would have sought out the grain of truth hid in every system, however debased, which man has erected between himself and an *Unknown God*; he would have been full of sensitive consideration for the most ignorant among those who were asked to receive a new faith at the hands of conquerors and rulers. He never heard a false religion inconsiderately or contemptuously denounced in the presence of its votaries without a jar in his own mind. Once, indeed, he wrote with more bluntness than was usual with him, 'If I were a Hindu, I am sure I should feel exceeding angry at hearing my religion so abused.' There was both strength and tenderness in the position of the Bishop's mind towards the spiritual cravings and intellectual doubts, the shattered faiths and philosophical systems, which have a place in those phases of thought through which the more educated Hindus are passing. To win such men to a knowledge of the truth as it is in Christ, was the work to which, without reservation, he believed the Church to be called, though he was the last to underrate the manifold obstacles that lay in her path. He was always perplexed and troubled by the inability evinced by some among those long accustomed to contact with minds in many stages of moral and spiritual progress, to estimate the length and strength of the conflict which so often precedes the acceptance of a new and transforming faith. With himself it was throughout his Indian life a subject of true interest to analyse the various arguments, or to observe the different mental bias, by which men were attached towards Christianity or withheld from it. He never accepted shortcomings in belief as an equivalent for Christian faith ; but he could recognise such shortcomings, and understand them. It is much to be regretted that so little of what he thought and felt on this subject was committed to writing. It was one less tangible, less bound up with direct and immediate issues, than many others of a more practical kind, and little now remains beyond the memory of his views on a point of supreme importance in the propagation of Christianity.

With regard to his theories on a subject of no less importance ;—that of native education, they are condensed in the following letter, written to a missionary in 1861. The opinions therein expressed lay at the root of all that he at any time suggested or stimulated in this branch of missionary operations :—

I think that you are quite right to throw yourself heart and soul into your first class. Think what an effect Arnold produced on his sixth form at Rugby mainly by the constant display before them of Christian principle, piety, energy, truth, justice, and an earnest devotion to their improvement. Do not be disappointed if as yet you see no spiritual life, no conversions. Work on in faith and hope, doing earnestly your own duty, and leave the result to the spirit of Christ. I believe that quite as many conversions have been produced by missionary education as by bazaar preaching. In any case, I am sure that lessons in Christianity, systematically given to intelligent young men, by one whose character they reverence, and to whom they are personally attached and grateful, must produce a mighty hidden effect, even though immediate fruit may be delayed. Besides, you have hardly been at work three months. Believing too, as I do, that the conversion of India must come from native agency, I think that such agents are more likely to be drawn out by the influence of a class-room than by words scattered over a crowd in a bazaar.

The other day, at a meeting of the Syndicate of the University, I expressed my hope that in time all the Government Colleges, except the professional colleges, might be abolished, and the money devoted to a great enlargement of the grant-in-aid system, and to the development of the University, as the two legitimate (because at once central and indirect) organs of Government education. One member announced his entire acquiescence; another said, 'The time has not yet come.' That may be true, because I doubt whether the missionary bodies are yet prepared to step into the gap; but it is the goal to which we should direct our efforts, instead of the impracticable scheme of introducing the Bible into all the existing Government schools. It is the view, too, to which the most thoughtful persons interested in missions are gradually and surely tending.

Thus was the Bishop's faith strong in those schools or colleges in which the respect and affection so readily yielded by the Eastern disciple to his *Guru* might be transferred to the Christian teacher. In them, too, he saw the most promising seedground for a native pastorate, of whose future he always spoke and thought with enthusiastic hopefulness. The ordination of three native pastors occurring almost immediately after his arrival in his diocese, was an early pledge of the reality of the work that had fallen upon him; and the vision of indigenous Stigands and Lanfrancs taking the place of the foreign Theodores and Augustines always mingled largely with his conception of the national Church of India. To native pastors, 'Christian pundits,' built up in sound learning, he looked for the real efficacy of that *disputing daily* in the thronged bazaars, and under the village tree, of which, while carried on only by Europeans, he often doubted the efficacy. In a native clergy ministering to those with whom they are identical in race and feeling, he discerned (in the words of one who once eloquently pleaded their cause in an English pulpit) 'the new vessels for the new wine, familiar with language, thoughts, and difficulties to Europeans so unintelligible, incapable of the mistakes and misconceptions with Europeans so inevitable.' *

When the Bishop went out to India, he was very doubtful as to the amount of prominence conceded to education in the machinery employed for the conversion of the country. On his first visitation tour, which covered a large part of Upper India, he carefully examined each successive mission school, and always made its condition a point of comparison with that of the Government school hard by. As time went on, missionary thought on this subject undoubtedly became progressive. The doctrine that secular knowledge must hinder the entrance of spiritual light into the soul, if still held in theory, was ignored in practice; and if there remained some missionaries who, as the Bishop used to put it, 'did not believe in schools,' there were others who were becoming increasingly dissatisfied with the share they had in native education. With these the eventual substitution of the system worked by them for that carried on by the State

* Sermon preached in St. Mary's Church, Oxford, June 10, 1860, by Arthur Penryhn Stanley, D.D., at the request of the Rev. T. V. French, Principal of Agra College.

was no mere vision or sentiment, but a practical measure to be kept steadily in view, and only needing time to bring it about. On the other hand, signs were not wanting of a willingness on the part of the civil powers to open a wider field for that education, combined with instruction in religion, which is the only kind that missionaries will administer. Here and there, in a small locality where two schools were not needed, the one set up by Government was closed, the other under Christian influence being left in exclusive possession of the ground: and this principle was carried out on a larger scale, in instances where the Government schools of a whole district peopled by hill-tribes free from caste prejudices were placed under the sole management of missionaries. By this arrangement the Church Missionary Society obtained a secure footing among the Santhals of the Rajmahal hills. A similar overture in behalf of the hill-tribes around Chittagong fell in so entirely with the Bishop's scheme for the occupation of Eastern Bengal by the Propagation Society, that he earnestly advocated the measure, 'trusting that the opportunity would be thankfully accepted by the venerable Society to whom it was thus offered.' An indefinite extension laterally of missionary instruction through the dense masses of the ryots or peasantry was facilitated by the relaxation of grant-in-aid rules, which was conceded by the Secretary of State to the representatives of the Church Missionary Society. In all such arrangements the Bishop heartily rejoiced, as steps in the right direction. He fully acknowledged the power and the soundness of the education diffused by the State; but he hailed with thankfulness, and stimulated by personal influence, every effort to overtake the State system in its strength, and to supply its one great deficiency. Among vigorous and independent efforts on the part of missionaries for the attainment of this end, none during his tenure of the See was more noteworthy than the establishment of the Cathedral Mission College in Calcutta; for through it the Church Missionary Society entered into competition with Government in the training of the upper classes of natives up to the B.A. degree in the University.

The years of his episcopate were not marked by any great accession of converts. The harvest reaped from seed widely sown was very scanty, and the baptisms were significant rather from the classes which supplied them than from their number. But the Bishop would not admit a tale of baptisms as the only test of advancing Christianity, and he never encouraged sanguine anticipations of any great and present ingathering into the Church. Rather he saw in the high intelligence of the native races an impediment to the passive and ready surrender of their minds and consciences to anything so momentous as a new faith.

On one occasion he wrote in reply to anxieties expressed about the small increase of converts:—

I allow, with sorrow and disappointment, that there seems to be a lull in missionary success generally in Upper India, except in some special cases, as that of the German Mission at Chota Nagpore, which is directed to an aboriginal tribe and not to Hindus. I allow that were there an entire stagnation of baptisms, we should have great cause for anxiety; but still we must not be too anxious to reckon up carefully the number of annual converts, and fancy that all the good we are doing must be measured by them. I trust that if there are not many actual conversions, a Christian influence is gradually spreading, and that agencies preparatory to the Gospel are becoming more and more powerful.

These general views upon 'quietness and confidence' being the motto for all missionary work converged to a point in the matter of Bishop's College, the central institution of the Propagation Society's operations in North India. Bishop Middleton was its founder, several home societies contributed liberally to its erection, and the Propagation Society was from the outset its sole trustee. The objects contemplated in its foundation were the education and training of European and native candidates for the ministry, and the promotion of Christian literature both in English and in the vernaculars. The high tide of Tractarianism which rose in England after 1840 cast a wave even on India, and produced some years of alienation between Bishop Wilson and the College. Calmer days followed, when its studies and discipline were guided by wisdom and moderation as well as by sound learning. The Church Missionary Society withdrew the prohibition against any of their missionary students entering the College, and Bishop Cotton, after five years' experience, recorded in his charge of 1863 'his unshaken confidence' in it. But the home Society seemed scarcely to share the revival of hopefulness which was felt in India. Greater results appeared to be expected than could be guaranteed by persons struggling with the constant interruptions and disappointments which surround all Indian work. A large proportion of the Bishop's correspondence with the Society's secretary in London was taken up with a defence of the College, and with the effort to dispel the distrust with which committees and sub-committees were apparently inspired. Disappointments no doubt had marked the career of some who had been educated within its walls; but, on the other hand, the education and training supplied by it had opened a door into the ministry for Eurasians, that neglected class of whom the Bishop always spoke as having long laboured under portentous disadvantages, and whom he earnestly desired to see raised in the social scale, and to be made to feel that a vocation in the Church was open to them. It has been already stated that in its literary department also, translations of the Psalms into Urdu and Bengali had emanated in quite recent years from its press, besides an able and remarkable book on Hindu Philosophy by the Rev. Krishna Mohun Banerjea, one of the professors. On all these facts the Bishop took his stand, and steadily maintained that, in spite of many disadvantages, the College was doing much good and useful, though not showy, work; and that, as the one institution in the diocese which supplied sound theological learning and opportunities for ministerial preparation, its position was unassailable. On the resignation of Dr. Kay, he wrote as follows to the home Society:—

. . . . I have reserved for the end of my letter a few remarks on the most important event which has lately befallen the Indian Church—Dr. Kay's resignation of the principalship of Bishop's College. I will not dwell on the loss which his departure is to the College, and, if he does not return to India at all, to the diocese; but I am anxious that the Society should appreciate the great importance of our College, of which I have a growing conviction. I am sure that it is getting more and more essential to the successful working of the diocese, and that people are beginning to feel this. The Church Missionary Society, in India at least, is now very friendly to it, and the son of one of their missionaries has lately been a student there. One of their clergy in Upper India told me that he had two or three promising native Christian boys in his school, whom he hoped in time to send down to Bishop's College, to finish their education, and, if possible, to be trained for the ministry of the Church. Besides its missionary functions, it discharges another of great and increasing utility. Several young Englishmen, Scripture-readers and others, have been sent there to be prepared for orders, and then placed under the auspices of the Additional Clergy Society, and other bodies, to minister to scattered communities of Europeans in different parts of the country. In this way, too, the influence of the Society for the Propagation of the Gospel and the College will, through them, make itself felt more and more. I hope, therefore, that the Society will believe that a really great and important work is going on in their College, that a thoroughly efficient Principal will be chosen, and that if any alterations are proposed they will be well considered, and perhaps I might ask that a sketch of them should be sent out to India before they are finally determined upon.

This letter was written in February 1866. At that time the affairs of the College were undergoing investigation at the hands of a sub-committee in London, and a report upon them was shortly afterwards sent out to India. Great divergence was manifest between the views of the home Society and those of their correspondents in India, on several points connected with the condition and prospects of the College. The Bishop had, however, become so convinced of its vitality and capacity for self-development to meet the growing wants of the country, that he had entirely adopted the proposal long advocated by those who in India were best acquainted with its working, that the institution should be severed from the parent Society in respect of direct control or management, and begin an independent existence. The letter to the London secretary, after the receipt of the report, was one of the last that he wrote, being dated September 1866. Its insertion here is, therefore, an anticipation of events chronologically, but it sums up his opinions on an important missionary institution which, through evil report or good report, was a prominent subject in his correspondence with the parent Society throughout his Indian life. The letter may also form a natural close to these brief notices of the Bishop's connexion with missionary work generally:—

. . . . It cannot be denied that Bishop's College labours under considerable disadvantages with regard to the constituencies which are to supply its students, and our chief effort should be to enlarge these, or at least, the one of them on which it ought chiefly to depend. At present it has three.

1. Students and probationers for holy orders of purely English blood. These are furnished chiefly by the Additional Clergy Society, being Scripture-readers and others, whom the

Society desires to see trained and ordained for ministering among the English settlers in India, and especially at railway stations.

In preparing such persons for the Christian ministry, the College does a very good work, and, as far as I have seen, does it very well. It is, however, necessarily a modern work, hardly foreseen by Bishop Middleton, and also a very limited one, since most of our additional clergy come from England. At present, there are two such probationers in the College, both gaining great advantage from it.

2. The Eurasian community. Of this body the sub-committee speaks, as I expected, in the language of distrust, and I am far from denying that they are justified in doing so. I admit that in more than one case the ordination of a Eurasian has turned out a matter for regret. Still, it seems to me un-Christian to despair of a whole race; and to open the clerical status to them is undoubtedly, under God's blessing, one means of improving and raising them. I trust, therefore, that there will be no discouragement given either to the admission or ordination of East Indians as such, though it is plainly necessary to be very careful in regard to the latter, and each individual candidate must be well weighed and tested before he is accepted either by the Society or by myself.

3. Since, then, the English and Eurasian portions of our constituency are necessarily small, we fall back on those who ought to be, on all accounts, traditional, national, and religious, the chief care of the College—the natives of India. But here we have a difficulty not noticed in the sub-committee's report. Our native constituency is almost limited to Bengal. It is more and more clear that the Hindustanis, i.e. the people of the upper provinces, have an almost insuperable aversion to the climate of Calcutta. If they can help it, they will not go there as students, and this must always be a difficulty in extending the circle from which Bishop's College is to draw its supplies. It is true that the lower provinces ought to supply plenty of students, but then, unfortunately, the College is practically almost limited to the missions of the Society for the Propagation of the Gospel. Now, the missions of the Society in Bengal, except Mr. Driberg's, are not very flourish-

ing nor numerous, so that the students cannot be numerous either. This is one of the main reasons why I have advocated the separation of the College from the Society for the Propagation of the Gospel—its independent endowment, and the formation of a separate trust, with the Bishop as visitor. It strikes me, that by making the College really diocesan, instead of keeping it attached to one particular Society, a large constituency would arise, from which its students might be drawn; more persons would be interested in it, its influence extended, and its usefulness increased. And I believe the only complete and satisfactory way of doing this would be to raise a large sum by way of endowment, to hand this and the College itself over to a Board of Trustees (of whom the Society for the Propagation of the Gospel should nominate a portion), to give to this Board or to the Bishop the nomination of the Principal, and to leave the College to work out its destinies in India without any interference from England. Should this be considered too sweeping a measure, a less satisfactory but tolerably hopeful form of the same general plan would be that the Society should be trustees of the College and its property, but that there should be a separate endowment, large enough to pay all College expenses, including salaries of Principal and tutors, administered, together with the whole discipline of the place, by the College Council, under the Bishop as visitor, the Society merely receiving an annual report of the state of the College and the use made of the money. To leave the men sent out to teach and rule the College as much as possible to their own unfettered judgment, controlled by that of the Bishop as their natural head, seems to me the best way of securing their undivided energies, and throwing them on their own resources for success. The committee of the Society for the Propagation of the Gospel in London is too distant, and generally too little acquainted with facts, to be an efficient governing body.

But, before all things, the great thing now to be desired is the appointment of a Principal.* The vacancy has now con-

* Dr. Kay resigned his post at Bishop's College early in 1866, but he had left India, from ill-health, eighteen months before. Hence the discharge of the work of the office by an *acting* Principal had been, as stated in the text, of long duration.

tinued for a long time, and its longer continuance is hardly fair to Mr. ——, and must be injurious to the College. Send out a good active man with some 'ideas' in his head, and his judgment and opinions, formed on the spot, will be worth many reports of sub-committees. Let him come out with the report and the proposal for endowing the College before him, and then, with his help, plans can be formed on the spot and carried out with the necessary assistance from home.

I hope that you will not think that my desire to make the College more or less independent of the Society rises from any distrust of the latter, or from insensibility to the great services rendered by it to the College and the diocese. With the Society I always have heartily co-operated, and always hope to do so; but I think freedom and local government essential to a place of education, and that rules and regulations framed without local knowledge must be theoretical and are often mistaken.

CHAPTER XII.

RESIDENCE IN CALCUTTA IN 1864—THE BISHOP VISITS SIMLA—MEMORIAL SCHOOL AT JUTOG—VISITATION CONTINUED TO LAHORE—LETTERS—RETURN TO CALCUTTA—CATHEDRAL MISSION COLLEGE—DEPARTURE FOR THE PUNJAB—ARRIVAL AT MURREE—TOUR IN CASHMERE—THE MARCH—SRINAGAR—MEDICAL MISSION OF THE CHURCH MISSIONARY SOCIETY—SIGHTS AND ANTIQUITIES IN THE VALLEY—RETURN MARCH TO ABBOTTABAD AND MURREE.

ALTHOUGH the vigorous and varied work which the last chapter has related went far to dispel the monotony of the hot months of 1864, many clouds hung over the residence in Calcutta during that year. There were deaths, some very sudden, others very mournful (especially, amongst the latter, that of Mr. Burn at Nainee Tal, in the Himalayas), which cast dark shadows round the Bishop's path. One trouble, too, which touched him very closely, was my departure for England, necessitated by broken health, and, with me, of the child also, who could not be left behind. The Bishop called the nine months of our absence 'his year of desolation;' and I never saw him so cast down as at the parting on board the steamer, when we were homeward-bound to see friends, and, above all, our boy, after five years of separation, while his only prospect was a return to the deserted house, to many weeks of most trying heat, and to daily cares and labours, uncheered by any remnant of family life, prized by him as the well-spring of his truest earthly joys. He was provided with the best security for his comfort that was possible, in the presence of Mr. Cowie (now Bishop of Auckland), as his chaplain, who to bright cheerfulness and untiring energy added a real attachment to the Bishop. In truth, the Bishop stood in need of much watchful care. As work grew under his hands he withdrew more and more from any share in domestic or personal arrangements; and except that he retained a careful supervision over his library, and exercised a close scrutiny over his banker's book and private finances, he renounced all concerns with the lesser, more practical details of life's business. It was not that he was lazy or luxurious; but a sense of dependence upon others increased gradually, almost unconsciously, upon him, and he was like a child in his reliance upon those about him for the arrangements, or comforts, or even the safeguards of his life. His even and unselfish temper, and the grace of character, in which affectionate ease was blended with much quiet dignity, made such ministrations a labour of love on the part of those who stood to him in the close and confidential relations of domestic chaplains, although, as he said, 'he knew they often sacrificed their comfort and convenience for his.'

In August he prepared to go forth again on visitation, The sharp illness of the preceding year was a warning that the season of extreme damp after the first rains had better be avoided, and matters of business had arisen to sound a distinct call for his presence at Simla. One point under consideration was a fresh local habitation for the Memorial School, carried on at that time at Jutog, where it had first been placed, and the Bishop's personal help was much desired to decide the question of a fresh site. Some ecclesiastical matters too were causing trouble and excitement in the station. So to Simla in due time he went, and spent September there with Sir Charles and Lady Trevelyan, who kindly offered him a hospitable home during his brief sojourn. With them he passed a very pleasant month, thoroughly enjoying a rest in an invigorating climate, and with society exactly to his taste, the supreme Government being then in residence. He was soon in the midst of the affairs of the school, and assisted at the selection of a site for the new buildings within the station of Simla, combining much beauty with salubrity and other advantages. The school then existing at Jutog was of course visited. He presented with profound pleasure his prize for divinity, after looking over the examination papers, to a Dissenter, one Carey, great-grandson of the well-known Baptist missionary, and with equal pleasure the second for the same subject to a son of the headmaster, an undoubted Churchman; the two together forming, as the Bishop trusted, a testimony to the catholic and equitable principles on which this school of his creation was governed.

He preached often to overflowing congregations; the number of communicants was very large; and he saw with thankfulness proofs of the beneficial influence of active work, and of the sight of upright Christian goodness in the highest quarters, in a place which has often been called the Capua of India. He had much private conversation with the Viceroy; he always considered opportunities of personally getting the ear of Government as eminently conducive to the good of the diocese, and was never disposed to agree with Bishop Heber's theory, that the Bishop of Calcutta was best placed in the centre of the diocese, as all business with the Government could be done just as well by correspondence.

After a month of mingled work and refreshment, he went by way of Dharamsala and Dalhousie to Lahore, thence retraced his steps, spent Christmas at Lucknow, and reached Calcutta early in 1865. A few letters here annexed may again supersede his journal.

To a former Pupil.

July 1864.

. . . I entirely admit your plea for not coming to me as my chaplain; indeed, it would have been ridiculous to urge it as a duty on anyone, least of all on one who has so many ties at home. I often think of you with pleasure and a kind of yearning to see you again. Indeed, considering how slight our connexion was when you were at school, there is no one among my pupils to whom I feel more closely drawn. Possibly that illness in —— has had some influence on my feelings to you; at all events, they are deep and genuine, and to hear from you or about you is a real pleasure. It is an inexpressible happiness to me to read in your letter words which imply that I exercised a good influence over you at school, and helped you to take a worthier view of life than you had done, and to recognise your duty to God and Christ. For as life goes on, especially now that I am a good deal alone, I often turn back in thought to the years that are gone, and ask myself whether all that long school-time of mine produced any really Christian fruit, or was at all an adequate exercise of my calling as Christ's minister. And such an acknowledgment as yours, spontaneously offered, is a consolation and an encouragement. I rejoice that you are all happy together at ——, and am sure that you are doing a good work there. Your influence, I trust, will always be fresh and practical; you will not trouble yourself with theological difficulties; you will teach boys to serve God and to lay hold of eternal life, undisturbed by the depth of the Nile mud, or the number of the first-born. It does sometimes provoke me to observe the vast interest which these questions excite, compared with the feeble efforts which are made to raise men's minds to the love of God.

To his Daughter.

July 21, 1864.

I have bad news for you to-day. Poor parrot is dead! I cannot make out why he died: certainly Maharaj took care of him, and gave him plenty of seed and water, and he always seemed to me very happy, till one day Maharaj observed that he was 'bimar' (sick), and next morning, when I went to see him, he was clinging to the lowest part of his perch, panting, and very unhappy. That day he died. I have sent him to the Asiatic Society to be stuffed for you, so that you may again look at his pretty green back and red stomach; but he will never frighten Aunt Julia again, or croak at us like a frog when we pass him on the verandah.

I have got your letter, written on June 28, when you were getting near Aden. I liked your letter very much, but I want to see you. O my pussy, my pussy, why don't you come and say 'Night night!' to papa?

What do you think?—Mr. Nesfield has carried off Dhulip Sing to Darjeeling. Peter does not want him; Dhulip had nothing to do, and was getting more like a pig than a pony; so I would not sell him, because I hope that you will want him at Murree next year; but I told Mr. Nesfield that he might use him till December, when he can buy another pony, and must then send him back to go up to Murree. So Dhulip and his syce started by the train on Tuesday night, and by this time I hope are at Purneah.

I shall want to know all that you think of Granny, and brother Edward, and Hyde Park, and the Pantheon, and the gold-fish, and the talking dolls, and everything else that you see.

P.S.—What do you think the cow has done? She and her calf were sent to feed in the cathedral close, and when the people went to bring them to their stall at night, where do you think they found them?—Inside the cathedral!

To his Wife.

Allahabad, August 1864.

. . . If you desire a general view of these weeks of desolation, I can say that, as to their occupations, they have been numerous and, I trust, useful. But it has been a mournful time. Besides the two near sorrows which came in such quick succession, the deaths of Scott, Smith, and Harris helped to complete a background of gloom. Yet the time went fast, and now sometimes the parting in June seems only a dream, and I can hardly believe that you are not now at the palace awaiting my return. I sometimes think that you must regard the humorous tone of my letters as inconsistent with the general character of these weeks; and even on looking over this one, there is doubtless an incongruity between its tragic opening and the sketch of the Patna visit; yet the letter is written in the natural strain in which my thoughts and words flow when turned to different themes. Till I actually begin to think about it, I am never conscious of anything comic in the grotesque phraseology of some of my narratives; so you must take all as you find it; for, in truth, in this busy world of ours, one thought soon thrusts back another, and tears and smiles follow each other in rapid alternation.

To the Same.

Simla, September 24.

. . . I have read the 'Apologia' with great interest, and though it gives me the impression that Newman has a subtle and tortuous mind, I do not think him dishonest. His victory over Kingsley is complete; his book is in beautiful English, his autobiography is a curious chapter of Church history, his defence of Rome places its pretensions in a clearer light than I ever saw them before, and perhaps on a more logical basis; but he entirely fails to convince me that I should find any refuge from modern difficulties under the auspices of the Pope. The questions of fact, critical and other, which disturb people now-a-days, are surely no more solved by the assurances of Pius IX. that they are not difficulties than by the assurances of the 'Record.' And this assurance of Pius IX. that all is right is, in fact, the sole security which Newman gives us. Strange that it should be a security to so able a man as he is.

To the Same.

Ferozepore, November 6.

. . . Two occurrences here have been of considerable interest, one on private, one on public grounds. The regiment here is the Royal Fusileers, who at this time of the year have an annual fête to celebrate their Crimean exploits, consisting of a grand mess banquet and some soldiers' games. At the mess dinner a large piece of old-fashioned plate was displayed —a kind of massive silver shield, with a portrait of Sir William Myers (a miniature on ivory), who was killed at Albuera, where the regiment gained much renown, for its central ornament, and the names of all its officers who died in the Peninsula engraved below. Among these was 'Thomas Davenant Cotton.' After dinner Major Marten, the commanding officer, made a speech about Alma and Inkermann, and then proceeded to say that they had not only met to celebrate these victories, but to receive me as their guest, and proceeded to tell the whole story of my father's death quite correctly. 'On November 10, 1813, at the battle of the Nivelle, a gallant captain of this regiment, by name Thomas Davenant Cotton, fell leading on his company,' &c. (with more description). 'There had been recently born to this captain in England an infant son, and that child is our guest of to-night, the present Bishop of Calcutta.' It was really very effectively done. My health was drunk, and with me were coupled the other clergy present, including Father Alfonso, the Popish priest, on whom I had therefore to bestow a sentence in my reply, which I did by stating that the Churches of England and Rome in the army must postpone all differences to the one great object of raising in every way the moral character of the soldier. The public matter of interest was a most wonderful native confirmation. You remember those Muzhibi Sikhs (the 32nd Native Infantry). There has always been a strong Christian tendency in them, varying and uncertain, from the few and far-between visits of the missionaries, and since these have ended, not growing at all. But all who were baptized have remained faithful, nearly all have fairly good characters, and their children, for whom there is a school, a very good one. Since the regiment came to Ferozepore, Smyth has held an Urdu service every Sunday for the Christians in it, visited them in hospital, regarded them as part of his flock, and prepared sixteen for confirmation. Though he has been unable to undertake any work with the heathen, yet these proceedings have roused again the Christian inclinations of the regiment, and they expressed a wish to come and see their comrades confirmed. Accordingly, on Thursday, November 3, the church was crammed: the chancel by candidates for confirmation and Christians of the regiment, the transepts by the people of the station, the nave by all the heathen soldiers; and we proceeded with our Urdu confirmation, Smyth reading the Litany, Cowie the preface, and I the rest. What the heathen thought, I do not know; but the station people declared that the sight was one of the highest interest, many saying that they could never have believed that they should see such a thing in India, and that it had quite opened their eyes to the reality of missionary work.

To his Daughter.

Ferozepore, November 9, 1864.

I cannot write to you a long letter, for I have been ill, and am still weak and lazy; but I must send a line or two to my dearest little girl on her birthday, and say, as you do to me, 'May God bless you and keep you from all harm!' Also I have to tell you of a birthday present. I told you that Mr. Cowie had brought a dog, named Dot, with us. One morning we found that Dot had got five children! They are very pretty little puppies, and Mr. Cowie means to give one of them to you. As they were born at Lahore, they are to be called after the five rivers of the Punjâb: Jhelum, Chenab, Ravee, Beeas, Sutlej; and you are to have Jhelum. If you come back safe to India, and go to the hills next year, he will be a nice little companion for you in your walks.

I want to ask you some questions about your travels in England:—

Did you go to Doncaster in a dhooly?

Which is furthest, Doncaster to Chester, or Coonoor to Metrapollium?

Did you find the 'Pearl' at St. Leonard's?

Do the ladies at Cheltenham go out in jonpans?

Did you go to Lichfield in a dák ghari or a bullock waggon?

Has Granny a good Khansáma?

There, that is all that I can write, except that I hope that you are a good and wise girl now that you are seven.

The beginning of 1865 found the Bishop again in Calcutta. From a brief 'journal' review of occupations during a few weeks' residence at the palace, the following extract is taken. It has an interest, because it records his thankful hopefulness in contemplating the promising start made by an institution, in the foundation of which he had been much associated with some able and prominent members of the Church Missionary Society's staff in Calcutta.

In Calcutta the most important missionary effort in connexion with our own Church recently made, is the opening of the Cathedral Mission College in a native house not far from the Amherst Street mission. I went to see it, found about 150 boys diligently at work, briefly examined and harangued them, expressing my hopes and aspirations for them in general language. I trust that God's blessing is upon it: it realises very completely some of my most cherished wishes—the committal of the higher education of India to good and earnest Christians, the union of secular and religious learning, the application of missionary efforts to the educated Bengalis, the greater prominence of our own Church in educational matters in Calcutta. I visited the College on a day almost wholly devoted to education; for in the evening the convocation of the University was held, when Maine, as vice-chancellor, made one of his wonderfully fluent and polished speeches, but inferior to that of last year, partly from its greater abstruseness, partly from his extravagant laudation of the study of physical science, by which, in a somewhat Comtian and Bucklerian spirit, he said that that of history was to be guided, and which must, he added, be the main instrument of university education. Surely to this there was a double objection, first the implied positivism, and secondly the comparison between the method and the results: for even if the discoveries of physical science are as grand as Maine says, it does not follow that it should furnish the best means of education. The results of theology are the most important of all results in the estimation of a believer in revelation: but a man trained exclusively in theology is half-educated and apt to be narrow-minded.

Almost immediately after my return from England, we all quitted Calcutta for the far North-West. Thanks to almost continuous railway communication, the continent of India was quickly spanned, ample rest to break the long journey being also secured. At Delhi, where a long halt was made, the Bishop laid the foundation-stone of a church for a mission of the Propagation Society. It was partly intended to serve as a memorial of the ruined mission of 1857, and thus its erection was some compensation for the disappointment which befell the project of the Society for a church of a similar character at Cawnpore. Passion Week and Easter were spent at Lahore, and before the end of April, Murree, the delightful hill retreat for the Punjâb, was reached. The winter in the Himalayas had been very severe, and snow was still lying deep in nooks and corners of the valleys, where the sun could not penetrate. The house engaged for the Bishop was uninhabitable, from the effects of snow and storms. It was left in the hands of workmen; but a temporary refuge was at hand in an unoccupied house, kindly lent by the late Mr. Roberts, Financial Commissioner of the Punjâb, and very shortly the great campaign of the year, the long contemplated and greatly desired expedition into Cashmere, was accomplished.

At 5 A.M., on May 2, a bright party quitted Murree. It included the Bishop and myself; the child and her governess; Dr. Lyons; the new domestic chaplain, Mr. Hardy, and the retiring one, Mr. Cowie, going to officiate for the season to the European sportsmen and tourists, who now annually frequent Cashmere. The usual endless tail of natives attached to camp life completed the retinue. The ladies travelled in dandis, i.e. litters of a very comfortable form peculiar to the Punjâb. They are constructed of leather or cane, and netted cord, slung on a pole, and carried by two men, and are so light and narrow that wherever a man can go, on the roughest path, a dandi can follow. The child had a special conveyance, duly described by her father. He also had a dandi as a resource on very bad roads; but a pony was likewise on duty, 'Toghluck' by name, 'on account of my pleasing recollections of a visit recently paid to the ruins of Toghluckabad, and also because the pony, like the Emperor, is a Pathan.' The *dinner-bell*, rung through the camp by the chaplain, broke all slumbers while it was still dark, and the daily start began very soon after 4 A.M.; for the marches were often long, or toilsome, from the steep ascents, and the tents were seldom reached, after a half-way halt for breakfast under a tree, until the sun was high and fierce in the heavens. Heat, dust, fatigue, were often trying; but the memory of these passed away like the morning mist. Not thus transient were recollections of that fine open-air life among the mountains, with its daily interest of the onward march, the new encampments; of social gatherings seasoned with some grotesque incidents of travel, of sunset strolls, and evening tea at the tent door, with the moon above and the foaming river below; of Sundays, true rest days for wanderers, whether man or beast, when the small congregation and the English liturgy made a visible, though transitory, church on the hill-side. Seventeen days were spent at Srinagar, the capital of Cashmere. The houses allotted by the Maharajah to Europeans lie beyond the confines of the city, which abounds in dirt and misery. They are dotted about on the green flat banks of the river, and are often shaded by plane-trees of magnificent growth, but they are strictly Asiatic in construction and cleanliness! It happened, moreover, that among the visitors of the season was a literally Egyptian plague of brown hairy caterpillars. In one long avenue the poplar-trees were gaunt white skeletons, every leaf, together with those of the vines which clothe their base, having been devoured. In the tents that were still in use the creatures swarmed, assailing all indiscriminately, invading everybody's dress, and dropping down from the canvas sides and roofs even into the episcopal cup of tea, the owner whereof calmly awaited them, and compared himself to Bishop Hatto and his rats.

To his Son.

Srinagar, Cashmere, May 14, 1865.

Here we all are in the valley which the old French traveller Bernier has seriously pronounced the original abode of Adam and Eve, and of which Moore sings—

> Who has not heard of the Vale of Cashmere,
> With its roses, the brightest that earth ever gave,

and which undoubtedly is sufficiently beautiful to merit a great deal of panegyric. The approach to it is not free from fatigue and exertion. We left Murree on Tuesday, May 2, and entered the valley on Thursday, May 11, reaching its capital the next day. . . . Our attendants are innumerable; personal servants of every kind. . . . And besides these the Maharajah of Cashmere has attached to us a superior official to see to our supplies and comforts, together with a jemadar and twelve of his sepoys to guard our person. After leaving Murree we had only twenty miles of British territory to traverse, and then we bade adieu to good roads and dák bungalows, and had to take to our tents and steep mountain-paths. The boundary is the Jhelum, at a small village named Kohala. The river looked so rapid that it was difficult to see how it was to be crossed; however, we were all stowed away in a great barge, then pulled by a rope some way up the stream, let go, immediately whirled round by the current, and finally propelled by about a dozen sturdy strokes of the oar to the opposite shore, where we were landed amidst rocks and mud in the territory of the Maharajah Rumbeer Sing. Here some of his officials received us with many salutations, and brought for my special conveyance a kind of litter furnished with red cushions, and shaded by a canopy of a Cashmere shawl. As I should have had to sit crosslegged in it, I preferred my humbler dandi; but the royal litter appeared the very thing for Ursula, whom it held in a convenient position, so she was immediately transferred to it, and called the *Rosherana Begum*—a princess whose splendid conveyance and dignified deportment are described by Bernier in his account of the journey of Aurungzib from Delhi to Cashmere, which he visited 200 years ago, partly to recruit his own health, partly to gratify the whims of the said Rosherana, with a train of 300,000 human beings, and elephants, mules, and other quadrupeds in proportion. Our road was excessively steep, going up the mountain-side straight from the Jhelum by short zigs and zags, but presenting to us beautiful views of different turns and reaches of the river. From this point eight marches, i.e. days, brought us to Baramula, where the valley begins. Details of the marches would be wearisome. Suffice it to say, that the scenery on the way had three great attractions: the foaming Jhelum roaring below us, pent between steep banks, which sometimes rose into magnificent red cliffs; occasional snowy peaks rising above the nearer hills; and the most beautiful vegetation, including some quite European—as roses, jessamines, horse-chestnuts, walnuts, mulberries, buttercups, clover, hawthorn, vines, and oleanders; some quite Himalayan, deodars and grand pines; some peculiar to Cashmere in size and umbrageousness, namely, plane-trees of height, width, and extent such as I never saw before, the trunk of one being 34 feet in circumference. Through country of this character we advanced at the rate, on an average, of twelve miles a day, seventeen being our longest, and six, a tremendously steep ascent, our shortest march, till we reached Baramula, where the river emerges from the valley and begins its descent into the plains of India. Here it is navigable, and we were accordingly transferred to a long narrow barge with thirty-six rowers, eighteen in front and eighteen to the rear of a sort of raised daïs, something like an enormous tea-tray covered with a red floor-cloth, and surmounted by a red canopy with curtains all round. In this we voyaged up the river. We were accompanied by seventeen other boats of ruder construction, bearing the other members of our party, together with all our camp, baggage, servants, and other appurtenances.

About 2 P.M. on Friday, May 11, our fleet entered the city of Srinagar, ('holy city'), of which the Jhelum forms the principal street, the houses being built on each side of it, and coming flush down to the water, with landing-places at intervals. So far it bears a distant resemblance to the grand canal of Venice; but, on the other hand, there are no fine buildings, most of the houses being in a most rickety, tumble-down condition, of wood or unburnt bricks—none with any glass in the windows, which are closed with wooden shutters or greased paper. Some few houses are better, chiefly the abodes of shawl merchants, and two buildings on the river are of some pretension, a mosque and the Maharajah's palace, the latter containing as a private chapel a temple of Krishna, with a gilt pyramidal roof, which glitters brilliantly in the sun. The river is crossed by several bridges, each of which consists of a narrow roadway supported on two or three piers, composed of logs of wood laid crosswise, increasing in width as they rise from the river, so as to form an inverted pyramid. One or two have shops on them like the Rialto or Old London Bridge.

Having passed through the city, we came to a flat district covered with a pleasant green sward and planted with planes and poplars, along which some bungalows have been built by the Maharajah for European visitors. One of these has been assigned for our use, but it will only hold your mother, Pussy, and myself, so we have pitched tents all round for the rest of the party, and use the largest of them for our dining-room. The valley is about 5,200 feet above the sea, it is very green and fertile, so well watered that in parts it looks swampy, and enclosed by a complete girdle of magnificent snowy mountains, which divide it on one side from Thibet and on the other from India. Just behind our camp a steep rocky hill rises about 1,000 feet from the valley, called the *Takht-i-Suleiman* ('Solomon's throne'), and from this the view in the early morning is certainly first-rate.

The English visitors here every summer are numerous: the young officers on leave amuse themselves by shooting (especially bears) and fishing, or rather spearing fish. This amusement is denied to the natives, at least in the neighbourhood of the city, by the Maharajah, because his guru, or spiritual preceptor, told him that his father's soul had migrated after death into a fish, and this fish might be killed. This we were told by one of the royal officials. 'But why,' we asked, 'is not the fish as liable to be killed by a European as by a Cashmerian?' 'That,' replied our informant reverentially, 'God only can explain.'

The contrast between the face of nature in this fair valley and the unhappy aspect of the people whose home it is, was truly mournful. Even the children had a worn and poverty-stricken look, as if the blight of the benighted rule under which they were born and reared fell upon them at an age usually impervious to care.

Both in the Mahometan and Hindu quarters (wrote the Bishop in his journal) the population seemed to swarm; in the latter I never saw a greater number and variety of the sectarial marks on the forehead. The people nearly all seemed in a state of dirt and squalor, and certainly the work of christianising such a population under such a sovereign seems at present, humanly speaking, impossible, no European being allowed to stay in the valley during the winter, so that any little good which might be done is annually suspended for six months. One man whom —— baptized was twice put into prison on some frivolous pretence, and one of the authorities sent for him and told him that he should have some money given him if he would declare that —— made him drunk, and in that state baptized him. He was at last protected by the Resident, and is now ——'s servant. The case seems one in which we can only say, '*Oh that Thou wouldst rend the heavens and come down,*' and leave in God's hands the means of rescuing these crowds from their miserable condition. Meantime I believe that Elmslie is knocking at the only gate which has any chance of being opened, and that his labours deserve all help and encouragement.

This 'one gate' was the medical mission, just started at Srinagar in connection with the Church Missionary Society.

In 1865 it was but the day of small things, with an attempt to set forth Christianity in that heathen kingdom through deeds of mercy. By God's blessing the work has been sustained since that time, though amidst many hindrances, requiring all the patience and faith of the good man who has returned year after year to continue his ministrations to suffering Cashmeries in temporal and spiritual things conjointly. The Bishop's journal thus describes the scene, at that time entirely new and strange :—

I went this morning to see Dr. Elmslie and his patients. When I saw the process which he adopts, it struck me that Christianity appeared in its most beneficent aspect. About twenty-four invalids were seated on the floor in his verandah at 7 A.M., and addressed by a catechist, who read and expounded to them in very plain and simple Hindustani a portion of the Sermon on the Mount. Most of them seemed very attentive, some made occasional remarks and assenting comments, a small minority were listless and uninterested. The address, which I could readily follow throughout, was thoroughly good and practical. After this, Elmslie retired into another room accompanied by two intelligent young native Christians, whom I confirmed the other day at Amritsir, and whom he is teaching to compound medicines. They were so sharp, careful, and modest that they formed a very pleasing part of the general illustration of Christianity in its effects. Then the patients were admitted one by one, kindly questioned and examined, and remedies administered. Many of them were abominably dirty, and were exhorted to wash all over—'tamám badan sáf karo.' One man suffered from chronic rheumatism, and a dose of physic was prepared for him by Sekander (one of the young assistants), but he entirely refused to drink it from an impure vessel, as contrary to the rules of his caste. As every vessel touched by poor Sekander or any other of us was impure, nothing remained but to give him the medicine in a solid state, and tell him to mix it with water in his own lota. Dr. Lyons, who was present, said that, according to his experience in the plains, all Sepoys, and nearly all who come to the dispensaries for relief, have got over this prejudice, though there indeed the men who mix the medicines are not Christians. Altogether, considering the ignorance and wretchedness of the patients, and the entirely disinterested character of the mission, the scene appeared to me most interesting and edifying, and could not fail to remind me of Him who went about all Galilee preaching the Gospel of the Kingdom, and healing all manner of sickness and all manner of disease among the people. It appears that there are some native doctors in Cashmere; but as Hinduism prevents them from learning anatomy, they are useless in all serious cases.

Only a minimum of pastoral or ecclesiastical work was possible in Cashmere. Beyond the consecration of a cemetery, and a share in the Sunday services held in the Resident's house, there was no work to break in upon a brief season of real holiday. The Bishop, like the handful of Europeans who adjourn to the valley for a brief period of the year, bent for the most part on errands of sport, had left all business behind him. While they hunted bears, he surrendered himself with keen enjoyment to the other attractions that were around. Some places of exquisite beauty lying away from the main course of the river provided the more distant expeditions, and sights within the city or in its immediate vicinity furnished full occupation for other days. They included Hindu temples, dating back to 200 B.C., revealing in their Doric architecture the Greek influence of the kingdom of Bactria; the Fort; the shawl manufactories; memorials of Mussulman supremacy in the Shalimar gardens and the Nishád Bagh or 'garden of bliss' (scenes of the loves of Jehanghir and Nurmahal), in the long poplar avenues, or again in the Jumma Musjid. Now that Hinduism is in the ascendant, this mosque is dirty and dilapidated; but it is one of the finest and most curious in India, with a cloister which is literally rather than figuratively a 'forest' of 384 pillars, each pillar being the trunk of a deodar pine. Temples at Bhaniyar, near Baramula, at

Pandrethan, and on the top of the Takht-i-Suleiman, were all visited and noted; as were also many fine ruins and temples seen in an expedition up the valley as far as Islamabad. These great architectural remains, complete specimens of a distinct Cashmerian style of architecture, and as yet only imperfectly examined, were to the Bishop an immense addition to the natural and more popular attractions of the country. General Cunningham's paper was in his hands as a guide-book. Incited by Mr. Cowie, he went beyond the investigations of 1848, became for the moment a practical antiquarian, and started fresh excavations to bring to light one of the finest of the ruins; but though he explored these sacred buildings with careful observation, looking at everything with his own eyes as well as those of other men, and even offered the substance of his journal as a contribution to the antiquarian lore of the Asiatic Society, he had neither the leisure nor the knowledge to be a scientific archæologist or to throw new light on the difficult and obscure subject of Indian antiquities.

On the return from Islamabad the camp at Srinagar was struck and the journey back to Murree commenced. The Maharajah's barge and boats carried the travellers down to Baramula. Here the Jhelum ceases to be navigable, and the marching life was resumed. The homeward route took the right bank instead of the left. In due time the vile paths and unbridged nullahs (brooks) of the Maharajah's territories were exchanged for well-made roads, types of British civilisation, and for the very pretty suspension bridge thrown across the Nansuck, by which the Hazara district and English territory were gained. A halt at Abbottabad broke the final journey to Murree, where by the end of June the patched-up house supplied repose and an acceptable shelter from the increasing heat. This record of a time of great enjoyment and of many blessings may close with one entry from the

Bishop's journal—a simple and spontaneous outburst of feeling, which, with the writer, always found a vent more readily through his pen than through words :—

June 2.—As I devote much of my journal to recording scenes of physical beauty, I shall to-day note one of moral beauty. As I was passing leisurely along the road above the strange bridge of a single rope at Uri, by which the natives sling themselves across the river, Hardy, who had gone on ahead to see to the breakfast arrangements, suddenly met me, breathless and hot with fast walking. 'Hurrah!' he exclaimed, 'I have caught you in the nick of time. I thought that you would like to look at the bridge through my binoculars, so I have brought them back to you.' It appeared that for this purpose he had returned two miles, so that, merely to give another person a moment's pleasure, he added to the day's march a long hot walk.

CHAPTER XIII.

FURTHER PROGRESS OF EDUCATIONAL PLANS—CAINVILLE HOUSE SCHOOL—TRANSFER OF ST. PAUL'S SCHOOL—PURCHASE OF MR. MADDOCK'S SCHOOL—LETTER TO THE SECRETARY OF THE BOARD OF EDUCATION—FRESH APPEAL FOR SUBSCRIPTIONS—FINAL EDUCATIONAL PASTORAL—LIFE AT MURREE—JOURNAL RECORD OF WORK—COLD WEATHER VISITATION OF 1865-6—DISTURBED STATE OF HAZARA DISTRICT—DESCENT OF THE INDUS—HISSAR—DELHI—AGRA—CORRESPONDENCE.

THE leading occupation during a four months' residence at Murree was a further prosecution of the hill-schools' movement. An earlier chapter in this memoir brought the movement down to the birth of the Simla school and of the Diocesan Board of Education in 1863. For some months afterwards the Bishop was comparatively resting on his oars, and was waiting until time and events should ripen for further personal efforts. There was, however, no lull in the educational activity of the diocese. The Board of Education was giving much aid in the establishment of boys' and girls' schools in the chief cities of the Presidency, thus supplementing the hill education by that corresponding education in the plains which those most friendly to the Bishop's special scheme desired should not be lost sight of. A girls' school in the hills, rivalling in efficiency and stability the schools projected for boys, was established solely by the energy of Archdeacon Pratt. He had co-operated from the first most actively and heartily in all the educational measures that were on hand, and in 1863, when the Bishop suspended for awhile his personal exertions, and declared that 'he was really ashamed to ask the public for money for any fresh object,' the Archdeacon seized a favourable opportunity for planting a girls' school at Mussourie. He set on foot a subscription throughout the diocese, which, when doubled by Government and aided by a grant of 100*l.* from the Christian Knowledge Society, and another of 400*l.* from the Board of Education, amounted in eighteen months to 60,000 rupees (6,000*l.*). With this sum a property was bought and a small reserve fund secured. The school when once opened was made over by deed to the Bishop and Archdeacon as *ex officio* trustees of the Board of Education. Thus Cainville House, Mussourie, was added to the trusts attached to the see of Calcutta, and a very important step was taken towards rolling away the reproach that in a great Protestant diocese a large share of the female Christian education beyond the limits of Calcutta was carried on in convents.

As 1864 advanced, the Bishop began again to take the initiative, and concentrated much of his time and attention upon what may be called the *second part* in this educational enterprise, with a view to the establishment of Himalayan schools, standing in the same relation to the North-West Provinces, Eastern Bengal, and Assam, as the Simla school did to the Punjâb. Circumstances had arisen to facilitate this further expansion of the work. St. Paul's School, in Calcutta, had long been in an unsatisfactory state. From various causes it had become unpopular, and was ceasing to pay its way. The remedy suggested for this state of decadence was either to amalgamate it with some more flourishing school in Calcutta, or to transplant it to the hills. The Bishop wavered long about this latter alternative. The temptation was great to take a step which might renovate a sickly institution and be at the same time subservient to his own plans. On the other hand, St. Paul's School was bound up with the memory of Archdeacon Corrie, who had founded it for the inhabitants of Calcutta, and of Bishop Wilson, who had enriched it by one of his many acts of munificence. Moreover this school was almost the only one in Calcutta representing distinct Church of England teaching. Elsewhere the influence exercised by the Church was of a hazy kind, being overpowered to a great extent by Presbyterianism or by a vague Bible Protestantism. On one occasion the Bishop wrote, in reference to this point, that 'he was fairly frightened by the Dissenting tendencies of some of the Calcutta places of education, fearing that a time might quickly come when disgrace and embarrassment might ensue from the absence of any distinctly Church school in the Presidency city.' However, a committee, who carefully and laboriously investigated the affairs of St. Paul's School, at length counselled a transfer to the hills as the best remedy for present evils, and the Bishop eventually did not dissent from the conclusion thus arrived at. In 1864, the school premises, standing on valuable ground in Calcutta, were sold, a property was bought, finely situated in the beautiful sanitarium of Darjeeling, in the Eastern Himalayas, and thus a second hill school came into existence.

In the case of a third, the question was mainly one of money. A large private school had been flourishing for some years at Mussourie, under the management of the late Rev. R. N. Maddock, its proprietor. It was for a higher class of boys than those educated at Simla or St. Paul's School, and the fees were higher in proportion. In 1864, Mr. Maddock was ready and willing to sell the school. The Bishop wished to buy it, and include it in the chain of hill institutions; 120,000 rupees (12,000*l.*) were asked for the property and goodwill. It became, therefore, a question whether the money could be raised. The Simla school was in full operation, its applications for entrance greatly exceeding its powers of admission; the Diocesan Board of Education was popular, and receiving large financial support; the Bishop deemed that the time was come when an onward step might be taken without undue rashness. Owing to delays inseparable from all Indian work, it was not until the following year (1865) that any definite scheme for the purchase was set on foot. The Bishop desired that the Board, as the centre of all educational enterprise, should be the agent in the transaction. Early in that year he hinted his wishes to the committee; subsequently he submitted a distinct proposal, which was strongly supported by the Archdeacon. Its purport was that the Board should at once make itself responsible for the purchase-money by sinking its reserve fund (about 2,500*l.*, in Government securities) in the property of Mr. Maddock's school, and trusting for the large remaining balance to a flow of private subscriptions, which the Government grant would double. In July he thus wrote to the secretary:—

I am desirous that, before the September meeting of the Diocesan Board of Education, the measures by which it is proposed to purchase the Rev. R. N. Maddock's school should be thoroughly considered.

. . . .

The Archdeacon and I have had a good deal of correspondence on the question, and the result is that he has drawn up the very clear and able minute which accompanies this letter, and with which I desire to express my entire concurrence, as containing the best plan for raising the money necessary to bring about this important end.

. . . .

It will doubtless occur to the Board to inquire whether the purchase of Mr. Maddock's school is so important an object that it is worth while to pledge the whole of their endowments for the sake of securing it, and whether we shall not thereby cripple our means of giving help to schools which may be projected in the plains. To this I can only answer that the present opportunity seems to me so very great, that it is worth while to risk something for the sake of securing it. By the permanent foundation of these three schools, at three important hill stations, in the three chief provinces of the Presidency, we provide a connected chain of Christian education, under the direction of the Church of England, for the middle class of the whole diocese; we thus actually realise what was spoken of six years ago as quite visionary. I well remember then the remark, that though nothing short of three schools would suffice for the actual want, yet that, if the present generation raised one, at Simla, this was all that could be expected. But here we have the power of securing the three, put before us in a manner which we may well regard as providential.

Again, I would remind the Board of the importance and standing which Mr. Maddock's school has acquired in the diocese; that by purchasing it, we secure not only the land and buildings, but its one hundred boys, its goodwill, its reputation, and also, through Mr. Maddock's liberal offer to restore 10,000 rupees of the price, the means of beginning at once the application of its advantages, in the form of scholarships to boys who cannot afford to pay the full charge for education.

Schools in the plains have already come into existence in considerable numbers through our aid: Calcutta, Howrah, Lahore, Allahabad, Rangoon, and Moulmein have all been helped by us to found cheap schools, and Lucknow, Singapore, and Nagpore are provided for in other ways. This list includes the seven seats of government in the Presidency, and two other important places. At present, owing to the impetus we have given to education, there is some fear lest, as in the case of ——, we may encourage abortive schemes which depend on the zeal of some active local official, and fall to pieces when he is removed. It is of great consequence that we should bestow our help only on schools which, from their proved importance, are tolerably sure to be permanent. . . . With these remarks I heartily commend the scheme to the favourable consideration of the Board, in the belief that to secure Mr. Maddock's school for the permanent advantage of the diocese, is one of the best objects to which they can apply their resources.

Much of the letter from which the above extracts are taken was devoted to the consideration of ways and means for raising the money, points which had only a temporary and limited interest. It will suffice for the general reader to catch sight through these extracts of the Bishop's mind in respect of this business, and to know further, that the managing committee met his overtures at once with ready attention, and shortly afterwards responded by a cordial assent.

The agreement entered into between the Board of Education and Mr. Maddock stood as follows:—

> 'That on January 1, 1867, one lakh (100,000 rupees, or 10,000*l*.) be paid to him for the school premises and goodwill. Half the profits of the school to be paid over in each succeeding year, on January 1, till the total purchase-money, 120,000 rupees (12,000*l*.), is paid off.'

This bargain very shortly cancelled itself. Contributions flowed in so freely during 1866 towards the Bishop's entire hill-school scheme, that by a very slight borrowing from the *general* fund, the purchase-money for the Mussourie school was realised before twelve months had elapsed, and in November 1866 the Archdeacon reported that the whole price of the school would be in the Bank of Bengal by the close of that year.

While still awaiting the decision of the committee, the Bishop had begun to make collections for another object which he had equally at heart. For each of the three hill schools actually or prospectively in his hands, he desired to raise and invest a moderate reserve fund, of which the interest only should be spent, as some security against an incumbrance of debt, should fluctuations in prosperity arise. A circular had been issued a short time before, commending the matter generally to the clergy and their flocks. The Bishop now followed it up by vigorous personal appeals, addressed during the sojourn at Murree to influential persons and private friends, both in India and in England. His action in this matter was a strong illustration of the quiet concentration of purpose with which he placed an object definitely before him, and then relaxed neither effort nor energy to secure its accomplishment. To his original appeal in behalf of the memorial school at Simla six years before, the remembrance of the crisis through which British dominion in India had just passed lent a spasmodic and popular force; but in 1865 the intrinsic importance of the cause was its only credential to public favour. Distrusting, therefore, the efficiency of printed appeals only, he supplemented them by private commendatory letters, as the only way by which, under God, his end could be attained, and these were written, two or three in a day, during the comparative leisure of a residence in the hills. Those who know the irksomeness of copying rather than composing letters, can estimate the weary labour of writing a hundred and sixteen, which were only slightly modified repetitions of each other.

The sum required for the combined purchase and endowment schemes was 250,000 rupees (25,000*l.*). The Government grant would reduce the demand upon the public to half this sum. The Viceroy in his private capacity promised 100*l.*; the Board of Education, 150*l.*, besides investing its reserve fund in the purchase of the Mussourie school property; and the Society for Promoting Christian Knowledge, 250*l.*; each subscription to be repeated annually for three years, during which the endowment fund was to remain open. These were substantial pledges of more general help, and the Bishop's labours did not go unrewarded. As Christmas 1865—the last of his life—drew near, he was cheered and encouraged by the receipt of many goodly contributions from donors both in England and India, friendly to himself or his projects.

The undertaking was no doubt large and comprehensive. Viewed on its financial side, it might be called hazardous, though not more so than kindred projects which are daily started in the world. Neither was it on a more extensive scale than in the Bishop's opinion the cause of sound Anglo-Indian education demanded; and in this opinion he had the firm and steady support of men whose judgment was equally calm and dispassionate with his own. As has been already said, the subject of extended education had begun to occupy the attention of English officials in the Punjâb before the Mutiny arose. The Bishop's special work lay in giving, when circumstances again became favourable, immense impulse to the movement then started, in developing it, and in extending to the whole Presidency what was in the first instance contemplated only for one of its provinces. Undoubtedly from the outset he entertained in his own mind the whole scheme, which was only carried out by instalments, and held that nothing less than three schools in the salubrious climate of the hills would attain the desired object. Existing interests were, nevertheless, from the first, carefully respected, and Mr. Maddock's private school would have been gladly accepted as the educational provision for the North-West Provinces; but the Bishop never lost sight of the necessities of Eastern Bengal and Assam, and as early as 1862 he took steps to secure a site for a school at Darjeeling, and was quite prepared for vigorous efforts to get it established. A concurrence of circumstances, however, as has been seen, led to the transfer of an existing school in one case, and to the purchase of an existing school in another. The work of creation became thus exchanged for that of absorption and consolidation, and in the end the only addition made by the Bishop to institutions already existing was the school established at Simla.

The schools have not been planned on any exaggerated

estimate of the numbers likely to fill them; that at Simla is the largest, and its quarters are calculated for less than two hundred pupils. Neither is the material fabric in either of the three hill schools pretentious or ornate. Naturally the Bishop desired and hoped that the Simla school (the one monument raised in British India to commemorate a general and almost national thanksgiving fo the restoration of peace after the Mutiny) might have a local habitation worthy of its memorial character; but, apart from this feeling, in one specific instance, and a general desire that the other school premises should be constructed with as much regard to the health of European and semi-European boys as the costly barracks that are occupied by English soldiers, he gave economical considerations their full weight, sought only to secure durable buildings adapted to their purpose, and carried every available rupee to the account of scholarships and endowments.

The last educational pastoral was dated from Delhi in January 1866. Written with the usual clearness and vigour, it had also all the fulness which was still necessary, for no abridgment of the oft-told tale would effect the desired object in a country where the supporters of any good work are widely scattered and perpetually changing. Patiently the Bishop retraced the rise and progress, and recapitulated the main features of the work he had in hand, dwelling upon the increasing numbers of middle-class Christians, the paramount necessity of healthful training for their children, the certainty that, if this were neglected, future generations of English and mixed blood would be distanced in knowledge and intelligence by Hindus and Mahometans. Acknowledging what had been done by contributions during the last few months in behalf of the purchase and the several endowment funds, he pressed on the notice of the public what still remained to be done, and with something of the peremptoriness of one who has a confidence that he will not ask in vain, he wrote:—

I shall not be satisfied that the work is properly carried out unless, in January 1867, the Diocesan Board enters on the possession of Mussourie, unencumbered with debt, and unless, in July 1868, each of these three schools is endowed with an invested capital of 50,000 rupees (5,000*l.*). To do this, 25,000 rupees will be required, of which Government will contribute half. Thus I must ask the public to raise the sum already subscribed to 125,000 rupees by July 1868.

In words expressive of sincere thankfulness for wide-spread liberality and deeply-valued support, and of earnest and devout hopes for the future, this, his last manifesto on a subject that had engrossed his Indian life, ended:—

It only remains that I should heartily thank those who have already come forward with their contributions, especially, perhaps—though, indeed, it is invidious to particularise—the Society for Promoting Christian Knowledge, which has now for more than a century been ever among the foremost in doing good to India; His Excellency Sir John Lawrence, for much public and private encouragement; the Venerable Arch-deacon Pratt, for the wise counsel and ready help which he has given to me in this as in many other works undertaken for the welfare of the diocese; and those headmasters in England who have shown a truly kind and brotherly sympathy with this attempt to spread Christian education among a neglected class, by making collections for it in the schools over which they preside. All, however, who have contributed have my hearty thanks; and I trust that the constant calls upon my time and thoughts made by the pastoral charge of this great diocese will serve as my excuse if I do not write a separate letter expressing this to every one who has actively promoted the scheme, which I now once more commend to the blessing of God, and the bounty of His Church.

This circular being issued, and the cause pleaded by it committed to the favour of the Anglo-Indian public, a lull came again over the Bishop's personal efforts, and during a few ensuing months he had little to do beyond registering the donations with which his appeal was answered. He was to the last anxious, but not despondent about the ultimate fulfilment of his wishes, though possibly he might have waited long for it. But it was not permitted to him to witness an early or remote realization of his hopes; it was willed, in the providence of God, that other men should enter into his labours, and that by his death, and not by his life, the unfinished work should be accomplished.

The general character of the life at Murree is described in one of those short sketches into which the Bishop usually expanded, at the end of any continuous sojourn, the brief 'three-line' journal, resumed when travelling was suspended, and devoted to a brief and quaint notice of each day's events. He liked Murree much, and enjoyed as usual the fine mountain walks and occasional expeditions, and the sight of range on range of hills meeting the eye on every side. He liked also the pleasant social circle, which included many able members of the Punjâb Government; men whom he used to delight in describing as 'simply and practically religious, and imbued with a strong sense of the supremacy of duty and of the majesty of work.' While, however, much refreshment was drawn from outward sources, the question of the usefulness and profitableness of his own life seemed to be gaining increasing ascendency in his mind, and the sense of the grave and solemn purposes for which his lot had been cast in India to be ever acquiring fresh strength. A brief review of a definite period inserted in the record of ordinary daily occupations, and disclosing simply and unaffectedly the earnest and devout principles by which he desired to guide his life, took the place with him in a great measure of more distinctly religious effusions. There were some years of his life during which, at long intervals, he committed to writing thoughts of a more devotional and contemplative kind; but the practice was not a congenial one—it never became habitual, and was deliberately abandoned. A passage written in a manuscript book in 1863, recording this intention, is so characteristic of the writer, that its insertion claims a place in a memoir which can only touch lightly upon points over which he who is the subject of it threw while in life a veil of reserve.

I have completely altered my method of writing in this book, and I doubt whether I shall ever return to the old way. Some time ago I read some religious biographies (especially one), in which extracts from private journals of this nature were printed. They certainly gave me an impression of unreality. The writers seemed often to fall into mere talk: into vague statements of doctrine, or expressions of feelings about themselves, which are at least unnatural, and which I can scarcely think were altogether realised. It is, perhaps, hard even to write in a religious journal without a secret fancy that it may some day be seen, without the intrusion of the unblest desire for human applause. This is dangerous to sincerity, to reality, to depth of Christian conviction. At least it is in my case, though perhaps not in the case of others. Therefore I resolved to give up all record of my private feelings in such a book as this. But, on the other hand, religious writing is a help to self-recollection, and a means of meditation, which is to me always a difficulty. I have therefore substituted for a record of personal feelings passages from the Bible, with a brief reflection on each. I trust that I have derived good from writing these, and from looking back at them from time to time. I hope to continue the practice, and may God be pleased to bless it to my growth in Christian wisdom and holiness, through Jesus Christ our Lord.

Thus turning away from elaborate introspective searchings of heart and spirit, the Bishop, with the true naturalness of his character, made his outward life the test of inward nearness to God and Christ, and in short passages like the following was wont to record little beyond the practical work which, wherever he found himself, he desired to begin, continue, and end in sole reference to his Master in heaven.

Murree, June 14, 1865.

I shall now discontinue my daily journal, returning, I hope, to a regular mode of life. After so much enjoyment, and so much experience of God's goodness in the uninterrupted health and safety of our party, some useful work becomes on all accounts a duty. My desire is, during the next four months, to take a considerable part in the Church services, both on Sunday and Wednesday, and to do something in the following directions: to read a great part of Augustine, 'De Civitate Dei;' to lay a foundation of Sanscrit, by going through Monier Williams's Grammar; to write an article for the 'Calcutta Review' on the education of Europeans and Eurasians; to push vigorously my scheme for the three hill schools, and to make a beginning of two works which I long to accomplish, or see accomplished, in the course of the next two or three years, if God grants me life and health, but which I approach with trembling, from considerable distrust in my own power to do much towards either—(1) a book of Christian evidences adapted especially to the nineteenth century and the Brahmo Somaj, and (2) a small book on Christian practice and devotion for young men coming from England to India. I have also plenty of books, such as the last volume of Merivale's 'Rome,' Rawlinson's 'Ancient Monarchies,' Max Müller's last set of Lectures on Language, Perowne 'On the Psalms,' &c., in which I hope to make some way at odd times.

Such is my purposed work, of which, if I accomplish half, I suppose I ought to be contented, and it rests with a higher will than mine whether I shall accomplish any part. But I humbly commit it to God's mercy and blessing, through Jesus Christ our Lord.

October 14.

The time is now approaching when we must quit this most pleasant place of summer sojourn. As to diocesan business and places, I have been mainly occupied with the scheme for founding the three hill schools, of which it is hard to overrate the importance. Besides this, in conjunction with Colonel Lake, I took measures for transporting the intended Punjâb Girls' School from Dharamsala to Simla. I also assembled at breakfast one morning all the Lahore officials, and Mr. Finch, the officiating agent of the Punjâb Railway, to consider how we can manage to place a clergyman at Naulakha, the railway-station of Anarkulli. A parsonage will, I hope, be provided by subscriptions in India; but, after the meeting, I drew up an appeal to the shareholders, requesting them to allow a certain percentage to be deducted from their salaries, to form a 'Punjâb and Delhi Railways Clergy Fund,' like that which, by the Archdeacon's exertions, is being gathered for the East Indian Railway. My definite pastoral work has included one sermon on nearly every Sunday, and pastoral visits to the Lawrence Asylum, and to Nunkote, about twelve miles from Murree. Service has been held in church every Wednesday, and during this time I have delivered a course of eight expository lectures on Joel, Jonah, and Obadiah, which I prepared with care by the help of Ewald, Pusey, and the Dictionary of the Bible. And lastly, I had every Friday a meeting for Bible reading and explanation at our own house, and went through the Epistle to the Galatians, my expositions being materially aided by the new and admirable edition of the epistle by Lightfoot, the best addition to our exegetical literature which has yet resulted from the critical movement in England. The meeting was well attended; and some of the higher officials of the Government were always present. Now as the administration of the Punjâb is certainly as able and vigorous as any in India, this fact at least shows that statesmanship and an efficient discharge of this world's highest and most difficult duties are entirely compatible with earnest Christian faith, spite of all the chatter of the day about the increasing repugnance of intellectual men to the ordinary religious teaching given in our churches. When the exposition of the Galatians was over, four weeks still remained, and during these, I went to the weekly bible-class established in the barracks, and attended by some twenty or thirty soldiers of the convalescent depôt. With them we read and discussed the last four chapters of St. John's gospel.

This brings me to record the degree to which I fulfilled my intentions as to reading which I set down on June 14. I have read thirteen books of the 'De Civitate Dei,' always with interest and instruction, even when it was plain that Augustine's arguments and criticisms were wholly wrong—for it is a book suggestive alike by its errors and its truths—but generally with great profit, and often with considerable benefit to my sermons, of which three were suggested and enriched by it. I have also gone through the greater part of the Sanscrit grammar, and can at least read the Devanagari character, and know what Sanscrit is like, besides having gained much ocular demonstration of its importance in comparative philology, and of the cousinhood of Hindus, Greeks, Romans, and Englishmen. The educational article for the 'Calcutta Review' is written, and the proof corrected. On the other hand, of the two works mentioned on June 14 as to be accomplished, God willing, in two or three years, I have done very little to (1), from lack of books, and nothing at all to (2), from lack of competence to the task. I collected a few notes and references on Evidences, but as to the book of devotion, though I read a good deal of Thomas-à-Kempis, and Bright's 'Book of Ancient Collects,' I always felt as if to begin it, I needed more quiet and deeper Christian experience than I have. The lectures on the Prophets too occupied time, which might have been devoted to these projected works. The last volume of Merivale's 'Rome,' Rawlinson's 'Ancient Monarchies,' Kaye's 'History of the Sepoy War,' Howard on the 'Travancore Syrians,' and Lathbury's 'History of the Prayer Book' (the last a truly dull, and somewhat prejudiced book), formed the chief elements in my armchair and sofa studies. I also went carefully through Fremantle and Brodrick's collection of 'Privy Council Judgments,' and was converted by it from distrust of the Judicial Committee to a contented acquiescence in it, and a strong sense of its impartiality. Not liking to let my Hebrew slumber altogether, I read the 'Book of Ruth' in Wright's edition, and I wrote for the 'Christian Intelligencer' short accounts of this, of 'Lightfoot on the Galatians,' and of the 'Privy Council Judgments.' So ends a quiet and happy time, for which I humbly thank our Heavenly Father, through Jesus Christ our Lord.

The cold weather visitation of 1865 began with an expedition into the Hazara district, which was then in a very disturbed state, through Mussulman fanatics and assassins who were keeping up a chronic state of alarm. Just at that time, a bandit chief, named Samundhar, from the independent territory of Mulkah, on the other side of the Indus, had been captured, and was lodged in the gaol at Abbottabad, awaiting his trial for divers acts of cattle-lifting and kidnapping Her Majesty's Indian subjects, conveying them encased in mussicks (buffalo-hides) across the Indus, and then demanding their ransom. On his capture, his followers sent a message, brigand fashion, to the officials of Hazara, that if he were not at once released, some European would be carried off and kept as a hostage. Hence guards and armed escorts were everywhere enjoined; the Bishop and his chaplain had a night and day attendance of soldiers with loaded carbines, and Samundhar's followers were kept at bay. At Attock the Bishop had again the great delight of seeing the fine junction of the Indus and Cabul rivers, with Akbar's fort frowning above; and at Peshawur, on his last birthday, he made the following entry in his journal:—

Peshawur, October 29.—My birthday found me at the furthest limits of my diocese. I spent part of its leisure in writing to and about my boy, whose long absence is the greatest trial of my Indian life. I trust that my work here may leave behind it some results to make up for a sorrowful and unnatural separation, and that he, in accordance with Christ's promise, may find the want of father, mother, and sister supplied by hearing and doing the Word of God.

From Attock the whole party, now reunited, descended

the Indus to the frontier of Scinde, then crossed to the left bank at Dehra Ghazee Khan, and travelled to Moultan and Lahore. The last week of December was devoted to a visitation of the Hissar district, south of Delhi. Once more, in January 1866, the Bishop visited Delhi; his journal bearing witness to the ever fresh enjoyment afforded by a sight of the Jumma Musjid, the palace of the Moguls, the grand tombs without the walls, and the general view of the great city. Once more he gazed on that 'thing of beauty,' that 'joy for ever,' the Taj Mahal, at Agra. Here, too, he held all but his last ordination. The admission to deacon's orders of two natives, on this occasion, raised the native pastorate to fourteen, nine of whom had been ordained by himself, in the course of seven years. From Agra he once more took one of those expeditions of combined work and pleasure which he loved so well, and making what has been called one of the finest marches in North India, he visited Futtehpore Sikri, to see again, as in 1859, the great palace of Akbar; Bhurtpore, for the sake of its history, and Muttra for ecclesiastical duties. Early in February he was again settled at Bishop's Palace, and the following letters present, in his own graphic style, the main points in the life and occupations of the preceding months:—

To the Dean of Westminster.

July 1865.

. . . I have just received, and am reading with much pleasure, the 'Guardian' of May 24, containing the Convocation debates on the Court of Final Appeal and the new Causes. I highly approve of your speeches, and of the friendly but characteristic interlocution between you and G. A. Denison. Moreover, I think you, Harvey Goodwin (possibly by this time Bishop of Chester?), Blakesley, and others very wise and public-spirited in taking so much interest in Convocation and its proceedings, thereby preventing it from incurring contempt as a purely one-sided assembly. At the same time it ought to contain laymen, and to be united with the York Synod. I trust that Dissenting rancour will not prevent the Clerical Subscription Bill from passing the Commons, which would be far more inexcusable than the shipwreck of the bishopric of Lahore, which it has already effected. The next ecclesiastico-political question which I desire to see taken in hand by a Royal Commission is an alteration of the Table of Lessons; and I trust that thus, by a moderate and gradual course of bit by bit reform, we shall greatly improve and emancipate the Church, without alienating and disgusting High Churchmen. I long to hold an ordination without the necessity of exacting the 'unfeigned assent and consent.'

I have read 'Lightfoot on the Galatians' with great admiration: it is at once candid and critical, and at the same time conservative of Christian truth and historical fact against theorists and hypothesis-framers, which is at present my ideal of apologetic theology.

To the Rev. H. Bell.

August 1865.

. . . This rejection of Gladstone at Oxford is a great scandal and a great misfortune. That the ablest statesman of the day, being at the same time an earnest Christian and Churchman, and devoted beyond all other politicians to practical schemes for removing the greatest blot on our national escutcheon—the degraded condition of the poor—should be turned out by a highly educated and mainly clerical constituency, is, I think, a real disgrace to us. I am afraid the Marlborough bridegrooms did not feel the duty of staying in England to vote for him.

To Bosworth Smith, Esq.

Kohat, November 1865.

. . . I delayed my annual letter to you till I had seen in the paper the actual announcement of your nuptials, which, owing to our distance from the sea, reached us late. I heartily congratulate you on the successful accomplishment of the marriage, and on being able thus early in life to enjoy the blessings and fulfil the duties of domestic life. A wife to take care of you, 'halving your sorrows and doubling your pleasures,' and a home of your own, are precious gifts of God, and I trust that His blessing will be upon you in the use of them. . . .

We are now, as you will gather from the date of this, engaged in the annual work of visitation, and I am going down all the stations on the frontier which separate us from the wild tribes of the Paropamisus, Afridis, Khyberees, Wuzeerees, Pathans of other kinds, and Belooches, and who form a long narrow border between us and the scene of our greatest crime and blunder of recent years, the kingdom of Cabul. Our main highway for this journey is the Indus. We embarked on this famous river at Attock, the place where Alexander probably crossed it, but not where he began his voyage down it, as he must have entered it from the Hydaspes (Jhelum), at the point where it is joined by that and the rest of the five rivers of the Punjâb. . . . A fleet of four vessels conveys us down the river, and they are not, I should think, materially different from those used in Alexander's time. They are merely clumsy barges, almost flat-bottomed, and drawing very little water (the river up here is shallow and rapid), propelled when necessary by four huge oars, two at the prow and two at the stern, but often left to float down the stream, which runs at the rate of six or seven miles an hour. . . . We all keep very near each other during the voyage, and can migrate from one boat to another without much trouble. We are off at sunrise, stop at about 9·30 for breakfast, and again as soon as it is dark, when we dine. During the night it would be unsafe to proceed. Hitherto, while we are in the mountainous country, the river has been picturesque, but its banks are soon, we are told, to become flat and ugly. The scenery is wild and peculiar: steep rocks and cliffs of a dark grey colour on each bank, generally wholly without vegetation, sometimes diversified by a few stunted trees. Peaked rocks, too, rise from the middle of the stream, which sometimes has been compressed into very narrow limits, one place being marked by the common legend of a horse leaping across the river, and not unfrequently the boats are carried briskly down rapids, where the water whirls and foams so as to cause a little excitement as we pass the rocks. . . . The boats themselves are comfortable; the time is spent pleasantly enough in reading, writing, talking, and looking about us; the mornings are bitterly cold; the heat at 2 P.M. is considerable, but not oppressive. All along the river, sometimes on its bank, sometimes at distances of thirty or forty miles inland, are the military stations, which I visit, an escort of native cavalry being always sent down to bring us safely in, and protect us from the fate of poor Mr. Moens; for an Afridi chief is very fond of carrying off anyone whom he can catch, generally some fat Hindu tradesman, whisking him up into the mountains, and holding him to ransom. In fact, they are just like Italian brigands, or Highlanders of Rob Roy's type. Kohat, from which I date, is one of these military stations: here a church and cemetery have been consecrated, service performed, ecclesiastical matters looked up; and civilities and hospitalities received from the officers. . . .

Since I began this, the telegraph has flashed to us the overwhelming intelligence of Lord Palmerston's death. I call it overwhelming, not from any great admiration for him, though I have latterly appreciated him more than I used to do, but on account of the crisis which must follow in English, and possibly in European, politics; in which view I suppose that his death is the most important which could happen except that of Louis Napoleon. You and the Radicals (unless the soft influence of a wife has mitigated your Radicalism) will probably rejoice in it. I do not mean in the death personally, which would be malignant, but in the removal of a drag from Liberalism. On the other hand, the Tories will also rejoice in the removal of the man who kept a great amount of floating uncertain demi-Conservatism on the side technically called Liberal; but they must execrate their luckless fate, which delayed the event till the elections were fairly won by their rivals. . . . I regard their present position under their present chief as a Nemesis upon them for their conduct to Peel, aggravated and repeated by their recent crime and folly in the rejection of Gladstone at Oxford. . . .

Edward is now in the agonies of his final cramming for

Woolwich: I shall be thankful if he succeeds, though I do not expect it; for if he fails, his heart is set upon the line, to my mind the most profitless and perilous of professions, except perhaps that of an Assam tea-planter, and one which I could only consent to his entering from my deep conviction that any profession which a boy deliberately chooses is more profitable and less perilous than one into which he is forced or persuaded by his father.

To Professor Conington.

November 1865.

. . . . In writing to you I always feel one doubt: whether you prefer my telling you of my travels and work in India, of which, except for my sake, you cannot desire to know much, or criticising public events in England, about which one is apt to utter platitudes which you have already seen in the 'Times' or heard in the Common Room. I shall give you a slight mixture of both this time, and shall, by a hysteron proteron, begin with the last of the two general topics, and say that as to a new Whig Premier, I should, on the whole, have been willing to give Gladstone the fair trial which he must have; or, if the time is not come for him, then I think that Lord Granville or Lord Clarendon would have been preferable to the actual chief, who however was probably inevitable. As to the Reform Bill, which will, I suppose, be proposed, I am no democrat, and all my prepossessions are in favour of the schemes of theorists like Lord Grey; but I conclude that any plan like his is impossible for a people who boast of being so simple and practical in our tastes as we do; and therefore the only question with me is this:—the great, crying, terrible evil of England is the pauperism, the enormous difference which separates classes, the practical heathenism and physical misery of the masses. Will a democratic Reform Bill remedy this? I certainly doubt it; but if there is any probability of it, I should feel it wrong to oppose it, even if it costs us the aristocracy and the establishment of the Church. But in carrying such a reform, I should trust Gladstone more than anyone else, because he, alone almost among statesmen, seems to have an adequate appreciation of the need that the spiritual and material welfare of the people should be provided for together. . . .

Turning now to ourselves, since we left our summer sojourn at Murree we have been travelling over the western extremities of India, and are now descending the Indus. . . . The river, which for the first few days flowed between picturesque mountains, has now utterly flat and uninteresting shores, the Suleiman Range which separates India from Cabul being too far off to be seen. In going inland to the stations, however, we have seen it, and especially admired one prominent mountain of the chain, the Takht-i-Suleiman (Solomon's throne), 13,000 feet high, very peculiar, and like a throne in shape; so that Solomon, when visiting the Jinn, is said to have selected it as the spot whereunto he desired his green carpet to convey him, that from it he might gaze upon the plains of India. This story reminds me, and may remind you, that I have now actually been gazing upon those plains for seven years; and one begins to ask, what have I done all that time? any good to make up for so utter a change of life? I should like to live to see four works in good progress towards completion; —(1) The organisation of a system of education for Anglo-Indians, through hill schools for both sexes, and the Diocesan Board, aided by Government; (2) a supply of clergy for the railway stations; (3) a better pastoral oversight of all classes of Christians in the city of Calcutta; (4) vigorous efforts, by lectures, schools, colleges, friendly intercourse, and in time more directly religious means, for evangelising the educated natives of Bengal. I mention these four, not as the only, nor necessarily the greatest, works which English Christianity should effect in India, but as those with which I have become most directly and personally connected.

To the Dean of Westminster.

Bishop's Palace, February 1866.

. . . . We left our Himalayan retreat on October 16, and proceeded in the first instance to Peshawur, then turned back, and commenced a long round, containing three distinct novelties:—(1) the descent of the Indus to the frontier of Scinde, with excursions from the river towards the roots of the mountain barrier which separates India from Affghanistan, and of which the grandest point is the Takht-i-Suleiman; (2) a journey through the desolate regions of Hissar, bordering on the great desert of India, chiefly effected by a carriage drawn by four camels; (3) a short but very pretty tour from Agra to Muttra, the birthplace of Krishna, by Futtehpore Sikri, the scene of Akbar's glories; Bhurtpore, where old Lord Combermere achieved greatness and threw a certain reflected lustre over his kinsfolk; Deeg, the most remarkable specimen of modern Hindu architecture and princely life; and Govadhun and Bindabun, altogether given up to Krishna and impurity. The heroes of the first of these three regions are Solomon, Alexander, and three Pathan chiefs of Humayun's reign—Ismail Khan, Ghazee Khan, and Futteh Khan—who established on the frontier three camps (dehra), which have now become the flourishing towns and English stations of Dehra Ismail Khan, Dehra Ghazee Khan, and the purely native and insignificant one of Dehra Futteh Khan, and have further given to the whole country the name of *Deraját* ('the encampments,' *ját* being a Persian plural). The heroes of the second region are Mahmoud of Ghuzni, who took the Hindu fort of Sirsa; the Emperor Ferozeshah, who used to hunt incessantly in the jungle, now cleared away, certain lions, of whom the last was killed by a Mr. Fraser, in 1828; and various English adventurers who tried to carve out for themselves principalities or large estates during the general break-up which began with the death of Aurungzib, and did not end till the Mahrattas were put down. Of the third region the heroes are yet more miscellaneous: Krishna, the giant Gunze, the Bhurtpore rajahs, Akbar, Lord Combermere, and a man probably descended from Gunze, being 7 feet 6 inches high, and requiring sixteen pounds of corn for a meal, who exhibits himself at Deeg to astonished and half-affrighted travellers. The mode of conveyance in the first journey was principally by four large native boats. . . . In the second journey we were, as I said, chiefly dragged over the desert by camels, the carriages being lent by the rajahs of Puttiala and Jheend, two Sikh princes who dwell in the territory between the Sutlej and the Jumna. This journey was very cold and fatiguing, and afforded less compensation than the others in the way of secular interest, but perhaps more interest of a higher kind; for from the rarity of religious ministrations there, our presence seemed nowhere more acceptable. Three churches were consecrated in this desolate region. The third journey was luxuriously performed in the carriage of the Maharajah of Bhurtpore, who in entertaining the cousin of the Poliorcetes of his territory, was not sheltering a member of a hostile house, since he is grandson of the infant whom Lord Combermere placed upon the throne which was withheld by a usurping uncle. The only great city, not included in the limits above indicated, which I saw for the first time during this tour, was Moultan, a place of some interest from the murder of Anderson and Vans Agnew, which sealed our possession of the Punjâb, and from abounding in tombs of Mahomedan saints, covered with beautiful tiles of varied colours like the encaustic works of Wedgwood and others in modern days. It is said to be the hottest place in India. On approaching the tomb of Shamach Tabreez (Shamach=the sun, cf. Beth Shemesh) we were told the reason of this excessive heat by the guardian of the shrine. Shamach Tabreez, he said, was a very holy fakir who came to Moultan 250 years ago, but the people refused to receive him, or to listen to his preaching, desired him to leave their city, and declined to supply him with any kind of food. A disciple, however, brought him some game from the jungle, and he begged from the churlish Moultanese fire wherewith to cook it. This they also refused, whereupon the fakir said that if they would not help him to cook his food, the sun should do so, and accordingly, by his prayers, brought the sun near enough to Moultan to provide him with an excellent roast hare. Once there, however, the sun declined to return to his former place in the heavens, and so the people of Moultan are still punished for the impiety of their ancestors by an extra allowance of heat. This, however, is the case only in the summer; when we were at Moultan the climate was cool and pleasant.

The tour, I trust, was not unprofitable; two at least of the missions—Agra and Amritsir—were in a state of great vigour and efficiency. I consecrated altogether sixteen churches for European worshippers, and laid the corner-stone of another. . . Altogether life here passes very happily, though of course with some drawbacks; but I have never felt otherwise than thankful that I came to India, and had so *great and effectual a door opened* for doing some good in life. My main regret has been that I have made so little use of it. However, that is a matter rather for oneself than one's friends.

CHAPTER XIV.

THE BISHOP'S OFFICIAL CORRESPONDENCE IN 1866—STATE AID AND VOLUNTARYISM—REVISION OF PENSION RULES—SUGGESTIONS FOR IMPROVING ECCLESIASTICAL SERVICE—INCREASE OF ARCHDEACONRIES—VIEWS ON EXTENSION OF EPISCOPATE—COADJUTOR BISHOPS—ALARMS FOR THE POSITION OF THE INDIAN CHURCH—LETTER TO THE BISHOP OF LONDON—THE CAPETOWN CONTROVERSY—LETTER TO THE BISHOP OF CAPETOWN—REMARRIAGE OF CONVERTS' ACT—TWO LETTERS ON THE SUBJECT.

A SPECIAL interest is attached to the Bishop's public correspondence in 1866. All that he wrote during these few months, before his sudden summons to resign his charge, has served to place on record his latest views and wishes for the work that he had in trust. Diocesan matters of mere routine, which usually largely occupied his pen, seemed for the time to recede before the exposition of broad and practical schemes formed and ripened during eight years, in the general interests of the Indian Church. In an article contributed a few months before to the 'Calcutta Review,' he had traced the rise and progress of the 'Anglican Establishment in India' from the days of William III., when, at the request of the residents in Bombay, 'two godly ministers' were sent out to administer the Protestant religion in all garrisons, and 'to instruct the Gentoos as should be servants or slaves of the Company.' After describing its progress down to the present time, he asks :—

And now what improvements and developments does our Church require in that branch of its operations which concerns Europeans and East Indians? . . . Undoubtedly, a Church establishment in India is as necessary now as it was when Wilberforce and Buchanan and Bishop Porteus and the Church Missionary Society clamoured for it. Its work would be mainly with the army and those in the employment of Government, though of course it must extend its charge to all with whom it is brought into contact. Obviously, too, this establishment, if it exists at all, should be an efficient one, and able to compass the objects above indicated; but, beyond this, the development of the Church should proceed from within, and the aid of Government should be given only in proportion to the liberality of its members. . . . The combined action of the State and of individual Churchmen, guided by the ecclesiastical authorities, will, under God's blessing, place the Anglo-Indian Church on a satisfactory basis.

Voluntaryism, thus put forward once more as a powerful lever of profitable Church work, was no new principle in India. Substantial charities, still in full operation, represent the helping hand stretched out in bygone days to relieve want and sickness among the Christian population. Bishop Wilson gave a new development to this same principle by the foundation of the Additional Clergy Society and the Seamen's Mission, a pastoral agency being thus provided, mainly through private support, for Europeans living beyond the reach of Government chaplains. His successor invoked it incessantly through his appeals to all members of the English Church to promote education within her borders, and to maintain her position as the foremost among Protestant communities in carrying the Word and Sacraments into the jungles of British India. A considerable augmentation of the reserve funds of the Church Building and Additional Clergy Societies; a threefold increase of agents employed by the latter society; an investment of 7,000*l.*, contributed by the shareholders of the East Indian Railway towards the support of pastors along the line, and the great increase of schools throughout the diocese, are all tangible results of the late episcopate, and to these results the steady flow of voluntary aid largely contributed.

But while thus successfully pressing on Churchmen the duty of self-help, Bishop Cotton none the less laid claim to a continuance of that support from the State which for 200 years has been a source of strength to the Anglo-Indian branch of the Established Church, gradually making that Church what it now is, a compact organisation, possessing, through its close and peculiar connexion with the State, foundations of stability, and a reserve fund of strength far beyond what falls to the lot of many struggling colonial Churches. One ecclesiastical measure, with which the Government were directly and exclusively concerned, was that of a revision of the regulations respecting chaplains' pensions. It was only completed in 1866, and demands more notice than the brief reference to it made in a former page. The movement was started in the Madras Presidency in 1862, and the case in outline was this. The changes impending after the Mutiny led the chaplains to review their position. The amalgamation of the Company's forces with the Queen's threatened the destruction of the Military Fund, subscription to which by Government chaplains was compulsory, and formed an insurance for a surviving family. Salaries were insufficient to afford a surplus for savings in days when the cost of living was constantly increasing; and the pensions, which had been reduced in 1834 from 365*l.* to 290*l.* a-year, were inadequate for the support of a family after retirement to England. The only prizes that gilded the service were the two senior chaplaincies in each Presidency, to which a somewhat higher salary was assigned. These posts, however, were but shadows of benefits to the service generally; the simple fact of seniority secured them to six members of the whole body. They exercised, moreover, in some degree, an injurious influence, by inducing chaplains to linger on, in the hope of succeeding to them, when it was evident that their energies had been seriously impaired by a tropical climate. The Madras chaplains carried with them a large majority of their brethren in the other Presidencies in desiring to surrender these senior chaplaincies, and to receive in exchange a return to the higher rate of pension that had prevailed before 1834. It was well known that the case would obtain no official consideration unless it were shown that no extra expenditure would be incurred, and the memorial of the chaplains was drawn up on a basis of careful calculation, which, it was believed, left no financial flaw. Lord Elgin's government, before whom it was laid in 1862, arrived at different conclusions, and while viewing the proposal favourably in its general scope, rejected it as entailing increased outlay upon the State. A stone, however, had been set rolling which was not likely to stop. The bishops and the chaplains were equally interested in the movement. The subject was discussed in many conclaves during the Metropolitical Visitation of 1863; and at Bombay a fresh scheme was drawn up, signed by the three Bishops, which, retaining the main features of the former one, and vindicating the correctness of previous calculations, was partially recast so as to have more chance of acceptance with the authorities. Its reception by Sir John Lawrence's government was more favourable, and it was forwarded to the Secretary of State. At the India House the question was mainly one of finance. Supporters of the measure in India advocated it in behalf of the chaplains and of the Church's welfare. To bring it into harmony with all these requirements was a work of time and difficulty; and long correspondence ensued. The proposed return to the former rate of pension after twenty years' service was conceded, but only as a substitute for the senior chaplaincies; the interests of existing incumbents had to be considered, and three years' grace was allowed, during which the next in succession might elect either to assert his claims, should a vacancy arise, or to relinquish them, for himself and for the service generally, in favour of the higher pension. Hence the operation of the new measure was prospective only, and liable to indefinite postponement. Many chaplains whose time of service was far advanced, having no inducement to remain when the senior prize had, for them, become practically already abolished, were willing and anxious to resign the service, and were only deterred from doing so by the fear that a premature retirement might permanently forfeit the new rate of pension. But the officials of the India House, alarmed by the prospect of a sudden enlargement of their pension list, long shut their eyes to this point in the case; and it was not until 1866 that the Bishop obtained the acceptance of his recommendation that all chaplains desirous of retiring on the completion of their twenty years' service, should be permitted to do so on the existing pension, and await its rise until such time as the senior chaplaincies should lapse. One clause in the scheme emanated solely from the Bishop of Calcutta—viz. that which made retirement compulsory after twenty-five years' service, for all chaplains, except such as might be especially recommended to the Secretary of State for prolonged service. This enactment was naturally unpopular with a few members of the ecclesiastical service, who, after long residence in India, had become indifferent about returning to England; but the Bishop looked upon it as an essential corollary of a measure intended to benefit not only the clergy but the Church. It would be invidious to say more than that his strong and repeated, and in the end successful, representations to Government on this point, rested on the conviction, formed through some painful experience in the earlier years of his episcopate, that less than any department of work in India could the ecclesiastical service afford to dispense with the regular infusion of freshness and vigour that England alone could supply. The small sum at issue in each case, amounting only to 70*l.* a-year, and the small number of Government servants at any one time affected by revised pension rules, might seem disproportioned to a correspondence which ran its course, at the rate of Indian progress, during four years. But distinctions of 'little and large' are rightly forgotten in the presence of a grievance to be redressed; and it may not be wide of the mark to infer that this special act of legislation owed much to the support afforded by a Viceroy whose former Indian career had been contemporary with that of a whole generation of chaplains, and who would be not less alive to inequalities in their position than to deficiencies in their ministrations.

Other suggestions having in view the well-being of the Church and her ministers, and resting, for the most part, on the principle of grants from Government supplementing voluntary efforts, were embodied in some of the Bishop's latest official correspondence. Such suggestions pointed to a more general erection of parsonage-houses; to the development of more lay co-operation in the Church by vestries and churchwardens; to the establishment of a pension fund for the widows and orphans of chaplains, to take the place of the military funds which, as was expected, were swept away in the great changes subsequent to the Mutiny. Another measure recommended by him as eminently conducive to the welfare both of the Church and clergy, was the raising of some two or three chaplaincies into archdeaconries. The expense would be slight to the State; for the extra allowances granted to the chaplains of Malacca and Singapore, on account of the great expense of living in the Straits Settlements, would revert to India on the transfer of the Straits to the Colonial Office, and become available for a slight increase of salary for archdeacons. The establishment of a few such posts, with a very moderate pecuniary advantage, the Bishop strongly recommended as a legitimate mode of breaking up the dead level of a service which he did not shrink from characterising as 'somewhat stiff and prosaic,' and of placing in the hands of the bishops an occasional piece of preferment for members of the clerical body who, by character and attainments, were fitted to advise and guide their brethren. He pressed such appointments also in the direct interest of the Church, believing that archdeacons placed at extremities of the diocese, such as Lahore, Nagpore, and Rangoon, would exercise a salutary oversight of the clergy, so long as there was no division of the diocese to insure a more frequent and regular episcopal supervision. The Bishop's latest view with reference to an extension of the Indian episcopate arose partly out of the collapse of the attempt to create a fourth see solely by the State. The subject had never been lost sight of since the subdivision of the one original diocese into three. Bishop Wilson, when in England in 1846, advocated a bishopric of Agra, with all the force of his personal character, and of his long experience of the needs of India. But the Court of Directors, languid in those days in building churches, were not likely to be forward in endowing bishoprics, and they did nothing beyond giving the venerable prelate a respectful hearing. A cry for more bishoprics mingled largely with the zeal which the Mutiny awoke among Anglican Churchmen. A clause providing for the erection of a new see was inserted in the Bill that transferred India to the Crown, but was withdrawn 'as irrelevant to the matter in hand.' The first Secretary of State for India under the Imperial Government, while pronouncing himself favourable to the question, cautiously removed it to a distance by suggesting, in an interview with Bishop Cotton, in 1858, that he should first traverse his ecclesiastical territory, and then pronounce upon its wants. Thus the matter was laid to rest during the first visitation, which lasted during three years and a half. The Bishop's own views on this question were set forth in the preface to his second charge, delivered in 1863, and they were expressed again with very slight modification in 1864, when he was consulted in reference to Sir Charles Wood's intention of bringing a Bill into Parliament for the erection of a new see in the Punjab. These views were characterised by his usual practical judgment and moderation. He had an abiding sense of the anomaly of Burmah being ecclesiastically administered from India, and of the needless toil imposed on the Bishop of Calcutta by unequal and ill-arranged ecclesiastical divisions of India itself; but he never took an exaggerated estimate of the fatigues and burdens of the metropolitan see, nor urged relief to himself personally as an argument for its subdivision. On the other hand, he was fully sensible of the benefit that both the clergy and their work draw from the near presence of one standing towards them in the position of an influential counsellor and guide. There was also the vexatious fact that the mere mechanical process of traversing so great a territorial area monopolized time, strength, and energies which might have been profitably devoted to more concentrated work in behalf both of Christians and non-Christians. It was on these grounds that he always supported a division of his see as a 'desirable and beneficial' measure. As time went on, the arguments for the creation of a separate diocese east of the Bay of Bengal lost much of their force, in consequence of the impending transfer of the Straits Settlements to the Colonial Office. The Bishop then warmly advocated the claims of North India to a second bishop, and when the project of erecting a see at Lahore was negatived in 1865, by parliamentary opposition, he sincerely regretted that an opportunity was lost for creating a fresh centre of Church work in one of the most encouraging provinces of India. An extension of the episcopate by the direct interposition of the State having thus become increasingly improbable, his suggestions for effecting it took a different direction. In writing on the subject, in these last months of his life, he recommended that an Act of Parliament should empower the Queen to permit in any part of the province of Calcutta the consecration of bishops to be wholly or in part independent of State support. Through such an enactment an extension of episcopacy would, he apprehended, become possible in localities where the English communities were prepared to meet State aid half way, or in others where the native Church would make itself wholly responsible for the support of a bishop. The needs of an indigenous Church, the future glory of India, were present to many minds. The organization of the increasing Church of Tinnevelly was engaging the attention of missionaries in South India, and to some of these it appeared that the time was fast approaching when, for a Church numbering its tens of thousands, and with considerable funds in trust for ecclesiastical purposes, the administration of these funds should be less in the hands of Europeans than of a largely extended native pastorate, headed by a native bishop. Two extracts may here be given from what the Bishop wrote in 1866 on the subject, in reference to the native Church. The first is from the article on the Anglican Establishment mentioned above, and has a special interest now that the arrangement therein suggested for India has been carried out in more than one home diocese:—

. . . . As to the appointment of 'coadjutors' to the present bishops, we do not mean coadjutors '*cum jure successionis*,' in which relation Bishop Courtney stands to the Bishop of Jamaica, but officers like the *chorepiscopi* of ancient times, or the suffragans instituted by the still existing statute of Henry VIII. The former, τῆς χώρας ἐπίσκοποι (country bishops), were appointed, as a diocese became enlarged by the conversion of Pagans, to execute the functions of a city bishop in villages at a distance from the cathedral.

The suffragans of the sixteenth century (who must be carefully distinguished from the ordinary diocesan bishops of a province under a metropolitan deriving their name from the votes or suffrages which they gave in his synod) were attached as assistants or episcopal curates to the several sees, and were to perform such functions as might be assigned to them by the diocesan. It is true that the *chorepiscopi* were abolished in the twelfth century, for 'arrogance, insubordination, and injurious conduct,' and that the English suffragans soon fell into desuetude; but we trust a better fate would attend the introduction into India of a class of assistant bishops, who might at once lay a foundation of independent self-supporting native churches, and relieve the diocesans of part of their work. . . . A suffragan appointed for such a purpose would, we hope, be a native, which would be a step towards the formation of an indigenous Church.

To the Rev. Henry Venn.

February 8, 1865.

As it is getting near post-time, I am hardly able to enter at length upon Mr. ——'s important letter. But would not one way of meeting his views, and removing my objections, be to consecrate a native as coadjutor to the Bishop of Madras, with such work as the diocesan bishop assigns to him? And it might be agreed that he should receive a salary from the Church Missionary Society, or from the Church Missionary Society and Society for the Propagation of the Gospel together, on condition that he ordinarily resides in Tinnevelly, and takes the charge of such native congregations as are handed over to him. Then he might also be employed in travelling at intervals about other parts of the diocese, and confirming the Tamil congregations more frequently than can be done now. He should be consecrated by the metropolitan and two of his suffragans, and not removable without the metropolitan's consent. In this way the geographical difficulty would be obviated, my serious objection to separating Europeans and natives into different Churches would be removed, the general influence and supervision of the Bishop of Madras would be retained for Tinnevelly, and the native bishop's position, in reference to the English missionaries residing near him, would be less ambiguous than on any other plan. Doubtless the question of discipline in connexion with such a bishop must be carefully considered, as we learn to our cost from the mass of troublesome technicalities now before the Privy Council; and I have no doubt that an Act of Parliament would be necessary. It seems to me that power might be given to the metropolitan, on the application of any diocesan bishop, with the sanction of the Crown, to consecrate such a coadjutor to the diocese of the bishop making the application; Government not being charged with his salary. In this way I might myself hope some day to have both a Bengali and Hindustani coadjutor. I think that some such plan as this would be at once ecclesiastically correct and practically useful.

The foregoing suggestions were for the most part thrown into the form of official letters by request of the Viceroy, and had been already discussed in private conversations with him. The Bishop did not live to see any of his counsels carried out, and it must be a matter of doubt how far they would have secured attention. As it is, they remain like bread cast upon the waters, to be found again perchance on a future day when the Indian Church shall have assumed some new aspect, or shall have taken up some new position; contingencies, under the shifting effects of the changes and chances of the world, of which the Bishop never lost sight. He was thus shadowing forth a future of gradual growth and expansion of the Indian Church from within, at a time when she appeared for a moment exposed to the danger of premature development through the ecclesiastical crisis with which all the dependencies of the British Crown were threatened. In the spring of 1866 he received intelligence from home that the Bill before Parliament for placing colonial bishops on a new and more independent footing would probably include India in its operation. The notion of the Indian Church being as yet ripe for an independent and self-supporting position was, to his mind, beset by practical difficulties. His opinions on this subject in the abstract were by no means rigidly Erastian. He regarded the principle of pure voluntaryism on which the infant native Church rests as a sure guarantee for eventual freedom and self-government. But the circumstances of English congregations are widely different. He looked upon a close alliance in their case between Church and State as productive of great mutual benefit, and as necessarily interwoven, under the present condition of things, with the whole civil and military administration of the country.

The following extracts from a letter which he lost no time in writing to Dr. Tait, then Bishop of London, contain his protest against any hasty or premature disturbance of the unique ecclesiastical system of India:—

I have been disturbed by a letter just received from Mr. Venn, of the Church Missionary Society, in which he says that, though the Bill just brought into the House of Commons by Government to decide about the status of colonial bishops does not refer to India, yet the lawyers think that it will override the Acts on which the Indian patent rests.

I wish to say very earnestly that, in my opinion, the principles on which the status of colonial bishops may be settled are at present altogether inapplicable, and that I should esteem it a serious and quite peculiar misfortune for the Church here if anything were done to unsettle its connexion with the Crown and Church of England.

It should be remembered that our Church in this country is in a state of transition, and that it would be quite premature to attempt to fix at present its permanent condition. We are a small Christian body in a heathen country, and the majority of Englishmen in India have no intention of remaining here permanently. These two facts are alone sufficient to show that the Church in India is in an entirely different position from the Church in a settled colony with a fixed Christian population. . . .

Special features in the external aspect of the Indian Church were then pointed out: the complete subordination of the chaplains, in respect of work and residence, to the exigencies of the State; the transitional and tentative nature of arrangements bearing on the organisation of the native Church; the danger of independently appointed bishops without synods as a controlling agency; the numerous difficulties of convening a synod in a country of vast size, and where clergy and laity are bound hand and foot by Government regulations; the futility of imposing synodical decrees, even were synods practicable, upon clergy who, for the most part, regard India as only a place of temporary sojourn, hoping eventually to resume ministerial work under the mother-Church at home. After dwelling upon these various difficulties, he continues:—

The above, I think, are reasons against hastily altering the present arrangements of the Indian Church, and I confess that I can see no reasons for so doing. In a colony which has an independent legislature, it is, I dare say, unconstitutional to issue letters-patent and create a jurisdiction without the consent of that legislature; and a colony, properly so called, where English people of all ranks are permanently settled, and where all as a rule profess Christianity, has an undoubted right to say what form of Christianity shall be established among them, or whether any shall. At all events, with such a colony the question is only one of time: it is probable that one day it will be an independent nation. The training of the mother-country is preparing it for this end; and then, at least, an English sovereign would no more issue letters-patent to its bishops than to the bishops of the United States. But India differs from such a colony in every particular: it has no independent legislature; the councils which exercise legislative functions are created, and may be destroyed, by Parliament, and are in no way representative bodies. The governors, judges, and councillors are Englishmen, appointed for a few years, and then going home. The permanently settled European population is quite insignificant; the country is heathen, its independence is not contemplated, or if contemplated, only as a distant possibility. The commonwealth of India is essentially part of the great English imperial system; and such also the Church had better remain, at least till it is fitter than it is now to walk alone. It seems hard that because grave difficulties have occurred in South Africa, in a case for which Parliament had made no provision at all, therefore the Church in India should be revolutionised, which is regulated by perfectly intelligible and straightforward Acts of Parliament, and in which, as far as I can see, such a difficulty could be reasonably and constitutionally met. For I consider that it would be a revolution to send out a bishop consecrated by the Queen's licence only, and apparently not bound by the ecclesiastical law of England (or at least not prevented from altering it); and further, for the reasons given above, that such a revolution would be altogether premature, although, doubtless, we look forward to a day when the Gospel will have spread in India, when the present anomalous condition of its European inhabitants will have assumed a more settled form, and when the Church will require more independent powers than we possess at present. That the revolution may not take place in our time (for I suppose that I should not be deprived of my letters-patent without my own consent, and that the clergy and I would retain the status and advantages which were promised to us when we came to India) is a reason why I am able to argue the matter from an independent position, with a view rather to my successor's interests than to my own, and to the Church of the future rather than to the Church of the present.

Thus for a brief moment the Bishop was brought into personal contact with questions and conflicts that were disturbing the Church at large. Any notice in these pages of his views with reference to the special controversies of South Africa, must be necessarily inadequate to a subject at once difficult and so profoundly and widely agitating. In common with all thoughtful men he watched the course of these controversies with anxious interest. He had spoken freely in his second charge of the reckless speculations that endangered the faith of the weak and unlearned; in the pages of the 'Calcutta Christian Intelligencer' (a small Anglo-Indian periodical, to which he frequently contributed terse and vigorous comments on passing events), he deplored the way in which, in one instance, these speculations were dealt with.

In 1864, while sympathising very really with the difficult and trying position of the Bishop of Cape Town, he recorded the thoughts and opinions to which the recent charge of that metropolitan gave rise in his own mind.

The reasoning pursued in that memorable charge appeared to lead to the denial of the Queen's supremacy (that great expression of the rights of the laity as members of the Church) within her own dominions, and to the assumption of a claim to decide grave theological and ecclesiastical questions by the will of a single bishop. The Bishop of Calcutta brought these theories home by putting the question, how would such a case work in India? With a tinge of humour, half inadvertent, half irrepressible, he contemplated himself sitting in all but solitary judgment on an heretical suffragan, and following up his condemnation by a summary deposition of the offender, and the consecration of another prelate in his room. Without venturing to assert that a crisis such as had arisen in South Africa was impossible and inconceivable in India, or hazarding any theory as to his own mode of dealing with it; without controverting Bishop Gray's able and powerful defence of his legal rights, he was prompted by all the instincts of charity and fair-dealing, and self-distrust, to deprecate for himself, no less than for other metropolitans, the possession or exercise of irresponsible powers, and to desire such amendments in English ecclesiastical law as should reach the points raised in the South African Church, and deal with them wisely and well. For, in commenting on the struggle which was rending that distant Church, he never lost sight of its twofold aspect: of the exhibition of doctrinal laxity on the one hand, and the assumption of ecclesiastical despotism on the other. His own profound faith in the power and majesty of the Bible revelation disarmed fears as to the ultimate result of what he did not hesitate to call the extravagances of latitudinarianism; but the question whether the Church was to be governed by law and order, or by the arbitrary will of individual bishops, was, to his mind, one of lasting importance,—one that ought not to be overlooked in the midst of excitement occasioned by a particular theological controversy. His own recoil, in mind and spirit, from conclusions to which the theories and teaching of the Bishop of Natal tended, enabled him to express with all the more freedom his disapproval of the measures taken by the Metropolitan of South Africa in condemnation of his suffragan. The perils and perplexities which during recent years had been gathering around the holiest and gravest matters, awoke in him, as in many others, a fresh burst of loyalty towards the Established National Church of England, and he mourned equally over the prevalence of loose doctrines within her borders, and over her inability to deal with them. Just as he greatly desired that some one should arise with the *spirit of power and of love and of a sound mind* to meet the times in defence of Christian faith, so also he urged, as one of the chief needs of the age, the construction of some tribunal through which the English Church, while avoiding dogmatism or persecution, might declare authoritatively the truth of which she claims to be the depositary.

The following remarks were written in connexion with this subject at the beginning of 1865:—

. . . . It is probably no exaggeration to say that never since 1689 has the English Church been so near a schism as at the present moment. The dissatisfaction felt at the judgment of the Privy Council in the cases of Dr. Williams and Mr. Wilson has been very deep, and in this dissatisfaction is of course involved the constitution of the Supreme Court of Appeal. At this we cannot wonder. A tribunal of which the majority consists of lawyers, will always be anxious to decide as little as it can, and to avoid theological difficulties as far as possible. These decisions on questions of doctrine are new, . . . and the result is that we are drifting, by a kind of negative process, into a fresh set of doctrinal definitions and declarations, not made by the Church, as a body, but by a lay tribunal, which is always inclined to guide itself by the principle of what may be called without offence political expediency—the principle, that is, of keeping things smooth, and avoiding all violent results. It is, however, very hard to see how the Judicial Committee can be remodelled in any satisfactory way. The Cape Town proceedings do not incline us, nor will they incline the laity and Parliament of England, to substitute a clerical for a lay judicature. . . . Probably Lord Brougham's plan, by which the Judicial Committee, perhaps with the episcopal privy councillors excluded from it, should consult the Bench of Bishops on questions of doctrine, just as the House of Lords consults the judges, would be the most feasible remedy, only with this modification, that they should consult a mixed body consisting partly of bishops, partly of divinity professors, and other eminent theologians. For the bishops neither are nor are likely to be (indeed, it is scarcely desirable that they should be) the most distinguished, still less the only divines in the English Church. In any case, we think that the Judicial Committee should be forbidden to embody any elaborate theological disquisitions in their judgments, and should merely declare (for example): 'We do not find that Dr. ———, in the passages of his recent work brought before us, has contradicted any article or formulary of the Church, and we therefore acquit him of the charge brought against him.' In this way the character of the judges, as mere interpreters of the language of our formularies, would be obvious, and no attempt made to give expositions of doctrine, which the judgment now under discussion certainly appears to do. At the same time we do not at all wish to make it easy to accuse and condemn a clergyman for heresy. The comparative freedom of the Scotch Church, for instance, has not always led to happy results. It would have been wise, we think, to have borne with so great a man as Edward Irving longer than the General Assembly did; and one of the ablest defences of Christian truth which has recently appeared is written by Mr. Campbell, who was ejected, we believe, for some offence against Calvinism. . .

What we want is some fair tribunal which shall do justice on both sides, repressing the extravagances of latitudinarianism on the one hand, and of hierarchical absolutism on the other; for at present the two evils are playing each other's game. We earnestly pray that God's Spirit may put it into the hearts of some wise and good men to devise such a solution of our embarrassments.

The following letter was an utterance from the East on the proposed Pan-Anglican Synod of 1867:—

To the Bishop of Cape Town.

Bishop's Palace, May 22, 1866.

I have just received your letter of February 18, containing an extract from that of the Archbishop on the subject of a meeting of all the bishops of the Anglican communion in London, to take counsel on the various difficulties which now beset our Church. You are quite right in saying that in my charge of 1863 I expressed my conviction that some general assembly representing the Church of England in its various branches and provinces was highly desirable; and that there is a danger in multiplying colonial and missionary bishops, without any organisation by which all may be kept in mutual dependence, and compelled to act in brotherly union, according to the Church's law. But I confess that in writing that sentence, I contemplated something more than a meeting of bishops convened by the Archbishop, without any power of enforcing its decrees. I spoke of a general synod of bishops, and of other clergy and laity fairly representing the whole Church of England, and meeting under the control of the English monarchy and Parliament, and under the presidency of the successor of Augustine. The decrees of an assembly of bishops, convened by the Archbishop of Canterbury, would no doubt be entitled to great deference, and have much moral weight; but I do not see that such a body could alter or adapt to colonial wants a single rubric or canon of the Church of England, or compel any single bishop to introduce into his diocese any one of its recommendations. Whether, therefore, it would be worth while, for the sake of such a meeting, to take so strong a step as to summon all the colonial bishops from all points of the world to London, is extremely doubtful.

But, however this may be, we in India are powerless in the matter. Our temporal position is regulated wholly by Act of Parliament, down to such minute details as furlough rules. No power on earth can enable me to go to England before November 1868, except an Act of Parliament, or the visitation of so formidable an illness that my medical attendant would be able to certify that I cannot safely continue in India. The Bishops of Bombay and Madras are tied down by similar rules. I do not know what the case may be with the Bishop of Colombo; but as he is strictly a colonial and not an Indian bishop, though in the province of Calcutta, and as no Act of Parliament was passed to give validity to his letters-patent, he is probably dependent for power to go home, or at least for retaining any part of his salary during his absence, on the Government of Ceylon. But with us in India it is not even a question of retaining or renouncing our salaries: to go home, except in accordance with the provisions of the Act, is an *ipso facto* resignation of an Indian see.

P.S.—Copies of your letter shall be sent to other bishops of the province.

It is with great diffidence that any reference is here made to so complex a question as that which was involved in the Bill for the 'Remarriage of Converts,' which in this year was a prominent act in the legislation of the Indian Government. The measure was intimately connected with the organisation and discipline of the native Church; and if it was right that the Bishop should take, as he did take, an active part in the discussions carried on outside the

Council chamber, it seems right not to pass by the subject entirely. It will be easily understood by those whose acquaintance with Indian matters is only superficial, that cases arise where Christianity is accepted by a husband or wife, while the other partner remains in heathenism. The tendency of such conversions being to produce desertion on the part of the latter, the convert is left to the alternative of enforced celibacy, or of a marriage of doubtful legality. This state of things had been under the notice of the Government of India for many years. Attempts to remedy it had been made without success, and laws passed from time to time for the regulation of Christian marriages failed to touch the peculiar circumstances of the native convert. For him, in the words of a high authority, 'the matrimonial law was immersed in doubt, and exhibited an amount of confusion that could only be described as chaotic.' A statute had been passed in the reign of George IV. under which it was possible that a native convert marrying during the lifetime of a heathen wife might be punished for bigamy. The operation, however, of this statute was always open to doubt; it was only in force in Presidency towns, and was eventually repealed by the Penal Code. The Penal Code affixed penalties to the contraction by a person, having a husband or wife living, of any marriage which should be void by reason of its taking place during the lifetime of such husband or wife; but prior to 1864 it was not clear that a marriage entered into by a native convert, forsaken by his heathen wife, was void, since no law, then existing for the regulation of marriages, decided how a Christian stood towards a marriage contracted when he was a heathen. It was through Christianity that the Eastern convert had learnt that a man cannot have two wives at once, and the canon law of the religion he had adopted seemed to favour the theory of the first union being in his case void, by its sanction of remarriage in the event of desertion on religious grounds. From this point of view, supplied by the Christian Church, a considerable proportion of native Christians had long looked upon the original union as dissolved, and had contracted fresh ones, which many missionaries had solemnized with such simple religious forms as they thought suitable to the circumstances. The uncertainty overhanging the law was tacitly admitted by the fact that no proceedings had ever been taken against converts contracting these second marriages, nor against any minister for performing them. In 1864, however, Mr. Anderson's Act was passed for the regulation of marriages between Christians, in which it was laid down as a condition of their validity that 'no husband or wife must be living.' Native converts came at once under the operation of this new law; from that time, marriages which could not previously have been said with certainty to be prohibited, which certainly never had been punished under any existing enactment, became at once punishable offences. It was, therefore, urgently necessary that the law should take cognisance of the native convert; should define the extent and weight of his obligations towards the first marriage, and legislate for his peculiar position as a Christian who had formed ties while still in heathenism, such ties having been repudiated by the still heathen partner. This the State undertook to do by a Bill brought into the Viceroy's Council, in November 1864, by the legal member, Mr. H. S. Maine. Though the proposed measure was at the outset stamped with a secular character, it was impossible to eliminate the arguments of Christian theology from a subject bound up with the condition and morality of the Christian Church. In the speech delivered when leave was asked to bring in the Bill, the subject was carried back into remote Christian ages. An ancient as well as a modern history was claimed for it; and attention was called to the fact, that the question of a dissolution of marriage on religious grounds was coeval with Christianity, having arisen from the moment when the first conversions had produced a condition of things analogous to that which presents itself in India at the present day. The further progress of the measure was suspended at its first stage, in order to afford time and opportunity for a free expression of opinion from Christian and non-Christian quarters. With Christians, the scriptural test was that by which the measure ought to stand or fall, and the application of this test made the Indian clergy for a brief moment controversial. Opponents of the principle and object of the measure were in a minority numerically; but in force of character and position, especially in the case of native pastors, the leaders of argument on either side were so evenly balanced, that, as was said, 'the Legislative Council might well decline under such a conflict of opinions to take upon itself the responsibility of refusing redress on the ground of theological reasons alone, to those who, but for these reasons, would be admitted to be entitled to it.' The scriptural ground taken by one party was the prohibition, in Matthew v. 32, of any separation except for adultery; the scriptural ground taken by the other party was the sanction of remarriage deduced from the interpretation of 1 Corinthians vii. 15, which maintains that the apostle contemplated not the unbeliever's own act of self-separation, acquiesced in by the Christian partner for the sake of peace, but a release from the original marriage-bond, with the liberty to contract a new one. The Bishop's views were embodied in a pastoral letter which he issued in 1865, while the Government measure was lying before the country. Beyond expressing strongly a desire that a judicial divorce should in every case precede the judicial permission to remarriage, he abstained from criticism on details in the Bill, for which he was unfitted through his limited acquaintance with native feeling and customs, and confined himself chiefly to the theological argument. For the sake of those who might look to him for guidance, he entered into a full analysis of the passage in the epistle to the Corinthians, and defended the interpretation which claims apostolic sanction for the lawfulness of remarriage under the circumstances that had raised the question. But while thus declaring his full concurrence with the principle of the proposed act of legislation on scriptural grounds, he went beyond a mere critical disquisition on a text; and a no less valuable portion of the pastoral was that in which he gave exhortation and counsel against a hasty abuse of the liberty about to be provided, and reminded missionaries, and native Christians through the missionaries, that the measure of the convert's legal rights was not the measure of his moral duties; that the liberty conceded by the law ought to be claimed only when patience, conciliation, and forbearance had failed to win back the alienated partner. On another point intimately bound up with Christian ethics, the Bishop's own words shall be transcribed :—

I will only notice one other point, which can hardly be called an argument against the measure, but yet is entitled to our most thoughtful consideration, since it is calculated to excite against it the feelings of some whose Christian experience is the deepest, and whose faith in Christ is the most earnest and practical. It is said, that this separation from a heathen wife is the cross which a new convert has to bear for his Lord's sake: and what, it is asked, is his conversion worth, if he refuses to bear it? And so he is urged to seek his consolation, not in remarriage, but in Christ's promise as recorded in Matthew xix. 29. Now we have seen that cases may arise in which a convert is bound to submit to this sorrow as well as to all the others which usually accompany his conversion. But it does not follow that this should be enacted by law and made compulsory. On the contrary, if it can be shown, as I think I have shown, that the author and first preachers of the Gospel did not intend that this particular cross should necessarily be borne by those whom God's Spirit calls from darkness to light, surely we have no right to force it upon them? Their difficulties and troubles are already sufficiently terrible; the impediments to conversion are numerous enough; a Hindu or Mahometan who comes to Christ for life eternal, must, as it is, generally give up father, mother, brothers, sisters, lands, and possibly children also. If his fellow-Christians can lawfully save him from one other privation—a privation which, above all the rest, touches his spiritual life, and endangers his Christian steadfastness—surely they are bound to do so, lest they fall into the condemnation pronounced against those who *offend one of the little ones who believe in Christ.* Doubtless, we look forward in faith and hope to a day when India will be a Christian country, and when therefore the liberty tolerated, or, as I rather believe, enacted by St. Paul for a state of transition like the present, will be necessarily withdrawn, because no case for its exercise can ever arise. Till then, it seems to me that just as Moses was permitted to enact for the Jews a temporary and exceptional law, so the Indian Legislature is bound, by some measure like that now contemplated, to remove this stumbling-block from the path of Christ's disciples.

When the Bill reached its final stage in the councils of the Legislature, there was little to impede its course. The theological scruples of a limited number of the clergy were powerless to arrest the passing of a measure which claimed to be based on the authority of canon law, and upon the general practice of the Christian Church; and the small amount of dissent emanating from the non-Christian population of India justified the opinion expressed at the outset, that the sentiments of this section of the community were those of indifference. Many of the provisions of the Bill turned upon abstruse points in Hindu law and custom, and cannot be noticed here; but in its general scope it was simple and intelligible, and had features which imparted a human interest to the dry technicalities of law. It was to be a law of liberty, and no man's conscience was to be constrained. Nobody would be compelled to marry converts if he had scruples on the point: but, on the other hand, the State would impose no penalties on a minister remarrying them; and again, the object of the Bill was to promote, not divorce, but the reunion of the married couples. The respondent in a suit instituted for this end was to appear personally, and under the shelter of the law, and withdrawn from the influence of her family, to decide of her own free will whether she would return to her husband or persist in desertion of him.

The object of this procedure was to ascertain how far the refusal to join her Christian husband arose from absolute alienation, caused through his change of religion, or, as was maintained to be frequently the case, from some miserable prejudice 'respecting meat, drink, or raiment,' implanted in her mind by the heathen relatives around her, and capable of removal by argument or persuasion. Should such procedure, renewed if necessary at intervals during a fixed period, prove ineffectual to win back the heathen partner, the convert was held by law to be no longer 'under bondage,' but free to marry elsewhere.

The Bishop's journal thus records the completion, on March 31, 1866, of a second great act of legislation distinctively in behalf of native Christians:—'The long disputed question of the remarriage of native converts deserted by their heathen partners was happily settled by the passing of a Bill legalising such marriages, after certain preliminaries, and with certain safeguards, in accordance with the obvious meaning of 1 Corinthians vii. 15, and the opinion of the Church catholic throughout the world. I attended the meeting of Council at which the Bill was passed, and heard a really admirable speech from Maine, unanswerable in its reasoning, and containing a noble piece of eloquence about the evil of neglecting and overlooking native Christians.' It is well remembered how the Bishop returned to the palace repeating the concluding sentence of that memorable speech—'We will not force any man to be a Christian; we will not even tempt any man to be a Christian; but if he chooses to become a Christian, it would be shameful if we did not apply to him and his those principles of equal dealing between man and man, of which we are in India the sole depositaries.'

Two letters may be here inserted. The first, addressed to the editor of a leading Anglo-Indian newspaper, affords in a small compass a glimpse of the divided feeling in India with respect to the Bill. The second has an interest as explaining why Mahometans did not come under the provisions of the Remarriage Act:—

Delhi, January 8, 1866.

. . . I have sometimes thought also of writing to you about the Remarriage of Converts Bill. I have abstained from doing so for two reasons better than want of time. The first, because I suppose that the Bill, or some satisfactory modification of it, is sure to pass. The second, because I said my say completely in my pastoral letter, and have never seen any real attempt, in all the writings against the Bill in the 'Christian Intelligencer' and elsewhere, to grapple with the answers which I there attempted to give to the objections alleged against it on scriptural or historical grounds. It would, of course, be very presumptuous and absurd in me to say that these answers of mine cannot be refuted; but I am sure that they have not been, but that much of the subsequent writing against the Bill has simply passed by the pastoral letter as if it were non-existent. This may, of course, arise from its dulness, or from the confused manner in which I have expressed my arguments; but the arguments remain untouched. For example, I saw the other day a restatement of the assertion that the early Christians tried to drag the case of desertion under that of spiritual adultery, in order to bring it within Our Lord's permission of remarriage, thereby proving that they did not interpret 1 Corinthians vii. 15 as all the sound commentators do now. But I showed in my letter, not on my own authority, but on that of Hefele, who is a great patristic scholar, that this was a mistake, and that the passages quoted about spiritual adultery really refer to the case of a converted wife or husband relapsing into idolatry. So, too, people go on saying that everybody would be contented with a Bill for dissolving marriage in case of adultery on the part of the recusant partner, wholly overlooking Mr. Maine's *moral* objection to the proposal, which, to my mind, is unanswerable, and also the notorious fact that the principal English High Churchmen, such as Archdeacon Wordsworth, are opposed to remarriage in case of adultery, but perfectly willing to allow it in case of a heathen's desertion, arguing (and justly) that the interpretation of 1 Corinthians vii. 15 is far easier than the explanation of the differences between the records of Our Lord's words given by the Evangelists.

. . . It may be well, too, for me to remark, in reference to the petition which has been presented against the Bill, that people have no business to call it the 'petition of the clergy of the diocese of Calcutta.' A clear majority of the clergy have refused to sign it, though there were very good reasons for not getting up a counter memorial. I had declared my own opinion in my pastoral; many of the clergy have announced theirs in letters, either to me or to Government; not a few have signed the petition from the Protestant ministers and missionaries, who, by-the-by, have rather unluckily designated themselves as living *in or near Calcutta*, for they have got signatures from Tinnevelly and Amritsir. This reminds me that all the Tinnevelly missionaries, both of the Church Missionary and Propagation Societies, have declared, in separate minutes, their approbation of the Bill, that of the Propagation missionaries, drawn up by Dr. Caldwell, being a very able performance. You will find it in the 'Christian Intelligencer' for December.

To a Missionary.

Bishop's Palace, July 9, 1866.

It is undoubtedly true that the reason why Mahometans were exempted from the Converts Divorce Bill is that, in the opinion of the authorities of the Mussulman religion, the marriage is *ipso facto* dissolved by the apostasy of either husband or wife. This has been repeatedly stated by Mr. Maine in council, by the select committee appointed to consider and amend the Bill, by Mr. Muir, by the Mahometan petitioners, who quote all the passages on which the opinion is founded, by Moonshee Amir Ali, and by the Mújtahid or chief priest of the Shiahs at Lucknow. On these grounds, it was thought unnecessary to pass a Bill authorising the remarriage of a convert from Mahometanism deserted by his wife, because such remarriage is not unlawful now. I have frequently stated that, in my opinion, the passage 1 Corinthians vii. 15 is sufficient to show that such remarriage is authorised by the law of God; and as this view is affirmed by the Roman, Greek, and Presbyterian Churches (i.e. by all which are bound by the Westminster Confession), by the followers of Luther and Calvin, and, not indeed by any formal decree of the Anglican Church, which has never pronounced upon the subject, but by many eminent men among its divines, and, to the best of my belief, denied by none of them, I do not think that I am presumptuous in adhering firmly to my own conviction, nor neglecting the rule *quod semper, quod ubique, quod ab omnibus.*

. . . It is of course possible, as the Mahometans are excluded from the Bill, that the lawfulness of the remarriage might be the subject of an action at law, and that the remarried husband might be required to show that he had not committed bigamy. I believe that it would be easy to show this, the Mahometan woman having ceased to be his wife by the act of his conversion; and that the Legislature assumed this in framing their Bill, is, as I have said, certain. Still, Mr. Maine frequently allowed to me, in talking over the matter privately, that such an action was possible, though he added that there could be no doubt as to the decision of the Court. In the present case, from what you say of the woman's friends, such a suit is highly improbable; but there will be a danger of it till the High Court has given a formal judgment to the effect that the conversion of a Mahometan operates as a divorce. Of course, therefore, this letter only gives you my authority to perform the marriage as an ecclesiastical act. I cannot shield, except by advice and evidence, either you or your convert from any possible, though very improbable, legal troubles which might follow the remarriage.

CHAPTER XV.

SOCIAL INTERCOURSE WITH NATIVES IN CALCUTTA—VISIT TO PÁTSHÁLAS—BUSINESS IN THE UNIVERSITY—LETTERS—DEPARTURE FOR ASSAM—JOURNALS AND LETTERS—RETURN TO KOOSHTEA—THE BISHOP'S CONSECRATION OF A CEMETERY—RETURN TO THE RIVER—UNPROTECTED CAUSEWAY—HIS FATAL FALL.

THE hot months of the year glided away peacefully and happily, though the few inmates of Bishop's Palace were unusually parched by the heat of May and June. The rains of July refreshed them somewhat, and the Bishop remained well in health, and found in constant work the best antidote to the relaxing effects of another hot season in the plains. There was the usual pleasant intercourse with the social circle in Calcutta, which he always liked to maintain, both from principle and inclination. An attempt was made to extend friendly hospitality beyond the limits of European society, by two soirées given, the one at the palace, the other at the house of a Church Missionary Society's missionary, to several of the leading Hindus in Calcutta. No Eastern ladies were present. One of the guests, who was a Christian, remarked, speaking for himself, and some members of his family, also converts, 'I wish we could get our ladies to come with us.' There are cases in which habit and national custom continue to assert, even after the adoption of Christianity, a singular power, and the freedom of the Christian religion seems almost to increase the reluctance to emerge from Eastern seclusion. It is a feeling which commands respect and sympathy in days when the tendency is rather to encourage a rending of the veil between the Eastern woman and the outside world, although, as yet, the safeguards either of Christianity or of education to fit her for the glare of a less restrained existence are few and slender. In spite of the absence of ladies, however, the evenings passed very pleasantly. The native gentlemen expressed a gratification, which their English hosts fully reciprocated; and the Bishop was well pleased to find in pleasant conversation and fruit ice a neutral ground on which educated men of different races and religions could meet under a private roof and exchange the courtesies of civilised life.

With great satisfaction the Bishop spent another day with the Rev. J. Long, of the Church Missionary Society, among his Pátshálas in a missionary district a few miles out of Calcutta. The Pátshálas are the original and indigenous village schools of India, reaching back to unknown antiquity; and when left only in the hands of the gurus or teachers, they are miserably neglected or mistaught, the scholars sometimes being unable even to read. In some places Government, in others the Vernacular Education Society, takes them in hand, places a circle of them under the charge of an inspector (in the latter case a native Christian superintended by a missionary), and establishes at once the system of payment to the guru 'by results.' In the Society's schools the inspector also introduces some elementary Christian teaching. A number of these gurus, 'much brushed up by contact with Long and his Christians,' had gathered at Thakerpukur to meet the Bishop, and in return he went with them round about the district, penetrating through damp jungle, and crossing nullahs or brooks, to reach some schools situated among the low lands that are almost a swamp in the rainy season. He was very much pleased with what he saw. The schools proved on examination to be quite as good as an average English village school, were thoroughly native in idea and appearance, and yet had received a most successful infusion of a Western and Christian element.

The Bishop took as usual his full share in the affairs of the University. One important piece of business before the governing body was connected with the munificent gift of two lakhs of rupees (20,000*l.*) from Premchund Roychund, a great Bombay millionaire. The disposal of the money raised a sharp contest, and the old professorship controversy of 1862 was revived. Many of the opponents of the proposed scheme were, as before, strongly in favour of the principle involved in Government education; and even those who might allow that the idea of University professorships was right in theory, still maintained that it would be premature to attempt such a sweeping change in the system of higher education. In their view, the University, though a great success, could in no sense be said to have as yet become an indigenous institution, for no colleges had as yet been founded by natives, and missionary colleges could not be considered permanent institutions, when a large proportion of home supporters still objected on principle to expending the funds on education instead of more directly evangelistic work. The Bishop again supported the professorship movement, both in the Syndicate and in the Senate, but in vain; and he had only the consolation of seeing the success of another plan suggested by himself, but only as a *pis aller*, for founding certain annuities in the nature of fellowships, to be called Premchund Roychund Studentships, and contended for by Masters of Arts in an examination equal in pretensions to one for Oriel or Trinity fellowships.

This year also witnessed the final arrangements for the memorial to Dr. Duff. The subscriptions were handed over to the University to found scholarships. The form which the memorial thus took was by no means that which the Bishop and many others had desired, and was a very disappointing substitute for the hall which had been originally proposed. In such a public hall, in the native quarter of the city, for meetings, lectures, conversaziones, all serving as links between the educated and intelligent of Eastern and Western races, many of Dr. Duff's friends had seen the fittest symbol of his life's work, and the most suitable memorial of the leading position he had held in native education. A letter of the Bishop's in 1863 will have served to indicate the difficulties which, from the first, embarrassed the scheme for a hall. It was taken up again, and pushed forward warmly in 1864, when he and many others amongst its supporters doubled their subscriptions. But stiffness of views among Europeans, and Bengali lukewarmness when a testimony of respect and honour is to pass from words into deeds, divided the counsels, and crippled the funds. The committee found themselves eventually compelled to accept a compromise, and to fall back on the foundation of University scholarships, useful in themselves, but very inferior, as a memorial, to the projected hall.

The few letters annexed find their right place here:—

To his Son.

Bishop's Palace, April 5, 1866.

We were very glad indeed to get your first brief sketch of Woolwich, and much interested by it. I quite appreciate the self-satisfaction with which you say you 'strut about in your uniform.' When the right of wearing it has been gained wholly by yourself, and not by my making interest with military magnates of my acquaintance to get you a commission in the Line, a little pleasure in the new costume is perfectly legitimate. I remember the intense satisfaction with which I began to exercise any small privileges when I was elected Fellow at Trinity: my delight in using the college plate when entertaining my friends at dinner, or in giving orders for the library; nay, even the secret chuckle with which I walked over the grass-plots, forbidden to less exalted persons. Such reminiscences seem childish and absurd, but there are childish and absurd elements in human nature, and they furnish, in spite of ourselves, some portion of the rewards of any success. However, it would not be well that we should confine our attention to these small results of our own exertions; and so I doubt not that you are rising from the contemplation of your uniform to the contemplation of your work, and to the duty of using these two years as a grand opportunity for preparing yourself for usefulness in the profession which you have deliberately chosen, and have, by God's blessing on your own efforts, been enabled to enter. We should like to know in your next something about the difference between Engineers and Artillery, the advantages of both, and the prospects that you have of obtaining one or the other. . . . Also I should like to know something about the ecclesiastical arrangements of Woolwich. Where do you go to church on Sunday? Is the service hearty and devout? By whom are you preached to? Have you daily public prayers? From the sketch of your time given in your last, you seem to be very seldom left alone. Do you ever play cricket or any other game? Again, Macaulay lays stress on the importance of a historian inquiring into the character of a nation's 'repasts.' Of what do the Woolwich dinners consist? Are they and the other meals taken in a hall? Do you have wine-parties and other academical entertainments? Is the discipline mainly that of a college or of a school? Have you each a separate room, or couple of rooms?

Having asked you such a multitude of questions, I proceed to impart in return a few facts. The main one is the flight of poor little Puss, by which name and not Polly she is designated in India. She departed from Simla on the evening of the Tuesday in Passion Week, in a copious flood of tears, accompanied by Miss Maclean, two male attendants, an ayah, and escorted to the station by Hardy. Such, you see, is the state in which she makes her Oriental progresses. . . . We have great confidence in the worthy chaplain and his wife to whose care we consign her, and I have myself experienced their tenderness, having been ill at their house at Ferozepore, when on visitation in November 1864, and nursed with the greatest devotion.

To-night I am going to give the Hindus a lecture 'On the Employment of Women in Religious and Charitable Works,' in which I intend to describe Sisters of Charity, beguines and deaconesses, and to suggest that, instead of burning their widows or condemning them to household drudgery, it might be better to see if they cannot be employed in acts of womanly beneficence. A quantity of glib talk and profusion of compliments will follow the lecture: of course nothing will result from it directly, but it may be considered as carrying on the dripping of water on the rock.

To his Daughter.

Bishop's Palace, Whit Sunday, 1866.

We have come back, you see, from Barrackpore, where we stayed in the Governor-General's house, but we thought it hotter even than Calcutta. It was pleasant, however, to take a nice walk at 6 in the morning in the garden and park by the river-side; and on Sunday I went across to Serampore, had tea with Mr. Stuart, and preached for him. As we were driving from the Sealdah station home on Monday evening, we came across a violent storm. The wind blew so furiously that I expected it to upset the carriage, and we were glad to find ourselves safe under the portico. Mr. Hardy followed in his buggy, but had been kept at the station by the folly of Pecko, who wished to get out of the train in some unlawful way, and was in consequence seized by the police. So Mr. Hardy had to stay and rescue him, and thus came in for a worse part of the storm than we did. He was nearly blinded with the dust, and also wet through. He could not get on in one place against the wind, but had to drive to the side of the road, and wait till the gust was over. So he, too, was very glad to get home. On Wednesday there was another storm, but that was chiefly rain, which came down in such bucketfuls that we could not get across to the cathedral service. And on Friday there was a third storm, when the thunder was like cannon going off close to us; so that altogether, you see, we have had a most disturbed week; and whenever there has been no storm it has been dreadfully hot. . . . Dr. Smyth tells me that you are getting fat enough to marry Sir John Falstaff. Edward will be quite pleased to hear it, for he was shocked at being told that you were so scraggy. Perhaps you need not go to England by the mail of June 23, if Dr. Smyth still finds your frocks unable to button.

Now, good-bye, my own little Puss; do not let us hear anything more about crossness at lessons, &c.

To his Son.

July 1866.

The frightful heat under which we were groaning when I last wrote to you has happily ceased. Ever since June 15 the weather has been cool and pleasant, with clouds constant, and showers frequent. But the change was too great and rapid for some people, and a good deal of not very serious illness has been the result. The thermometer, standing at 96° in the afternoon of June 14 in my library, was at 82° at the same hour of June 15. . . .

June 14, the last day of the great heat, was the first of a much direr calamity; for on that day the telegraph conveyed to India the terrible news of the failure of the Agra and Masterman's bank. I say terrible, for in truth the suffering consequent upon it will, I fear, be spread very widely, especially among the widows and children of old Indians; for it was the favourite bank of the civil and military services, and its shares were a common investment of the savings of Indian officers. It was an immense concern, with branches in France and China as well as in London and India; it was thought immovable, paid dividends of 8 per cent., and had just erected (or rather, had not quite finished) a real palace in Calcutta, in the Venetian style, with an open *loggia* by way of verandah—one of the few buildings in the city showing at once solidity and originality of design. The depositors, of course, only lose their money, but the shareholders will have to pay up the full amount of their shares, whereof only half had been paid before the crash. . . . Personally I had, happily, nothing to do with it, but several of the diocesan and other charities and trust funds were more or less involved in it, which will have to be replaced by larger subscriptions. Several of the clergy have lost remittances which they had just sent through this bank to wives and children in England.

Meantime, since I began to write the above, a telegram has come from England, which nobody can understand, saying that things there are turning out better than was expected, that the ultimate loss will only be a million sterling, and that there is to be a voluntary liquidation. If so, depositors will ultimately, I suppose, be paid in full, and even shareholders will not lose everything. But again, if so, it is asked, why did the bank stop? for the million could have been realised by calling the remainder of the money due on the shares? Altogether business men are puzzled, depositors and their wives are fluttering with hope, and we wait anxiously for the mail. . . .

You cannot think in what a fever of excitement we are kept now by the fitful flashes of the telegraph. I decidedly hold that, for the ordinary imparting of news, this Indo-European line is a mere nuisance. Of course for grave emergencies it is very important, but for the common everyday intelligence it is only a source of unsatisfied curiosity and frequent blunders. We know, for instance, that war has broken out in Saxony, Silesia, Venetia, and near Frankfort, that the ministry were beaten on the borough franchise, and that they have in consequence resigned. But what led to the immediate outbreak of the European struggle; who has been 'sent for' in consequence of the retirement of Lord Russell; why, if he has resigned, another telegram should predict a dissolution of Parliament; how it came that the ministry were beaten on the borough franchise, when they had carried their more important change in the county franchise—on all these, and a multitude of other elucidations of the bare facts announced, we are left in complete ignorance. . . . Our state was pleasanter, I think, when we first came to India, and the telegraph only united Calcutta and Galle. For then, a week before the arrival of each mail, we had a summary of news from Galle, like the headings to the chapters of an interesting book, and afterwards, on the actual arrival of the steamer, we received the details of the matters which we had been discussing and speculating on during the intervening seven days. . . .

To the Rev. R. Duckworth.

Bishop's Palace, Calcutta, July 6, 1866.

I was very glad to get your letter, and am much obliged to you for your valuable exertions at Oxford on behalf of my hill schools, carried on in conjunction with my worthy cousin of Worcester. When you have completed the collection, you will enhance its value if you will kindly send it as soon as you can to —— ; for as soon as it is transmitted to us we invest it, and the securities of the Indian Government are now so low (owing to the failure of the Agra Bank and other commercial disasters), that the time is particularly favourable for the investment of money.

By this time I suppose that you have left Oxford, and have your home in one of the royal palaces. I congratulate you on being selected for so important a post; a great proof of the esteem in which you must have been held at Oxford, and a great opportunity for doing good. For, as in a constitutional monarchy the true function of kings and princes is to influence society, it is a blessing when they are so trained that their influence may be Christian and intelligent. I hope that you will make your Leopold as wise a man as his great-uncle of Belgium, and a considerably better one than most of his great-uncles on the Brunswick side. You will, no doubt, see a great deal of interesting society, and watch the course of many interesting events, and I trust that the connexion will be alike profitable to yourself and to your pupil, in whom we must all be truly interested, from that feeling of loyalty which, if it sometimes degenerates into flunkeyism, is yet in itself one of the safeguards of England.

I have now begun to date official documents 'in the ninth year of our consecration,' and though such whiskers as I have are grey, and my hair considerably mottled with the same tint, yet I am thankful to say that I have on the whole very good health, and that the climate has dealt very mercifully with me. . . . We start in August, all being well, on a two months' expedition by river into Assam, the great tea province, where there are a number of scattered tea-planters who should be looked after, and provided, if it may be, with clergymen and churches.

Just now the weather in Calcutta is pleasant, as we are in the midst of the rains, which have come down so copiously as to wash away a great part of the East Indian Railway, and stop communication between Bengal and the upper provinces. It is fortunate that no mutiny is going on.

On August 1 we left Calcutta for Assam. Half a day's journey on the Eastern Bengal Railway took us to Kooshtea, where the Government steamer 'Koel,' having the barge 'Rhotas' in tow, was awaiting us. The latter had been again kindly lent by the Lieutenant-Governor of Bengal, and this comfortable private yacht became the luxurious mode of transit during the last visitation as during the first, seven years before. As the Rev. R. Norman, one of the cathedral chaplains, was at that time prostrate under severe illness, Mr. Hardy remained behind in Calcutta to take his duty, and Mr. Vallings, secretary to the Society for the Propagation of the Gospel, went in his place as chaplain to the Bishop. Dr. Powell was in medical charge of the party, which also included Mr. and Mrs. Woodrow as guests, for whom the spacious barge afforded ample accommodation. As a school inspector Mr. Woodrow did some work for Government by looking at the Assamese schools, and profited by two months' leave to visit some private property in the Cachar district. For the Bishop, the expedition was for the most part a repetition of the earlier one through these same watery regions in 1861, all contemporary notice of which was suppressed, for the general features of the two visits were the same, and to the second was imparted a peculiar interest from being the Bishop's last visitation. Except for some increase in tea-planting, five years had made no difference in the condition of a province which has been called the Bœotia of India. The Assamese inhabitants of the plains, few in number, and stupified with opium-eating, are useless for the development of the country's great resources; and the wild hill tribes of Garos, Merees, Nagas, &c., are as yet scarcely approached either by civilisation or Christianity. A few small and detached European settlements and missions carry on existence, under difficulties, amidst the fever-giving jungles of a region in many parts fair and beautiful in outward aspect, but years behind the rest of India in the conveniences or comforts, or even necessaries of life. Almost at the outset of the voyage a fatal event occurred as a strange prelude to that which marked its close. On the first Saturday, August 4, as evening prayers on the barge were ended, about 10 P.M., the party were startled and saddened by news from the steamer anchored ahead that one of Mr. Woodrow's servants had rolled over in his sleep on deck, and fallen overboard. A buoy was thrown out at once in the dark, and a boat put out immediately; but all search was fruitless. The catastrophe remained a sad memory till its disastrous repetition, exactly nine weeks from that evening. The steamer and barge passed from the river Gorai, on which Kooshtea stands, into the Poddah, another branch of the Ganges, and thence into the Jabooma, leading into the Brahmaputra, of which it forms, indeed, the main channel at this southern part of its course. The stations visited were Goalpara, Gowhatti, Jeypore, Sibsagor, Nazeerah, Nowgong, up to Dibroghur, each place being situated either on the great river, or on some tributary; for as yet Assam has not advanced beyond that normal condition in which nature's watercourses form the only highways. Descending the Brahmaputra, the party reached Dacca early in September, and thence threading through another network of rivers, they made their way to Cachar and Sylhet. After leaving Sylhet, the 'Koel' anchored in the Surma, a broad muddy river; row-boats were put in requisition for navigating a smaller tributary, and finally mere canoes took the travellers up a most lovely, but very shallow, mountain-stream, overshadowed by rocks and tropical vegetation; and thus, still by no way but that of water, the foot of the Kossiah hills was reached, and they were ascended for a brief sojourn at Cherrapoongee and Shillong. At every halt, weekday or Sunday, services were performed, and the holy communion administered; confirmations were held, and native schools visited; and considerable collections were realised for the Additional Clergy Society or the hill schools fund. For these two objects the Bishop had for a long time, when on visitations, deliberately preached, as standing in greater need of support and advocacy than mission work, which has a reserve fund of stability through connexion with home societies. The following brief journal extracts and a few letters will suffice to describe some characteristics of life in a somewhat dreary region; they will serve to exhibit also how the lonely life of the English settler, with its few safeguards and its many temptations, remained to the end an object of the Bishop's unceasing care and anxiety.

Wednesday, August 22.—To-day the Captain desired to take the 'Koel' down to Dickomukh, to have plenty of time for gathering in coal enough for the voyage, not only to Dibroghur, but back to Gowhatti. And as Sibsagor is very deficient in means of accommodation and supplies of food, the ladies were carried off in the steamer, and the circuit house made decently comfortable for the gentlemen of the party. Moreover its principal room was very neatly arranged as a temporary church, by Mrs. Sconce. . . She hung texts in illuminated characters on the walls, and made two platforms, one for the pulpit and one for the communion table, strange to say, out of opium boxes, which come into Assam in large quantities containing food for the untameable, but now somewhat restrained, appetite of the Assamese; and when their contents are emptied, are sold and used as a moveable flooring to keep away the damp which exudes through the ordinary brick floors. These platforms were covered with carpets, and the communion table with a purple cloth and surmounted by a picture of the Crucifixion. Yet in spite of these skilful arrangements the service furnished an extraordinary example of the destitution of Sibsagor. We had assumed that the station would supply the bread and wine for the sacramental elements, and it was only just before service that we discovered that there was none. We applied to Captain Sconce, whose house was close by. He said that he had some sherry, though no port, but that at that time of day (10 A.M.) it was impossible to produce a morsel of bread. So Woodrow had to spring on one of the few ponies that were in waiting, to gallop down to the steamer (a mile off, and just getting up her steam for starting), and to bring up a bottle of port wine and some bread. Many other arrangements of the station show it to be on the very confines of civilisation. Time, food, and servants are equally unknown at Sibsagor. There are no clocks. Fowls cost an immense sum; there are no sheep, because the grass will not support them; and gram is very dear; beef is unknown, because the death of an ox nearly causes a mutiny amongst the Assamese. Ayahs are unattainable; so the ladies work, dress, teach, feed, and take out walking all their children, with no help but that of some girl who consents for large wages to come and do ayah's work for a portion of the day. Altogether it is a dreary place, but its inhabitants were cheerful, and ready to make the best of it.

Thursday, August 23.—At 4 A.M. the heavens looked gloomy for the expedition to Nazeerah. It poured as if it never meant to stop. At 11 four elephants arrived, and as the rain had diminished, we packed ourselves up in waterproofs and ascended the beasts, which, as most things in Assam, are arranged in a most comfortless way, with no howdah or pad, but a simple seat, on which you are perched sideways, with feet hanging down unsupported. Soon after leaving Sibsagor we plunged into a dense jungle, with only a path left (of course deep in mud and slosh), which was wide enough for the passage of an elephant. There were large trees in the jungle, such as peepuls and banyans, with a very thick undergrowth of tall grass, bushes, and creepers; among them magnificent convolvuluses, and other climbing flowers. Beautiful butterflies, too, were buzzing about when the rain ceased. There were some clearances for tea, but William Sconce said that they had not turned out profitable. We also passed several cottages and shops, and one very large break in the otherwise uniform jungle, where there was an abundance of rice fields. After two hours and a quarter of considerable discomfort, the elephants deposited us on the bank of the Dikho, and a ferry boat came across and conveyed us to Nazeerah. This place is wholly the property of the Assam Company, who, though now exclusively occupied in making tea, have the right to carry on in their land any operations developing the resources of the country. Hence they decline being called the Assam *Tea* Company, as they not unfrequently are. The station consists of their godowns and offices, and the bungalows of their officials, of whom the chief, a Scot named John Smith, drove down to meet us, and conveyed me to his house in a buggy. He came out nine years ago from Aberdeen, in the service of the Company, and is now superintendent of all its large concerns, with twenty-three tea-factories under his immediate direction. Though the day was as unfavourable for our purposes as it could be, twenty-six assistants and others engaged in tea-making assembled for service besides our own party. I preached, and the holy communion was administered. . . . Afterwards I had a long talk with John Smith about the means of placing a clergyman here, which he allows to be most desirable; for, as he says, 'among all these scattered young men there really is no one to exercise any good or improving influence, and the solitude of a tea-planter's life is a great temptation.' I am to state my plans in a letter, which he will forward to the Directors of the Company at home. At 7.30 we left Nazeerah, after a visit which, though short and hindered by bad weather, was long enough, I hope, to remind the inhabitants that there are Church ordinances in India, and to inform me of their wants. We could not have stayed longer for lack of sleeping accommodation. Our ride from it was as tiresome as our ride to it; we had one heavy shower of rain; the moon struggled from behind dark clouds, the forest looked weird and ghastly, fireflies took the place of butterflies, and the strong smell of decaying vegetable matter reminded us that to pass in the night through a dense jungle in the rainy season is not altogether a healthy process.

Dacca, Sunday, September 9.—The fever was better this morning, and I was happily able to take my usual part in the service, though I doubt whether I have felt such difficulty in doing so since 1859. How thankful I should be for the change that has taken place in my health since that disastrous autumn! . . . On the whole, we of the English Church have reason to be ashamed of our position at Dacca. The fragments of Hæberlin's mission, which existed in 1861, have now vanished, the chaplains here having done nothing to keep it together, and everything has passed into the hands of the Baptists. Next to Calcutta there is no place in Bengal where education has made so much progress as at Dacca; for besides the college, there are several good aided schools, and a large body of Brahmoists is forming in consequence. The fields seem white to harvest, but we Anglicans are doing nothing to gather in the crop. Doubtless, we must not hinder the Baptists in the work, but I wish that there was a chaplain who would come here in a missionary spirit, and, having but a small English congregation, lay hold of the educated young Hindus. The race of Corries and Martyns is perhaps necessarily extinct; the zealous men who would act if they could in their spirit are sent to large stations, where regiments and hospitals take up all their time, and the incumbents of small places are often past their prime. Mr. Wise dined with us, who has known Dacca for forty years, and laments its fallen state. In his early days a Court of Appeal for East Bengal sat here, four judges driving to court in their carriages, with silver sticks carried before them; now a single judge walks down to cutchery in a solah topee. He not only remembers Heber's visit, but Lord Combermere's, who arrived with a grand aquatic procession of twenty large pinnaces.

To the Rev. J. Thomas.

Barge 'Rhotas,' August 1866.

I was, as always, very glad to get your letter, especially as it gave cheering accounts of the gradual disappearance of the debt, which, if I live to return to England, I hope to find utterly vanished. I used never to be quite easy about that ninety-nine years' lease under which the College is held. Of that I suppose that twenty-three have expired, and how can Marlborough take its place by the side of Eton and Winchester if in seventy-six years (the days of our grandchildren) its property might be resumed by the Lord Ailesbury of the day? I should rejoice to hear that, when the debt has gone, the attention of the council is turned to the work of acquiring the property in freehold. The money would not be sunk on a mere fancy; the rent of the buildings would be saved. . . . I have started to Assam on visitation, chiefly to look after the tea-planters scattered through that province, where, however, there is also a fairly successful mission of the Propagation Society, and some native Christians. The tea-planters are, I fear, too often a godless set, and I should be glad to place a new clergyman and church in one of the less accessible parts of the country. The highway is the vast river Brahmaputra, and we travel luxuriously in a great barge, or, as it is called, a 'yacht,' towed by a steamer, which is allowed to the Lieutenant Governor of Bengal to visit the watery parts of his territories, but which he, not wanting to use it this year, has lent to us, . . . and as the weather in the rainy season is, as a general rule, cool and pleasant, our existence is sufficiently easy and enjoyable. Of course, when we reach Assam there will be work to do, but during the ten days or so of our voyage to it we have a complete holiday.

I heard from —— the other day, who seems very happy, and though still vehement (one could hardly wish him otherwise), less denunciatory than usual, which I trace to the influence of a gentle and sensible wife. I should be very thankful if he could feel himself comfortable in taking orders, which the relaxation of the terms of subscription may perhaps render possible, as I do not think that his difficulties were ever fundamental, and he always seemed to me to retain a firm hold on Christian faith and hope. . . . I am very glad to hear that Edward is going to Stafford Rectory again; it is a place where he gets nothing but good.

To Arthur Watson, Esq.

On board the 'Rhotas,' river Brahmaputra, August 4, 1866.

. . . Let me thank you for the continued liberality of your response to my appeals for the hill schools, which are still, and will be till 1868, if I live so long, my chief object. I will say nothing about its recent progress, because I hope to send you a report early in 1867. . . . As the journey from Calcutta to Gowhatti (the chief town in Assam) occupies ten or twelve days, and as during that time we are quite excluded from post offices, European information is unattainable except at long intervals. At present, on this 4th day of August, we have only read newspapers up to the return of the Queen from Balmoral, her fruitless effort to patch up the Whig ministry, and her sending for Lord Derby. The telegram, however, has informed us that he is in power; that Lord Stanley has the Foreign Office, and Lord Cranborne, India. I trust the latter will send out zealous and sensible chaplains, recommended by the tutors of colleges at Oxford and Cambridge. In like manner, as to the greater contest in Europe, the newspapers have only brought us to the seizure of Hanover and Saxony, and the defeat of the Italians near Verona; but the telegram speaks of the complete triumph of Prussia, the withdrawal of Austria from the Bund, and the surrender of Venetia to France. . . . As to the war, I am altogether on the Prusso-Italian side. I even half repent of having joined in the ordinary abuse of Bismarck; not, I trust, from any disposition to worship success, but because he seems to have conceived, held firmly, and carried out vigorously a great and noble idea—the unity and nationality of Germany—so that his policy in the north of Europe is precisely that for which Cavour and Ricasoli have been justly admired in the south. The Austrian cause is plainly indefensible on any principles of right and justice; indeed, all pretence to them was thrown away by the occupation of Holstein.

Turning to domestic matters, Edward's success at Woolwich was a great pleasure to us. Not that either of us had the least wish for him to go into the army ἁπλῶς, but as he had set his heart upon it, we wished him to enter in an honourable way. And the separation from him has been such a sorrowful drawback to the happiness of the last seven years, that a proof that he has been using his time profitably was a most blessed consolation to us both.

To Bosworth Smith, Esq.

Shillong, in the Kossyah Hills, September 26, 1866.

. . . You also urge me to pay England a visit. I do not want urging on that head, for I desire not only for my own sake, but because I think that I might, with God's blessing, do some good to the diocese by interesting people at home in its wants and welfare. But I am fettered by no less formidable an impediment than an Act of Parliament, through which it is impossible to drive a coach and six, or rather to steer a P. and O. steamer. The Act empowering the Crown to found and endow the See of Calcutta, provides that the bishop shall in no possible case leave the country till he has dwelt and worked in it for ten years. My ten years expire on November 12, 1868, and if I live so long, I hope then to avail myself of the liberty which the Act concedes, and to go home either on eighteen months' furlough or permanently, according to health and a variety of other circumstances, which need not be considered till they are developed in the course of Providence; not indeed that I should sail on November 12, or for some months after it. All doctors say that after ten years in the tropics, it would be very unsafe to arrive in England in midwinter (it was probably the cold after India that killed Lord Canning); but I hope, if no untoward event occurs, to be in England before many months of 1869 are over. It is a long time to look forward to, and the anticipation of such a return to friends and country is so delightful, that I often doubt whether it is right to indulge it; but in India the scale of my work and plans is so large that I am absolutely compelled to forecast more than is desirable: and as we believe in a Father who is in Heaven, and not in jealous Nemesis, I trust that as long as I form any scheme in submission to His will, I do not displease Him by looking forward to a legitimate source of happiness; and though I speak with rapture of even this distant prospect of England, you need not fear that I am getting weary of my work in India. I take as much interest in it, and feel its importance as much as ever, though I believe that the time is coming when a short intermission of it, and the refreshment of intercourse with those at home, would be good both for me and for it. As for the sentence above, in which I contemplate the possibility of resignation in 1869, you need not infer from that that I desire an old age of idleness. I think it very unlikely that I shall resign then: but health and other things are uncertain; a Bishop of Calcutta must be capable of a good deal of physical endurance in the way of travelling, and putting up with discomfort; and I thought it better, as your letter had extracted from me a statement of my future intentions, to state them fully, and impart to you the future contingences which they may involve.

To Mrs. Tomkinson.

Shillong, on the Kossyah Hills, September 22, 1866.

I have been a long time in acknowledging your very acceptable present of 'Bernard's Lectures,' but I can thank you very sincerely for the book, not only generally because it was your present, but for its own sake. I read it with great interest, and I hope profit. I thought it clear, logical, often eloquent; and as I was at the time preparing four sermons for our Wednesday evening services in the cathedral, on the date and origin of the four gospels, I often found in the lectures, which travelled over the same ground, hints which facilitated and improved my own work. These lectures, and Hessey's on Sunday, are very satisfactory recent results of the Bampton endowment, which has often been wasted on singularly profitless discourses. . . . With regard to Ursula, whose return to England at the end of this year has been urged both by you and Edward. I will say a few words to prove that we are not regardless of your exhortations, but there are some considerations in favour of keeping her until 1868. It certainly is, or ought to be, a great advantage to a child to be with her parents as long as possible, unless the parents are worthless folk; at all events, it is in accordance with the laws of nature and will of God, and I always consider the separation generally necessary not only one of the great *pains*, but one of the most glaring *evils* of Indian life. As soon as I return to our steamer at Chattuck, on the river Surma, where I have left the mass of my books, I will transcribe for you a passage from Southey, quoted and highly commended by Thackeray . . . .

Where is Shillong? you will ask, and where the Kossyah hills? The Kossyahs are a wild mountain tribe, not Hindus, with language, religion, and customs of their own, tamed by forty years' contact with Europeans, and occupying a range of mountains 6,000 feet high, and containing wide plateaux of table-land, rising from the Brahmaputra in Lower Assam, and stretching over to Sylhet and Cachar, and the river Surma. Cherra Poonjee has long been an English settlement and sanitarium in these hills, but the rainfall there is scarcely credible (from 500 to 600 inches a year); moreover, it is at the end furthest from Assam (now rising in importance on account of the tea), and is on a small piece of table-land, so as to be incapable of wide expansion. Hence, the Assamese officials have set up a new sanitarium on their side of the hills thirty miles from Cherra Poonjee, with a more reasonable amount of rain, where they are building houses, cutchery, &c., are projecting barracks, and are hoping to be allowed to reside during the hot months, and even to transfer the native troops from Cherra. S—— is at Cherra, and I have come over here to see after the ecclesiastical wants and capacities of Shillong, the road being rough and the accommodation limited, so that she was left behind. To-morrow I hope to return, and then, after giving the Cherra Poonjeeites a Sunday, we all intend to descend on our steamer, which is left on the bosom of the Surma, and begin our voyage to Calcutta. I am enjoying, and so, from a note just received, is she, our whiff of mountain air at the end of a somewhat hot and muggy journey; the country is fresh, open, invigorating, not unlike the Downs of Surrey or Sussex, only with the grassy hills better defined, and more peak-like and mountainous in outline. There are some very pretty spots indeed. Last night we had an eclipse of the moon, and the hills echoed with the drumming and shouting of the people, endeavouring to drive away the wicked giant who had laid hold of it. . . .

October 2.

We have again reached our steamer, and after being aground for some time this morning, are proceeding down the Surma or Barak (in this maze of rivers it is hard to know where one name begins and another ends) at the rate of ten miles an hour. I send you the passage from Southey's letter to his wife:—

'If your feelings are like mine, I will not go to Lisbon without you, or I will stay at home and not part from you. For though not unhappy when away, still without you I am not happy. For your sake, as well as my own and little Edith's, I will not consent to any separation; the growth of a year's love between her and me, if it please God she should live, is a thing too delightful in itself, and too valuable in its consequences, to be given up for any light inconvenience on your part or mine. On these things we will talk at leisure; only, dear, dear Edith, we must not part.' [Quoted by Thackeray as a proof that Southey was a 'true gentleman.']

However, I do consent to part at the end of the cold weather of 1867–8, when I am quite willing, and think it better, that U. should precede us to England by a year. 1868 must, if possible, be spent in Calcutta, and the trouble of arranging for a third season for U. at Simla would be greater than it would be worth while to encounter for the sake of the (I trust) few months' interval between her descent from Simla and our own flight.

These letters were among the latest that were written. The last entry in the journal bore date October 1. With an unfinished sentence the manuscript page ended; the book laid aside for the ink to dry was never to be resumed. Thus the pen of one who was truly a ready writer, rested from its work: thus, with mournful suddenness, was closed the journal so regularly and accurately kept, that for eight years it had formed an autobiography—the correspondence in which a shy nature found a vent for all its earnestness and all its bright humour, and in which so much of the mind and life of the writer were faithfully pictured.

The few remaining days need only the briefest record. Dacca was reached in the steamer on Wednesday, October 3, and the whole party again transferred themselves to the 'Rhotas,' which was at once attached to the steamer for the return voyage to Kooshtea. The Bishop had a fresh touch of the fever, which he invariably caught during any protracted sojourn among river damps. On Saturday, October 6, he got up far from well; but he mended as the day wore on, and had a long conversation in the forenoon with Mr. Woodrow on some school matters. The vessels were anchored at Kooshtea by mid-day, when the party broke up, some proceeding at once by train to Calcutta; the Bishop and myself, with Mr. Vallings, remained on board for the evening work. The Bishop ate his luncheon, and appeared decidedly better. Between three and four, when lying on the sofa in the pleasant sitting room of the 'Rhotas,' he said suddenly, 'Shut all the windows.' They were open to let in the cool air, for the day was cloudy and pleasant. His hands were very cold, and a fresh fever fit seemed coming on; but some strong hot tea revived him, and at five o'clock he left the boat for the consecration of the cemetery, feeling not otherwise than equal to the exertion. He expected to return by seven, dine, and leave by the night train. At the service of consecration he gave, as was his wont, a short extempore address. In words remembered and recorded by the very few to whom he last spoke as a bishop and minister of the Church, he reminded his hearers 'that such consecrations were for the benefit of the living, not of the dead; that departed souls suffered no injuries if their bodies were left in a desert place, or on a field of battle, or in any other way were unable to receive the rites of burial; that the solemn ceremony of consecration was to enable the living in a better manner to pay the last tribute of affection, and to retain a more solemn and permanent impression of the awful truths which give eternal importance to the questions of life and death.' After the service was over, he lingered to discuss some ecclesiastical arrangements with the very few residents of the small station, and twilight was fast passing into darkness when he reached the river-bank. Owing to currents, churs (sand-banks), and the precipitous nature of the bank, it was impossible to bring any vessel up close. The 'Rhotas' was lying in the full stream; an intervening flat was at anchor between it and the shore, and this flat the Bishop prepared to reach. But, between himself and all to which he was looking forward as perhaps still to be permitted to him in this world—unfinished work and fresh formed plans; active labour yet for a space in India; dawning hopes of England and English friends—between himself and all except the Master he had striven faithfully to serve, there lay many yards of the rapid rolling river. Somewhere on the perilous causeway of planks bridging the waters his foot slipped; he fell, and was never more seen. The increasing darkness, an unsteady platform, his near sight, the weariness of a frame enfeebled for the time by fever, had all doubtless a share, humanly speaking, in the great calamity foreknown in the counsels of Him 'who moves in a mysterious way.' Every effort was made to rescue, to recover him: all who are acquainted with the current of an Indian river will know how infinitely slight would be the chance of success in the one endeavour or the other.

There were those to whose lips, on hearing the mournful tidings, the simple Bible words arose—'*And Enoch walked with God, and he was not, for God took him.*'

CONCLUSION.

Thus he passed away, at a time when, beyond dispute, his powers were at their highest. It was only in the somewhat bent figure, in the hair flaked with white, that signs of age, almost prematurely revealing themselves, testified to the effects of sojourn in a tropical climate. His strength continued equal to the demands of a life involving frequently much bodily exertion and fatigue. His constitution had shown an unexpected degree of elasticity in India; for though illness overtook him from time to time, his power of rallying seemed to increase, and he could throw off an attack of fever better in 1866 than in 1860. His mental energies, far from suffering any abatement, had for long appeared to expand under the demands laid upon them, to rise year by year to a higher level, and to become continually more fitted to deal adequately and comprehensively with the numerous matters that came within their range.

Any brief and general summary of the Bishop's work in India will naturally first take note of that work in connexion with the intellectual movement among educated Hindus. It is a movement which, dealing in its spiritual aspect with the inner life, stands wholly apart from the civil polity of the country, and yet appears to contain the germ of a sway over the national heart, deeper and more extensive than that attained by many other regenerating influences. Among those who in these days watch with keen interest the development of this remarkable product of European rule and civilization, the position assumed towards it by a leader in the English Church justly challenges scrutiny and criticism. The Bishop assuredly never underrated the vast importance of this movement, nor of the responsibilities of the Christian Church towards it; but results, great or tangible, were scarcely to be hoped from it in the work of establishing Christianity as the all-sufficient solution of moral and spiritual perplexities. Many influences now contend for mastery over minds roused from the torpor of centuries into an activity of intellect which the free thought of an enquiring age is constantly stimulating. Christianity is only one amongst these influences, and the Bishop, like any other observer of the tendencies of modern views, knew well how long and arduous must be her contest for supremacy. There are many, doubtless, for whom the interchange of argument with subtle, though often superficial, thinkers, would have a peculiar fascination; but the Bishop, whose mind was far more practical than metaphysical, had no taste for controversy for its own sake, and, capable as he was of large-hearted sympathy with doubts and difficulties, he never cared to encourage transcendental speculations which have so much attraction for the dreamy and imaginative Oriental. Moreover, the points at issue between himself as an upholder of Christianity in its integrity, and those who inclined towards intuitive philosophical systems, were too vitally important to be handled simply as disputed intellectual problems. He would have been utterly untrue to himself had he ever sought to win the native mind through any surrender of the fundamental tenets of revelation. In the course of this memoir it has been plainly indicated how alien to his own convictions were those views current in modern theology which, professing to expand the Christian system, tended, in his estimation, to lower it. It would have been at the cost of harsh inconsistency if, in the interests of an all-comprehensive toleration, he had lent his sanction to those partial approximations towards Christian faith which clearly reveal their Western origin; for one remarkable feature in the higher religious thought of the East at the present day is the outward form and coherence which it has rapidly and quite recently acquired, keeping pace, as it were, and assimilating itself, with the latest developments of liberal theology in Europe. When the Bishop went to India in 1859, a small band of disciples, now known as the Brahmo Somaj, the highest and purest of those sects which have discarded heathenism, were, for the first time, giving an outward expression to a theistic faith in an organised devotional worship of great purity and simplicity. It was not until 1866 that the famous lecture of Baboo Keshub Chunder Sen, on the character of our Lord, brought that teacher into wider prominence as the leader of the sect, and stamped the creed of the Brahmo Somaj with a conception of Christianity plainly reflecting the teaching of a modern school of European writers. That the lofty sentiments and inspiring religious enthusiasm which distinguish some of these writers should find a quick response in cultivated Oriental minds, no one could more entirely understand and acknowledge than the Bishop. But so far as the tendency of such teaching was to substitute an eclectic theism or an æsthetic morality for the evangelical truth of the New Testament, he was at issue with it. Varied are the portraits now drawn by sentiment or philosophy of the Son of Man; but it was the Christ as portrayed and apprehended by St. Paul, by Augustine, by Luther, by Arnold, whom alone the Bishop could offer for the acceptance and refuge of Eastern minds thirsting for the Water of Life. It may perhaps be safely and correctly said that the Bishop found his most congenial and satisfactory point of contact with Hindus through the sure and firm paths which a liberal education had opened. He ever cherished the sound and solid intellectual training involved in the theory of that higher education which has now full play in India, as the main instrument for bracing and invigorating the native mind, and securing that mental discipline which must be preparatory to an impartial and reasoning acceptance either of the truths of science or of the facts of history, and among such facts he of course classed those which belong to Christianity and its history in the world. In his fearless advocacy of all broad educational measures; in his efforts to expand and invigorate the education administered by missionaries; and to influence, from a Christian standpoint, that education which is in the hands of the State, the strength of his position in reference to the native community is mainly to be found. But the more indirect influence exercised by the force of a character so steadfast and so true, cannot be overlooked. As Bishop Heber's name is to this day remembered and venerated by Christians in India outside the pale of the Anglican communion, so it is certain that Bishop Cotton's name will be handed on through many generations of Asiatics, whether Christians or not, as one who desired that, in default of higher grounds of union, forbearance, charity, and goodwill should be the bonds of connexion between men of different races, nationalities and religions. The highest hopes entertained in 1858 by friends in behalf of the Bishop pointed to his fitness at a peculiar crisis, 'to heal the wounds and assuage the strifes' caused by the recent mutiny, and to exhibit a 'large-hearted philanthropy, bounded by no distinctions of race or creed.' After he was gone, the verdict alike of English laymen, missionaries, and natives, testified how fully a brief career had fulfilled those hopes.

It is in the domain occupied by the European portion of the Church in India that the labours of the late episcopate were truly and substantially fruitful. The mark left by the Bishop on Asiatic intellectualism may have been fainter than some perhaps expected. Direct missionary operations may have been characterised more by the silent growth of broader views than by manifest results in a great accession of converts; but the hold which he maintained over the Church among professing Christians was firm, vigorous, and effective beyond all gainsaying. He had the diocese, so far as Europeans were concerned, thoroughly in hand; he had learnt its distinctive peculiarities; he had gauged its wants, and if he could not fully meet these, he kept them incessantly in view, and was gradually multiplying ecclesiastical resources to bear upon them.

From this point of view, the contrast is great between the first and the last of the letters written annually to Government on the affairs of the diocese. That of 1859 dealt merely in a general way with ecclesiastical matters, which were just beginning to flow again in ordinary channels after the convulsion of the two preceding years. In 1866 a similar report was a thankful record of schools increased, clergy multiplied, and a general development of ecclesiastical agency, through the harmonious co-operation of State aid and voluntary effort. To the latter the Bishop was largely indebted; his appeals were constant, and never in vain; but his great strength lay in the official support so liberally and consistently extended towards him. The times were doubtless favourable. During some years there was a buoyancy in Indian finance which now seems almost mythical, and much good work that the Bishop had at heart reaped the benefit of large grants from the public revenue. In a higher sense also the age had improved. A desire for respectability and godliness among nominal Christians was no longer limited to the few who, on leaving England, did not leave all religious instincts behind them; and the Bishop's views and wishes received attention and co-operation in quarters where zealous leaders of the Indian Church had of old met only obstruction or indifference. The highest civil power recognised duties and responsibilities towards Europeans in India of every class, and discharged them by consistently aiding and trusting the chief pastor, throughout his active and progressive administration of the ecclesiastical department of the State. Valuable for its own sake was the financial assistance of the Government, but it was almost more valuable as a pledge of moral support. It does not fall to the lot of many men to receive so marked a tribute to capacity and influence as that which was rendered to the Bishop by the acceptance of his educational scheme within one year of his arrival in India, and its adoption by the Government, in every detail, before two years were over. Thus the firmly established schools in which that educational scheme was embodied, remain a conspicuous monument of the Bishop's tenure of the see; but they no less represent the influence which, quickly acquired, he quietly but surely sustained, and by which, as it has been happily said of him, 'he made public functionaries, either in the army or the State, not his suspicious opponents, but his natural friends and allies.'

Yet he did not make his way by qualities that were dazzling or commanding. His abilities were good, and had been constantly cultivated, but his intellectual powers were sound rather than showy. He was not a rapid nor an especially fertile thinker. In acuteness of intelligence and quickness of perception he was deficient, and work so successfully prosecuted was evolved out of patient and industrious reflection, rather than inspired by any flash of genius. The great personal weight that he carried lay in the mental energy and practical ability which eminently distinguished him, and in the breadth and sound common sense of his views, combined, as these were, with powers of conciliation that were proof against the jarring elements of daily life, and with a sincerity of aim and purpose on which others rested as on a rock.

Far too guileless to possess that form of vanity which makes some men strain after leadership and prominence, he knew no ambition except that of being an instrument for the furtherance of God's kingdom in the world, and of turning his occupancy of the see, whether for a longer or a shorter time, to some high and definite account. He knew by many unmistakable signs how secure, in working for this end, his self-created position in India became. There are expressions in his journals or letters which under this aspect might, to a general reader, seem to be tinged with a spirit of vanity. The inference would be erroneous. Few people could be more wholly devoid of self-consciousness than the Bishop. When any work was accomplished, any onward step secured towards the ends he had at heart, he deeply and heartily rejoiced; but it was with a joy that first rose in a rush of thankfulness to Him who gives all good things.

One source of his ever-widening influence arose, undoubtedly, from the marked spirit of earnestness with which he adopted the great interests of India as his own, living and working, so long as he was spared, for these alone. He realised the lessons read to England by the great mutiny, with a force quite equal to that felt by those who had lived and suffered through it; but had there been no mutiny, he would none the less have felt all that is involved in the fact of England holding India; and he brought to bear on his own share in that mighty trust, a statesmanlike sagacity and breadth of view, no less than the philanthropy of a Christian. In his mind there was no distinction, as regards the motives and principles of action, between the work of the missionary and that of any soldier or civil servant of the State. The disinterestedness and self-abnegation by which the former are characterised were to him the rule of life to be followed by all. Every influential word that he uttered, either as a preacher, or as the projector of some useful work, or as the exponent of the duties of England towards India in some more popular form, was a protest against the miserable notion that an Englishman's existence in India is an untoward and unwelcome accident, with no obligations beyond a perfunctory discharge of duty. He spoke as he felt, when at any time he sought to stimulate in others that power of studying and enjoying a great country, which was to himself a personal blessing, so far as it tended to diminish the sense of exile, which he never wholly lost, and to fill the void in his life caused by the want of the warm friendships of England. It would be difficult to overrate his keen interest in the historical antiquities, the many noble sights, the merely external features of India. To find in every successive visit to her great cities some point overlooked, or forgotten, or imperfectly understood, was to make all objects minister to his own thirst for knowledge, to draw from the treasures of this world *things new and old.* 'The more,' he once wrote, 'residents in India feel how wonderful a country it is, how rich in scenery, architecture, historical recollections, the more they will feel that it is worth living in, worth working for, worth restoring to the greatness from which it has fallen.' These are words that may fitly stand as the motto of a life full of active and faithful toil, but redeemed from all that was narrow or merely practical, by high mental culture, and enriched by intellectual tastes of marked purity and correctness. Yet it is the grace of a deeply Christian spirit that casts the brightest halo round the Bishop's memory. In the first burst of general sorrow, in October 1866, it was said that his sudden removal had made men brothers through a common grief; so many were there who could remember some special link wrought by a word or act of personal kindness. For from the depths of his essentially gentle soul there had often issued, as occasion arose, the language of justice and fairness, recognising the rights of all; the conciliatory expressions tempering remonstrance or rebuke, the words of condolence and sympathy, so happy in their form, so relieved from everything that was commonplace, that they supplied to mourners their choicest consolations in the hour of bereavement. Such outward graces were the truest index of an inward Christian faith, working so secretly and unobtrusively, that few beyond those who shared his daily life knew its strength and steadfastness. The following words, written to a correspondent in 1858, are expressive of the principles that guided him to the last, and indicate how entirely a sense of the necessity and of the sufficiency of Christianity to meet moral and spiritual needs overpowered intellectual difficulties:—'I do not overlook, and have from time to time been disturbed by difficulties connected with the details of Christianity, but I suppose that my turn of mind is too practical to enter into the subtler disputations which disturb others; for myself, I feel rest in the conviction that outside Christianity all is blank, desolate, hopeless, and that with faith in Christ all true holiness is inseparably connected.' Of this inseparable connexion in his mind between two things not to be *put asunder*, the ordinary course of his life afforded constant illustrations. One may be given as a sample of many others. He was blessed by nature with a remarkably sweet and even temper; but in India—a land of many irritations and small worries—it was often tried, and was especially liable to be discomposed if anyone's carelessness or forgetfulness occasioned a breach of that punctuality which, out of regard to others, he was scrupulous in maintaining in all business arrangements. A cloud would gather for a few minutes on his countenance; he looked angry because he felt so, but ordinarily, by entire silence, he arrested the hasty word on his own lips, and forbade altercation or argument in others. Sometimes, though very rarely, expressions of annoyance escaped him: his self-condemnation afterwards was truly the *godly sorrow that worketh repentance*, and could spring only from the heart and conscience of one who feels that he has for the moment failed in allegiance to Him in whom alone lies the strength for a sinner's struggle and victory. No traits in the moral and spiritual side of the Bishop's character were more consistently developed than those of self-restraint and self-discipline. His outward career ran for the most part tranquilly and happily. None of those sorrows that shatter a life and lay it low, fell to his lot; it seemed as if his gentle nature needed not such fiery chastening. In lesser trials common to all, in transient visitations of illness, in circumstances of vexation or perplexity, he heard and obeyed the call for the exercise of patience and self-government; in the most trivial temptations, he strove to maintain that warfare against sin for Christ's sake which made his whole life, as it ripened towards its close, a religion, a devotion, an act of faith. While still a young man, the exchange of faith here below in the things that are not seen for the visible presence of the Saviour hereafter, was an anticipation dwelt upon by him in more serious moments with a fulness of assured trust and joy, not always the possession of one on whom the world, through a goodly heritage of temporal blessings, has a strong hold. The habitual sense of the near though invisible presence of Christ which pervaded his whole earthly life, is well drawn out in the following passage, written by one well-known in the Indian Church:—

I could say much, and with truth, of many excellent traits in the Bishop's character—his never-failing gentleness especially; his quiet cheerfulness; his carefulness in economising fragments of time; his patience in working out the details of any plan of practical usefulness which he had resolved on; and, most marked of all perhaps, his habitual endeavour to form an *equitable* judgment on all things and persons.

This last prevailed so strongly, as sometimes, if I mistake not, to be a source of weakness to him.

But the main distinctive thought which is associated with him in my mind, is that he was one who seemed to me more than any other person whom I have known, to labour systematically to embody in his life the precepts and character of Christ.

Should I be liable to be misunderstood if I said that, of the two successive Bishops of Calcutta under whom I laboured (and whom I both loved and reverenced), the one seemed to me to have had his religious life moulded predominantly on the first eleven chapters of the Epistle to the Romans, the other on the remaining five? Bishop Wilson was, I am sure, truly zealous of good works, and Bishop Cotton truly evangelical in doctrine; but the impression left by them on their diocese corresponds, I think, to what I have described above. The one seemed animated by an ever-present sense of God's wondrous mercy in the redemption of fallen man; the other by a lively conviction that Christ was carrying on a great regenerating work upon earth in, and by means of, His faithful servants.

I will only add,—*Sit anima mea cum illis.*

The Order in Council notifying the Bishop's death ran as follows:—

Home Department—Ecclesiastical.

Simla, October 10, 1866.

The Right Honourable the Governor-General in Council has learned, with the deepest sorrow, the death, through a calamitous accident, of the Right Reverend George Edward Lynch Cotton, Lord Bishop of Calcutta.

There is scarcely a member of the entire Christian community throughout India who will not feel the premature loss of this prelate as a personal affliction. It has rarely been given to any body of Christians, in any country, to witness such depth of learning and variety of accomplishment combined with piety so earnest and energy so untiring. His Excellency in Council does not hesitate to add the expression of his belief that large numbers, even among those of Her Majesty's subjects in India who did not share in the faith of the Bishop of Calcutta, had learned to appreciate his great knowledge, his sincerity and his charity, and will join in lamenting his death.

By command of the Right Honourable the Governor-General in Council.

E. C. BAYLEY,
Secretary to the Government of India.

The outburst of private regret and sorrow which found so general an expression in India when a bright career was suddenly cut short, is almost a more solemn remembrance for all who cared to observe and note it. The Bishop's active, zealous work, the sincerity and guilelessness of his life, the attractive charm of his character, seemed to assume at once fresh proportions in the minds of many who spoke from their hearts, as they mused on him who was gone from their midst. A chaplain whose intercourse with the Bishop had been only brief and occasional, thus wrote :—'In my retired and isolated life, I have met with very few able or distinguished men, and certainly never had the privilege of friendly intercourse with one who was so thoroughly in earnest, whose life was so consistent, and whose soul was so engrossed in the work his Master had given him to do. Whatever improvement recent years may have witnessed in myself, any increased interest and diligence in the discharge of my duties I may attribute, under God, to the influence of the late Bishop. His preaching and his kind familiar intercourse during one brief period, the interest he has always taken in the circumstances and concerns of his clergy, no less than the general character of his whole life, have greatly endeared him to me.' A layman wrote ;—'. . . The loss of one whom I always found a wise counsellor and a sympathising friend is a real personal grief to me, besides which I cannot but feel that there was no one whom India could less afford to lose. There is no one whose influence for good was more widely spread and more deeply felt than his. He was at the same time so thoroughly in earnest in his own convictions and deeds, and so wisely tolerant in his dealings with the convictions and prejudices of others.' The above extracts are but fragments of much that was expressed in the freedom of private correspondence by those who more immediately shared his work. But from many likewise of those outside the English Church there came the same recognition of his comprehensive charity and far-seeing wisdom, and of the bright and holy example of his life. From these came also the testimony, at once honourable and memorable, that to the late Bishop other Protestant communities had learnt to look up as to their natural head.

The local Anglo-Indian Press, usually devoted to purely secular topics, freely opened its columns to a feeling and accurate review of the life so suddenly closed. Its tribute of respect to the Bishop was just and generous when it spoke of him as 'pre-eminently a man for the times,' and 'in whose short tenure of the See more active work for the Church in various directions had been set on foot than usually falls to the lot of most men;' or, again, as one who, 'a teacher by training and by choice, was having gradually but surely yielded to himself the lead in the great educational movement now quickening India.' One passage from the 'Indian Daily News,' comprising much in a short compass, and full of affectionate reverence, deserves a less abridged notice. 'Few persons occupying so high, and at times so delicate, a position have been more generally or more deservedly popular. Nor was the late Bishop's popularity of sudden growth; it was rather the result of his steady consistent walk in all things sound and good, combined with vast powers of conciliation. An admirable tact was one of the great causes of his almost uniform success in what he undertook. Few have possessed in so high a degree the calm patience which works while it waits; few have exercised that discriminating power of using rightly times and seasons with such shrewd wisdom and care. Thus, step by step, Bishop Cotton triumphed over prejudices raised by a manner at first deemed stiff and reserved, and won upon the hearts of men. . . . Years hence, long after the excitement and shock occasioned by the suddenness of his death shall have passed away, the name of Dr. Cotton, associated with much that was calm and dignified, yet meek and gentle, will be a household word; his great efforts for the improvement, socially and intellectually, of the most neglected in India, will be bearing fruit in abundance, and he, whose material presence has been removed so suddenly and mysteriously, will live in the grateful memory of thousands.'

Missionaries mourned for him with a wholly filial reverence; they spoke of him as one who had been to them a 'good gift from God.' As individual men, or through the united voice of conference or committee, they recorded their sense of his fatherly counsels; of his broad and suggestive views touching their great work; of his fresh and ready sympathy with their successes or their disappointments. Now that his name, his life, his sudden loss are rapidly passing out of sight, there are missionaries who still speak of him as one who was 'the beloved and revered head of the Indian Church.'

The sentiments of regret, at once so warm and so general on the part of the native community, are best condensed by a brief reference to the proceedings of the Bethune Society. This Society, it will be remembered, is for literary and intellectual objects, and styles itself 'a great lever of progress in India, aiming to achieve the total annihilation of race-feeling and race-hatred.' It was a curious coincidence, that, on the occasion of meeting for a fresh session in November 1866, the Christian Bishop shared with a non-Christian Hindu—the Rajah Pertap Chunder Sing, late vice-president of the Society—the expressions of regard and regret awarded so freely in the minutes of the day's proceedings to the philanthropy and large-hearted toleration of the one, to the enlightenment and great munificence of the other. Baboo Kissorychund Mittra, in seconding the resolution of which the Bishop was the subject, thus concluded :—

'. . . Benevolence was the distinguishing trait of the character of the lamented Bishop, and it was a benevolence fettered by no distinctions of creed or colour or clime. He never ceased to exercise that divine attribute of which his exalted office made him minister. While Dr. Cotton was sincerely and unaffectedly religious, he was entirely free from that narrow-minded bigotry which curtails the usefulness of so many members of his profession. His toleration, his freedom from sectarianism, and his zeal in the cause of progress, endeared him, while living, to all classes of his fellow-citizens, and will associate his memory, now that he is no more, with their esteem and gratitude. He was one of those happy but rare natures which could embrace all that was good in the latitudinarian tendency of his age, its aversion for all bigoted religious exclusiveness, and its large philanthropy.'

The following valued passage, commenting upon the possible impression made on the native mind by the Bishop's life and character, is from the pen of one who in 1866 held the office of president of the Bethune Society. The manly gifts of an English officer were in the writer's case combined with the literary tastes of a student, and he possessed all those qualities of head and heart which fitted him no less than the Bishop, of whom he so warmly speaks, to bridge the gulf between Eastern and Western races, and to earn the confidence of the most cultivated section of the native community :—

'. . . We question very much if even the most intimate friends of the late Bishop in the least degree expected that spontaneous outburst of regret which the news of his sudden death evoked from the educated natives of Bengal. This is at least a testimony to his character which his surviving friends may regard with profound satisfaction. It is the unbought and unsought for testimony of the non-Christian portions of the community to the practically Christian character of his life and doctrines. . . . Many years have passed since the confidence of the natives of Bengal was gained by any European gentleman so completely as by this Christian Bishop. . . . Their feeling amounted to more than common regard. We never met an educated native who did not speak of him with respect and affection. The reception he met with at a meeting of the Bethune Society in April this year was enthusiastic and respectful. . . . His sudden death, cut off as he was in his prime, in the midst of his career of usefulness, has caused a feeling of general mournfulness throughout India, which the mention of his name and the recollection of the great things he was contemplating cannot fail constantly to recall. Still, as his life was a pattern and example to all, influencing thousands for their advantage, it is possible, we think, that his death may not be without effect upon even the most indifferent among the community. Cold and callous must be the man who cannot deduce some profitable reflection from the contemplation of that pure and spotless life, that unselfish devotion to duty, that untiring energy on behalf of others. His was the white plume, ever foremost in the good fight of faith, which it becomes every Christian to labour to follow. And not alone every Christian. That which is to them a natural duty, will come, we think, with advancing time, to be regarded by the natives of India as a sign and beacon in the distance, towards which it will be their privilege to shape their now wandering course. We may be sure at least that when they talk, as talk they do, of Englishmen, they will never mention without respect and affection the name of the late Bishop. Nor will it be possible for them to recall that name without recollecting that bright example he set them during his lifetime, that noble charity which drew their unconverted hearts towards the Bishop of the Church.' *

* 'Dr. Cotton,' *Calcutta Review*, 1866.

Of all the former distinguished occupants of the great Indian See, the one whom Bishop Cotton undoubtedly most resembled was Heber. In brilliant gifts of imagination he was of course inferior to him, though he probably had the advantage in useful practical powers; but they were much alike in the cultivated tastes which invested a life of exile with many fresh interests, and still more alike in those attributes of urbanity and peculiar gentleness through which the varied classes and races that crossed their path were attracted towards them.

It is now a matter of interest to trace some earlier links in a chain of associations connecting the one with the other, and finally completed by the tenure of an office which formed the work of each unto death. At the beginning of this century intimacy and intercourse between the families of the Hebers and Cottons was close and frequent. The rectory of Stoke in Shropshire, held by George Cotton, Dean of Chester (Bishop Cotton's grandfather), was within a short distance of Hodnet; his son James, afterwards Dean of Bangor, and Reginald Heber were contemporaries, and when young curates they served together as volunteers in a regiment raised in Shropshire in the time of the Peninsular war. Years passed away, and from 1840-44 George Cotton had the Cholmondelys, Bishop Heber's nephews, as pupils, in his house at Rugby. Between him and their mother, the Bishop's sister, a warm friendship arose, which was strengthened by an occasional visit paid in the Rugby vacations to Hodnet Hall, where she, as Mrs. Macaulay, was living until her death in 1845. Mrs. Macaulay was a woman of much ability, and possessed also a keen sense of humour. The visits to her house were of the most joyous character, and contemporary letters show how thoroughly she and her guest understood and appreciated each other. The hereditary reverence and admiration which George Cotton had through life felt for the pure and beautiful character of Reginald Heber, was naturally profoundly intensified when he was suddenly called to fill his chair in India. While feeling how great an example of zeal and devotion he had before him in his immediate and venerable predecessor, his frequent allusions to a still earlier one seemed to indicate a sympathy engendered by kindred temperament and tastes. In one of his earliest letters to a chaplain who was changing his presidency, and who had somewhat invited counsel and admonition, the Bishop closed a few words on charity, moderation, and consideration for the feelings or the prejudices of others as follows:—'You are now going to minister by the side of Heber's grave; I trust you will remember how completely this was Heber's spirit.' At the close of his much enjoyed South India visitation, he had two regrets—that he had failed to see the temples of Madura, and that he had not been able to look upon the tomb of Bishop Heber at Trichinopoly. A cheque signed in the last month of his life was for a donation towards the repair of that same tomb. When the mournful news of October 1866 was wafted to England, there was one to whose memory rose a passage from a sermon of Dr. Arnold's, in reference to the equally sudden removal of his predecessor forty years before. The words it contained seemed to belong equally to either of the two, whose lives, though in the annals of time far apart, had been knit together by the same holy grace of character, by the same sacred office, and by the strange likeness of their deaths.

Not by words only, but by many munificent deeds, the Bishop's memory has been honoured. The Council of Marlborough College at once founded a scholarship of 50*l.* a year bearing his name. Memorial windows at Rugby and at Marlborough will long connect his name with the two school chapels, the services in which had been so fruitful in building up his own inner life.* In the school

* The Rugby Memorial is represented by four windows placed in the eastern apse which forms one portion of the alterations in the school chapel, completed October 1872.—Ed.

of his own creation at Simla his portrait in oil now hangs. Subscriptions for the purpose were gathered in by the headmaster, Mr. Slater, chiefly from the parents of boys, and therefore from a quarter where wealth does not abound. The amount collected, though inadequate under ordinary circumstances, was accepted by Mr. Eddis. He had painted in 1852 the original portrait which has now a final home in the Arnold Library at Rugby. Taking in 1868 this picture as a basis, he made the painting of a modified copy of it his own work, and not only produced a very successful likeness, but added a picture, of which any institution might be proud, to the few fine works of art that are very gradually decorating the British possessions in India. But any local memorials, substantial and valuable as they were, became subordinate to the great collective effort that was made to carry on the consolidation of the hill schools up to the point at which the Bishop had ever aimed. The work had yet two years to run when all scenes of this life closed for him, but it was not for a moment allowed to drop to the ground. In his name, and for his sake, it was taken up in India and in England. Archdeacon Pratt on one side of the world, a band of faithful friends on the other, started fresh appeals. In England old Rugby and Marlborough pupils were its secretaries and treasurers. Through contributions munificently given in both countries, that undertaking was accomplished from which the first projector and organizer had been removed with solemn suddenness. By the solid foundation of the three schools, it is humbly hoped that a pledge has been afforded of God's continued blessing on a work indissolubly connected with the Bishop; on a work, begun by him as a memorial of a great deliverance, and completed as the worthiest memorial that could be raised to himself.

APPENDIX.

The allusion in the concluding chapter to the financial position of the hill schools was brief and general. A few statistics, in the form of an Appendix, may possess interest for some among the numerous subscribers in England whose liberality materially contributed to the consolidation of the schools. It has been stated in the text of the memoir that the sum which in 1865 the Bishop announced as necessary for his purpose was 25,000*l.* Of this only a portion was raised during the last year of his life. Upon his death the work at once assumed a memorial character, and the sources from which a large sum was eventually derived were four in number: (1) the proceeds of his own three years' appeal, started in 1865, amounting in round numbers to 14,262*l.*; (2) the fund subscribed as a memorial to him in India, which, after deducting 1,802*l.*, appropriated, according to the terms of the appeal issued in November 1866, to schools in the plains, amounted to 1,868*l.*; (3) the English Memorial Fund, 4,032*l.*; (4) the Government grant, 20,162*l.* (equivalent to the amount of the foregoing subscriptions), in all a total of 40,324*l.* This sum of 40,324*l.* was that with which Archdeacon Pratt had to deal, when from October 1866 he acted as sole treasurer and trustee of the Hill Schools' Fund. The first great charge that came upon it was the purchase money of the Mussoorie School, viz. 12,000*l.* From the residue must further be deducted 265*l.*, the amount disbursed for postage and printing, and for legal expenses connected with ascertaining legal modes of investment, and with the drawing up of the final trust deed. 28,059*l.* remained, which purchased 26,420*l.* of 5½ per cent. Stock, and this sum was sunk in *Endowment Funds*, distributed as follows:—

Simla Endowment Fund	. . . .	£9,830
Mussoorie "	. . . .	5,360
Darjeeling "	. . . .	11,230

From these figures it will be seen how greatly financial results outran the Bishop's expectations. In 1865, 5,000*l.* was the amount of endowment for each school that he allowed himself to contemplate; yet before 1868 had closed, the amount available for the two schools that most needed help had doubled that figure.

The three hill schools have now been in working order and in regular operation for the last few years. In that at Simla, the boys, besides receiving general religious instruction, are educated usefully in Latin, English, one Indian vernacular, history, geography, a short course of mathematics, and certain optional studies to suit distinct tastes. The English language has a much more important place in the curriculum than the Bishop, from want of acquaintance with the deficiencies of Indian boys in this respect, had originally contemplated. Fifteen exhibitions are annually distributed by the Governors, of sufficient value to reduce the annual school expenses from 36*l.* to 24*l.*, and are provided by the grant-in-aid given on the report of the Government school-inspector. The building debt, though in process of liquidation, still burdens the finances. This was incurred when a Government loan became necessary to complete the present buildings, the first stone of which was laid by the Viceroy, Sir John Lawrence, on September 26, 1866. The premises, now finished, include dining-hall, class-rooms, and dormitories for 150 boys, a head-master's house, and rooms for under-masters, hospital, chapel, and a play-ground. The following extract from a letter, dated February 1872, from the head-master, the Rev. S. Slater, gives the present condition of the school, financially and otherwise:—'On December 31, 1870, the balance of the building debt against the school was 40,856 rupees (4,085*l.* 12*s.* 0*d.*). On December 31, 1871, it was 29,166 rupees (2,916*l.* 12*s.* 0*d.*). This sum is at 10 per cent., so that the interest of it is a heavy drag on us. Last year I paid out of the school funds 4,300 rupees (430*l.*) Our prospects for this year are 10,000 rupees (1,000*l.*) from Government, some hoped-for subscriptions, and perhaps 3,000 rupees (300*l.*) saved out of the school funds. I do not think the school can do more than that, for our numbers are increasing, and we shall probably have to build a house for a married second master. I anticipate nearly 120 boys as against 104 last year. Our success at the Calcutta University Examination was fair; at Roorkee, most encouraging. My three candidates stood second, fourth, and fifth, amongst 50, and the second was first in mathematics.'

The school at Mussoorie still remains a higher class school of nearly 100 boys. The fees are higher than at Simla, and the standard of instruction is more advanced both in classics and mathematics. There are two very good exhibitions, founded by the original proprietor, the late Rev. R. Maddock, who liberally remitted for this object 1,000*l.* of the money he received on the sale of the institution. From an account of the school supplied this year by the head-master, the Rev. Arthur Stokes, its present condition appears to be satisfactory. Boys sent to the Roorkee Civil Engineering College are doing well there, and one candidate sent up for the First Arts Examination of the Calcutta University in 1871 passed sixth in the first class and gained a scholarship, while out of five sent up for the Entrance Examination, four passed in the first class.

With respect to the third school, St. Paul's at Darjeeling, either from the miscarriage of letters, or from some unexplained cause, information which was solicited has not been received. It is believed, however, that its general character approximates to that of Simla rather than Mussoorie, the pupils being for the most part drawn from the lower ranks of Government officials, and requiring a middle class education as the best preparation for their future career. This school has in some respects had more difficulties to encounter than the sister institutions, but in all probability when the long talked-of railway through Eastern Bengal facilitates communication with the foot of the hills, the school will attain a prosperity worthy of its healthy and beautiful site.

All the three schools, in their efforts for real success as

places of education, have still to contend with many difficulties incidental to India. These arise partly from the premature removal of boys, from causes dependent on the fluctuating fortunes and frequent change of residence among middle class Anglo-Indians, and from carelessness and negligence in homes in which tenderness rather than wisdom often prevails. Time will prove the best corrective to this latter class of impediments to the success of the hill schools. The effects of good moral and physical training, though as yet in some cases needlessly interrupted, or prematurely cut short, will declare themselves more hereafter. Boys even now join the Himalayan schools from Sukker, far down the Indus, and from other equally remote places of North India; and it seems impossible but that they, when grown to manhood, will not in their turn seek to place and to retain their sons in institutions designed to be fruitful in health both for mind and body. The new schools will amply fulfil their mission for this generation if they succeed in kindling that sense of the value of education which must be the parent of consistent efforts to secure it for the children yet to come.

Difficulties in the way of education which arise from the changing circumstances of Anglo-Indian families are more intelligible, and excite real sympathy. So rapid are the attacks, and so sudden the results of illness in India, that families living in affluence, and respectably maintaining their children at school, are constantly reduced in a day to pauperism through the death of the head, the 'bread winner,' of the household. It was with a view of meeting such cases, and also of increasing as far as possible the usefulness of the schools, by bringing them within the reach of persons of respectable social position, but possessed of very limited incomes, that the late Archdeacon Pratt issued an appeal in 1869 in behalf of a 'Hill Schools Nomination Fund.' The object of this appeal was to raise a sum of money which should be invested in safe securities, and of which the interest only should be available; such interest to be administered in the form of *grants in aid* to assist and encourage private liberality. For it was hoped that in many stations the richer residents would be found willing to subscribe a certain sum towards the annual school charges of poor or orphan children, if such voluntary efforts could be supplemented by assistance from a central fund. The subscription list remained open during two years, and brought in 43,378 rupees, (4,338*l*.). The collecting and organizing of this fund continued to engage the Archdeacon's attention almost to his death in December 1871. It was among the last works of his long and honoured Indian career to draw up in his usual clear and business-like manner the rules whereby the interest of the above-named sum (such interest being doubled by Government) is henceforth to be administered by the Diocesan Board of Education. Through the kind response made to an appeal in the closing paragraph of the first edition of this memoir, some substantial remittances have been sent from this country to India, in aid of this special fund. It will be satisfactory to these contributors to learn that a correspondent in India, writing early this year, speaks very hopefully about the fund, 'as just beginning what it is expected will prove an active and healthy existence.'